Frederick the Great
of Prussia

Absolutism and Administration

MEN IN OFFICE

General Editor:
Professor Ragnhild Hatton

WALTHER HUBATSCH

Frederick the Great
of Prussia
Absolutism and Administration

with 40 illustrations

THAMES AND HUDSON

LONDON

3/83 10,50

*Printed in Great Britain by Cox & Wyman Limited
London, Fakenham and Reading*

Contents

Introduction

Frederick the Great of Prussia is reckoned one of the the most important rulers of the period labelled 'Enlightened Despotism' or 'Enlightened Absolutism' in European history. Either label tends to make the general reader and the student assume that the ruling princes of the time governed according to their own will, that they were free to pick and choose which of the ancient laws of their state they wished to obey or disobey, or even that their word was law. In Frederick's case, quite apart from the unhistorical character of this interpretation in general, there is total ignorance of the manifold dependent relationships within which he had to operate as a ruler of a German territorial state inside the boundaries of the Holy Roman Empire of the German Nation. His own foreign policy, the wars in which he became involved, and the often difficult economic situation of his various territories, were in themselves checks on his freedom of action. More fundamentally, however, he was circumscribed by the Imperial constitution to which he – though king in Prussia outside the Empire – was subject by virtue of the majority of his possessions inside the Empire which he held in his capacity as elector of Brandenburg. To give but a few examples of the way in which he was tied: his legal reforms necessitated permission from the Emperor who alone had the power to grant 'exemptions' from Imperial law; the peacemakings of Breslau and Hubertusburg forced him to maintain a separate minister of justice for his newly conquered province of Silesia; his financial innovations were hindered by the decrees governing Imperial coinage.

Further restrictions existed through the different privileges of the individual provinces which made up the state known in the eighteenth century as 'Prussia'. These varied in every province in respect of law and taxation, in the incidence of military service and the duty to quarter the ruler's soldiers; but all had to be respected under the Imperial constitution. It is thus a mistake to speak of Prussian 'centralization' in Frederick's reign. Other labels, often applied, prove equally misleading when examined. That of the 'machine-state' does not fit since Frederick's Prussia was a highly complex organism, made up of living parts in the process of continuing development. The 'mechanical' connotation of this label seems downright false when we recall that such gifted administrators as the experienced Saxon Heinitz and the strongly independent (not to say obstinate) Imperial Freiherr vom Stein worked with and for Frederick: neither would have agreed to be mere spokes in a wheel where they could exert no control over direction. The 'military state' label falls to the ground when we take into account that the larger proportion of the Prussian army was in peacetime 'on leave' so that the trained soldiers could earn their main livelihood on the land or in the manufactures. The 'police-state', yet another label, conjures up a draconian executive devoid of compassion and takes no account of the strict observation of the many and varied privileges already mentioned.

Indeed, the most marked characteristic of the Frederician absolutism is the ruler's being bound by the law. The codification of the various laws, and their further development through legal reform, had been attempted and begun by Frederick II's father, Frederick William I. Frederick followed in his footsteps and was speeded on his way since 'enlightened' Europe expected and even demanded reform from the 'Philosopher of Sans Souci': the encouragement he received gave wings to his ambition for *gloire* as a reformer. The final result, the Prussian General Law, achieved at the very end of Frederick's reign, was no rhetorical construction but an organic growth sprung from practical administrative measures undertaken in the spirit of the Enlightenment. In the very moment of its promulgation the Prussian General Law was already familiar and in force, being based on the sum of cabinet decisions of a long reign. Frederick could be confident that in his legal reforms he had acted in accordance with the dictates of reason, on enlightened principles, and that he was backed by, and expressed, the consensus of educated men as to what constituted 'good government'.

Frederick's cabinet decisions were not empty declamations of high principles. They were concerned with practical administrative and constitutional measures and were deeply anchored in the reality of the state. The administrative organs of the executive were as bound as Frederick by the limitations which operated on the king: but the administrators were, on the whole, also spurred on by the goals of the Enlightenment. The complex and varied structures of the several provinces demanded not only that the *Generaldirektorium* (the General Directory) should be arranged on a territorial basis, but also that the presidents of the provincial governments should retain a large measure of responsibility. They made their own decisions after mature consideration, taking into account alternative proposals transmitted to them, and adapting the king's directives to local conditions. Here is no mechanical process of executive action following, without question, upon orders from the centre. The breaking down of regional peculiarities by means of a superior state law was not at this time the issue; rather the task was conceived of in terms of accommodating local laws within the state law. Not till Napoleon had swept aside all regional and personal privileges could Freiherr vom Stein reap the fruit thereof in a sweeping reform of the Prussian legal system.

In spite of the many obstacles to change in Frederick II's reign, reforms were carried out – in so far as legal constraints permitted – in all spheres of Prussian life: in administration where the aim was uniformity, in the operation of criminal law, in agricultural, church and school policies, in the management of the royal domains and forests, in mining and manufactures, in trade and shipping. The king was, naturally, dependent on the intelligence and unremitting cooperation of his co-workers, the administrators. How they worked, what were the goals of the reform work, what was achieved and what could not be carried out, is the subject of the pages which follow this introduction. This book is not a biography of Frederick the Great, but a history of the Frederician administration set against the background of the political events of Frederick's reign and the developing personality of the king himself. Frederick's statesmanship had to adapt itself to the pace of political events. His generalship kept the enemies of the state at bay, but the main and lasting result of his reign was the administration. In the Frederician period, as always, administration was an enduring, flexible process, an interplay between challenge and response, a dynamic game played according to constantly changing rules. Both the object and the instigator of administrative order were subject to this. It takes more than a discussion of the development of Frederick's youthful character to deal adequately with his mature personality. We must not halt at that threshold where the *Bildungsroman* leaves its subject: Federick's real struggle began once he had shouldered the responsibilities of office.

I wish to thank, as in the German edition of my work, Professor Ragnhild Hatton for her invitation to write on this topic as well as for her encouragement and criticism as my work progressed. It only remains to be said that it is based mainly on the huge printed series of archive material, *Acta Borussica* (which till now has not been systematically exploited for my purpose), complemented by unprinted archive material from the former Prussian state archives, expecially those of Berlin-Dahlem, Münster and Königsberg (which have now been moved to Göttingen).

1

The Crown Prince

PROVINCIAL ADMINISTRATION AT KÜSTRIN AND REGIMENTAL DUTIES

Frederick's introduction to the Prussian administration can be pin-pointed to the exact day. On 20 November 1730, rehabilitated as crown prince of Prussia, he began work in the War and Domains Chamber (*Kammer*) of the Neumark at Küstrin. His token submission to the will of his father, Frederick William I, had brought to a close an episode which had escalated from a personal crisis into an affair of state. Not all the blame for the unhappy family life of the Prussian royal house can be laid at the door of the irascible king. Two political marriages linking the Hohenzollerns with the proud House of Guelph – not counting Frederick's own later marriage with a member of one of its collateral branches – led to domestic tensions, the ultimate source of which was Hanover's connection with England. The coronation of his grandfather, Frederick I, in 1701 had nearly suffered a last-minute cancellation because of the obstructiveness of his Guelph wife;* and the frequent extolling of English ways by Frederick's mother, Queen Sophia Dorothea,† at the Berlin court could not but impress the vivid imagina-tion of the young crown prince. There is no doubt that the children were turned against their father; within a family atmosphere of intrigue, hypocrisy and shifting confidences Frederick sought and found a life-long ally in his sister Wilhelmina.

Frederick William I, who on his accession had immediately swept away the shallow pomp and expensive trappings of his father's court, saw his over-delicate heir, with his predilection for poetry and the flute, as a frenchified aesthete, adept at evading more serious pursuits. What, the worried father asked himself, went on in that little head? Was it a

* Sophia Charlotte of Brunswick-Lüneburg, sister of George, elector of Hanover since 1698 and king of Great Britain since August 1714.
† Sophia Dorothea of Brunswick-Lüneburg, daughter of George I.

bad omen that the boy bore the same name as his grandfather? Would
that easy-going way of life, so inimical to Prussia's survival and development, return when Frederick became king? To his grief he could find
no trace in his son of Frederick I's strong – if intermittent – attachment
to Pietism. That inheritance was his own strongest link with his father.
He forbade masked balls and comedies, and even tried to banish sacred
music from the churches since, in his view, it did nothing to promote
conversion or improve morals.

All Frederick William's anxieties and inner anguish, his aspirations
and ardent expectations, were condensed in the instructions written for
his heir's tenth birthday in 1722, the day Frederick was gazetted a
lieutenant in the Prussian army. But, to the king's great disappointment, the boy managed to disengage himself from its spirit. Nor did
his confirmation classes seem to touch his inner life. In 1726, to move
Frederick into his own orbit, Frederick William took him along on
tours of inspection to Westphalia and to Königsberg. Two years later
he permitted Frederick to accompany him to Dresden, though only
at the express desire of his host, August II of Saxony-Poland.

At the Saxon court a new world, utterly different from that of Berlin
and Potsdam, opened up for the crown prince. Here life consisted of
light gallantries, webs that glittered but did not bind, playful *joie de
vivre* and music. For Frederick, the subsequent return to Prussian
frugality and austerity was a torment. Refusing to live within his
meagre allowance, he irresponsibly piled up debts. The conviction
that elsewhere a much better life was possible grew stronger, all the
more so as his own obstinacy and insubordination provoked his father
into ill-treating him. The king, in impotent fury, insisted on demands
which Fritz – with his mother's encouragement – refused point blank.
Matters came to a head in August 1730 when the crown prince was
caught while attempting to flee to England. Court-martialled for
desertion, Frederick was imprisoned, while his fellow-conspirator
Katte was executed. With an Old Testament sense of justice, and a
concern lest army discipline suffer, the king insisted that both sentences
be carried out.

The crown prince's subsequent detention in the fortress of Küstrin
was not spent in idleness. For the first time Frederick was completely
in the power of his father who took advantage of the opportunity to
have his son trained, if rather late, for some of the duties of kingship.
In the morning Frederick attended the discussions of the local *Kammerkollegium* (collegial chamber) under the guidance of Hille, its director.
In the afternoon he had to copy and study documents, in a way remi-

niscent of that in which he had earlier been given selections of letters
from foreign princes to read in order to familiarize himself with their
content and style. To channel his energies along the desired paths
reading of any other kind was forbidden: if he wished to read, there
were sufficient documents in the Küstrin archives from the time of
Margrave Hans* or Elector Frederick William† to occupy him. He was,
however, forbidden to study plans of fortifications: these came under
the heading of 'amusements'. Even the topics on which Frederick might
converse with his tutors were limited to 'the Divine Word, the state of
the province, manufactures, social welfare regulations, cultivation of
the soil, the auditing of accounts, litigation over tenancies and court
procedure'. The crown prince's life in detention was simple and monotonous. For an eighteen-year-old it was deadly dull, but it was as useful
as it was difficult. In the daily routine of the *Kammer*, the future ruler
saw for the first time the workings of the economy and the fiscal
system, the nature and content of contracts, and the operations
of the administrative machine. In spite of his many earlier failures,
Frederick now learned how to manage his own small allowance
and how to present his accounts neatly in a way pleasing to his
father.

After nine months of tedious routine Frederick was forgiven. There
followed a second stage in his Küstrin training, as deliberately and carefully planned as the first. Under the tutelage of its president, Christian
Ernst von Münchow, Frederick attended the sessions of the War and
Domains Chamber three mornings a week; and regular visits were
arranged to crown domains for the study of the practical details of
estate farming: tilling, sowing, harvesting, stock-raising and beer-
brewing. Theoretical economy also had to be pursued, but recreation
in the form of duck shooting was permitted. The programme had a
Pietist framework. There were morning and evening services with
prayers and hymns; readings aloud from the scriptures, to be performed 'with seemly devotion and piety'. Secretly Frederick remained preoccupied with the radical theories of predestination. The
boundaries of human free will was a problem which never ceased to
fascinate him; his interest in it, nearly morbid in intensity, continued to
increase throughout his life.

His thoughts at Küstrin were, however, hidden from his father.
Superficially, he appeared to have adopted Frederick William's views.
In a series of letters written to the king between mid-August 1731 and

* Johann (Hans) I (1513–71), margrave of Brandenburg-Küstrin.
† Frederick William, the Great Elector (1620–88).

the end of February 1732, he demonstrated his new-found knowledge. He wrote of the management of the *Amt* (the royal domain) of Wollup and the *Vorwerk* (the outfarm) of Carzig, on soil conditions and the improvement of cow-byres and meadows, on the terms of the lease at Marienwalde where he had established a glassworks. His observations and recommendations may have been compiled with the help of his tutors, but the crown prince, expressing himself succinctly, proved that he was familiar with the topics under discussion. During this same period Frederick – in private letters not intended for the king's eyes – showed a genuine interest in affairs of state which went far beyond the management of a domains chamber. There is no doubt that the year in Küstrin made him face his future task of governing the Prussian state.

On 26 February 1732 Frederick left Küstrin for Berlin to celebrate his betrothal to Elisabeth Christina of Brunswick-Wolfenbüttel. The match had been arranged by Franz Stephan, duke of Lorraine (and future consort of Maria Theresa), according to the wishes of Frederick William. The next phase of the crown prince's training was, by the king's orders, military. In December 1731 Frederick had been re-admitted to the army with the rank of colonel. On 29 February 1732 he was given command of the Christoph Heinrich von der Goltz infantry regiment, stationed at Nauen and Neuruppin, though he did not join the regiment until 5 April. Again he felt an initial dislike for his allotted task, making ironic comments to the effect that 'the university of Potsdam' was 'the high school of the art of drill'. To Grumbkow, his military mentor from Küstrin, Frederick reported more factually from Nauen, 'We drill here *comme il faut*, new brooms must sweep clean, and I must justify my rank and demonstrate that I am "an efficient officer".' And, again, from Neuruppin on 23 October: 'I devote my time to the regiment. Drill and financial matters occupy my time till the midday meal. After the password has been given, I am free to visit nearby villages or to spend my time reading and playing music. About seven o'clock I meet my officers and we play cards. At eight o'clock I sup, at nine I go to bed and thus one day passes much like the rest.' By the spring of 1733 the routine had scarcely altered: 'I have drilled, I drill, I shall drill! That is all the news I have for you, but I enjoy it too much to allow myself a respite from it and I prefer to drill here from dawn to dusk than live the life of a rich man in Berlin.'

In the *Mémoires pour servir à l'histoire de la Maison de Brandenbourg* (1751) Frederick, casting his mind back to this period of his life, wrote:

In all regiments the officer corps was purged of elements whose behaviour or background made them unsuitable for a position of honour. From then on the officers themselves only accepted men who were beyond reproach. Drill practice went like this: the manual exercise was first performed, followed by the loading of muskets by platoons and divisions. After that, while advancing at slow march, volleys were fired. Retreats were conducted along similar lines. Then two squares, impracticable for use against an enemy, were formed. An utterly useless *feu de haie* completed the drill. All battalion exercises were, however, executed with clockwork precision.

As a military instructor for the crown prince the king chose the thirty-eight-year-old Lieutenant-Colonel Kaspar Ludwig von Bredow, a tactful officer whom Frederick initially suspected of being 'an informer at court'. Because of this he attached himself after 1734 to Colonel von Camas and Engineer-Major Senning and these men became Frederick's real teachers in military matters and in the art of fortification. Extensive reading of the military classics in French translation was part of the training, important not so much for what they taught the prince about changes in techniques as for the fundamental lessons in the art of war which they offered.

Neuruppin, 'the beloved garrison' as Frederick later called it with a mixture of nostalgia and irony, was an unimportant, out-of-the-way, none-too-clean small town which the king had prepared as best he could to house the first battalion of the crown prince's regiment. As commander Frederick chose quarters close to the house of Colonel von Wreech, a cuirassier officer to whose wife he had taken a liking during his stay at Küstrin. Beyond the walls of Neuruppin Frederick laid out a garden as a rural retreat, though it was not much used as his brother officers tempted him into escapades of many kinds. He was still delicate and often ill, but his intellectual superiority soon taught him to curtail inessential activities. Theatricals, reading, music and composition filled his spare time, but without fully satisfying him. His extreme sensitivity kept him in a state of irritable nervousness. He longed to express himself fully through his work and was consumed by ambition. But at every step the pull of his service responsibilities restricted the independence he craved. He had not yet succeeded in spanning the gap between his drab and demanding physical duties and the serene dream-world of poetry and music. Moreover, the eyes of his father were always upon him.

Frederick was not allowed to forget his administrative tasks. At first he made excuses to postpone work on the new leases for the Neuruppin *Amt* which the king had ordered him to undertake; but in the last

instance his pride prevented him from handing over the chore to someone else. These administrative tasks, such as the settlement of Swiss
colonists in the Ruppin district, the inspection of the mirror factory at
Neustadt on the Dosse and of the glassworks at Zechlin, were additional
to his military duties. He continued these until his accession, though
he gave up the day-to-day command of his regiment in the autumn of
1736. On 1 June 1740 he honoured his regiment by designating it one
of the elite regiments of guards. For four and a half years – broken
only by a brief period on his marriage in June 1733 – he exercised all
the duties of a regimental commander, which he took more seriously
than his letters to Grumbkow would suggest. Each of the two battalions
stationed at Neuruppin and Nauen had 20 officers, 55 non-commissioned
officers, 3 fifers, 15 drummers and 540 musketeers, as well as a grenadier
company of 108 men. Frederick's instructions to his company commanders in 1737 laid down guidelines for training and were also concerned with details of equipment, especially with footwear. In 1739
the crown prince informed Voltaire that he was practising the art of
educating men:

> a constant study of the human character, the ultimate purpose of which is to
> render the dullest minds sensitive to glory, to make rebellious natures sub-
> missive to discipline and to imbue dissolute youths, libertines and criminals
> with morality. As thankless as this task may appear, one undertakes it with
> pleasure.

Yet the prospect of an inspection by the king made the crown prince
uneasy: he feared that the regiment would 'not come up to scratch,
even if we drill ourselves to death'. But Frederick William, observing
the improvement in his son's physique and character, was impressed
by his efforts. He could not conceal his satisfaction from Prince Leopold
of Anhalt-Dessau, the foremost infantry expert of the age: the crown
prince's regiment was now 'in better order, with good recruits and
everything just right'. In 1735 the king embraced his heir before the
assembled troops and promoted him to major-general.

From July to August 1734, during the War of the Polish Succession,
Frederick was given the opportunity of taking the Prussian contingent
due to the Emperor to Prince Eugène's headquarters near Heidelberg.
This visit to a war zone, and the course of the campaign that followed,
had a somewhat unexpected result. Despite a deep respect for the veteran
Austrian commander, the critical Frederick, with the eye of a regimental
officer, found himself unimpressed by the quality and striking power of
Prince Eugène's forces. His was a superficial, even frivolous assessment;

but it had important consequences. Knowledgeable, though still relatively inexperienced in administrative and military affairs, the twenty-two-year-old crown prince was already dreaming of the path to fame for which his ambition yearned.

EAST PRUSSIA AND RHEINSBERG

When Frederick returned to Neuruppin it was not to become immersed in the spit-and-polish routine of the barracks but to lay down a detailed training programme for the regiment with an eye to the future. What he had seen in the Austrian camp fell short of his expectations, yet he was intrigued by Prince Eugène. When, in the spring of 1735, the latter began preparations for a resumption of the campaign on the Rhine, Frederick was eager to visit him once more. The old commander, who had favoured him with stories of past campaigns, had brought history alive; he represented human greatness and everlasting fame, qualities the younger man hoped to emulate. Perhaps he, at the head of a military contingent better disciplined than the Austrian one he had seen in 1734, could make a name for himself and display greater initiative, boldness and determination than the ageing hero. In May 1735 he asked his father's permission to join the Imperial force, as other ambitious young princes were doing. He argued that the indecisiveness of the previous season's campaign made his return all the more necessary; military experience was not to be gained by staying at home.

The summer passed and Frederick was not given the permission he had requested. Frederick William had many reasons for withholding it. His earlier good relationship with the Imperial court had cooled. There was a feeling in Berlin of having been both deceived and used by Vienna in respect of the Jülich succession issue. Frederick William would, in fact, have liked to lead a Prussian contingent, five times as strong as that he owed Charles VI as a prince of the Empire, to the Lower Rhine to back up his claims to Jülich, but he felt too ill and weak for such a challenge. Were his inexperienced heir to visit the Austrian camp, he might be tempted into playing politics and – so the king feared – become the tool of Austrian diplomacy. The king was also saddened at the physical and mental decline of Prince Eugène, his brother-in-arms of Höchstädt and Malplaquet: he did not wish Frederick to see the prince at close quarters in his present state. When, at the end of August, Frederick pressed his father to let him go – 'I am a young man and if I have not the chance to gain experience now it will be too late when I

am old' – the king, politely but firmly, turned him down. As compensation Frederick was offered 'a pleasure trip' to East Prussia:

> so as to study and become familiar with the economy and the way of life
> there, also to find out why things are not progressing there. Since one day
> you will rule this territory, it will be most useful for you to take a good
> look at what is happening in the towns and on the land as well as in the
> administration. ... You shall be authorized to obtain whatever information
> you require from the War and Domains Chamber and other bodies. At the
> same time you should take the opportunity to check if the regiments stationed
> in Prussia are as I expect them to be; whatever is not in order you can put
> right.

These instructions carried power. The king had, after a sudden illness
during the previous year, already authorized the temporary transfer of
some of his governmental responsibilities to his heir. Now he intended
introducing Frederick to what had been his own main work, the *rétablissement* (resettlement) of East Prussia.

From 1709 onwards this province had been devastated by several
outbreaks of the plague, which had almost wiped out human settlement
in its northern *Kreise* (administrative districts corresponding to English
counties). From the moment of his accession in 1713, Frederick William
had endeavoured to help East Prussia by drawing on the central resources
of the state, and over a period of two decades he had personally supervised a generous reconstruction programme. Thousands of peasant
families immigrated from neighbouring territories to settle in East
Prussia; they also came, on the king's invitation, from French Switzerland, Nassau, the Rhine Palatinate, the Magdeburg-Halberstadt region
and, in particularly large numbers, from Salzburg. As a result, the
population increased from less than 160,000 to 600,000. Difficulties and
set-backs in such a vast undertaking were unavoidable; even after the
major crises had been overcome, Frederick William visited the development areas almost every year so that important issues could be decided
on the spot. Since illness prevented the visit planned for 1735, Frederick
was to be his substitute: officials were 'to show the crown prince whatever he wished to see, to keep him fully informed and to accept his
instructions as if they had come from the mouth of the king himself'.
The War and Domains Chamber was instructed to see that the king's
portrait was hung in every one of its offices to remind East Prussian
officials of him during his absences. The East Prussian Chamber's
pressing application for an extra subsidy of 175,000 talers was to be
particularly scrutinized.

Although inwardly reluctant, Frederick resigned himself to the task:

'Being sent to Prussia is somewhat more respectable than being sent to Siberia, but not much.' The views of father and son did not yet coincide; but when, on the day after his arrival in Marienwerder, he reviewed the squadrons of Buddenbrock's Cuirassiers stationed there, he did so with his father's eyes. In the evening he assured the king by letter that 'the soldiers ride like mechanical puppets' and that 'the regiment is in good trim' in spite of having suffered a recent epidemic of the bloody flux. Nor did he forget to mention the presence of some exceptionally tall recruits, a subject close to his father's heart. Further reports dealt with domains and villages. Via Mohrungen, Bartenstein and Angerburg Frederick travelled to Gumbinnen, where he stayed five days. He paid surprise visits to the royal domains, their outfarms and to the newly-founded towns of Stallupönen, Darkehmen and Pillkallen; he also attended a meeting of the Gumbinnen Chamber Commission (*Kammer-deputation*). Then, via Ragnit, Tilsit, Insterburg and Wehlau (where he reviewed four cavalry regiments on the parade ground), he reached Königsberg. There on 14 October he attended a session of the War and Domains Chamber. He sent the king samples of peasant bread, proposed improvements in the school system and advocated a fairer allocation of labour services. 'The towns are fine, full of people and houses. Most of them have had to extend into the suburbs. In short, both towns and rural areas are milling with people and in about eight years' time the province will be better populated than Switzerland or Franconia.' During recent years, however, the harvest had been worse than expected. To Grumbkow Frederick wrote, certain in the knowledge that these letters would reach his father just as quickly and surely as the official reports:

> I will sum up by saying that I have visited all of East Prussia. I have seen its good points but have also witnessed its wretched poverty. If the king does not decide to open the granaries before the New Year, you can depend upon it that half the population will starve to death, so bad has the harvest been for the past two years.

Frederick thought it his duty to state the facts without mincing matters, but, as reports from the Chamber show, his misgivings were somewhat exaggerated. The crown prince had, however, been forced to face the current problems of East Prussia. His reports pleased the king, especially because 'you go into details and try to get to the bottom of things, the most sensible thing to do'. But soon after his return, Frederick, in a confidential letter to Grumbkow, spoke with irony of his mission:

In my reading I came across a passage from the life of the Emperor Julian
that exactly fits my mission to East Prussia. Here it is: 'The emperor wished
only to turn him into a purple-garbed phantom which could be paraded
before the army and exhibited as the ruler's image in town after town.'
When you read this, please recall my mission, the purpose behind it and the
figure I cut in East Prussia. Have I not impersonated my precursor? Have I
not warned both the army and the administration in a thundering voice that
their king is alive, that in the near future he will come either to strike them
with lightning or to pardon them?

Yet the journey had been worthwhile. In the realm of foreign affairs
it provided Frederick with fleeting impressions which in time had a
decisive and lasting effect on his judgment. He saw the exiled Polish
king, Stanislas Leszczyński, father-in-law of Louis XV of France, who
was sitting out the War of the Polish Succession at Königsberg. On
Sunday, 8 October 1735, the crown prince was present at the service in
the Schlosskirche, 'which was packed', and afterwards at the parade.
What happened next he described in a letter to Grumbkow:

> On the way back I met a few hundred men on horseback, all Poles ... the
> horses of superior breed but ridden by the world's filthiest mudlarks. Not
> far behind came King Stanislas in Katte's carriage, on his way back from
> Mass. We greeted each other with great courtesy and then each went his way.
> Following his carriage were a dozen others containing Poles, ugly apes of
> both sexes. ... In the afternoon Count Tarlo appeared with all the con-
> federates* to pay their respects. These people are not at all like those you meet
> in Dresden; hardly any of them speak anything but Polish and they are
> covered in grease and dirt. In my address to them I assured them that my
> father, the king, was very much in favour of their freedom and wished for
> nothing more than that they should be happy during their stay in his terri-
> tories. I felt entitled to say at least that much to them; anyway it was only a
> civility.

On his return journey though West Prussia, 'the royal Polish part',
Frederick encountered hordes of refugees, fleeing northwards before
Russian troops, and Saxon cavalry on their way to Danzig. The second
seizure of the Polish throne by the Wettins, this time with Russian help,
was under way.

As yet, Frederick's role was that of a spectator with no real influence
over government business at home or abroad. He fretted that his life
lacked purpose. The regiment, to which he returned as colonel, was not
enough. In the spring of 1736 he wrote, in evident bad humour:

* Members of one of the confederations formed by groups of Polish magnates after
  the death of August II.

Day after day we drill ourselves to death here, without achieving anything; for although the Margrave Heinrich [von Schwedt] regiment today performed miracles during the review the king was still not pleased. . . . I long for the day, the hour, nay the minute when I can get away from here, so that I can have peace and enjoy life.

What fate brought him was another visit to East Prussia. Frederick William, recovering from his illness, decided to travel to the province and take Frederick with him – music and books would have to be rationed.

This journey, in the summer of 1736, was a visible triumph for the king. The experiment of the Salzburg settlement had been successful. In Gumbinnen the Chamber Commission was promoted to a second East Prussian War and Domains Chamber with the able Blumenthal (later to render good service to Frederick) at its head. With the Salzburgers, as previously with the Swiss, a contract that freed them from labour services was signed; twenty-six village mayors (*Schulzen*) were nominated, received a *Freihufe** of land each free of all tax and were given powers to lease abandoned farms and encourage the establishment of new farms. The church and school regulations of the province as a whole were improved.

Having crossed the Vistula on 7 July, the king travelled over Saalfeld, Seegertswalde, Mohrungen and Liebstadt to Amsdorf, always two hours ahead of his party in his eight-horse carriage. At the relay stations the horses were changed and the hot axles cooled with water; then he pressed onwards, covering up to twenty German miles between four in the morning and the late evening. The *Landräte* (the rural commissioners) and domain officials through whose area the king passed rode alongside the royal carriage to answer questions put to them. In addition to the crown prince the king's entourage included Prince Augustus William (the king's second son), the margrave of Schwedt, Prince Leopold of Anhalt-Dessau and his son, General von Grumbkow, the French envoy, the marquis de la Chétardie, an adjutant-general and five other officers, two cabinet secretaries, twelve mounted pages and four mounted messengers. For the riders and the twenty-one conveyances (which included the kitchen, provisions and baggage wagons) 198 horses were changed every two German miles. The planning and functioning of this relay service was, with success, entrusted to the provincial administration.

---

* *Freihufe*: a unit of land, about 41 acres in extent, exempt from charges or labour services.

The crown prince, still not in tune with his father's plans and policies, considered his own presence superfluous. Indeed, the gulf between Frederick William and himself widened during these weeks. Frederick, engrossed in a French translation of Christian Wolff's work on metaphysics, later confessed that he 'had not let this work out of his sight for a single minute' throughout the journey. Even with allowances for exaggeration this shows a desire on Frederick's part to remove himself from reality. He found the visit with its military duties in summer thunderstorms unrewarding. Yet he had profited from the reading for which he had stolen time: immediately after his return, on 8 August 1736, he began his correspondence with Voltaire on the theme of Wolff's philosophy.

At the end of the month Frederick moved house from Neuruppin to Rheinsberg, where, in the company of his wife and a small circle of friends, he was able to devote himself to his literary and musical inclinations. While still at Küstrin – though against the rules laid down for him – he had begun to read avidly if indiscriminately in French literature. At Rheinsberg he built up a select library which, apart from the classics, was devoted to philosophy and ancient history, with some enlightenment theology. That he read the books he purchased is evident from his later letters. Of Prussian and Imperial law and the flourishing cameralism of the period we find no trace. Neither his tutor the Huguenot Duhan de Jandun, nor his reader-companion Karl Stephan Jordan, was interested in those subjects and if they had been they would in all probability not have awakened any interest in Frederick. Everything conspired to divert the crown prince from his given *métier*, to side-track him from the world of *raison d'état* to the delights of aesthetics and the imaginative life. In the autumn of 1738 he described 'Remusberg-Rheinsberg' as 'my Sans Souci, my little cloister', where he sought 'only freedom of the spirit and tranquillity of soul'.

But were these ambitions natural for a young man of twenty-six? In the summer of that same year he was admitted through Count Adalbert Wolfgang zu Schaumburg-Lippe to the first German freemason lodge. He wanted to encompass the movement intellectually, but it had no influence on the *raison d'état* philosophy which he later evolved. Though Frederick's urge to widen his educational horizon was genuine, he may be said in his Rheinsberg days to have deceived himself as to his real needs: his life's work was not to consist in the satisfaction of his literary ambitions. 'He always sought to find in his own understanding the answers to the great questions posed by history, nature, and life, and to illuminate with the highest attainable measure of rational clarity the darkness that envelops the active man.'* Could this in the long run be anything more than a dilettante though well-meaning effort? At best it was the enclosure of a territory within which he could take refuge from pressing problems, to give himself the illusion of escape and a source of relaxation.

'Every day I become more economical with time. I begrudge its loss and hold myself accountable for its use.' But to what effect? 'My mind is steeped in philosophy,' he wrote in the summer of 1737. If that were all, Frederick would not have become Frederick the Great. 'The happy Rheinsberg years' were not as idyllically removed from Frederick's *métier* as is often assumed. When we study them closely, we find the germs of later political decisions and at times are even made to sit up sharply. Prussia's neutrality in the War of the Polish Succession worried him. The country, he argued, would lose out to her neighbours, the Saxons and the Russians, if it remained inactive in great power politics; the latter could overrun Poland and take Danzig. 'I love the king, his reputation means much to me. . . . Our military position is strong but our negotiations lack vigour.' In 1737, pondering the unsuccessful outcome of Prussia's negotiations on her claims to the Jülich-Berg inheritance – where concessions had been made both in 1728 and 1732 – he looked forward to a solution by military action: on the death of the present ruler both Jülich and Berg could be occupied from Cleves as long as forty squadrons of dragoons and sufficient infantry were betimes stationed in Mark. In the summer of 1738 Frederick spoke even more clearly when he confided to an army friend his desire to experience battle:

> Thank God our review went off very well. The king was satisfied and his satisfaction caused jubilation throughout the regiment from the Zeder to the Ysop,† from the colonel to the junior fifer. I wished for nothing more fervently than the same satisfaction after a battle in which I had utterly routed enemy troops. I hope this will come true and that on the plain of Düsseldorf I may congratulate both you and myself on a victory won under the king's command.

In the meantime musters and exercises meant days of emotional torment lest he lose Frederick William's good opinion. He concentrated on making a good outward show: 'My regiment was superb; so was the rifle drill; a little flour sprinkled on the soldiers' hair; men over six foot and numerous recruits proved stronger arguments than those of my slanderers.' He accepted, coldly and cynically, the methods of the

* Gerhard Ritter, p. 40.
† Old Testament, I Kings, Chapter 5, verse 13.

press-gang and the fact that money talked. In a letter in which he
discusses spiritual satisfaction and inner peace he also mentions 'a
physical phenomenon': 'It consists in this, that with the attractive power
of 6,000 talers I have made a body over six foot nine inches gravitate
towards me from deepest Holland.' On another occasion he refers to
the fact that his father has made him a 'magnificent present of 10,865
talers' as recompense for five recruits from his own regiment. Frederick,
himself reprieved as a deserter and an eye-witness of his friend's execution, employed in his regiment deserters from other states, and justified
the execution of a deserter from his own regiment with the pitiless
military logic that 'this example will have some effect'.

These quotations all date from the Rheinsberg period and we may at
first sight find them difficult to reconcile with the Frederick who is
supposed in his 'Remusberg' to have prepared himself for the role of 'a
philosopher on the throne'. What we must remember is that Frederick,
as crown prince and as king, kept the two spheres, aesthetics and the
exigencies of state, separate. Neither influenced nor penetrated the
other, though both were contained within a single person able to enter
either of them at will. Frederick's 'Considerations on the Present
Political Situation in Europe' of 1738, as well as the 'Anti-Machiavel'
of 1739 with its borrowings from Fénelon's *Télémaque*, were philosophical writings. Frederick's only political writings were his Political
Testaments, the first unexpurgated edition of which was not published till
1920.

From 7 July to 18 August 1739 Frederick paid a third visit to East
Prussia. Once again he accompanied his father. Their speed was as
before, as the king pressed restlessly on. 'For the past three weeks',
Frederick wrote to his sister Wilhelmina at Bayreuth, 'we have been
rushing through lands as large as two-thirds of Germany and we have
not yet finished our business.' But the relationship between them had
changed. His father, Frederick confessed – all irony and cynicism forgotten – behaved towards him 'as I have always wished that he would'.
This was the eleventh and last time Frederick William saw East Prussia.
He was gratified to find the *rétablissement* completed and the province
now on the same footing as the rest of the monarchy. The visit made a
strong impression on Frederick; Voltaire became the recipient of his
impressions. From Insterburg on 27 July the crown prince sent the
French philosopher a deep appreciation of his father and his work to
repair the damage caused by the plague: fifteen towns and five hundred
villages had been depopulated, but now there were half a million
inhabitants in the province:

There are more towns and herds than formerly, more wealth and fertility than in any other place in Germany. And all this is thanks to the king, who gave the instructions and watched over their execution. He alone outlined the plans and brought them to fruition; he spared neither effort, nor care, nor immense amounts of money, neither promises nor rewards, to secure life and happiness for half a million sentient beings. To him alone they owe their prosperity and their security. ... I find something heroic in the generous and zealous way in which the king has colonized this desert and made it fertile and useful and I feel certain that you will be of my opinion when you read of this colonization.

This homage to the king goes deeper than literary flourish. The crown prince had been moved and wanted the most enlightened man of his age to accept his experience. In his father's activity Frederick became aware of true sovereignty. Could there be any higher expression of it than for a monarch to further the happiness of his subjects? The theories of the 'Anti-Machiavel' seemed to take on reality: here was a king who actually lived for the service of his state. Frederick William as an enlightened monarch? What a reversal of his son's earlier opinion!

Frederick was not yet ready to shoulder such responsibilities himself. The six weeks' journey with its monotonous series of inspections appeared endless. He longed to be back at Rheinsberg with his flute and his books: 'Perhaps this land is not fit for thinking, nor has the god of poetry looked on it with benevolent eyes.' This observation was both superficial and unjust. Kant and Hamann had grown to manhood in East Prussia and Herder completed a triumvirate of talent. The Albertus university at Königsberg was at that time laying the foundations for the European-wide fame it was to win in the second half of the century. By 1740 Frederick seems to have sensed something of this when he said of Quandt, the court preacher at the Schlosskirche and rector of the university, 'I have never heard better German, more beautiful phrasing, more fluent or elegant language.'

This visit was to be the last occasion on which Frederick was able to shrug off his fate; only a few months later complete authority became his and was to remain so for the rest of his life.

FREDERICK WILLIAM I's HERITAGE

The conflict between father and son was settled by 1739; the generations complemented one another. Only contemporaries whose knowledge of Frederick was slight could have expected an abrupt change of

system with his accession. As crown prince he had learned to appreciate
what his father had built up for him. As early as the autumn of 1737 he
had written in connection with the impending Jülich dispute:

> It seems that heaven has destined the king to make all the preparations
> demanded by prudence and wisdom. Who knows whether providence is
> not preserving me to make glorious use of these preparations, to utilize them
> for the execution of those plans for which the king's foresight has destined
> them?

Frederick William, for his part, had accepted his son. In the spring of
1740 he acknowledged that his successor would be a good manager:
he would not squander his money; furthermore, he took an interest in
the army and cared for it. The king died on 31 May 1740, fifty-one
years old, 'content, as I leave such a worthy son and successor'. In his
usual orderly fashion he had, several days previously, talked to his heir
for an hour and a half, familiarizing him with the state of affairs and
explaining his own domestic and foreign policies.

Much earlier, in 1722, in the only written instructions he left, he had
listed the main qualities needed in his successor, with numerous references to religion and with examples taken from the history of the House
of Hohenzollern: 'You alone must deal with income and expenditure
and the command of the army must be in your hands alone'; if 'you
alone hold the purse strings' this will earn you the reputation of being a
'skilled and upright ruler'. Detailed instructions for the maintenance
and improvement of the army followed. The various regions of the
monarchy were next considered. East Prussia, 'a very beautiful and
extensive territory and very fertile', must remain firmly under royal
sovereignty: under no circumstances must the Estates government,
with its tax-assessment privileges, be permitted to re-emerge. The
nobility must be employed in the state service: it must 'know no lord
but God and the king of Prussia'. Its service in the army, which should
as far as possible be recruited from natives, was especially important.
More towns ought to be founded, and manufactures, especially for
textiles, must be established. Hither and Further Pomerania were also
fertile; the domains there were in good shape and the income of the
state could be increased through profitable leases. The situation in the
Neumark was much the same, but there the domain estates would have to
be improved. In the Kurmark the review of the domains showed that
the province could make greater contributions; forestry in particular
could be made more profitable in an expanding timber market, and
stricter measures must be taken against illegal felling. The inhabitants

of the Altmark were inclined to be obstinate, and unreliable rural commissioners ought to be relieved of their office: 'That will show them that you are the lord and they the vassals and that they have no vested rights.' Some old families were listed as having to be carefully watched. The Magdeburg area was beautiful and its towns were fine; but the domains, though well-managed, could be made to yield more. It was wisest to employ royal domains officials from Magdeburg in East Prussia, Pomerania, Minden and Cleves as well as in the Mittelmark, but because of their family connections in Magdeburg not in Magdeburg-Halberstadt or the Altmark; domains officials from other parts of the kingdom should be sent to work in these provinces. The Wettin saltworks and coal-mines could increase their output – already good – by a third. Vassals in Minden, Ravensberg, Tecklenburg and Lingen were troublesome, but were easier led than those of the Altmark; the domains there were in good condition. The people in Cleves and the county of Mark were difficult to deal with and determined to keep their special privileges: to make 'well-behaved, clever and worthy lads' out of them they would have to be educated in Berlin. The domains should produce more, but most of the leaseholders were bad managers who wasted money. People in Moers and Guelders gravitated towards the Dutch Republic and the Emperor and must, therefore, be closely watched. All the lands and provinces should be visited yearly, as had been done up to the present, so that the ruler might get to know territories and peoples, the administrators and the military commanders of the garrisons. The review of the domains must be carried out in an orderly fashion: within a span of six years the accounts of the crown estates of all the provinces should have been examined; an annual increase of income of between 600,000 and 800,000 talers should be possible without any special effort.

This survey of 1722 had served Frederick William as a kind of stock-taking and had led to the introduction of important new administrative measures, most of which were completed during his reign. Much had happened between 1722 and 1740; many of the statements in his political testament on administration, finance, the economy, the Church and foreign affairs had been rendered obsolete by the time of Frederick II's accession. In 1722 Frederick William had described, for the benefit of his successor, the bad condition in which he had inherited the state from Frederick I: plague had almost denuded the largest province of people; everywhere the domains were mortgaged; bankruptcy appeared imminent; the army – as far as numbers went – was unimportant and weak:

I cannot adequately describe how bad things were. It is a masterly achievement that in the nine years up to 1722 I have brought everything into order
again, so that you do not owe anything as far as the domains are concerned;
the condition of your army and artillery is as good as that of any in Europe.
And rest assured that I had little help from my officials.

The remaining two-thirds of Frederick William's reign were equally
active. Apart from the rebuilding of East Prussia, the king's most significant achievement lay in the creation of an effective administration: a
central organizing authority was established and a class of able,
dependable, keen and hard-working officials was trained. Already in
the first year of his reign authorities that had evolved from the *Staatsrat*
(Council of State) were merged into a central ministry with the long-
winded title of the *General-Oberfinanz-Kriegs-und-Domänen Direktorium*
(the General Supreme Finance War and Domains Directory). It was
called for short the *Generaldirektorium* (General Directory), and dealt
with domestic policy, finances and army administration; provincial
affairs were also put under its control. The three great territorial divisions of the monarchy, completely separate from one another, were,
however, too different in structure to be successfully governed by
schematic centralized authorities. Prussian absolutism, even at the height
of unfettered royal rule, had to take into account the regionalism –
explicable by historical, demographic and economic conditions – of the
diverse parts of the state.

The General Directory, which became effective in 1723, proved
successful in its mixture of functional and territorial administration. It
was divided into four departments, each with a minister, assisted by four
or five councillors. The First Department embraced the provinces of
East Prussia, Pomerania and the Neumark, and had no special functional
responsibilities. The Second Department dealt with the Kurmark and
Magdeburg, as well as with the march-orders, billeting and victualling
of the whole army, and was also responsible for provisioning policy
and for the *Mühlsteinregal* (the royal tax on mill-stones). The Third
Department was in charge of Moers, Guelders, Cleves, Mark, Neuchâtel,
the Orange inheritance, the salt monopoly and the postal service. The
provinces of Minden-Ravensberg, Tecklenburg, Lingen and Halberstadt, as well as the Mint and the care of disabled soldiers, were the
concern of the Fourth Department. A (fifth) Department of Justice
had no territorial limitation: its task was to exercise jurisdiction in all
provinces. Four times a week the departmental heads, with their
councillors, met together for general collegial deliberations in the
Berlin Schloss. Each department had its own registry, but the *Geheime*

Kanzlei (the Secret Chancery) was responsible for the General Directory as a whole. There were two general treasuries, one for the 'war revenues', excise and contributions, and one for the 'domains revenues', the regular revenues of the state. The king reserved for himself the control and use of the *Staatsschatz* (the state treasure), the minted gold kept in the cellars of the Schloss.

The day-to-day administration of the centralized state in the separate regions was the responsibility of the *Kriegs- und Domänenkammern* (the War and Domains Chambers). The authority of a chamber usually embraced a whole province, except in East Prussia, where in 1736 a second chamber was constituted at Gumbinnen to administer the resettlement areas. For the entire state there were from then on nine War and Domains chambers: those at Königsberg and Gumbinnen for East Prussia; Berlin for the Kurmark; Küstrin for the Neumark; Stettin for Pomerania; Magdeburg with Halle's collegial commission (*Deputationskollegium*) for Magdeburg and the county of Mansfeld; Halberstadt for the principality of Halberstadt, the county of Hohenstein and – through a commission – for the county of Wernigerode and the lordships of Derenburg and Hasserode; Minden for the principality of Minden, the county of Ravensberg and the lordships of Tecklenburg and Lingen; Cleves for 'the provinces beyond the Weser', i.e. Cleves-Mark with Moers and Krefeld as well as the duchy of Gelderland which had its own War and Domains Commission. Neuchâtel and Valangin were jointly administered by a governor from the native nobility and a privy council, though their financial affairs were controlled by the Third Department of the General Directory.

The examining and checking of chamber management was done by the *Ober-Kriegs- und Domänen-Rechenkammer* (Chief War and Domains Audit Office), a subordinate organ of the General Directory. The main duties of the War and Domains chambers were to collect, administer and utilize the revenues, in so far as these were not regulated from the centre. The chambers had a duty to encourage production by every possible means, so as to maintain and increase revenue from taxation, to promote agriculture and trade, to maintain law and order, to regulate traffic and to guarantee that security on which confident trading was based. Land reclamation, forestry and construction work underground – in so far as these were matters for the chambers – were advised on by experts, as were mining for salt and metals. The chambers were organized on a collegial basis. Each councillor had a limited functional or regional responsibility while *generalia* were reserved for the directors and presidents. Decisions were reached by vote and decrees were signed

by all. Each chamber had, as its name indicates, a military section which
dealt with the marching of troops, their billeting and victualling; it also
organized the relay of post-horses, assessed compensations and supervised
the magazines.

The basic feature of this administrative structure was subject-related
governmental activity, serving both the fisc and the general good.
Instant success was not to be expected since new and unfamiliar areas of
administration had to be explored. Remnants of the administrative
agencies of Estates government survived everywhere, as did even older
local traditions of princely rule. Older, traditional ways had to be
changed gradually; new objectives had to become the common concern
of those in authority; future work had to be planned and prepared. In
all provinces the older institution of the Estates government, the *Regierung*, continued to function alongside the new institution of the centralist
state, the War and Domains Chamber. Its jurisdiction was now in
theory limited to sharing the administration of justice with the chamber,
the *Regierung* retaining control of such subordinate authorities as the
ecclesiastical consistories, the criminal collegia and the *Hofgericht* (the
provincial superior court); but matters concerning sovereignty, frontier
disputes and questions of feudal tenure, as well as church and school
supervision, also remained the responsibility of the *Regierung*. Its
representational duties, such as hereditary homage, the recessing of the
Landtag (provincial assembly), acts of grace and public mourning,
continued. In these circumstances friction developed which negate any
comparison of the absolutist state with a well-oiled machine. Much that
was irrelevant, irrational, inadequate and antiquated persisted; work was
duplicated and even counteracted; only slowly and with difficulty was
greater order created. The steady imposition of new tasks demanded
an ever increasing adaptability from the administrators, but old routines
and professional jealousy hindered the process. Yet, from the foundation
of the General Directory administrative reforms at all levels of government were the means by which the Prussian state advanced decisively
into the eighteenth century.

Because of the differing ways of raising taxes, separate administration for towns and rural communities was maintained. In the towns –
which were not numerous and usually small – the power of the old
Ratskollegien (town councils) had already in Frederick William's reign
given way to the authorities of the central state, and royal officials
administered police and justice. The excise tax (*Akzise*) raised in the
towns had become a state tax, the town's financial administration being
restricted to its own landed property. The administration of the town

and the collection of the excise became the responsibility of the *Steuerrat* (the tax councillor or commissary), a locally-based representative of the relevant War and Domains Chamber. It is characteristic that he was responsible not only for the supervision and control of taxation but also for the development of taxable produce within his district. The state itself insisted on land reclamation, on the establishment of brickworks and mills and the equipment of workshops with the most up-to-date tools; trade commissions were appointed to explore the market for local products, doubtlessly giving at times more weight to local considerations than to the economic plans of the central government.

The rural areas of almost all the provinces had been divided into administrative units (*Kreise*) on the Brandenburg pattern. In charge of each *Kreis* was the rural commissioner (the *Landrat*) who combined in his person the functions of a royal official and those of a representative of the local Estates. Frequent decrees from the central government on action to be taken by the commissioner strengthened and developed the office so that by the end of the 1740s it transcended regional differences: throughout the state the commissioner had become the chief agent of the crown. The manorial estates and villages that were privately owned were administered as the crown domains, the owners having legal and fiscal powers. Crown tenants, whose leases came up for renewal every six years, also had certain official duties to perform.

State officials, as a rule, held their posts for life. There was not as yet any formally prescribed training or security of tenure, but background, practical experience and local needs were taken into account on appointment; the 'royal servants' were, for the most part, placed in posts suited to their capabilities. Appointment and promotion lay with the king alone but he acted on recommendations from superiors who kept records of the behaviour and abilities of their juniors. During the reign of Frederick William I the majority of officials had been of non-noble stock, as had half the ministers and five-sixths of the councillors of important chambers. Promotion above a certain grade usually brought ennoblement. Since state salaries were low, it was presupposed that private means were available to supplement them. Ministers received from 1,000 to 2,000 talers annually, chamber councillors half of that, subordinate officials up to 100 talers in ready money – but perquisites in naturalia often went with their post. Pensions and holidays were not given as by right but granted on individual application; in time regulations governing such benefits were laid down.

Subordinate positions in the public service were, for the most part, reserved for retired soldiers, particularly non-commissioned officers.

Pensions were thus effectively provided and the aim of drawing closer together the military and civil establishments furthered. Frederick William desired not to militarize the state but to raise the status of the soldiery, to make honest men of the despised and feared *Kerls* (literally 'chaps', 'fellows', used to designate a private soldier) and promote their assimilation with the subjects of burgher status. On his accession in 1713 two-thirds of the army consisted of 'foreigners', i.e. non-Prussians, who had been more or less forcefully conscripted and who could be kept loyal only through the most draconian measures. By the *Kanton-Reglement* of 1733 the number of natives was increased to about two-thirds of the army.

In 1739 the army consisted of thirty-two infantry regiments, twelve cuirassier, seven dragoon and two hussar regiments: including garrison battalions the total number of troops was 81,000. Prussia had 2,700 heavy guns, counting fortress artillery. The troops were spread over the provinces of East Prussia, Pomerania, Magdeburg-Halberstadt, the Mark Brandenburg, Westphalia and Wesel. Garrisons were stationed within their cantonal districts, from which troops were recruited by the regiments, as a rule for a period of two years. Officers were drawn from the Prussian nobility, members of which were forbidden by the king to join the forces of other states. They began service either in the regiments or in the cadet corps. After three months as recruits they served three years as non-commissioned officers before being eligible to fill vacancies as ensigns. More often than not a long wait ensued before a vacancy became available; there were non-commissioned officers from noble families who never received a commission while non-noble non-commissioned officers were sometimes commissioned by the king. We find at times as many as thirty noble non-commissioned officers in a regiment, one-third of them with more than five years service. In the engineer and artillery corps most of the officers were of non-noble stock.

Punctual payment of soldiers, in full, mitigated somewhat the stiff discipline and the brutal punishment meted out to deserters. Soldiers received new outfits annually, so that good uniforms and headgear went far towards the development of an *esprit de corps*. The assimilation of the social orders which Frederick William I desired was promoted by the billeting of soldiers in burgher households. This was, at first, felt by the householders as a heavy burden; but the example of his host had long-term beneficial effects on the soldier, while the house-owner, who had a guest – although one forced upon him – share his meals, usually learnt to trust and like him. The army was kept at full strength only during the period of annual training between April and June. For the rest of the year more than half the troops were on leave: during 1739, for instance, 13,000 of the 23,000 musketeers in the infantry regiments were on leave, employed on the land or in trade – some of them even as journeymen.

During Frederick William's reign his initial strong preference for the military – a policy the consequences of which had not been fully realized – gradually gave way to the experiment of assimilating the army into the general structure of society. The success of this later policy was not complete, in part because the king, who passionately collected *lange* (tall) *Kerls*, even for the cavalry, at times contradicted his own instructions. Jurisdictional disputes – sometimes of the most trivial kind – between the civil and military courts were, however, greatly reduced in number if not altogether halted. In the cantons men of military age eligible for call-up required the permission of the local commander before getting married. This had its reasons: regimental commanders wished to limit, to one-third of the total, soldiers with family commitments. The military 'marriage-permission' which extended over the whole of the young peasant population had undesirable consequences. Frederick William I's conception of justice was a naïve one. For him God's commandments were of supreme importance: the chaplain, who taught his soldiers their catechism, received a warmer welcome than the *Auditeur* (military judicial official). The king's two distinguishing characteristics, a Calvinist asceticism in professional life and a Pietistic sense of the transiency of earthly joys, permeated Prussian life.

No trace of this could be found in the crown prince's 'Anti-Machiavel'; and the Enlightenment, with the materialism of such men as Voltaire and Maupertuis, was almost as far removed from the world of Frederick William I as were the Middle Ages. It was assumed with almost mathematical certainty that the accession of 'Frederick the Philosopher' would usher in an era of change. But those who predicted this were to be proved wrong.

II

The Young King

Frederick II first astonished a watching world by explaining, in elegant and persuasive phrases, the functions of kingship which Frederick William I had practised in such a silent and morose, if constantly active manner. He made it clear that the administrative system would continue unchanged. He disbanded the 'giant guards' and ended recruitment by force, while at the same time expanding the army and accepting presents of regiments from other German princes. His Rheinsberg friends, though given court appointments specifically created for them, were denied real influence, while all his father's trusted collaborators were retained in office. Court ceremonial was curtailed and was conducted, as before, with sobriety and economy. Following the example of his father, Frederick refused to be crowned but his bearing was never without dignity. The order *De la générosité*, founded in 1667, was transformed into a more general distinction, *Pour le mérite*, awarded on merit: the cross of the Knights of St John, the Prussian eagle and Frederick's monogram surmounted by a crown were incorporated in its design.

The Rheinsberg days had ended, abruptly and irrevocably. Because Potsdam had been so much his father's foundation Frederick wished to honour his memory there. A battalion of grenadier guards in old-style uniforms continued to mount guard there in a spirit of reverence. At this time, Potsdam did not become Frederick's residence; neither was he drawn to the old Jagdschloss in the Grunewald nor to the castle at remote Oranienburg on the Havel; and he avoided the hunting lodge at Wusterhausen, haunted by unhappy childhood memories. The queen mother remained at Monbijou, her Berlin palace. The new king went direct from his father's death-bed to the old Schlosss by the Spree; the next day he moved to Charlottenburg where he decided to take up residence. Directly opposite the palace he had new barracks built for his mounted life-guards.

Rural Lietzenburg had lost little of its village character since the first Prussian king had built a summer palace there for his Guelph wife, Sophia Charlotte, and named it after her. Arnold Nering had designed and supervised the main building between 1695 and 1699, and the Swedish architect Eosander von Göthe had enlarged the palace, adding a new wing. There was a garden laid out in the Dutch fashion, but the whole was still unfinished on Frederick II's accession. Another wing, originally planned as an orangery, was now built to house the royal apartments. For this Frederick employed Georg Wenzeslaus von Knobelsdorff, who had rebuilt Rheinsberg in a manner that pleased the king. This wing, with its delicate rococo decor, was not completed until 1746 when the great banqueting hall, the Golden Gallery, was formally opened. Frederick took a close interest in the work and influenced it strongly: the interiors are fine examples of early Frederician rococo. Intended for the king's daily use were a panelled study, a bedroom and a library, all facing the gardens and less ornate than the sumptuous banqueting hall, with ceilings painted by Antoine Pesne.

In the event, Frederick never lived in the suite of rooms whose building he had supervised with such great expectations; but he spent the first months of his reign at Charlottenburg where the peaceful atmosphere encouraged undisturbed work. There, on 2 June 1740, he explained to his ministers, who had just taken their oaths of office, the principle that would guide his reign: 'We do not recognize any distinction between our interests and those of the realm. . . . in fact the interests of the realm must take precedence over our own, should they fail to coincide.' With work on Charlottenburg, somewhat neglected during his father's reign, restarted, Frederick spent some autumn weeks at Rheinsberg; then he left for the campaign against Austria, not to return to Charlottenburg until July 1742. During the Seven Years War Charlottenburg was sacked by the Russians (in 1760), but it was restored on the express instructions of Frederick.

Although the royal apartments in the Berlin Schloss were refurnished while Charlottenburg was being completed, no important rebuilding was undertaken there. After the Second Silesian War Frederick decided to transfer his residence from the noise and bustle of Berlin to Potsdam. The period of peace after that war saw the transformation by Knobelsdorff of the Town Palace (the Stadtschloss) in Potsdam. Originally a cluster of buildings, some of which dated back to the time of Elector Joachim I (1483–1535), the Town Palace had been completely renovated by the Great Elector (1620–88). Now Knobelsdorff added corinthian pilasters to the façades and corner portals and fitted an outside terraced

staircase decorated with colonnades to the front of the palace. He raised
the wings to three storeys – to match the main building – and surrounded
the parade ground with pergolas, yew hedges and statuary. Johann
August Nahl the Elder and Christian Hoppenhaupt the Younger
designed the interiors and the furniture, counted among the glories of
German rococo. Already in 1747 the king was able to receive Johann
Sebastian Bach in the new concert hall.

During the same year the little palace of Sans Souci outside Potsdam,
an enchanting, intimate palace on a miniature scale, was built after the
king's own designs. It was conjured into being by Knobelsdorff and
furnished by Nahl. With its terraces and parks, its temples and statues,
Sans Souci blends into the landscape of the Mark Brandenburg with its
brooding northern sky in a perfect harmony of nature and art. During
the years of peace the table-talk and flute concerts at Sans Souci were
the king's pleasures and limited to a small circle of friends. From Berlin
through Charlottenburg to the Town Palace in Potsdam and onwards
to Sans Souci, stretched a kind of escape route, a striving for ever
greater solitude. The style of the New Palace (the Neues Palais), built
at the far end of the park of Sans Souci in the straitened years after the
Seven Years War, belongs to the same sequence, though Frederick never
resided in its cold marbled magnificence. Nor did he wish to do so. He
disassociated himself from any *fanfaronade* and remained at Sans Souci,
his *monrepos*, with his music, his poetry and the works of Voltaire. It
was there that lonely old age – and death – awaited him.

Can these palaces, from which the absolute monarch carried on his
government, be considered residences? Such a question reveals the
insufficiency of our conception of absolutism. In fact, government
demanded more than the exercise of the royal will and the issuance of
decrees; for these necessarily presupposed the perusal and evaluation
of relevant documents, assembled by competent and well-informed
subordinates. Even if the monarch wanted to govern from his study
or 'cabinet', he could not possibly remain in permanent seclusion: the
proximity of a readily available, easily controlled and closely supervised
secretariat was indispensable to his office. Sans Souci, strictly out-of-
bounds to the inhabitants of Potsdam, was a sanctuary, a place for
relaxation and recuperation. The king naturally concerned himself
with affairs of state while staying at Sans Souci; he drew up programmes
there and contemplated questions of fundamental importance; his
Political Testaments, for instance, were written there. But the act of
ruling demanded direct, continuous and intimate contact with the
executive organs of the state. Therefore, near the royal palaces we find

the *Residenzstadt* (literally 'the town of the residence', i.e. royal capital), and that, indisputably, was Berlin. Although Potsdam also carried the title *Residenzstadt*, it housed only a few outposts of the central administration.

While the king needed hardly more than his study, his bedroom, his library and a patch of garden, apart from a few rooms and a kitchen for his servants, the administration expanded so much (despite the most stringent economy in the employment of personnel) that only a large city could provide the facilities necessary for the permanent accommodation and efficient functioning of its various branches. Berlin, made up of five originally separate towns (Berlin, Kölln, Friedrichswerder, Dorotheenstadt and Friedrichstadt), in 1740 had a population of 98,000. By 1786 it had grown to almost 150,000, despite the casualties and consequences of war. In 1740 the Berlin garrison numbered 25,000 men (including those on leave) with an equal number of dependants. The French colony remained fairly constant at 5,000 members; the Bohemians numbered about 1,000 and the Jews 3,000. There were 12,500 Calvinists and 8,000 Catholics; the rest were Lutherans. Domestic servants numbered 3,000 men and 10,000 women. In 1784 Berlin had 35,000 inhabitants employed in trade, counting master-craftsmen, journeymen and labourers. Officials accounted for only a tenth of that figure, 3,500 in all. The public relief funds supported 7,000 people. The prisons held forty-seven short-term prisoners and fifty-one dangerous criminals. After the inner defences had fallen into disuse the whole city, including the suburbs, was surrounded by a wall.

In 1784 the king's household – taking Berlin and Potsdam together – consisted of five court officials, seven masters of the horse with a hundred and twenty-seven coachmen and grooms; a royal orchestra of thirty-six musicians, an Italian opera company of thirty-eight singers, with another twenty-four dancers and actors in the ballet and theatre companies; nine gardeners, twenty-five cooks, four servants in charge of the plate and, taking all the palaces into account, ten stewards and an indeterminate number of lower servants. The courts of Frederick's wife and of his brothers and nephew, 'the Prussian princes', were much smaller.

At this period Berlin housed the following government organs: the *Geheime Staatsrat* (the Secret State Council), the Department of External Affairs, the *Generaldirektorium* (the General Directory), the Chief Audit Office (the *Oberrechenkammer*), the General Supply Office (the *Generalproviantamt*) and its different *Kassen* (literally 'chests', i.e. treasuries); the Department of Justice (*Justizdepartement*) and the Supreme Court (*Kammergericht*), the Ecclesiastical Department with the Lutheran

General Consistory (*Oberkonsistorium*), the department dealing with Calvinist affairs, the *Lehnsdepartement* concerned with feudal matters, and the 'French Department' for Huguenot affairs; the *Oberkuratorium* (supervising the universities) and the department charged with the affairs of the Palatinate settlements. There were also the General Directory of the Post, the General Excise and Customs Administration (the so-called *Regie*), the Supreme Medical Board, the Office of the Fiscal (*Fiskalat*) and the General Directorate of the Mint (*Generalmünz-direktorium*). Of the administrative army agencies the *Generalauditoriat* (which supervised the administration of justice in the army), the *Kriegskonsistorium* (the army chaplainate supervisory body), the *Geheime Kriegskanzlei* (the Secret War Chancery) and the *Intendantur* (Commissariat) had their offices in Berlin. The city also housed the Kurmark's *Landschaftlichen Kollegien* (the colleges of the Estates) and Berlin's own municipal authorities. Bodies specifically related to Berlin's status as a *Residenzstadt* had also been created: the Court Post Office, the Royal Firewood Administration, the Commission for Royal Buildings in Berlin, the Berlin Saltworks, the Berlin Fire Society, the Court dealing with the Porcelain Factory, etc. Social welfare institutions included the *Invalidenhaus* (hospital for disabled soldiers), the Institute for Poor Widows, the Public Alms Houses with their Relief Centres, and the sick care organization of the garrison.The Academy, the libraries, the art collections and the galleries proclaimed the city's status as a *Residenzstadt*. The Royal Library and the Schloss collection of royal paintings were open to the public.

In Potsdam petitions to the king were promptly dealt with by a staff of three privy cabinet councillors. A public notice of 1786 reads: 'Petitions to the king should be submitted to one of the cabinet councillors on duty. Immediate consideration will be given to petitions. Those handed in during the morning are answered in writing by 5 p.m. if the petitioner is in Potsdam; others are answered by post.' The *Feldjäger* (couriers), who carried dispatches between Berlin and Potsdam, exchanged bags half-way, at Zehlendorf; the distance between the capital and the king's Potsdam *Residenz* could be covered in two and a half hours. Frederick, travelling in an eight-horse carriage – as had been his father's custom – could make the journey in just over an hour. The *Journalière*, a daily public post-coach, took five hours each way.

Quite apart from building palaces, which tell us much about his taste, Frederick modernized Berlin and Potsdam, giving them public buildings worthy of their position at the centre of the monarchy. The first phase of building activity, beginning in 1745 after the Second

Silesian War, was set in motion by the 10 million talers paid by East Friesland. The fortifications by the Königs Tor (the King's Gate) and the Spandauer Tor (the Spandau Gate) having been demolished, the new Friedrichstrasse was financed from this money. Around it a new residential quarter was developed and a new Friedrichsbrücke was built over the Spree. In 1748 the old cathedral was pulled down, the Schlossplatz enlarged and the building of a new cathedral in the Lustgarten was begun. In the same period the *Arbeitshaus* (workhouse) and the *Invalidenhaus* were built near the Oranienburger Tor. Four years later the Neuvogtland suburb took shape.

When, after the Seven Years' War, the second phase of the building programme got under way, it was essential to remedy the housing shortage. Nearly 150 *Bürgerhäuser* (apartment houses for eight families) were erected between 1769 and 1777. Work on the new porcelain factory had begun already in 1763. In the following year the *Ritterakademie* (an academy for young nobles), a Manchester textile manufactory and a lacquer works near Monbijou were built. In 1769 a stone bridge, the Pomeranzenbrücke, was constructed, but it was not till 1774 that it was followed by the Royal Library and the Comedy Theatre (the Komödienhaus); the Friedrichstadt square (now the Gendarmen Markt) with its French theatre, flanked on either side by the twin domes of the French and German churches, was planned at the same time; the Unter den Linden with its Academy buildings was reshaped as a splendid thoroughfare incorporating the Opera Platz with St Hedwig's Catholic Church and Prince Henry's Palace. To the west of the Unter den Linden the Tiergarten was laid out as a public park, its many paths meeting in the Grossen Stern (the 'Big Star'), close to Bellevue, the residence built for Prince Ferdinand, the king's youngest brother. These developments transformed Berlin, giving the capital magnificent boulevards, avenues, squares and groups of public buildings.

The redevelopment of Potsdam, which at the end of the Second Silesian War had a population of 25,000, was carried out simultaneously under the supervision of the king and his architect Karl von Gontard. The changes effected accorded with the wishes of Frederick William I expressed in his political testament, though his request that Potsdam should be renamed 'Wilhelmstadt' was ignored. Frederick II demolished half the modest half-timbered terrace houses built during his father's reign to make way for streets of massive buildings distinguished by individually designed façades. The new buildings were financed by the state, but their upkeep was the responsibility of the burghers. By razing whole streets, carefully siting new roads and balancing the long vistas of three-storey houses with their connecting squares, Frederick created a harmonious north German baroque town. The public buildings strikingly demonstrate Italian influence (though Frederick himself never visited Italy): from the Town Hall (*Rathaus*) opposite the magnificent portal of the Nicolaikirche and its presbytery, the Huguenot Church, the palace-like orphanage and the Barberini Palace – a copy of that in Rome – to the triumphal arch and the marble obelisk in the Altmarkt (Old Market). Close by the Town Palace was the small arms factory with its heavily-ornamented façade. Strenuous efforts were made to attract trade to Berlin and Potsdam: the manufacture of tapestry, faience and silk were thought particularly suitable. The majority of the soldiers were taken out of private billets and concentrated in barracks built for them in Potsdam. Such barracks, as well as stables and magazines, were also built in various districts of Berlin. The Potsdam garrison, counting those on leave, numbered 8,000 men. Frederick William I's Potsdam had been a purpose-built utilitarian centre. Frederick II transformed it into a city of great charm and individuality. During his reign the number of buildings in Berlin increased fivefold, those in Potsdam eightfold. Both cities confute the legend of 'sober, inartistic, Prussian thrift'. Potsdam was no Sparta; and under Frederick II Berlin became a veritable 'Athens-on-the-Spree', the enlightened philosopher of Sans Souci proving himself less of a rationalist utilitarian than his strict father.

News-sheets first made their appearance in Berlin in 1727, giving the public information on price-changes, exchange rates and the arrival and departure of foreign visitors. In time vacant positions, sales notices and details of church services were added. After Frederick's accession in 1740 the *Berlinischen Nachrichten von Staats- und gelehrten Sachen* (Berlin news on state affairs and learned matters) made its appearance. Published by A. Haude and edited – from 1772 – by J. K. Ph. Spener, this paper, like the *Vossische Zeitung* (published by royal privilege), was delivered to its subscribers three times a week. The French-language *Journal de Berlin*, later renamed the *Gazette littéraire de Berlin*, also began publication in 1740. Serious newspapers were, in Frederick's opinion, an essential element in the proper education of the capital's inhabitants. He did not share the objections of his ministers to political articles: gazettes must not be 'harassed' if they were to retain the interest of their readers.

Frederick looked upon his residences as an embodiment both of the state and of the royal will guiding the state. His vigorous building programme was concentrated on Berlin and Potsdam, the focal points of his territories. The style and elegance of these cities enabled them to outshine Prussia's few other large towns. The embellishment of Berlin and Potsdam added – though perhaps unnoticed at the time – laurels of renown to those Frederick had already earned on the battlefield.

RECEIVING HOMAGE

During the early days of his government Frederick was strongly affected by his father's last words and by the opening and reading of the Political Testament Frederick William had left him. The continuity with his father's reign is strikingly evident in his decrees and orders in the realm of policy as in the administration. But, since a change of system was expected on Frederick's accession, the king's every word was scrutinized in a climate of opinion in which contemporaries read reform and innovation into acts which owed more to the will of Frederick William than most were prepared to admit.

The new king's expansion of the army followed in every detail his father's Political Testament of 1722. The abolition of torture, advocated by Samuel von Cocceji and proclaimed by Frederick in 1740, was enthusiastically welcomed by the disciples of the Enlightenment throughout Europe, especially since other governments of the time did not consider such a reform feasible. But in Prussia it had already been foreshadowed by a decree of 1720 which permitted torture only after the king had given his express permission. It should also be noted that complete abolition did not come in Frederick's reign – the use of torture was kept for very serious crimes. No new law was necessary; the reform was effected by modifying existing regulations. Another case in point is religious toleration. Frederick William's reign had not been intolerant. His Political Testament stressed the fact that the Prussian army had many Catholic soldiers and urged his successor to permit them their services: 'As far as the Catholic religion is concerned you must tolerate it.' Frederick's famous marginal note of 22 June 1740, in answer to complaints from the Ecclesiastical Department of proselytizing in Catholic garrison schools, was wholly in the tradition of his father – in spirit as in choice of words: 'All religions must be tolerated. The Fiscal shall only keep an eye open lest one encroaches on the other, for here everyone must be allowed to choose his own road to salvation.' His fundamental maxim for governing he also owed to his father: 'A ruler who wants to govern with honour must do everything himself. . . . You alone must deal with income and expenditure and you must keep the command of the army in your own hands.'

The firm and speedy way in which the twenty-eight-year-old king put these principles into practice caused great and general astonishment.

Yet Frederick had been preparing himself for his *métier* ever since 1734. The twenty-second chapter of his 'Anti-Machiavel' of 1739 expressed his personal conception of the duties of a ruler:

> There are two kinds of princes in the world: those who see everything with their own eyes and who really govern, and those who depend on their ministers, allowing themselves to be led by those who have gained influence over them. Princes of the first kind are, so to speak, the embodiment of the state. On them rests the burden of government, like the world on the shoulders of Atlas. They direct internal as well as foreign affairs; all orders, laws and instructions emanate from them; they are, simultaneously, ministers of justice, commanders-in-chief of the army and ministers of finance: in short, every aspect of policy demands their decision. Following the example of God, who uses beings higher than men to carry out His Will, they employ men of shrewd and energetic temperament to execute their intentions and to put their great designs into effect.

The earliest act of homage paid to Frederick came from the fusilier guard of the Glasenapp regiment, whose shouts of *Vivat* woke him on the first morning of his reign. Later that day he spoke to his assembled generals on the necessity of their setting an example by carrying out their duties to the letter and by the strictest self-discipline: 'The troops must be as effective as they are smartly turned-out, but they must not be allowed to become a burden to the land they are meant to protect.' When Prince Leopold of Anhalt-Dessau expressed his hope of being permitted to retain the 'authority' he had enjoyed in the previous reign, Frederick frostily answered that he knew nothing of such an authority and declared his determination not to share his royal power. From his ministers the new king demanded punctuality, thrift and 'promptitude in the execution of business'. He incurred their displeasure by confirming August Friedrich von Boden (a former domain tenant who had become Frederick William's cabinet secretary) in his post as minister of finance, thus signifying his adherence to stict cameralist principles. But where *Plusmacherei* (literally 'plus-making', i.e. extortion) had in the king's opinion gone beyond bounds, filling the royal coffers by ruthlessly exploiting the people, he took drastic action. Johann Gottlob von Eckart, a native of Anhalt, a dyer by trade and later a *Sparkommisar* (savings commissioner) whom Frederick William had ennobled and made a finance councillor, was expelled from Prussia to set an example: he had been a 'project-maker', typical of those at all courts of the time, whose lack of compassion and desire to please the king had made him an extortioner.

Frederick employed three colonels from the active list, in preference to the customary diplomats, to announce his accession to the three most important European courts. This was a challenge, one which the 'Soldier King' had not permitted himself. Moreover, by choosing his military emissaries for their abilities rather than for their family trees, Frederick flouted convention. Colonel Count Truchsess von Waldburg's mission to Hanover angered Versailles. Colonel von Camas, the king's special confidant but of less distinguished lineage, was sent to France: this was seen as an indication of Prussia's preference for the hated rival Hanover-England. The dispatch of Colonel von Münchow to Vienna was precisely matched to the degree of respect which the Emperor had shown Frederick William. The young king in Charlottenburg noted with wry amusement that the European courts, usually so punctilious in matters of ceremonial, made no protest. Truchsess was instructed to send 'two kinds of dispatches', one meant for the king alone and marked *soli*, 'the other with the news for the ministry'.

In July 1740 the Marquis de Valory, French envoy in Berlin since September 1739, reported 'that the new monarch is even more impenetrable than his father; he does everything himself, and his ministers are mere drudges of middling importance'. Frederick left nobody in doubt that he intended to be his own finance minister, his own field-marshal, and his own minister for home and foreign affairs. 'His character is such', wrote the Marquis de Beauveau whom Louis XV sent to Berlin to congratulate Frederick on his accession, 'that he believes intellectual power is the key to knowledge, that he needs advice from no man; and, more particularly, that he is determined to play a leading role in Europe, whatever the cost.' An absolute ruler, then, but admittedly – and nobody doubted this – an enlightened one. Frederick, however, was less influenced by the Enlightenment as a guideline for action than by *raison d'état* interpreted in an enlightened way. The general principle was trimmed to suit the particular circumstances of his own state. There were, certainly, limits to his absolutism. As ruler he was dependent on collaborators and on the excellent administrative apparatus built up by his father. His ability to control this apparatus and his independence of ministers, senior officials and military officers would be of decisive importance.

Before setting out on his royal progress to receive homage from his three main provincial territories, Frederick made some characteristic administrative reforms. All reversionary interests in estates held in fee, in directorships of domains and in prebends were abolished. All officials were instructed to make their reports shorter and more business-like, to dispatch work more speedily and, above all, to exercise stricter supervision in respect of building programmes, demands on public funds and claims for damages: officials, while maintaining contact with the public in these matters, must not allow themselves to be deceived. Arrears were to be made good from within each bureau from its own resources. On 2 June 1740 Frederick scotched rumours, which had been circulating since the spring, of impending changes in the administration itself by this pointed marginal note: 'It seems to me as if the General Directory wants to throw all old principles to the winds.' A request from the Directory that a journeyman should be allowed to go abroad to get married was returned with the comment: 'The Directory's job is to bring people into the country, not to let them out. The enquiry is both foolish and ridiculous. They must not bring such requests forward again. Fr.' Royal vassals were expressly forbidden to take up positions outside the state, and those working abroad were to be cajoled into returning by promises of advancement at home.

Costly formal ceremonies were abolished so that the money saved could be diverted to more sensible uses. One example of this was the omission in the official seals of the many coats of arms of territories to which Prussia held hereditary claim: as far as the young king was concerned the welfare of the state did not depend on such trivia. Like his father Frederick refused a solemn coronation, holding that 'ampullae of holy oil and useless, empty ceremonies owed their introduction to ignorance and their survival to custom'. For his royal progress he requested that there should be 'no ceremonies or fuss with processions; neither fanfares from church towers, nor firing of salutes, speeches, strewing of flowers, foxtail grass or such like, no matter what it is called; everything is to remain as it was before' – that is, 'as it was in my father's day'. As in Frederick William's reign the electoral cap and sceptre were not exhibited when the Estates of the Kurmark paid homage. Kingship as an embodiment of the state was in any case remote from the Prussian mentality. Carl Hinrichs is certainly right in stressing that Prussia's kings wished to be no more than the state's highest officials, able to travel incognito so as not to be diverted from their duties and, more importantly, not to interrupt their subjects in their daily work. Such a conception of the state is the ultimate in rationality: on the one hand alien to the earlier baroque age and on the other impossible to maintain once the French Revolution had introduced public spectacles and mass demonstrations.

Frederick's acceptance of his people's homage was, therefore, hardly more than a constitutional safety precaution. It was offered not so much to himself as to the holder of his office. On 1 and 2 June the leading ministers of the General Directory and the ministers of state took the oath of allegiance. Then, between 7 and 9 June, these same men conducted the swearing-in ceremony of their own officials in accordance with the customary formulae used in 1713. The oath taken by the privy finance councillors, the privy secretaries and registrars of the General Directory and of the Kurmark War and Domains Chamber, contained – apart from the usual emphasis on the secrecy attached to their office and the prohibition against the acceptance of gifts – a caution against the communication of official correspondence to outsiders. On 4 June orders were issued to the following authorities to take the oath of allegiance: the War and Domains chambers, the Gelderland (Guelders) Commission, the *Regierung* in Moers, and the High Courts in the Altmark and the Uckermark. A similar order went to the Secret War Chancery on 28 June. On 13 June officials of state ministries and of other official bodies of East Prussia took the oath in Königsberg.

On 7 July the king left Berlin with a small retinue to receive the homage of East Prussia. He shared his own carriage with his adjutant-general, Count von Hacke, his Rheinsberg friend Dietrich Freiherr von Keyserlingk, and the Venetian Francesco Algarotti, a writer of some elegance and a companion on whom he was to confer the title of count in 1747. Frederick also took with him his own chefs. The journey proceeded along an already familiar route: from Berlin via Lebus, Frankfurt on the Oder, Landsberg on the Warthe, Soldin, Pyritz, Stargard in Pomerania, Köslin, Stolp, Lauenburg, Wutzkow, Marienwerder, Riesenburg, Preussisch Holland, Mohrungen, Liebstadt, Preussisch Eylau, Wandlacken (near Gerdauen), Angerburg, Insterburg, Gumbinnen, Trakehnen and Tilsit to Königsberg which the king entered on the morning of 16 July. Following his father's example he had inspected regiments en route: at Landsberg, Stargard, Köslin, Stolp, Marienwerder, Preussisch Holland and Angerburg. The cuirassier regiment stationed at Angerburg was commanded by Hans Heinrich von Katte, father of the young lieutenant who had been beheaded for his part in Frederick's escape attempt. The king promoted him field-marshal and conferred on him the hereditary title of *Graf* (count). In every large village along the king's route the chief officials of the royal domains were ordered to ride alongside Frederick's carriage to give an account of their stewardship. At Marienwerder, Wandlacken, Trakehnen and Königsberg, where there were royal quarters, the king made use of these; elsewhere he usually put up at the local parsonage.

In Königsberg on Sunday 17 July the service of homage was held at 10 a.m. in the Schlosskirche, conducted by the senior court-chaplain,

Johann Jakob Quandt, whose sermon pleased and impressed Frederick. It was followed by a military parade in the Königsgarten. On the following two days representatives from Kurland, Orange and Elbing (mortgaged to Prussia by the Polish-Lithuanian Commonwealth forty-two years earlier) were received in audience; prisoners were pardoned; and the king visited the Customs House (*Licenthaus*) and the harbour where he counted more than a hundred and eighty ships. Frederick also walked round the town. The pupils of the orphanage were presented to him and the university students fêted him with a torchlight procession and a serenade after which he treated them to wine. On 20 July official business began. Following the swearing-in of the ministers of state the general homage took place in the courtyard of the castle where the rural commissioners, the *Ritterschaft* (the nobility below the rank of count), the magistrates of Königsberg, the representatives of the towns of the province, and of the guilds and the university professors, had gathered. Minister Heinrich von Podewils had already come to an agreement with the Estates which had been holding their *Landtag* during the previous eight days. No open opposition was voiced but the leader of the Estates (the *Landesdirektor*), Wilhelm Ludwig von der Groeben, hinted in his address of homage that Frederick ought to meet the Estates to settle their grievances. This hint was ignored. The king accepted the homage and let commemorative medals, boldly inscribed *Borussorum Rex*, be scattered among the people. After the midday meal, however, before Frederick set out for Danzig on his return journey to Berlin, a secret state council was held to discuss proposals put forward by the Estates.

By delaying the announcement of the homage ceremonies to the king of Saxony-Poland Frederick had ensured that his visit to Königsberg would not be marred by the presence of Polish commissaries: a clause (not abrogated till 1772) in the Polish-Brandenburg Treaty of Wehlau of 1657 laid down that the duchy of (East) Prussia was, in the event of the extinction of the House of Hohenzollern, to revert to Poland; and that Prussian officials, when doing homage to each new Hohenzollern ruler, were to take an oath acknowledging this clause in the presence of representatives of the king of Poland.

Frederick's previous visits had made him familiar with the situation in East Prussia. He knew that thanks to Frederick William's particular concern the province was flourishing, having benefited from reforms in many fields. Now, for decades to come, it had to take second place so that the pressing problems of other provinces could be dealt with in the interest of the unitary state (*Gesamtstaat*). Frederick did plan an important administrative reform for East Prussia (building on an idea of his father's from 1737*) whereby the Masurian districts would have a separate administration centred on Osterode, housed in the old castle of the Teutonic Knights; but money could not be spared for the salaries of the necessary officials and the project had to be dropped. Had it come into effect there would have been a tripartite division: the Königsberg Chamber administering the old Prussian districts, the Gumbinnen Chamber the Prusso-Lithuanian ones, and the Osterode Chamber those of Masuria. As it was all districts (including the Masurian ones) remained, though more rationally distributed, under the Königsberg and Gumbinnen chambers until 1905 when, with the creation of the county of Allenstein, Frederick's project was implemented.

The written grievances presented by the Prussian Estates on such questions as military conscription, the judicial powers of royal domain officials, the salt monopoly and the tax on flour, the exodus of craftsmen from the villages and the return of escaped serfs did receive royal consideration. Most of them were dealt with in the general legal reform of 1750, in the improvements made in the cantonal system, and in the standardization of economic regulations. The king was always prepared to accept regional variations and to make exceptions to general regulations. Temporary decontrol of grain exports was, for example, allowed on the petition of Königsberg merchants. The right of the university of Königsberg's theological faculty to issue testimonials to prospective teachers and ministers was not curbed, and the pietistic decrees issued in 1734 by Frederick William remained in force. This was a set-back for orthodox Lutheranism which had hoped to use the Enlightenment to strike a death-blow at Pietism. The Estates' attempts to have the office of the rural commissioner defined according to the Kurmark tradition did not succeed; the king's concept of the office prevailed. Frederick showed no interest in the question of the rights of the *Landtag*; for him they were of no importance in the *Gesamtstaat*.

On the afternoon of 24 July Frederick arrived back in Berlin and on Tuesday 2 August the Estates of the Kurmark did homage. The homage sermon in the cathedral, which began at 8 o'clock in the morning, was by order confined to a quarter of an hour. Among the hereditary officers of state the king gave a place of honour to von Münchow, the former president of the Küstrin Chamber, his first tutor in the practice of administration – a token of regard and reconciliation which compensated

* Frederick William had then proposed the establishment of a *Kammerdeputation* (that is, a commission subordinate to the War and Domains Chamber) for the Masurian districts in either Neidenburg or Osterode.

the old man for the troubles and tribulations he had experienced in his relationship with Frederick as crown prince. In Berlin, in contrast with Königsberg, traditional ceremonial was strictly observed. In the hall of homage the king sat with covered head on a throne, flanked right and left by the hereditary chamberlain holding the sceptre and the hereditary marshal carrying the sword. The *Ritterschaft* spoke the words of their oath loudly with raised right hand, and a triple 'Vivat Fredericus Rex' followed. The king stepped on to the balcony of the Schloss where, after a short speech by the chief city official (the *Stadt-Präsident*), the assembled citizens (the *Bürgerschaft*) acclaimed their king. Frederick had ordered that the splendid ceremonial of 1688 – when the electoral cap had been carried in procession and guns had been fired in salute – should be replaced by the short and simple ritual used by his father in 1713: everything must be arranged 'in such a way that, by avoiding all useless formalities, the whole business can be quickly dispensed with; for wasteful ceremonial is of no use to me'. But gazing down on the surging crowd in the Lustgarten the king was suddenly struck by the significance of the occasion. In the words of an eye-witness he became 'lost in contemplation'.

At the ceremony of homage the Estates of the Kurmark presented grievances and requests. They asked for their own (as opposed to royal) right of presentation to prebends and for the curbing of the power of consistorial courts to overrule church patrons. They demanded exemption for the nobility, and also for the *Ritterschaft* of the Uckermark, from customs duties, from taxes levied in lieu of soldiers' billet and board (the so-called Potsdam 'bed-money' and 'cavalry-money') and from the duties of helping to build royal castles and representing the ruler on missions abroad, basing their demands on the Brandenburg Recess of 1653. They further requested that their peasants' share of military and staging service should be curtailed, that the salaries paid to legal officials should be raised, that they themselves should be accorded an advisory role in all reforms of the law, and that the *Fiscus* (the fisc) should be prohibited from interfering in the decisions of the manorial courts. These grievances were reminiscent of those already submitted by the East Prussian Estates. Frederick did put a stop to the resumption of alienated domain land, a policy pursued by Frederick William to increase the crown lands at the expense of noble estates. In other respects, however, the Estates of Brandenburg fared as those of East Prussia: 'As their remonstrances are extremely verbose and appear to contain many useless and, in the present state of affairs, impracticable and questionable *gravamina*', the king decided that they should be examined by the relevant authorities and put before him in a more presentable form.

Despite yearly reminders from the Estates up to and including 1746 they received no satisfaction. Legislation could not proceed in the modern state by decrees embodying local privileges; enacted in the interests of the *Gesamtstaat* it could not make exception for Estates or individuals. Official regulations and the administration of justice, reformed and controlled from the centre, were held sufficient to remedy grievances. The 'right way' was to place grievances before the appropriate authorities and have them considered along with other petitions in 'the normal manner': in the Frederician state the Estates had ceased to have special rights in this respect.

On the day of the Berlin ceremony the Prussian part of Hither Pomerania also did homage. Hille, former director of the Küstrin *Kammer*, was honoured on this occasion by being nominated one of Frederick's plenipotentiaries. In February 1741, after long negotiations with the Estates, the *Regierung* of Stettin sent a list of the provincial privileges claimed by Hither Pomerania to Berlin for confirmation; but neither this nor a reminder in June 1745 brought any answer from the king. The act of homage in Further Pomerania and the Neumark was indefinitely postponed to avoid the attendance of Swedish commissaries, since the Peace of Westphalia had given Sweden the right to residual allegiance: as in East Prussia Frederick ignored old constitutional forms which did not suit his concept of Prussian independence. Not until 5 April 1743, at a time when Sweden was preoccupied with internal party strife and at war with Russia, did Frederick instruct the Stettin and Küstrin chambers to hold their homage ceremonies. His officials assured him that as far as Neumark was concerned homage had sufficiently been done in 1740. For Further Pomerania, as a substitute for the ceremony of homage, a special commission toured the province from 2 to 30 September 1743. Vassals who failed to appear before it were held accountable under feudal law. To coincide with the homage ceremony in Lauenburg and Bütow on 26 September – at which Frederick was represented by Philipp Otto von Grumbkow, president of the Pomeranian War and Domains Chamber – the towns and *Ritterschaft* of the region held a *Landtag* at which grievances were presented demanding freedom from cantonal obligations and army service for noblemen, and tax relief for the towns.

Homage ceremonies had been held in the duchy of Magdeburg on 2 August 1740. On the same date ceremonies had also taken place at Halle in which the saltworkers traditionally participated, in the county of Luckenwalde, in the town of Burg, and in the lordship of Rosenburg and the domain of Rosenburg. There were good grounds for painstaking observance of all legal formalities: since several magnates with estates or residences in these areas tried to avoid doing homage Frederick insisted on the fulfilment, however belatedly, of all homage obligations. The Magdeburg Estates had carefully co-ordinated their *Landes-Desiderien* (literally 'wishes of their land') with Kurmark and Halberstadt and presented a thick volume of over four hundred folio pages of documents at the homage ceremony. They demanded the preservation of old privileges, control through regional commissions of their own administration, the re-establishment of their territorial treasuries, and participation in lawmaking and in the workings of the new church ordinance of 1740. They opposed reform of the administration of justice: 'A multiplicity of laws only gives rise to greater prevarication'; formerly 'an old German, i.e. an honest heart, presided over the law courts', now 'parsons and tricky Italian lawyers' destroy it (i.e. the heart) 'by the introduction of laws the artificiality of which have already caused much damage in their own countries'. They also held that there was an urgent need for drawing clearer lines of demarcation between the jurisdiction of the Chamber and that of the army authorities if widespread abuses were to be stopped: 'almost everywhere the *miles perpetuum* forms a special *état* and *corpus* within society and is separate and independent of any other constitutional authority'. They desired the abolition of cantonal obligations and wished the army to be recruited from foreign mercenaries, while the provinces themselves should be responsible for an adequate militia force.

From such demands it is easy to deduce what changes were desired by provincial Estates still regional in outlook and preoccupied with class privileges: exemption from imposts, favourable trading conditions with 'foreign lands', including the other Prussian provinces, freedom from taxation for the nobility, the strengthening and extension of manorial jurisdiction, freedom of the hunt, and patronal rights with unlimited administration of ecclesiastical property. Between December 1740 and March 1742 Magdeburg several times reminded the king, in vain, that he owed them an answer.

The principality of Halberstadt also rendered traditional homage on 2 August 1740. At the request of the Estates a special ceremony was held in the county of Hohenstein, while Derenburg in the Harz (which in feudal law belonged to the Kurmark) rendered homage in Berlin. Brandenburg's right to dissolve the Catholic monasteries at any time, guaranteed in the Peace of Westphalia, was publicly reiterated, though it was not invoked in Frederick's reign. The Halberstadt Estates had handed their requests and grievances to the local *Regierung* which forwarded them to Berlin, thus making the examination of the bulky documents easier. As their contents were similar to the Magdeburg *Desiderien* we need not consider them in detail apart from mentioning demands specific to Halberstadt: permission was sought to leave the town gates open at night on the grounds that their closure harmed trade and agriculture; freedom of appeal to the Imperial courts (never legally rescinded) was demanded.* The Protestants wished to have the feasts of the Virgin Mary and St John restored; the 'abolition of the special privileges of artists' was demanded as was the abolition of the minting rights of the cathedral chapter, the magistrates of Halberstadt and others. Although royal assent to these and other demands was not forthcoming, the General Directory tried to remedy abuses (where they agreed that abuses existed) through the normal channels of law and administration.

Other western territories to render homage on 2 August were Moers and the principality of Minden. The prelates and *Ritterschaft* of Minden included in their grievances complaints of cantonal obligations and special taxes, and claims for taxation rights for the Estates and exemption of the nobility from taxation and from various administrative duties. In October 1740 a polite but firm reply was received from the Directory postponing consideration of the Minden requests until 'better times'. The ceremony of homage in Guelders was held in the market place on 2 August. There Frederick's representative, the president of the Cleves and Minden War and Domains Chamber, stressed the promise of protection given to the Gelderland Estates by the Emperor Charles V in the Treaty of Venlo of 1543. In the county of Ravensberg trouble arose when the *Ritterschaft* found that the Prussian *Regierung* councillor Pott, who was to administer the oath of allegiance, was not of noble birth, but their protests were of no avail. The Ravensberg Estates, apart from demanding to have their military burdens eased and their taxes reduced, desired the restoration of their own separate administration with a *Regierung* in Bielefeld. They complained bitterly of the 1719 administrative union with Minden which occasioned difficult, costly and time-consuming journeys. The Directory, mindful of the economies which had resulted from the amalgamation, turned down this request: the concept of the *Gesamtstaat* implied unification of the different territories rather than division and isolation.

Cleves was in a special position and Frederick intended to visit th

* To this the General Directory replied that the Prussian courts were quicker and better – which was probably true.

province in person as soon as possible. The homage ceremony, observing ancient traditions, took place on 2 August though for reasons of economy the county of Mark held a separate ceremony at Hamm. The towns of Soest and Lippstadt also rendered homage, although they did not belong to the county of Mark, a point they asked to have confirmed. Lippstadt was under the joint administration of Prussia and the counts of Lippe-Detmold. Moers, where meetings of the Estates took the form of *Erbentagen*,* also rendered homage on 2 August, the king being represented by a commissary from the Cleves Chamber.

On Frederick's accession the Estates *Regierung* in Cleves had sent a memorandum to the Prussian resident in their province on the position of Cleves-Mark within the Lower Rhine-Westphalian Circle of the Empire and on the question of renewal of Imperial enfeoffment. Mention was also made of the still unsettled claims of the House of Brandenburg on Jülich-Berg. As far as domestic affairs were concerned the memorandum stressed that there was hope of a flourishing free trade within the river basins of the Lippe, Ruhr, Rhine and Meuse if only taxes and military obligations were abolished. The *Regierung* was also of the opinion that the general ordinance survey being carried out by the War and Domains Chamber should be discontinued on grounds of economy.

These and a number of other issues were also among the *gravamina* discussed at the Cleves *Landtag* on the occasion of the homage ceremony: thirty-eight separate motions were carried against taxes and *Mühlenzwang* (the compulsory use of the manorial mill); the Estates *Regierung* demanded the restoration of the *Indigenatsrecht* (the *jus indigenatus*, the reservation of official posts for native-born nobility); it also wanted local entrepreneurs and carters to be allowed to participate in the state postal service; it further asked that the sale of the Duisburg news-sheet through compulsory *abonnements* (a practice also prevalent in Magdeburg) should be discontinued and that the transport of building material to domain buildings – a duty characterized as 'an unheard of obligation' – should be dropped to be replaced by a money payment raised by the Estates.

These resolutions were handed to Frederick on 4 September, during his visit to Wesel, on behalf of the Estates of Cleves and Mark. The minutes of the Cleves *Ritterschaft* record that the king 'accepted them and put them in his pocket. Otherwise the reception was gracious'. The deputies waited for a royal answer, but word was brought them

---

* Small local assemblies attended by local nobility, domain officials and peasant representatives.

that they need not remain and should bring the *Landtag* in Cleves to a
close. Frederick took the opportunity to have the president of the Cleves
Chamber provide him with facts about the province and the prospect
of the harvest so that he need not depend on out-of-date reports
deposited with the General Directory.

Frederick had begun preparations for his journey to Cleves as soon
as the homage ceremony in Berlin was over. From Charlottenburg he
instructed the General Directory on 4 August that, en route to his
western territories, he was not to be delayed 'with processions, triumphal
arches, parades by the citizens, the ringing of bells, salutes, fanfares
from towers and other ceremonies'. On 15 August 1740 he left Potsdam
and travelled via Leipzig to Eilenburg that day; two days later he was
with his sister Wilhelmina at Bayreuth. He left Bayreuth on the evening
of 19 August and travelled through Erlangen, Ansbach (where he met
his second sister, the Margravine Frederica Louise), Crailsheim, Heil-
bronn, Durlach and Rastatt to Kehl, which he reached on the afternoon
of 23 August. His small personal retinue consisted of Algarotti, his
younger brother, the eighteen-year-old Augustus William, and his
adjutant-general, Colonel Count Leopold Alexander von Wartensleben.
Frederick had toyed with the idea of going as far as Versailles to meet
Cardinal Fleury, then Louis XV's chief minister, before proceeding to
Cleves, but as no invitation came from the French court, the plan had to
be dropped. He decided, however, that having come so far he would
pay a visit to Strasbourg.

On the evening of his arrival at Kehl Frederick and his companions
crossed the Rhine and ventured on to French soil, putting up at the
Sign of the Raven inn under assumed names. Seemingly uninterested
in the history or architecture of the 'wonderful city', Frederick sought
out some French officers with whom he struck up an acquaintance.
From them he learned many things about their army. He watched the
changing of the guard, looked at army barracks and equipment, visited
the arsenal with its cannons and, on 25 August, was shown round the
citadel by the commandant who suspected his real identity. That same
evening Frederick left Strasbourg unexpectedly, driving northwards
along the left bank of the Rhine as far as Drusenheim, where he spent
the night. The following day, while the post-horses were being changed
at Landau, he took the opportunity to inspect the town's fortified ramp-
arts. On the road to Speyer he met by chance the Polish envoy who had
been sent to Berlin to condole with him on the death of Frederick
William and congratulate him on his own accession. In Strasbourg a
number of Prussian deserters and a citizen had recognized Frederick; in

Landau his identity also became known. News of Frederick's visit to Strasbourg travelled quite rapidly and reached the Saxon court on 2 September. On a sudden impulse the young king had made a reconnaisance of French military positions on the Upper Rhine, trying (as during his visit to the Austrian camp in 1734) to gather information through his own observations. He looked at French troops and their equipment and experienced at first hand something of the French way of life, uncoloured by the literary imagination.

From Landau he continued his journey – through Speyer, Worms and Mainz – to Koblenz. There he took a Rhine boat to Cologne. From Cologne he went via Düsseldorf to Duisburg and on 30 August was once more on Prussian soil.

Frederick's visit to France meant that the Estates of Cleves, which were to have paid their respects to the king at Wesel on 24 August, had their meeting postponed by order of Frederick's adjutant-general. A further postponement became necessary on 1 September when the king, watching the changing of the guard at Wesel, caught a chill. His meeting with the Estates of Mark and Cleves eventually took place – as related above – on 4 September.

Colonel von Camas had returned from Versailles with nothing more substantial than highflown compliments; Truchsess' visit to Hanover had failed to strengthen Anglo-Prussian relations. Frederick thus had reason to suspect that Prussia was as negligible a factor in the calculations of the great powers as it had been in Frederick William's reign. An opportunity to demonstrate that this need not remain so was at hand. In 1732 Prussia had acquired, as part of the Orange inheritance, the lordship of Herstal, near Liège. The unruliness of its inhabitants, brought on in large measure by the counter-claims to the lordship advanced by the bishop of Liège, made it almost impossible to govern. Frederick William had suggested selling the lordship to the bishop but that prelate had declined the offer. Now, on 4 September 1740, Frederick demanded a clarification of the bishop's intentions: did he wish to pursue his claims to Herstal and undermine the loyalty of its inhabitants? When his envoy returned without an answer Frederick sent a Prussian regiment of more than full-strength from Wesel en route for Liège; its soldiers distributed leaflets extolling self-help as an instrument of justice. The leaflet ended with a sentence that was most unusual in the diplomacy of the period: 'Despite so many manifestations of ill-will on the part of this prince, the king will not be unrelenting; content to demonstrate his ability to punish him, the king is too generous to crush him.' The bishop, failing to find any support among the powers, promptly yielded; and in October 1740 he paid Prussia 200,000 talers for the lordship of Herstal.

From Wesel Frederick travelled to the little castle of Moyland, near Cleves, where he had arranged to meet Voltaire on 11 September. The mutual highly-pitched expectations were not fulfilled. Frederick was suffering from fever and Voltaire was tired after his journey. But personal contact had been made and their relationship survived. Frederick was now ready to return to Berlin. The journey back took him through Brunswick-Wolfenbüttel where, on 20 September in the castle of Salzdahlun, the betrothal was celebrated of Prince Augustus William of Prussia to Princess Louise Amelia of Brunswick-Wolfenbüttel, sister of Frederick's queen. On 23 September the king arrived in Potsdam, the ceremonies of homage at an end. It had been an odd kind of 'royal progress': it had served purposes and objectives foreign to its nature and age-old customs had been viewed with the cold logic of reason of state.

Frederick was given little time to recover from the fatigues of his travels; on 26 October he received word that the Emperor Charles VI had died in Vienna. This brought the threatening question of the Austrian succession to the forefront of European preoccupations. The Pragmatic Sanction was now open to rejection or confirmation. The great political question, which Frederick had already decided to solve in his own way, was put before him at a time when he had scarcely received the homage of his own subjects. The inspection of his territories had shown him that, thanks to his father's work, he stood on firm and solid ground. War would be a gamble. It would have to be tested whether or not Prussia's economic strength would be sufficient to survive a long and serious crisis. Everything depended on the assessment of Prussia's economic position.

PRUSSIAN CAMERALISM

The addition of a fifth department to the General Directory soon after Frederick II's accession can in retrospect be seen as a most significant change in the administrative system inherited from his father. For the new ministry, set up alongside the old territorially-orientated departments, was a purely functional one. Its purpose was the formation, implementation and supervision of policies for trade, communications and the economy as a whole. The creation of a centrally-directed economy thus complemented the centralized administrative authority which Frederick William had created to direct the regional divisions of the monarchy. The necessity of a supra-regional economic structure capable of giving both inspiration and direction to cooperation between the individual provinces had been brought ·home to Frederick during his royal progress. The grievances submitted by the various Estates strikingly illustrated their limited horizons and their inability to see beyond petty local issues to the larger interests of the *Gesamtstaat*. The advantages inherent in the centralization of the state's resources had, however, already been demonstrated by Frederick William I's *rétablissement* in East Prussia. Seen in that light, the foundation of the Fifth Department was less a change than the necessary extension of the existing administrative machine.

The purpose of the new department was clearly explained in the Instruction of 27 June 1740: the improvement of existing manufactures in number and quality, the establishment of new ·industries and the recruitment of skilled foreign artisans. While priority was given to the woollen and linen industries, other manufactures – such as silk, brocade, velvet, good quality paper, sugar, Nuremberg-type dolls, boxes, brooms, tools and implements – were also encouraged. There was little 'system' in this programme. Though geared to consumer demands, early directives seem tentative, hesitant and advisory rather than commanding. The problem has been nicely analysed by Otto Hintze:

> The kings of Prussia, in attempting to make some, at least, of their provinces self-sufficient and to organize an economic unit free from the domination of neighbours and the exploitation of more-advanced foreign countries, had to cope with extraordinarily difficult problems. ... Everything depended on the development and expansion of Prussia's own productive capacity, on human effort and the internal movement of goods.

The utilization of cameralist concepts was in keeping with the spirit of the age, as was the belief that only a tightly-controlled, state-directed mercantilism could transmute these concepts into reality. There was nothing new about this. Frederick still subscribed to the economic principles of Chamber director Hille, the mentor whom his father had chosen for him at Küstrin. He hoped to persuade Hille to take charge of the Fifth Department; but old age and ill health made it impossible for Hille (who died shortly after the offer was made) to accept.

The post went to von Marschall who became the energetic exponent of the state's mercantilist policy. Ennobled by Frederick William I, Marschall had served as a councillor in the General Directory and had been head of the *Rekrutenkasse* (the recruiting fund) and *Landrat* for the county of Niederbarnim. In 1745 he was given the added responsibilities of managing the Prussian Postal Service and directing the Kurmark's mortgage bank. It was in the Fifth Department that he found full scope for his talents which he used to the king's satisfaction and to the exhaustion of his own strength. Within the limits of his office Marschall was allowed a free hand, for it was part of Frederick's style of leadership to allow unusual freedom of action to individuals he particularly trusted. That this should have led to demarcation disputes with other departments of the General Directory was inevitable, but Marschall overcame these difficulties with skill, tact, tenacity and expertise. Nor did he have to resort to the cabinet orders dealing with division of responsibility – apart from the fundamental directive of 16 March 1747 which left him the final decision in all matters that straddled departmental boundaries. The *Generalia*, that is, the issues which affected the state as a whole, were dealt with by Marschall, while *Specialia*, matters of regional interest, were left to the ministers responsible for individual territories.

With the support of his colleague Manitius, whom he had transferred from the First Department, Marschall sent a questionnaire to the various War and Domains chambers as early as August 1740 to ascertain the actual size and productive capacity of industrial concerns in each province, to discover which branches of industry were not represented there, to list the foreign imports needed and make proposals for their replacement by home production, and to suggest improvements for internal movement of goods as well as for transit trade. Other questions dealt with the planting of white mulberry trees for the production of silk and the growing of dye-producing plants. At the same time Marschall's industrial agents in Italy and the United Provinces were busy recruiting manufacturers of velvet, silks, metals, leather goods and good quality paper. This was not an easy assignment, for competent entrepreneurs were unlikely to be tempted to leave their own regions unless forced to do so by unforeseen circumstances, wars or religious persecution. The settlement in Prussia in 1748 of the Brabant lace-makers was therefore exceptional. By making spinning looms available in small towns Frederick sought to develop an efficient industry aimed, hopefully, at the export market. Improvement in the quality and sales of manufactured goods was made possible by imposition of tariffs for the protection of home industries, by stringent supervision of work regulations and by the gradual removal of those obstacles which had prevented the free internal flow of goods.

Until Marshall's death on 11 December 1749 the Fifth Department not only controlled the entire economy of the state, but also furthered private enterprise by advising on production problems and helping to find sales outlets. The king took an unflagging interest in this work, contributing an unending stream of suggestions, hints and demands and using every means at his disposal to promote an increase in productivity. He expected women and children to utilize their winter evenings by spinning flax and demanded that 'officials should give the necessary guidance to those subjects who were not sufficiently industrious'.

Reliable statistics, necessary for the running of a systematic state-directed economy, were not yet available. Frederick William had made the General Directory responsible for the regular compilation of reports on harvest yields, price fluctuations and cattle-breeding, but only the domains had kept exact records. Frederick encouraged the chambers and ministries to collect useful statistical information; but, as the criteria on which this was based varied from province to province, comparable data for the monarchy as a whole were not obtained. Improvement came only towards the end of the reign with the refinement of cameralist techniques. The king therefore remained dependent on personal observation and on practical information gleaned on his tours of inspection. The state's measures for the development of the economy consequently lacked system; they were, for the most part, a blend of intuition, compromise and experience.

In the early days of his government Frederick was already faced with the need to decide whether he should continue to pursue the existing mercantilist grain policy: unseasonable weather had almost completely ruined the harvest of 1739 in many parts of the state and several provinces were threatened by famine. The usual relief measures, to help out with grain from the Königsberg and Gumbinnen Domain Chambers and open the already heavily-depleted army magazines, were not enough to bring the situation under control. The restrictions on the importation of grain from Mecklenburg, Livonia, Poland and Russia were therefore lifted, but were reimposed at the beginning of the next harvest. Temporary relaxations, as permitted after the bad Pomeranian harvest of 1744, or for the purpose of stocking the Silesian magazines, were intended as exceptions to the rule of self-sufficiency. In industrial Silesia grain had to be subsidized as transport costs made its importation from the older provinces of the monarchy prohibitively dear.

The disastrous harvest of 1746 clearly demonstrated the ineffectiveness of Prussia's grain storage policy: importation of essential foodstuff also had to be made in later years. Yet strongly protective duties remained the basis of the grain trade policy; indeed, higher duties were put on all imports. The infrequent permits granted were given only in individual cases and after exhaustive investigations, the king reserving decisions for himself. Wherever possible the magazines had to give temporary help and bridge over the gaps in supplies. During 1771–72, when rye rose to five talers a bushel in Saxony and Bohemia, it cost only half that in Prussia. There were heavy penalties for private hoarding and stock-piling. To undermine speculators the authorities introduced fixed prices; the king proceeded relentlessly against those who 'wished to profit from the plight of the poor'. The distillation of brandy was drastically curtailed in times of bad harvests – despite losses to the fisc in excise duties – and from 1756 the consumption of brandy was further discouraged by the imposition of high rates of duty. The tentacles of the state's grain trade policy extended to market regulations: in 1747 dealers were forbidden to buy grain from the growers, and at markets private citizens had priority over dealers for their purchases. The most effective measure against grain profiteering was the imposition of an export ban, though by this time Prussia was no longer an important exporter. The abolition of inland tolls and the suppression of staple privileges along the Oder in 1751 did not therefore do much to help Stettin's trade; but the linking of Magdeburg to the Oder's network of waterways through the construction of the Finow canal – drawing the Oder–Elbe traffic to the Baltic – did benefit Stettin at the expense of Hamburg and Lübeck.

In his Political Testament of 1768 Frederick had this to say about harvest yields and the export of grain:

> I have had calculations made in my state which tell me how much grain each province consumes, how large its surplus is, and how much it needs to import to feed its inhabitants. To ensure that this information is as precise as possible a register has been compiled for good, average and bad harvests. From this I can estimate when the sale of grain should be allowed and when its export must be prohibited.

Such registers were drawn up in 1766, 1776–77 and 1783–84, enabling Prussia to cut back her grain exports and avoid the necessity of having to buy back at inflated prices during times of scarcity. Lesgewang, president of the East Prussian Chamber, lost his post for failing to take prompt action to counter the effects of a bad harvest; Winckel, president of the Magdeburg Chamber, met a similar fate in 1785 for allowing the export of more grain than was justified in view of the needs of his own province. The disappointing performance of the Elbe and Oder grain trading companies made the Vistula – after 1772 – increasingly vital for Prussia's grain policy, and Fordon became an important trade centre. Frederick had learnt by experience that conditions varied from province to province and that regulations must therefore be flexible enough to allow for regional variations. Frederician Prussia was administered neither in accordance with mercantilist doctrine nor by an insistence on equality of treatment for the sake of a 'unitary' policy: in the central provinces and Silesia foodstuffs were subsidized, while East Prussia was a free trade region. Care was taken, however, to avoid measures which might provoke economic retaliation on Prussia's scattered and therefore vulnerable western provinces by their neighbours.

In the last years of his reign Frederick returned with increased determination to a policy of grain storage. His father had maintained numerous depots in all provinces so as to supply the regiments in their cantons. In times of war or scarcity magazines, aptly named *Landmagazine*, became state reserves and were at the king's disposal. Frederick, arguing that the magazines were inadequately protected in the event of war, concentrated stores of flour – rather than grain or corn – in the two central fortresses of Magdeburg and Küstrin. The fortress of Spandau was designated a 'peace-time depot' (*Friedensmagazin*) for Berlin and its environs: it was to contain sufficient stores to supply Berlin's wants for one whole year. Reserve supplies were also kept at Stettin, but at Wesel and Minden stocks were either much reduced or completely withdrawn. Silesia's main depots were the fortresses of Breslau, Schweidnitz and Neisse. The large magazines at Tangermünde, in the strong fortress of Graudenz and in the small fort of Lyck at Spirdingsee in Masuria, were only partially completed in the years 1784–86. Each of these depots was planned to hold supplies to sustain an army of 30,000 men for one month.

On the whole Frederick's storage policy was a success. At the end of his reign the magazines contained ten times the amount stored at its outset, in all 120,000 *Wispel*.* Enough cash to purchase an equal amount was held in reserve. The magazines were also ready to distribute grain and flour to the population; this was done repeatedly in the 1770s and 1780s for the purpose of keeping the price of bread within tolerable limits. Here we see the social aspect of the Frederician grain policy. The king emphasized that 'it is not my intention to make a profit; I care only that the reserves for future needs be replenished and kept at the right level.' To put this simple sounding principle into effect proved, however, a difficult task, since the demand for grain always fluctuated. All the same, the Fifth Department succeeded with a skill and flexibility that reflects creditably on its efficiency, professionalism and *esprit de corps* in the task Frederick put upon them. Quite apart from practical experience the department was, in time, able to add useful insights gained

* 1 *Wispel* = 24 Berlin bushels = 1,000 modern kg.

from the rapidly developing science of political economy. The heads of the department were all open to modern trends of thought and, though Frederick himself was suspicious of innovations, tried to interest the king in them whenever the opportunity arose. In the grain policy as a whole those irreconcilable opposites, free trade and protective duties, played as big a role as attempts to restructure agrarian policy.

Next to the provision of a regular supply of bread for the population and the securing of markets for the agricultural products of a state still basically agrarian in outlook, Prussia's most important economic problem was the satisfaction of the clothing needs of the population. The export of surplus raw materials for textiles had been stopped by Frederick William I, who established the Berlin *Lagerhaus*, a warehouse for wool. This *Lagerhaus* developed into a state-run model workshop for woollen manufacture, the largest in Prussia, though it was not granted a monopoly. It employed 500 workers to man its 240 looms, and also gave work to 5,000 outworkers. The Warehouse Commission, run by Marschall and Manitius, learnt by practical experience the advantages and the drawbacks of a state-directed economy. The lessons learnt were utilized by Frederick II in the Fifth Department. The king, who preferred to work through private enterprise, leased the Warehouse to an entrepreneur from Aachen, and was pleased to find that the change from state to private management did not cause the woollen industry to decline.

The provincial towns had undergone a modest measure of industrialization ever since the times of the Great Elector. After 1750 Frederick gave Luckenwalde, situated almost on the Saxon border, financial help to build mills and settle more than a hundred and fifty families of weavers of woollen fabrics and unfulled cloth from Saxony and Gera. Supervision of the Luckenwalde enterprise was carried out by an entrepreneur who had taken an oath of loyalty to the state. The colonists were given hereditary tenancies of houses and gardens and were exempted from taxation for fifteen years. The raw materials were chosen and bought by the master weavers in the wool market at Luckenwalde or in the Whitsuntide wool market at Breslau which handled best-quality clips. A special Wool Depot Fund (*Wollmagazin-Kasse*), set up by Frederick William I, financed these purchases under the supervision of the *Kammer* and magistrates of the Kurmark. Since the county of Luckenwalde was a sheep-rearing area, the wool production benefited the Luckenwalders themselves. Between 1776 and 1786 the manufacture of woollen fabrics and unfulled cloth rose from 1,800 pieces to almost double that number, of which one-third was exported. Luckenwalde thus held pride of place among Prussia's cloth-producing towns. The manufacture at Cottbus was also important; and weaving colonies were founded at Brandenburg, Nowawes, Rathenow, Neuruppin, Wusterhausen, Eberswalde, Fürstenwalde, Beeskow, Storkow, Strausberg, Gransee and Köpenick. After the establishment of a 'wool depot' (*Wollmagazin*) in thirty-three other towns in the Kurmark, Luckenwalde acquired one of its own in 1774, but only a few spinners and weavers were able to take advantage of the credit facilities it offered. Many cloth makers who applied to the *Wollmagazin* took an over-optimistic view of temporary periods of growth and thoughtlessly ran up debts, with the result that their enterprises ended with losses to the fisc. Technical guidance was provided by state-employed factory commissioners who periodically visited the woollen mills. Despite all the care taken by the state, however, basic problems remained and prevented the hoped-for rapid industrialization: regular markets for Prussian woollen goods and credit for large-scale, long-term planning proved equally elusive.

Yet the strict prohibition of imports of foreign cloth and the unremitting efforts to improve quality laid the solid foundations of a Prussian woollen industry, the products of which could stand comparison with those of their foreign competitors. It is often thought that the industry worked only to supply the needs of the army. This was, indeed, the secure framework within which the industry developed, but the Fifth Department envisaged the supply of all Prussia's needs, civil as well as military, and a profitable export trade into the bargain. At the end of Frederick's reign the industry employed some 58,000 workers and made a profit of almost 4 million talers from its exports. By this time nearly all the provinces had cloth manufacturers, who sold their products, when possible, at fairs and markets in neighbouring states so as to avoid transport costs. The relative non-availability of such markets explains why the manufacture of unfulled cloth in Pomerania and of fine woollens in East and West Prussia developed slowly, while in the county of Mark, despite restrictive guild practices, the linen, woollen and cotton industries developed fast. In 1744 the Bielefeld bleachworks was exempted from the provision of recruits and from the billeting of soldiers. Premiums were paid for quality linens and cottons, and in 1765 a royal credit fund (*Darlehnskasse*) was set up to aid its linen industry. Two years earlier the first statistical survey of the linen trade was carried out in Bielefeld. The Westphalian linen industry was protected from Silesian imports. In Silesia itself the manufacture of fine woollen cloth and the cotton-spinning industry made steady progress; this was brought about and fostered by Frederick's policy after 1742 of attracting skilled workers by favourable tariffs, exemption from tax for a number of years and the granting of burgher and master-craftsman privileges. The installation of spinning-looms in the military barracks by shrewd entrepreneurs provided even soldiers and their wives with an opportunity to earn extra money. The state paid export premiums to the mills.

The Fifth Department had, from its very foundation, been ordered to devote special attention to the manufacture of high-grade luxury goods in Prussia. From this derived an entirely new industry, the manufacture of silks. The beginnings of such manufacture go back to the period before Frederick's accession, but throughout his reign the king devoted special attention to its promotion. For him the silk industry symbolized Prussia's economic advancement, the achievement of great power rank among the states which produced luxury goods. Since in the Frederician system the furtherance of industry was a government task, commercial and administrative history inseparably intertwine. It must be stressed that the production of essential commodities and of luxury goods was carried on simultaneously and was regarded as of equal importance. It is symptomatic of the system that during the great crises of the Seven Years War the production of silks and the payment of state premiums for quality and export sales were fully maintained. Frederick did not intend, however, to build up a state industry: he was concerned with the creation and support of efficient private industries. The state's part was to give all possible help by protective duties, import restrictions and expert facilities; to take care that the specialist silk-workers, often recruited at great expense, were found regular employment, and to make sure that the quality of Prussian silks was controlled, improved and brought up to a standard which would enable it to compete with its rivals. Financial and administrative measures, as well as the occasional dispatch of factory commissioners to the silk-mills, ensured that the industry served the fiscal objectives of the *Gesamtstaat*: the main aim was to end Prussia's dependence on foreign trade, though the desire to show that Berlin, the Kurmark and the other central provinces could do what France, the United Provinces, and even Krefeld in his own western territories, had done also played a role.

With the ending of the Second Silesian War Frederick was able to devote all his energies to the economic development of his state. More than a thousand weaving-looms were already in use producing fine-quality cloths, half of them engaged in the production of silks. The driving force behind the planting of mulberry trees and the training of peasants and labourers was supplied by the king, the tireless Marschall and, after his death, the Konitz-born Berlin businessman, Johann Ernst

Gotskowski. The big economic crisis of 1766 made a new start necessary. The 'silk depot' (*Seidenmagazin*), first opened in 1749, was re-established, technical experts were co-opted to the Manufacture Commission, production bonuses were skilfully used, and internal excises that hindered sales were abolished. Altogether Frederick spent 2 million talers on the silk industry: the strongest support for any branch of manufacture in his reign. At the end of his life he had the satisfaction of knowing that 4,200 silk-looms were in use in Prussia (1,300 of them in the western provinces) and that the annual value of the fine fabrics produced amounted to more than 3 million talers. Yet Prussia produced only one-sixth of the raw silk the industry needed and silk-production was still largely a cottage-industry, employing also child-labour – of which the king disapproved.

An important centre of the silk industry, apart from Berlin and the Kurmark, was Magdeburg where in 1742 one woollen and one poplin mill, employing 1,000 people, had been founded by Saxon entrepreneurs. In Stettin and Königsberg, where more than 30,000 mulberry trees had been planted, the production was concentrated on the weaving of silk ribbon. At Schidlitz, near Danzig, there was a small silk mill; and Iserlohn, in the county of Mark, produced silk ribbon and also kerchiefs. It should be noted that silk production failed to establish itself in Silesia alongside the important linen industry. Nor did Frederick succeed in drawing the prosperous Krefeld silk workshops to Berlin as he had first thought possible. The managerial system of the Krefeld silk industry, concentrated in large workshops and controlled by a small number of families, differed greatly from the state-protected enterprises in Prussia's central and eastern provinces. To protect the latter Frederick forbade the importation of Krefeld silk into the rest of the monarchy. Yet Frederick's appreciation of the Krefeld silk for the export trade was vivid. He granted privileges to the famous von der Leyen silkhouse which gave it a virtual monopoly of such trade, and in 1751 and 1763 he inspected its workshops to satisfy himself that all was well. He refrained, however, from interference by regulation. The freedom accorded to Krefeld and the strict control of the silk industry in Kurmark contrast sharply, but they illustrate perfectly Frederick's economic policy. Flexible enough not to fetter initiative, it concentrated attention on those areas where support was needed in order to achieve success.

Gotskowski, the entrepreneur whose keen interest in the silk industry was much valued by the king, also rendered substantial service in the founding of Prussia's other large luxury industry, the manufacture of porcelain. At the instigation of the king, a porcelain manufactory had been opened in Berlin in 1751 by a Swiss, Wilhelm Caspar Wegely. Its products proved not to be to Frederick's taste and it ceased production six years later. The king considered it essential, however, that Prussia should possess so significant and prestigious an industry as that of porcelain manufacture and in 1761 (the darkest period of the Seven Years War) persuaded Gotskowski to refound the porcelain manufactory. The technology of the manufacture and the artistry of decoration was perfected under Gotskowski, but since he was unable to make the business pay the king in 1763 bought the manufactory for 225,000 talers. It was now renamed the *Königliche Porzellan-Manufaktur* (the Royal Porcelain Manufactory). The production of elegant fine quality porcelain giving employment to skilled craftsmen, was supplemented by the making of goods for every day use much in demand in the post-war years. The king's preference for flower-decorated services gave distinctiveness to the products of the *K.P.M.*; though popular taste changed, the patterns of the 1760s persisted till the end of Frederick's reign. Perhaps this explains why despite its high quality Berlin porcelain did not sell fast. The king had to support it by mercantilist measures.

In 1754 the importation of foreign faience products, especially from Sweden and England, was prohibited to help the faience (false porcelain) manufactory established in Potsdam; imported faience, if discovered, was confiscated by the state and sold – not in Prussia, but abroad. The porcelain works proper were exempt from taxation. Its products were stocked in depots in all the provinces of the state from East Prussia to East Friesland; its export to the United Provinces was eased; it received firewood free of charge from the royal forests; it had its own court and enjoyed a monopoly in the production and sale of porcelain throughout Prussia, prohibition against trading in foreign porcelain being reiterated in 1768, 1774 and 1785. From 1765 the importation of Saxon Meissen porcelain was prohibited; even its transit through Prussian territory or its exhibition at fairs was forbidden. In 1775 similar measures were taken against porcelain from Württemberg. Conversely, credit was promised to foreign trading houses (e.g. those of Hamburg, Frankfurt on the Main, Genoa, England, Spain, Portugal, Riga) that accepted Berlin porcelain on commission. In return for the renewal of their privileges, some protected Jews were obliged to stock and sell the products of the Royal Porcelain Manufactory. Monthly reports on production, sales and artistic designs were sent to Frederick. The profit of 24,000 talers made in 1785 was not a remarkable sum, but it does demonstrate the tenacity with which the king endeavoured to avoid losses in the management of state-owned industries.

Difficulties were also encountered in the Prussian production of glassware. The mirror factory at Neustadt on the Dosse, the only one in the state, enjoyed a monopoly from 1741 onwards; but demand was too low and production costs too high. On 18 August 1764 the king instructed the General Directory to lower prices: 'Even if 3,000 talers instead of 4,000 flows in, the *Kassen* can still make a profit and the public can buy at bargain prices, which is a *privilegium regulativum*. It is easy to raise the revenue by increasing the price of goods but that is an expedient I will never knowingly allow.' In 1785 a Breslau entrepreneur was given the privilege of manufacturing small mirrors for the Silesian market, provided he used the products of the domestic glass industry. The quality of glass produced in the glassworks of the Kurmark, the Neumark and southern Pomerania left much to be desired, whether it came from the royal glassworks or from the often primitive private works: numerous estate-owners had established glassworks on their property or had sought permission to do so. During the Seven Years War glassworkers, many of whom had been recruited – often with difficulty – from rural areas, were sacrificed to the needs of the under-strength regiments. With the peace, works often had to be re-established from scratch. It is true, of course, that such re-establishment offered a chance to improve the quality of the product. Import of Bohemian glass was prohibited, and the highly efficient Silesian glass industry was not allowed to sell its wares in the other Prussian provinces, lest the small manufactures of the central provinces should suffer: Silesia had to sell within its own province or abroad. To succour the existing non-Silesian manufactures Frederick refused permission for the establishment of new glassworks, a decision probably motivated by a desire to conserve the supply of wood: uncontrolled cutting of firewood needed in the glass-works was frowned upon. But he remained adamant that those glass-works already in operation, barely profitable though many of them were, should remain in production.

Frederick could not bring himself to sanction the establishment of a comprehensive, centralized organization to supervise the glass industry throughout the *Gesamtstaat*. He realized that a necessary prerequisite for such an organization was a good road network, and this was lacking. From Berlin large parts of the monarchy could be reached only via foreign territories. Even after West Prussia had been acquired (1772) and the central and eastern provinces were – with the exception of numerous and at times large enclaves – joined to each other, Frederick proved reluctant to build paved roads, partly because they could be utilized by enemies in time of war. Waterways were, however, systematically developed in a west-east direction; an efficient network came into existence from the Elbe to the Oder via the Plauer and Finow Canal completed in 1746 and the Bromberg Canal of 1776 via the Warthe and the Netze to the Vistula. Other canals of importance were the Mietzel-Floss, cut in 1740, the new Oder Canal of 1753, the Templin, Werbellin and Ruppin Canal of 1766 and the Johannisburg Canal of the same year. In 1780 the Ruhr was made navigable by the building of locks. As a general rule navigation on these waterways was confined to the inland shipping guilds, though in exceptional cases foreign guilds were allowed to use them. The load carried by 1,000 six-horse wagons could be transported more cheaply by twenty barges. The Prussian postal service, which carried passengers, parcels and letters, had been so well organized in Frederick William's reign that all his success or had to do was to extend it to the new provinces.

Forestry products depended on rivers and canals for their transport to saw-mills and manufacturing centres. In an edict of 10 March 1742 the king stressed the need for rational utilization of wood, even in privately-owned forests; and in 1754 he commissioned a plan for the afforestation of the sandy soil of the Kurmark with oak and pine. Good-quality timber was highly profitable in an age of busy shipbuild-ing: one large English merchantman or man-of-war required at least 4,000 oak trees. The life-span of wooden ships being limited there was a constant demand for ships' timber. In 1764 the General Directory estimated that Hamburg merchants were asking 25 talers for fir trees bought in Prussia for 6 talers a piece. The formation of a Prussian trading company to deal directly with the customer was clearly desirable. Ephraim and Itzig, former mint concessionaires, were invited to par-ticipate in such a company but they declined, regarding it as too risky: transport costs were frighteningly high, at times 400 per cent the price of the timber. A timber trading company which was formed in 1766 for a five-year period did indeed fail, and on the expiration of its con-tract in 1771 the state took over the task of overseeing the sale of timber. But this state enterprise had to be terminated with considerable losses. Illicit trading undermined its efforts and the competition from English merchants, buying directly from Russia, was more serious than had been expected. Nor could market fluctuations in timber prices be exploited since only well-seasoned wood was used in the shipbuilding industry. Nevertheless some minor successes had been scored along the lines of the king's instruction of 12 October 1770 to the General Directory, 'On the Re-stocking and Conservation of the Forests to the Benefit of Future Generations'. The state put into reverse the trend whereby private companies and aristocratic forest-owners alike had almost completely denuded the forests near log-floating waterways. Now the chambers supervised the use of fire-wood, and in order to preserve timber, peat, charcoal and hard coal were used whenever possible in industry and army barracks. Frederick regarded coal-mining as the most important branch of the mining industry in his territories. Just a week before his death, on 10 August 1786, he wrote to minister von Heinitz, the head of the Mining Department: 'Our best mines are the coal-mines and the most sensible solution to our problem is to make the use of coal universal. That would save our wood. I do not think our other mines are of much use.' In 1779 the first steam pump for mine-drainage was installed by war councillor Gansauge, at his own expense, in the Altenweddingen district. Prussia's oldest mines were in the county of Mark, where mining regulations promoting efficient mining had been in force since 1737. In 1756 Mark had 108 coal-mines in production, but a further 104 had been closed down, including the two state-owned collieries. As the total number of miners in the country was 688, the usual complement for each pit was only five or six men. A revised mining ordinance, comparable to those in force in Saxony and Brunswick-Lüneburg, was not decreed for Mark, Cleves and Moers till 1766 when the Mining Office (the *Bergamt*) was transferred to Hagen in the county of Mark. That county profited from experience gained in the Silesian mining industry, and when the Ruhr was made navigable in 1780 new markets were easily found for the produce of the Mark coalfields. Freiherr vom Stein, Prussian mining director and a man of great initiative and energy, worked under Heinitz's supervision at Wetter on the Ruhr during the years 1784 to 1786. There was a Prussian Mining Office at Tecklenburg-Lingen as early as 1740, and the mine at Ibbenbüren was taken over by the state in 1747. Other Prussian coal-mines were those at Wettin and Löbejün in the Saale district, but their output was less than half of those in the county of Mark. In 1768 the copper-bearing slate quarries at Rothenburg on the Saale, in the Mansfeld district, came under state control, and were once again made to yield a profit. As far as salt-mining was concerned, the royal saltworks at Halle and Schönebeck (at that time the largest in Germany) were technically very well equipped, and thus more efficient than the privately-owned saltworks at Gross-Salze and Stassfurt. Other well-run saltworks were the Gradier works at Königsborn in the county of Mark and Neu-Salzwerk near Minden. By use of mercantilist tariffs Prussia made herself independent of French sea-salt and of salt from Lüneburg.

Finally, we must briefly survey the armament industry. This was not, as is often claimed, the prerequisite for mercantilist economic management in Prussia, but its result. The armament industry benefited from all branches of industry, but Frederick's first directive to the Fifth Department shows that the army was neither an end in itself nor the *fons et origo* of public life. Indeed, armament works did not increase significantly beyond their number in the reign of the Great Elector: Berlin had a cannon foundry and a gunpowder works, there were a few ironworks for the manufacture of artillery shells in the Mark Brandenburg, and a copperworks and a brassworks at Eberswalde. Frederick William I had established a small arms manufactory, situated in part at Spandau and in part at Potsdam. In 1752 new ironworks were built at Schadow (near Storkow), Gottow (in *Amt* Zinna), Torgelow (in Pomerania) and Vietz (near Küstrin), but all four manufactured iron goods for everyday use. Even for the Silesian works Frederick decreed that they 'were not to be allowed to spend their whole time just producing bombs'. Military requirements were on the whole left to entrepreneurs who imported gunpowder and arms from the United Provinces and iron cannon from Sweden. The Berlin bankers Splitgerber and Daum in particular had charge of this trade on the state's behalf. As in the other branches of Prussian economic life, we find in the very modest armament industry that close, 'almost personal relationship between king and entrepreneur which was characteristic of Frederician industrialism' (S. Skalweit).

In cases where entrepreneurs could not be found to establish industries Frederick invested large sums of money in order that manufactures should have a chance to prove themselves. At times he incurred heavy losses. The Manchester textile mill near the palace of Monbijou and the clock factories in Berlin and at Friedrichstal (near Oranienburg) lost him nearly 200,000 talers; the fustian works in the town of Brandenburg and the steel mills at Eberswalde, both of which were run by Thuringian colonists, swallowed heavy subsidies. The king also contributed to the paperworks at Spechthausen (near Eberswalde), the Berlin lacquer works and the turkey-yarn dyeworks at Kaputh (at Belzig near Potsdam). Such industries depended, to a large extent, on Prussia's ability to attract and retain reliable and skilled artisans from abroad. Frederick was indefatigable in his efforts to encourage collaborators and in the engagement of experts for their specialist knowledge of equipment and techniques. Entrepreneurs and merchants received only limited and occasional financial assistance from the state, but they were always helped to keep their workers in regular employment: during periods of crisis (as for instance in 1766–67) state subsidies were provided for this purpose.

In his *Essai sur les formes de gouvernement et sur les devoirs des souverains* of 1777 Frederick demanded that the ruler 'keep in mind the condition of the poor; for he must imagine himself in the situation of a peasant or industrial worker and ask himself: "If I had been born into the social class, where one's hands are one's sole asset, what would I expect from my sovereign?" Whatever his common sense tells him ought to be done, that he must do if he is to fulfil his duty.'

The Fifth Department (the *Manufaktur-, Kommerzien- und Fabrik-Departement*), which from its inception had been freed from the routine work of the General Directory, developed into a versatile instrument of economic management and, simultaneously, into a committee of the king's most farseeing advisers. After Marschall's death the department had a succession of temporary heads: von der Horst, von Bismarck, von Werder and – for two periods – von Heinitz. These men, often combining their office with the control of other departments and aided only by an understaffed secretariat, dealt with difficult, unclassifiable, constantly changing matters. In 1750 a Swiss, Johann Rudolf Emanuel Faesch, formerly the department's representative in Amsterdam, was made its director, though he was not given the rank of minister. Not till 1764 did the Fifth Department acquire a ranking minister as its director. During the intervening years Frederick himself was, and did the work of, the head of the department.

Before the Seven Years War, which nearly shattered the economic foundations of the state and necessitated almost complete restructuring, Prussia's central provinces had grown together into an economic unit. The five *Kammer* administrations of the Kurmark, the Neumark, Magdeburg, Halberstadt and Pomerania applied the same regulations to commerce, trade, duties and excise. Silesia, however, still had her own laws and as a province had not yet come within the jurisdiction of the General Directory. It could neither import wool nor export glassware. East Prussia, together with Prussian Lithuania, the most populous parts of the monarchy, also maintained a special position because of the free and transit trade which they alone were allowed. The king visited Königsberg between 10 and 16 June 1750 and 4 and 10 June 1753, but a close and constant supervision of the manufacturing enterprises was lacking and the province had, on the whole, to rely on its own resources. It was imperative for the *Gesamtstaat* to concentrate its energies and to accomplish that which was necessary before that which was merely desirable.

Only after the occupation of large parts of Poland by Austria and Russia in 1772, when English, Dutch and Saxon merchants sought new markets in what was left of independent Poland, did Frederick begin to take much notice of East Prussia. The Prussian gains of the first partition of Poland – direct connection of East Prussia with the rest of Frederick's territories via West Prussia – played an important part in a wave of state-aided manufacturing enterprises now begun in the provinces of West and East Prussia. The most important of these were cloth mills and factories producing sail-cloth, earthenware and leather. Equality with the central provinces was now achieved in domestic trade. Such equality was not extended to the Prussian territories west of the Elbe: the steel industry in the county of Mark could produce goods far superior in quality to those of the Brandenburg workshops, but the western territories were treated like foreign countries because the roads leading to them passed through non-Prussian states. Yet even in respect of the western territories a complicated system of regulatory exceptions, special privileges and exchange procedures attempted to link Prussia's internal trade relations from Cleves via Stettin and Königsberg to Berlin, though without infringement of separate markets. East Friesland, a maritime province, was able to maintain an undisturbed, untaxed connection with Prussia's Baltic ports.

Despite Prussia's striving for profitable foreign markets for her products, the monopolies enjoyed by whole sections of industry harmed trade. The fairs, particularly the Frankfurt on the Oder fair, were hampered by transit taxes on exhibits and did not attract enough buyers. Import and export restrictions, cumbersome controls and constricting regulations made the ideal of free trade all the more enticing; but for Prussia it had to remain an ideal. Its implementation would have exposed the carefully-nurtured infant industries to the chill winds of more efficient foreign competition and prevented advancement beyond the agrarian stage. Only the most rigorously-enforced import restrictions enabled Prussia's own industries to find their feet; and the understandable reluctance of undercapitalized merchants to take chances could only be overcome by the state acting as protector, guaranteeing the security and limiting the risks throughout the whole of the economic sphere. No money must be paid to foreign countries for goods that could be manufactured at home and would therefore benefit the economy.

When the French financial expert de la Haye de Launay advised Frederick to dismantle the Prussian system of industrial protection the king produced the following counter-argument:

> Your intentions are good but you are ahead of your time. When the right moment comes I shall do as you advise but to anticipate that time would ruin everything. You know my territories. The soil, for the most part, is

sandy, dry and infertile. Grain production is too low to meet the whole population's needs, and the more fertile regions cannot completely supply those less favoured. Grazing lands are similarly insufficient. Cattle are small, scrawny and few in number and my subjects are compelled to buy from Poland. As oil, spices, sugar, coffee and hundreds of other products have to be imported they impose a considerable drain on the resources of the state. Were I to allow my subjects to import manufactured goods from abroad – which would please them very much – where would the process end? In all countries luxury tends to gain the upper hand. Soon all our foreign reserves – from our exports of wool, linens and wood – would be spent. Sheer necessity compels me to watch carefully our balance of payments and to open my hand not to give money to foreigners, but to receive from them. I prohibit imports as much as I can so that my subjects shall be encouraged to produce those things which I forbid them to get from elsewhere. Admittedly their early efforts are crude, but time and practice will bring perfection and we must show patience with first attempts. ... I have poor soil; therefore I must give the trees time to take root and grow strong before I can expect them to produce fruit. ...

These principles, and in particular their practical application, corresponded less to mercantilism (many presuppositions of which did not, in any case, exist in Prussia) than to the flexible operation of the cameralism of the princes of a former age adapted to the changing needs of the state. They had evolved in the cameralist teaching of the universities of Halle and Frankfurt on the Oder which aimed not at the accumulation of surpluses (*Plusmacherei*) as such, but at the planned extension of the state's economic possibilities in order to produce higher revenues. The growth of the state and the development of its economy were, in cameralist terms, inseparable. Thanks mainly to Frederick's own initiative, and despite unfavourable conditions, opportunities for private enterprise were developed; the Prussian state, primarily agrarian in structure, became self-sufficient in the production of industrial goods during his reign. That Prussia's unfavourable balance of trade could, within a relatively short period of time, be converted into a credit balance was, however, due to the acquisition of Silesia.

III

The New Provinces

SILESIA

A full treasury, a powerful army and a thirst for fame – these were the
public reasons Frederick II later gave for his attack on Silesia. These
motives certainly played a part, as did the legal claims of the House of
Hohenzollern to Silesia. Indeed it is worth noting that Frederick immediately, and forever, dropped his equally good claims to Jülich-Berg
to press those to Silesia. Even so these motives do not enlighten us as to
the *arcanum*, the driving forces, of his policy. Additions to his scattered,
unconnected western territories did not tempt him. Prussia's existing
foundations were too weak to support the superstructure of a modern
state, and if Saxony-Poland had been able to encompass the desired
acquisition of Silesia Prussia would have been crippled politically and
economically for a long time to come. Frederick was not the first
Hohenzollern ruler to have contemplated a conquest of Silesia. The
Great Elector had harboured such a design; and when news of the death
of Emperor Charles VI, still in the prime of life, reached Halle, Cleves
and Prussia two of Frederick's experienced high officials felt compelled,
independently of one another, to call the king's attention to the 're-
opening of the Silesian question'.

Not for a moment did Frederick doubt that the way to his 'rendez-
vous with fame' would be short and safe. He took it for granted that the
administration and the economy of his state would function just as
smoothly while he led his army in the field as when he ruled Prussia
from his cabinet. On 3 December 1740 he left instructions for the period
of his absence, warning his ministers against slackening their efforts and
reminding them to keep the finances in good order. Ten days later he
was at Frankfurt on the Oder; by Christmas he stood before Glogau;
and on 3 January 1741 he entered Breslau. He returned to Berlin at the
end of January but had to leave for Silesia once more in mid-Feb-
ruary; in April the Austrian army gave him battle at Mollwitz. His

brother, Prince Henry, deputized for him at the laying of the foundation-stone of the Berlin Opera House, and he did not see his capital again until mid-November. Two months later he was on his way to Bohemia. The Prussian victory at Chotusitz on 17 May 1742 brought about the preliminary peace of Breslau which on 11 June ended the First Silesian War. In mid-July Frederick was back in Berlin, but after the 28 July signing of the Treaty of Berlin he travelled to Wesel (through Minden) in August and in September he went direct from there to Silesia. From October 1742 to August 1744 he stayed at Charlottenburg and Madgeburg, apart from some short visits to Pyrmont and Bayreuth and three inspection tours of Silesia. His abortive march on Prague, from August to November 1744, was followed by 'winter-quarters' at Charlottenburg and Potsdam until March 1745. On the day after the laying of the foundation-stone of 'the summerhouse at the top of the vineyard near Potsdam' (Sans Souci), he set out to join his army in Silesia; not until the Austrian and Saxon attempts to reconquer Silesia had been repulsed – in the battles of Hohenfriedeberg, Soor and Kesselsdorf – did the Second Silesian War end. The Peace of Dresden was signed on 25 December 1745. The next day Frederick celebrated the Christmas feast in the Frauenkirche in Dresden.

Years of peace followed, years which saw administrative reforms, expansion of trade and commerce, artistic accomplishments and, above all, the incorporation of Silesia in the Prussian *Gesamtstaat*. Frederick made annual tours of inspection in the conquered province; indeed, no other part of the monarchy was visited so frequently by the king. He bought the Spätgen Palace in Breslau and enlarged it into a royal Schloss between 1750 and 1752.

By the preliminary peace of Breslau, confirmed by the final Treaty of Berlin, Austria ceded to Prussia the county of Glatz, hitherto part of the Bohemian patrimony, the Moravian (previously Jägerndorf) enclave of Katscher and, most importantly, the greater part of the duchy of Silesia with the exception of the principality of Teschen, the lordship of Hennersdorf, part of Jägerndorf and the town of Troppau. These conquests were confirmed to Prussia in the Peace of Dresden in 1745, but the acquisition of northern Bohemia, to the Elbe, promised to Prussia by Emperor Charles VII,* did not materialize. Saxony ceded to Prussia the town of Fürstenberg on the Oder and the village of Schildlow, thus giving up her enclave and toll-house on the Oder. Maria

* The Bavarian Elector Charles Albert had been elected Emperor in 1742 by Maria Theresa's opponents in the Empire; he died in 1745 and Maria Theresa's husband Franz Stephan was elected in his place.

Theresa had already in 1742 renounced the Bohemian crown's feudal sovereignty over part of the (Prussian) Lower Lausitz. No territorial changes were made as a result of the Seven Years War – the Third Silesian War – and the Peace of Hubertusburg of 15 February 1763 confirmed the treaties of Breslau, Berlin and Dresden. The boundaries settled by the Silesian Frontier Recess of 6 December 1742 (laid down at the Klein Schnellendorf Convention of 9 October 1741), and ratified at Leobschütz on 20 January 1743, remained unchanged. The border passes between Silesia and Moravia remained in Austrian hands, as did the lordship of Hennersdorf, belonging to Freiherr von Bartenstein, the Austrian secretary of state. The partition of Silesia and Maria Theresa's retention of the title connected with the duchy of Silesia were confirmed in the Peace of Hubertusburg.

The duchy of Silesia and the county of Glatz, of which Prussia now held 40,000 square kilometres, had, when part of the Habsburg hereditary lands belonging to the Bohemian group of territories, enjoyed a fairly independent regional administration. The Lutheran confession in large areas of Silesia, strengthened by the Swedish guarantees of 1707, had deepened the province's separation from the Austrian monarchy. Even so the Silesian *Oberamt* (territorial government) had provided an administrative authority which had successfully held together for Austria the Silesian crown domains, principalities, nobility and towns. The king of Bohemia was the titular duke of Silesia and the Emperor Charles VI united in his person both titles till his death in 1740. The Wittelsbach Emperor Charles VII laid claim to the Bohemian crown from November 1740; it was not until 1743 that Maria Theresa received it. The town of Breslau enjoyed a large measure of independence, having its own administration, jurisdiction and town militia. In 1740 the director of the Austrian *Oberamtskollegium* was Count Hans Anton Schaffgotsch, a privy councillor (*Wirklicher Geheimer Rat*), hereditary chief steward, and also *Landeshauptmann* of the Bohemian crown in the principalities of Schweidnitz and Jauer, Imperial chamberlain and Silesian landowner. By order of the Emperor he headed the provincial government, supervised the judiciary and, together with the Estates, was responsible for taxation and military affairs. The middle level of administration consisted of regional authorities (*Land* governments), while the lowest level was that of the *Weichbildern* (Silesian equivalent to Prussian *Kreise*).

On the Prussian conquest of Silesia this cumbersome set-up, in which the Estates still had power, was abolished. The formal take-over was signalled by a ceremony of homage by Lower Silesia in Frederick's presence on 7 November 1741 in the Princes Hall of Breslau's *Rathaus*. He had forbidden what he regarded as inessentials: a formal reception, the draping of the walls of the homage chamber in red cloth and the firing of salutes; but in all important matters the ceremony followed the regulations laid down by Emperor Matthias in 1611. Representatives from all parts of Silesia were present. Frederick, in the uniform of his *Gardes du Corps*, stood before the throne – his brothers Augustus William and Henry beside him – listening to the address of minister von Podewils and the reply of *Landeshauptmann* von Oels. The provost and dean of the cathedral, the nobility, the cathedral chapter, the other Estates and the towns then swore allegiance. Nobody refused to take the oath. In the evening Breslau and its gardens were gaily illuminated: more than 250 transparencies were displayed by the population. On 6 May 1742 the Prussian commandant of Breslau accepted the homage at Neisse of eleven towns, eleven outworks and 150 villages of the border strip along the river Neisse; when the border had been settled the flood limits of the Neisse had been used as an excuse to include the dependencies of all villages which could be said to fall within the Neisse basin.

An important ceremony of homage was held on 20 February 1742 in the county of Glatz, where the prince of Anhalt-Dessau deputized for the king. Upper Silesia, because of war damage in its own territory, rendered homage at Neisse on 18 March 1743 quite simply with the commandant of Breslau deputizing for Frederick. The bishop of Olmütz and the prince of Liechtenstein, who had possessions in Upper Silesia, were represented by plenipotentiaries. The bishop of Cracow, mistakenly believing that he had been released from the duty of rendering homage, sent no representative; but no action was taken against him. Once peace had been concluded and the agreement regulating the frontiers ratified – at which time Prussia received an additional fifteen villages – the Bohemian Estates on 14 August 1743 made an explicit renunciation of authority over Silesia to Count Dohna, the Prussian envoy in Vienna. The archives of the annexed territories were then handed over to Prussia. Frederick regarded the preliminary peace of Breslau as 'a great and happy event which at the end of a most glorious war brings one of Germany's most flourishing provinces into the possession of my House. One must know when to call a halt. To force good fortune is to lose it'.

Hand-in-hand with the conquest of Silesia went the introduction of Prussian administration. While the fighting lasted this was done through the *Feldkriegskommissariat* (the War Zone Commissariat), a civilian-staffed authority whose function was the provisioning of the

army and the supervision of the local inhabitants in matters of taxation.
It negotiated with the Silesian Estates on the dismantling of the existing
administration and the setting up of Prussian War and Domains
chambers, judicial and financial administration, and the division into
Kreise. Co-directors of the *Feldkriegskommissariat* were privy finance
councillors von Reinhardt and von Münchow, both on secondment from
the General Directory. Privy finance councillor Deutsch, the *General-
Proviantmeister* (the General Supply Master), was also a member and
charged with responsibility for stores and march routes.

The *Feldkriegskommissariat*, over-burdened by the task of provisioning
the army and coping with the near-impossible demands of the king,
could hardly devote much attention to the administration of the province. It was not until 11 October 1741 that a cabinet order was sent to
the General Directory ordering the establishment of War and Domains
chambers at Breslau and Glogau. The heads of the *Feldkriegskommissariat* were appointed presidents: Reinhardt to Breslau and Count von
Münchow (son of the former president of the Küstrin Chamber) to
Glogau. Directors for the new chambers were provided by the Königsberg and Küstrin chambers, deputy-directors by those of Cleves and
Stettin. In 1743 the fully-staffed Breslau Chamber had, apart from a head
forester (whom it shared with Glogau), eleven councillors, four secretaries, three registrars, two record-keepers, eight chancery clerks, three
copyists, three chancery servants, and ten advocates and nine procurators
for legal affairs. The Glogau Chamber was not so well staffed: it had six
councillors, two registrars and two chancery servants, the same number
of secretaries and chancery clerks as at Breslau, but no copyists. It was,
in any case, difficult to find suitably qualified officials, especially for
senior posts. Chambers in the older provinces were ruthlessly raided,
and had as great a difficulty in keeping up with their work as in finding
replacements.

The two Silesian chambers, installed on 27 November 1741, were
ready to begin work on 1 January 1742. The areas covered were quite
large, a total of thirty-five *Kreise* even though only Lower and Middle
Silesia came within their jurisdiction. Under the Breslau Chamber
were the district of Grottkau which stretched across the river Neisse
and included the towns of Neisse and Schurgast, the principalities of
Münsterberg and Brieg, the county of Namslau, the lordships of Warten-
berg, Goschütz, Oels, the town and principality of Breslau, and
Schweidnitz. The Glogau Chamber embraced the principalities of
Jauer, Liegnitz, Wohlau, Glogau, the lordship of Beuthen, Sagan,
Schwiebus, Trachenberg and Militsch.

Hardly had the new administration begun to function when Reinhardt, who had not yet informed his subordinates of the king's intention
to help the war-ravaged areas, was recalled to the General Directory in
Berlin. On 19 March 1742 Münchow was promoted to minister of
state, made president of the Breslau Chamber, and named president-in-
chief of both Silesian chambers. The Silesian provincial administration
was not placed under the General Directory, but under the direct
control of the king. Thus Frederick could exert the greatest influence
on the future development of Prussia's largest province, an arrangement which favoured Silesia when compared to other parts of the
monarchy. Its organization, first regarded as temporary, made it possible
to avoid bureaucratic controls and deal promptly with administrative ordinances; during the period of reconstruction extraordinary financial aid
flowed easily from the state's central funds. The king's personal concern
and his frequent presence in Silesia made the inhabitants trust his administration and facilitated incorporation of the province in the *Gesamtstaat*.
This was not 'cabinet' government by abstract decrees. Frederick's on-
the-spot observations taught him what was or was not practicable. His
methods differed little from those of his father: during the *rétablissement* of
Prussian Lithuania Frederick William I had taken charge in the stricken
areas, using the state's central funds to give help where it was most needed.

The energetic Ludwig Wilhelm Count von Münchow, went about
his task politely and diplomatically. He was only twenty-eight years
old but was already among those Prussian administrative officials who
enjoyed the king's unlimited trust. That this trust was justified is clear
from Münchow's address to his colleagues at the opening session of the
Glogau *Kammerkollegium*:

> our constant endeavour must always be the best interest of the province, its
> happiness, the growth of its population, the furthering of trade and transport,
> the maintenance of order in town and country. . . . we must exert ourselves
> for king and country, without ulterior motives, without thought of our own
> convenience and with all our strength and ability. . . . we must find real
> satisfaction in performing our daily tasks to the best of our ability and in
> making sure that not a day – not even an hour – passes in which we have not
> truly served the king in some way. . . . only in this manner can our efforts
> bear fruit, and we must hold this reward in greater esteem than improve-
> ments in our own standards of living or other external advantages. My only
> consolation in this difficult post is my firm conviction that those about me
> share my aims. Everyone here is free to voice his opinions; indeed, I implore
> you never to suppress your own point of view. I especially ask you, my most
> worthy colleagues and friends, not to conceal anything critical of myself or

my policies. Should anybody be dissatisfied with his changed circumstances or with his present salary I would like to remind him that disappointment is no excuse for refusing to carry out his duties to the best of his abilities or for seeking to supplement his income by forbidden means. My own reaction if this happened would make his position worse; were verbal and written warnings to have no effect, there would have to be an unpleasant interview and I would have no alternative but to exercise the authority vested in me by His Royal Majesty to dismiss the culprit. Whatever good flows from the exercise of this authority I shall attribute not to myself but to you; to see His Royal Majesty's orders carried out everywhere would make me very happy. To the worthy gentlemen at the Treasury, the Chancery and the Building Department I especially recommend accuracy, industriousness, discretion and, above all, bearing in keeping with our oath, and I warn them especially against usury, bribery and oppression.

Münchow lived and worked by these principles. When the king refused him permission to marry, on the grounds that the work of reconstruction required his complete dedication to the task in hand, he bowed to the king's will – a telling characteristic of total service to the sovereign which should not be interpreted in personal terms, but in terms of serving the interests of the state. The merchants of Breslau wanted to show their appreciation of Münchow's work on their behalf by giving him a present of money, but he refused it. When they complained to Frederick about this refusal, they received an answer which they hardly expected: 'I approve of his behaviour and I think you should keep the money and use it for some other purpose. This should teach you that I do not allow my officials to plunder the country; every one of them must be satisfied with his salary.'

From 1744 onwards each of the two Silesian chambers had a *Collegium Medicinae et Sanitatis* attached to it. Three doctors, two surgeons, two apothecaries, and a lawyer under the direction of a chamber councillor made up the staff of each collegium. It published medical regulations, fixed fees and exercised a certain measure of independent jurisdiction. For the rest the Silesian chambers tackled tasks similar to those in other regions of the monarchy. They administered revenues and domains, customs duties, taxes and excises; supervised depots, billeting of troops and recruiting; looked after trade, commerce and the protection of Jews. The *Steuerräte* – two to each chamber and one for the county of Glatz – acted as urban commissioners. A *Kammerdeputation* was set up in Oppeln to act as the nucleus for the administration of Upper Silesia. On 31 July 1743 the Silesian postal service was removed from the jurisdiction of the General Post Office and placed under the Breslau

Chamber where it remained until the introduction of the *Regie*. A transit agreement was concluded with Saxony on 24 August 1743.

One month after the opening of the Breslau and Glogau chambers Prussian rural commissioners were appointed to each of the 35 Silesian *Kreise* and to the principalities. Administratively, the county of Glatz came directly under the provincial minister for Silesia. The rural commissioner, responsible to the chamber for the execution of administrative directives in his county, was chosen from the Silesian *Ritterschaft* and in each county two deputies (the *Landesdeputierte*) were appointed to assist him. Although the rural commissioners were royal appointees they were regarded by their fellow-nobles as the delegates of their Estate. So successful was this innovation that during the administrative reforms of 1748 it was extended to the entire monarchy.

On the day following the Breslau ceremony of homage Frederick announced to representatives of the Estates and of the churches the abolition of religious discrimination and of forcible conscription. He had to use Prussian experts to coordinate Silesia into the financial system of the *Gesamtstaat*, but he was keen to have Silesians participate in the administration of justice. Civil and canon law were therefore at the beginning of 1742 brought under the control of two *Oberamts-Regierungen* at Breslau and Glogau (which, despite their names, were exclusively courts of justice) staffed almost completely by Silesians, from president to councillors. In 1743 another *Oberamts-Regierung* was established at Oppeln, in which two out of the three councillors had to be Catholics.

The development of Silesia's judicial system was entrusted to the sixty-three-year-old Samuel von Cocceji, the Prussian minister for justice. Cocceji, born at Heidelberg to a family which originally came from Bremen, was also made minister of justice for Lower Silesia; at the end of 1743 this post was transferred to minister Georg Dietloff von Arnim, a difficult colleague who also created problems for Münchow and brought the reform of justice in Silesia to a premature halt. Cocceji, however, was now able to give more time to his major work, the *Corpus Juris Fridericiani*, published between 1749 and 1751. This did not affect Silesia much since Prussian Common Law (*Landrecht*) had only a limited validity there. Prussian supervision of advocates and the introduction of fixed salaries for the judges did, all the same, help to expedite the cases pending in the Silesian courts. The courts of first instance remained the prerogative of the princes, the *Standesherren* (nobility), and the town magistrates, in accordance with promises made at Frederick's homage. Courts of first and second instance were both controlled by the *Oberamts-*

Regierungen, as were the General Consistories for Ecclesiastical Affairs (*Oberkonsistorien*). At the opening of the Breslau *Oberamts-Regierung* in 1742 Cocceji stressed that 'Law and Religion are the main pillars of a well-established *res publicae.*' His attitude to the administration of justice can be deduced from an instruction for councillors of the *Oberamts-Regierungen*: 'During sessions he [the councillor] is not to read memoranda or acta or write decrees and sentences. These are to be read and worked on at home; decrees, sentences and opinions are to be written on separate sheets of paper and taken with him to court; while at court he is to listen carefully to the pleadings.' Changes were also introduced in sentences: the practice of deporting criminals was dropped in favour of detention in prisons and workhouses at Glogau and Brieg.

The prerequisite for a regular tax system was the preparation of reliable assessment-rolls (*Katasters*). In the spring of 1742 a systematic survey of Silesia was begun under the direction of the cameralists von Ziegler and von Thile. The roll for Lower Silesia was completed in less than twelve months and the tax assessment was ready for Trinity Sunday 1743; by the end of the year Upper Silesia and Glatz had also been dealt with. The productivity of the land was carefully assessed and comparison made with the findings of the Austrian tables, which were opened to public inspection so that mistakes could be rectified. The exemption from taxation previously enjoyed by nobility and clergy was abolished: Frederick held that, since the state extended its protection to all subjects, all should contribute to its expenses; even the royal domains were liable to tax. Taxation rates – varying from 28 to 34 per cent of net proceeds – were, as the Silesians acknowledged, carefully adjusted to actual profits. Even with the urban excise tax (*Akzise*) and the tax on rural traders' profits (the *Gewerbesteuer*) the Silesian tax-income did not suffice to balance the provincial budget; the annual deficit ran at 3 per cent of the estimate. Provision had to be made for crop failures, cattle disease and damages from hail and flooding, and the state took on most of this burden in order to restore high productivity as quickly as possible. Losses from fire were covered by self-help within communities by the so-called 'fire societies', which provided building materials, transport and labour. State ordinances on fire-prevention were aimed at wood-shingle roofs, especially those of the towns, and at half-timbered houses in general. The need for administrative initiative for reconstruction-work necessary in ravaged Silesia can be gauged from the report on Upper Silesia compiled in October 1742 by Lautensack, the commissioner for war damages: 'The harvest has been poor; the towns, in part destroyed, have lost their trade, fallen into debt and can not pay their taxes; conditions are particularly bad in the villages of the mediatized nobles where the population seem apathetic, half-starved and utterly depressed by the burden of billeting; the mines have been abandoned, and the whole land is so impoverished that tax quotas must be considerably lowered.' Much state help was provided for Silesia during the Seven Years War and, though that war bled the province dry, plans for its post-war recovery were so carefully laid that they could be put into speedy and successful effect.

The principles of the Silesian administration and the important role of the provincial ministers in charge of it survived Münchow's death. His successor was Joachim Ewald von Massow, a former army officer, whose career as president of the Königsberg Chamber had been both prudent and successful. Opposition from the Catholic clergy, however, ended his usefulness in Silesia as early as 1755. He was replaced by Ernst Wilhelm von Schlabrendorff, whose industriousness in the Magdeburg Chamber had favourably impressed the king. Schlabrendorff conscientiously guided Silesia through difficult times. He was a strict bureaucrat, who enforced the royal will, weeded out unsuitable subordinates, kept a sharp eye on the various branches of industry, and acted with vigour against all carelessness and sloth. In 1770, after Schlabrendorff's death, thirty-one-year-old Karl George Heinrich von Hoym was appointed provincial minister for Silesia. He ran the province on a much slacker rein. Under him the Silesian administration, which already enjoyed considerable freedom, was to acquire even greater independence, especially after Frederick turned his attention to the problem of developing West Prussia, and was content to leave Silesia, which was getting on quite well, to its own devices. Hoym at times succeeded in deceiving the overburdened king through reports which skilfully explained away the non-appearance of the great economic expansion for which Schlabrendorff had so painstakingly prepared the ground.

Only those elements of the Silesian economy which fundamentally differentiated it from the rest of the monarchy need to be discussed here. Its agriculture, capable of much expansion, was aided by the cultivation of fallow land, encouraged and even enforced by the government. Decrees also prevented the buying up of peasant holdings by the large estate-owners; others strongly encouraged the planting of fodder crops, oil-producing plants, mulberry trees and potatoes. The rural masses were not serfs; but they were tied to the land and dependent on the lord of the manor unless – as was often the case – they possessed large thriving farms which guaranteed them independence. The crown domains, being strictly supervised, were the most progressive agricultural units but their number was quite small since the Habsburgs had sold off most of their Silesian lands. The Catholic Church possessed more land than the crown, but towns and burghers also held large tracts of land with villages, farms and outfarms. The service obligations owed by the rural inhabitants to their landowners varied considerably: free peasants had no obligations; *Zinsbauern* (peasant farmers who paid rent for their land) were liable to small payments, either in money or in kind; 'gardeners' had small allotments of land; cottagers for the most part owned only their dilapidated huts; and the so-called *Freileute* (literally 'free people') were dependent peasants tied to a specific privileged estate. Most rural inhabitants were liable to limited services and many of them even to unlimited ones. In addition they had obligations to the state: the transportation of building material to fortresses, and the burdensome provision of staging horses for officials and for the royal baggage train. Frederick tried in 1748 and 1763 to abolish hereditable subjection, or at least to alleviate its harshness, but in vain. The density of settlement and intensity of agriculture depended on the degree of dependence and the amount of war damage. Silesian soil was in any case better utilized than that of the neighbouring countries: only one tenth of the land was not cultivated. One in four of the inhabitants found their living in industry, the rest in agriculture.

Great attention was paid to forestry. To combat indiscriminate felling and to preserve valuable timber prohibitions were issued even against the cutting of the first green shoots for Whit Sunday and the cutting of bushes for Laetare Sunday. The king issued special orders to preserve the valuable oak trees. The income from Silesia was considerable. In the financial year 1745–46 the domains *Kassen* of Silesia yielded 687,000 talers, of which more than two-thirds derived from the salt monopoly. Even more important were the profits from Silesian trade and manufacture. Linen weaving, carried on in mountain villages and in some town mills, took pride of place. The linen industry, in any case not well organized for export, had been severely hampered by the Silesian wars. It was put on its feet again by state subsidies and by regulations to improve quality and to diversify the fabrics: calico, gold and silver cloth, braid, velvet and parchment now became part of Silesian output. The state's attempt to distribute the Silesian linen trade more widely was not successful. The Breslau merchants proved uninterested in the Oder network of waterways which led to Stettin, but the old markets in England, Spain and South America remained stable; in 1783 the Silesian linen trade made a profit of 3·5 million talers. The woollen mills of the province had long been famous for high-quality cloth, and the Breslau wool fair soon regained its old reputation. Austrian protective tariffs, however, deprived them of much of their original markets; the old Prussian territories were not allowed imports from Silesia lest this lead to the closure of their own mills. After the Seven Years War Schlabrendorff did much to further the Silesian woollen industry. Grünberg and the county of Glatz increased their sales of cloth by between 25 and 50 per cent. The pottery trade, centred on Bunzlau, also prospered. New glassworks were established, nine in Upper Silesia and two in the county of Glatz, and old ones improved to satisfy the demand created by the prohibition against importing Bohemian glass. Ten years after Prussia's annexation, Silesia exported products to the value of 10 million talers. The province produced 45 per cent of Prussia's total exports and bought 44 per cent of her imports. The attempted industrialization of Upper Silesia, promoted by high state subsidies, proceeded by fits and starts: a profitable stocking factory was built at Pless, cloth mills and mills for unfulled cloth were started at Oppeln and Tarnowitz; but other towns remained backward, squandering their state subsidies on speculative housing while entrepreneurs and workers procured for them were forced to leave.

For the monarchy as a whole Silesia's most important industry was mining. In 1740 twenty-seven foundries and twelve blast furnaces were in operation. Metallurgy was well developed; of special importance was the brassworks – with an associated tin workshop – at Jakobswalde near Schlawentzütz in the county of Kosel of Upper Silesia. The Kreuzburg ironworks was founded in 1755. Prussia's first mining decree for Silesia was dated 19 February 1756; in it the state's mining rights were extended to cover the hard coal, almost all of which was at that time mined in the twelve pits of the Waldenburg district. In 1763 the whole of Glatz had only eighteen coal-miners, and there was no coal-mining at all in Upper Silesia. Thanks to the untiring Schlabrendorff a systematic survey was begun in 1755 to assess the output, economic importance and the future possibilities of the whole of the Silesian mining industry. The foundries increased to forty-six and the blast furnaces to twenty when the outbreak of the Seven Years War brought this flourishing branch of industry to a halt. In 1763 Schlabrendorff began the tedious task of rebuilding the industry. The meagre state subsidies available were, however, embezzled by a swindler in 1778. In the same year the first Prussian mining director, the famous cameralist Johann von Justi – since 1765 director of state mines – was imprisoned in the fortress of Küstrin because the Vietz foundry in the county of Landsberg on the Warthe and the Kutzdorf forge in the county of Königsberg/Neumark had not fulfilled their targets, and also because of alleged financial deficits. Justi died in prison three years later.

The responsibility for the state mines was too much for one person: on 9 May 1768 Frederick founded the Seventh Department of the General Directory to take charge of mines and foundries. To head it he appointed his most competent administrator, minister Ludwig Philipp Freiherr von Hagen, who also retained control of the Third and Fourth Departments. Separation from the general business of the Directory was of great advantage: correspondence could be dealt with speedily and without the need for collegial decision-making. Hagen had mineralogy and mining law placed on the curricula of the Prussian universities. The *Immediatkommission* (commission which reported directly to the king) established in August 1768 to prospect the Silesian mountains for minerals, and the cabinet order of 1 February 1769 which brought all mining matters, including those of Silesia (to the intense annoyance of the Silesian chambers), under Berlin's authority, can both be traced to Hagen's advice. On 3 December 1769 the Silesian *Oberbergamt* (provincial mining office) was set up at Reichenstein and in 1779 transferred to Breslau.

The 'Revised Mining Ordinance for the Sovereign Duchy of Silesia and the County of Glatz', modelled on that of Cleves, was published on 5 June 1769; in its turn it became the prototype of the mining ordinances of 7 December 1772 for Madgeburg-Halberstadt, Mansfeld and other places. Prospecting for useful minerals including hard coal was declared to be free; but the state, which issued all licences, retained first rights to any minerals discovered on state property. Mine management, since at that time it lacked experience and training, was put under the control of the mining offices with their *Berggeschworenen* ('mine-juries'): they appointed foremen and overseers, fixed prices and taxes, and exercised criminal jurisdicton within the mining communities. Each miner was registered with a miners' society, enjoying a certain amount of self-government, which paid sickness, accident and unemployment benefits from its own funds, and – in cases of death – paid for funerals and provided for relatives. The mine-owners were subject to numerous high taxes, which lowered the profitability of the mines. The Miners' Charter (the *Privilegium für die Bergleute*) guaranteed, in Prussia as in the western provinces, the miner's freedom to settle wherever he wished, and exempted him – and his sons – from military service, billeting obligations, communal taxes and the jurisdiction of manorial lords. To prevent an acute shortage of farm workers migration into the mines was, however, made dependent on the written consent of the manorial lord.

general scarcity of workers meant that miners were in short supply, but the practice of allowing serfs to buy their freedom eventually helped to ease the labour shortage in the mines.

Hagen died from overwork in 1771, before he had reached his fiftieth birthday. Friedrich Wilhelm Freiherr von der Schulenburg-Kehnert was his successor, while continuing to take responsibility for two other departments. His ignorance of mining led to his replacement in June 1774 by minister Sigismund Freiherr Waitz von Eschen. Waitz, a former chamber councillor from Kassel and an *Obersalzgraf* (official in charge of the salt monopoly), had in 1742 been offered the Prussian Mining Office at Wettin; but he preferred to remain in Hessian service where he became a minister of state and was ennobled as a Freiherr of the Empire. Waitz was a mining expert and despite his age – he was already seventy-six – energetically set about ridding the Seventh Department and its subordinate mining offices of dead wood and turning it into a highly efficient and professional body, achieving some success before he died in office in 1776. The king, still dependent on 'foreigners' for his mining department, appointed Friedrich Anton von Heinitz as Waitz' successor. A Saxon by birth, Heinitz had been in charge of Brunswick's mining operations in the Harz, had played a decisive role in the foundation of the Mining Academy at Freiberg in Saxony, and had studied contemporary mining practice in Sweden, Hungary and France. His appointment, at the age of fifty-two, with a high reputation as an outstanding organizer, shows not only Frederick's acumen but also the attraction of Prussian service. In addition to running the Seventh Department he had, at times, to take care of the Fifth Department, a circumstance which led to some differences of opinion with colleagues on the direction of the Prussian economy as a whole. The mines, however, remained his main interest; here he was supported, especially in Silesia, by his nephew and pupil, Friedrich Wilhelm Freiherr von Reden who although twenty-seven years younger than himself became his closest collaborator. Reden, educated in France, England and at the Mining Academy at Freiberg, had been made chief mining councillor (*Oberbergrat*) in the Seventh Department in 1778 and was the next year appointed provisional director of the Silesian *Oberbergamt*. In 1781 chief mining councillor Karl Freiherr vom Stein completed a triumvirate of able leaders.

On taking up his post Heinitz had divided Prussia's mining operations into four main districts; these later became the *Oberbergamtsbezirke* (main mining regions) of Berlin (the Kurmark, the Neumark, East and West Prussia), Halle (Magdeburg, Halberstadt, Hohenstein and Mansfeld), Breslau (Silesia and the county of Glatz), and Dortmund (the

Westphalian provinces). In 1779 the Silesian district was sub-divided into the mining domains of Reichenstein, Waldenburg and Giehren (county Löwenberg), to which later was added Tarnowitz, where the mining of lead ore on a large scale had begun in 1784. Heinitz established the foundries at Gleiwitz and Königshütte, installed the first steam engine, built the first coke furnaces, and introduced many practical innovations based on scientific principles. Drawing on his Silesian experiences he modernized mining techniques and foundry practice throughout the entire state. Frederick, a thrifty monarch, allowed himself to be convinced by Heinitz' arguments to the extent of investing almost 500,000 talers in mining from 1783 onwards. This heavy investment would, the king believed, bring ample future rewards. In a memoir presented to Frederick in the last year of his reign – and accepted by him – Heinitz argued that mining was no less important than trade and agriculture, those other pillars of the economy.

Frederick was during his lifetime, and even more so after his death, violently criticized for his mercantile policy, his personal manner of running the state (*Staatsdirigismus*), his cabinet government, his obstinacy, impatience and injustice. Schlabrendorff, himself a rather authoritarian provincial minister for Silesia, wrote to a friend in Berlin in 1765: 'If one cannot express freely, without being exposed to the greatest slander, what one considers best for the sovereign and the state, one is unable to contribute that of which one is capable.' Mistakes were certainly made by the king, imprudent measures were frequently passed, harmony and infallibility did not reign. Orders, decrees and laws, as historians realize, never mirrored reality. But were they therefore unnecessary? Thanks to its truly functional administration Prussia possessed a dependable executive; and the king's cabinet orders, despite the umbrage they sometimes caused, contained so much purpose, guidance and good sense that they were not as insignificant as some have judged them. The way in which Schlabrendorff was treated, and the probably unjust imprisonment of Justi, were major blunders of Frederick's and cannot be excused. But we also have evidence of exceptional achievement, generosity, clarity of perception, and a joy in decision-making. The historian has other material at his disposal than newspaper reports meant to flatter the king, who was in any case himself shrewd enough to question and put to the test their rosy optimism. Frederick was not easy to deceive in the matter of his own success. He was enough of a sceptic to realize the limits of human dependability, including his own. He reacted angrily to timid misgivings and pessimistic reports from his officials, not because he wanted to ignore reality but because he demanded from his collaborators that they should tackle unfavourable circumstances with all the strength they possessed and ease his burdens by informing him of the measures they had taken to help solve problems. Frederick put his officials through a hard school; his aim was not to supervise them, but to train them to accept responsibility within their own departments, to root out the habit of passing difficult decisions to the ruler and then waiting for instructions. On 2 June 1782, when Heinitz was put in charge of the Fifth Department in addition to his heavy responsibilities in the Seventh, he noted in his journal:

> It is the will of God that I shall be kept busy and I must therefore look upon this task as a service to God: to contribute to God's honour and to the true interests of my fellow men. In this I have the king as an example, for there are few like him. He is industrious, prefers duty to pleasure, gives priority to his responsibilities and has been endowed by God with the most superior gifts. There is nobody like him among his peers, nobody with his abstemiousness, his single-mindedness, his ability to occupy his time fruitfully. He does not have the reputation he deserves, yet he is superior to other rulers.

EAST FRIESLAND

Time and time again France, Sweden's ally, had deprived the Great Elector of his conquests along the Pomeranian coast. Because of this he adhered to the Emperor after the humiliating Peace of Nijmwegen of 1678, demanding as compensation for his services against France the reversion of East Friesland on the expected extinction of its ruling house. This reversion was only formally granted in 1694 to his successor but the Great Elector had, with the permission of the Emperor, as early as 1682 sent a contingent of Brandenburg troops to East Friesland in order to protect his interests. The next year he founded a Brandenburg Admiralty *Kollegium* at Emden and also a Brandenburg overseas trading company, the African Company. He planned to canalize the Upper Ems, thus linking Cleves-Mark with Emden and diverting general Rhine traffic to that port; he also hoped to found an East Indian trading company based on Emden.

A succession treaty had been concluded between East Friesland and Brunswick-Lüneburg in 1691 (which eventually led to Hanover's being awarded East Friesland in 1815), but the reversion of East Friesland was all the same confirmed to Frederick William I in 1714. After 1732 the principality was included among his titles and appeared on his coat of arms. Prussia, Calvinist as was the principality, was indeed welcomed in East Friesland, a land frequently flooded by the sea, long torn by domestic strife and exploited by its unscrupulous nobility. The king's most trusted representative was the able *Syndicus* of the Emden Collegium, Dr Sebastian Anton Homfeld. Of local peasant stock, and a *Gerichtsschulze* (military judicial official) to the Prussian battalion, he became after 1733 Prussian *Direktorialrat* (directorial councillor) in the Lower Saxon and Westphalian Circle. He successfully warded off Austrian and Hanoverian interference in East Friesland and won influential sections in the principality for Prussia, also securing in the process an indispensable position for himself. On his accession Frederick II confirmed Homfeld's full poweis and, after long negotiations, an agreement was reached on 28 November 1742 with the town of Emden and sections of the *Ritterschaft* wherein the Prussian right of succession was unreservedly acknowledged. In return Prussia guaranteed the existing Estates government. The agreement was not ratified till 1744 and Frederick, while maintaining his claim, tended to look upon it as of lesser importance than his claim to Jülich-Berg: he considered exchanging it for other areas and as late as 1744–45 toyed with the idea of selling the town of Emden.

In 1744 East Friesland comprised eight separate domains: Emden (including the town, the only important one within the principality that had autonomous rights), Aurich, Norden (both including the towns of the same name), Leerort (including the market town of Leer), Greetsiel, Berum, Friedeburg and Stickhausen with the lordship of Pewsun and the islands of Borkum, Juist, Norderney, Baltrum and Langeoog. All eight were administered by bailiffs (*Vögten*) appointed by the *Landesherr* (territorial lord). In the north-east, governed directly by the *Landesherr*, was Harlingerland with the domain, town and fortress of Esens and the domain and hamlet of Wittmund with its fortress. As a trading town Emden had declined in importance in the course of the seventeenth century, and its population had fallen from 30,000 in the sixteenth century to 8,000. Domestic troubles and difficult relations with neighbouring states had contributed to this decline, but the main reason was the shifting of channels of the lower Ems. The only industrial activity was the now ailing linen manufacture at Leer. For the rest the region lived from cattle-rearing on the rich marshlands and from its fisheries. Agriculture was in a backward state and the utilization of the fenland had hardly begun. With barely 100,000 inhabitants East Friesland's population was lower than that of the county of Mark.

No sooner had the ratifications of the Emden Treaty been exchanged than the inheritance fell vacant. Karl Edzard of the House of Cirksena, last prince of East Friesland, died on 26 May 1744. That very day the

king of Prussia's succession was proclaimed and the Black Eagles nailed
to the fortress. In the domains too the coats of arms were speedily
changed. The Emperor Charles VII immediately recalled the Imperial
detachment. The Dutch garrison in Emden was persuaded to keep quiet
and later to withdraw, while the forlorn attempt of the small Danish
garrisons at Aurich and Berum to prevent the Prussian occupation of
the principality came to an end when a company of Prussian soldiers
advanced on them from Emden. With the withdrawal of foreign troops
and the incorporation of the late prince's few soldiers in the Prussian
army East Friesland had been annexed in less than a week.

Frederick himself was at Pyrmont spa at the time. He ordered the
reinforcement of the Prussian troops in Emden by the Wesel garrison
to show that he intended 'to maintain without fail possession of this
[the East Friesland] principality'. On 30 May War and Domains councillor Caspar Heinrich Bügel left the Minden Chamber with the king's
detailed instructions for the inspection of East Friesland and its
domain lands and directions as to the principles on which it was to be
administered. Bügel was soon followed by minister von Cocceji whose
experience of Imperial law proved invaluable during the negotiations
with the principality's Estates on their *gravamina* and homage. The king
wanted East Friesland's transfer to Prussia to be accomplished as
smoothly as possible and was anxious that a mood of friendly expecta-
tion should be awakened in its inhabitants, not least because of the close
proximity of the United Provinces. Thanks to the discretion of the
Prussian officials this was successfully done. The *Landtag* met on 20
June. The ceremony of homage, which was held 'without the slightest
festivity', with Cocceji deputizing for the king, followed three days
later. The Estates offered Frederick an annual sum of 48,000 talers (double
the amount they had paid to the late prince), with an additional 12,000
talers (later increased to 18,000) in lieu of army recruitment in the
province. The king, for his part, assumed responsibility for the late
prince's heavy debts: to help defray these Karl Edzard's library was sold
and the post of librarian abolished. Frederick undertook to pay the
appanages of members of the princely family, the expenditure for the
army, churches and schools, building costs and the requirements of the
domain administration, in all more than 56,000 talers a year. The costs
of the domain administration were carefully examined and the large
number of *Drosten* (local noblemen who carried out some police and
military functions), councillors, county-court judges, district officials,
Rentmeisters (treasury officials) and governors of the castles – all with
vaguely defined functions – was, wherever possible, reduced or abolished.

Frederick held that 'generally the more people there are of that type, the more disorder, drudgery and exactions grow . . . especially as we here can get on well enough without such people.'

The new administration (including that for Harlingerland whose Esens chancery was amalgamated with that of Aurich) consisted of one chancellor, Homfeld, appointed on 27 June 1744 with the rank of privy councillor, four councillors,* an *Advocatus Fisci*, an archivist, a secretary, four chancery clerks, one beadle and two messengers. Two clerics had as consistorial councillors (*Konsistorialräte*) formed part of the *Regierung*. One was transferred and the position of the other was abolished on the appointment of a town pastor to a superintendancy. Salaries and emoluments were maintained at the level of the previous reign though those for the lower grades were slightly lowered. They could not be regarded as sufficient in any case; the *Advocatus Fisci* received 100 talers and two pigs per year. Order was brought into the *Drost* institution of East Friesland, first by a new list issued in the spring of 1745 and then by the regulations of March 1748 which brought the functions of this office as closely as possible into line with those of the Prussian *Landrat*. A cabinet order of 6 July 1755 laid down that *Drosten* were to be appointed by the ministry of justice and supervised by the General Directory. Their duties corresponded to those of the former Prussian domains officials; within the domains they had the highest authority, acted as commandants of the 'strong house' (of which every domain had one), were responsible for the economic management of the services due by subjects, filled vacant posts, supervised officials, controlled roads, bridges and dykes, guarded the frontiers, maintained the royal prerogative, watched over hunting and fishing rights, and participated in the administration of justice. Originally they could be dismissed on six months' notice but this was later allowed to lapse.

A formal agreement, known as the Aurich Convention, was concluded with the Estates on 7 July 1744 and ratified in Berlin on 31 July. The institution of the *Landtag* was retained, its decisions upheld, and royal assurance given that in times of general flooding or other natural calamities something would be deducted from the *quanto contribuendo* for the duration of the emergency. Cocceji's observation proved correct: 'Unity and peace are so great here that the inhabitants could not be more content. And nothing could give greater satisfaction than Your Majesty's declaration that recruits need not be supplied *in natura*.' The king was pleased at his success. Chamber councillor Bügel reckoned on a yearly

---

* Two councillorships were left unfilled, since their previous holders had been incarcerated in the fortress of Gretsiel for anti-Prussian intrigues.

surplus from East Friesland of 80,000 talers: most of this found its way into the Potsdam building fund.

East Friesland's administrative structure was so old-fashioned and differed so much from the rest of the monarchy that it was not possible, as in Silesia, to introduce many permanent changes. Cocceji abolished the princely privy council as 'superfluous in a *Gesamtstaat*'. His judicial reforms proved valuable in East Friesland, as in Silesia: hundreds of protracted lawsuits were either dismissed or speedily settled. The *Reichskammergericht* (the Imperial Supreme Court) was replaced by the *Oberappellations-Gerichtshof* (the High Court of Appeal) of Berlin. Other Imperial legal problems remained, such as the question of East Friesland's seat and vote in the *Reichsfürstenrat* (the Imperial Princely Council).

In European diplomacy local interests had at once to yield precedence to those of the *Gesamtstaat*, but Prussian administrative practices needed time to take root in the province. Some assimilation occurred at an early date. The old princely *Oberrentkammer* (the Chief Treasury Board) was, on Bügel's justified insistence, changed into a War and Domains chamber on the Prussian model at the time of the abolition of the Harlingerland chancery in 1745; Bügel, with Aurich as his base, became its director. But, while in Prussia the provincial *Regierungen* had long lost most of their importance, in East Friesland two parallel executive authorities continued: the Estates government, also based in Aurich, had charge of internal administration and of police matters, functions which elsewhere were exercised by the chambers. Homfeld, the chancellor of East Friesland's *Regierung*, had in 1725–27 written a 'Comprehensive Guide to the Rights of East Friesland's *Landtag*'; and as a native of East Friesland he naturally upheld the rights of the Estates as guaranteed by Frederick after 1744. To Homfeld Bügel was a foreign observer, a small-minded snooper who wanted to transfer administrative legal authority to the Chamber. Bügel, for his part, found the whole entangled, nepotic business of the Estates with their murky and selfish business practices and racketeering intolerable. He suspected Homfeld – not without reason – of 'the vain ambition of becoming Governor-General of this province'. When Bügel was appointed a royal *Landtag* commissioner (*Königlicher Landtagskommissar*), the Estates applied the *jus indigenatus* to have his appointment revoked. Against the inclinations of the General Directory Frederick gave in and named a native East-Frieslander in Bügel's place.

Bügel remained director of the Chamber, but had to stand by while the various groups within the Estates, by their quarrels and intrigues, brought local government in the province to the point of absurdity.

Without involving himself in these squabbles Bügel concentrated on the most pressing problems. East Friesland came under the Third Department of the General Directory, along with Cleves-Mark, Moers, Gelderland and Neuchâtel; the minister in charge was August Frederick von Boden, a financial genius, whom Frederick William I had discovered, advanced and ennobled. Boden appreciated Bügel's worth. The regulation of East Friesland's entangled monetary system proved a monumental task which had to be carried out against intense opposition from the Estates. Bügel, however, succeeded in removing payment in worthless coinage from the administration, and from 1746 onwards assessments were paid regularly and in full. The land being agrarian the payments in kind could be farmed out and a regular chamber estimate obtained. In the same year successful fen cultivation was started. On the other hand standardization of weights and measures made slow progress, as did the regulation of fisheries, forestry and horse breeding: the *Landtag* opposed all change. Thirty-six dyke associations had long administered their own affairs. Their failure had been demonstrated during the great tidal wave of 1717. Inspections had failed to reveal the corruption, carelessness and nepotic practices which concealed the unpreparedness of this antiquated system. From 1749 reforms in the administration produced some improvement, and the rebuilding of the fortifications of the off-shore islands, bashed to pieces by tidal waves, was now undertaken.

Bügel, to the annoyance of the Estates, kept Boden informed of developments in East Friesland; but the Chamber, intent on concentrating on the most important reforms, advised Bügel in the summer of 1745 to remedy abuses 'in the course of time and by and by, and in a convenient manner'. In 1751 the Estates *Regierung* was still in debt to the tune of one and a quarter million talers, and the attempts by the *Landtag* commissioner Sebastian Eberhard Jhering to improve the situation achieved little. In May 1748 the General Directory had threatened 'to take measures which will bring order into their affairs, something which has not yet been done; for we will finally be forced to interfere in order to protect the interest of our faithful subjects.' As East Friesland was still within the purlieu of the Department of External Affairs the opposition between Chamber and *Regierung* in Aurich continued at a higher level between departments in Berlin. Eventually it became necessary to set up a mixed commission to examine the East Friesland position. On 18 August 1746 a departmental regulation (a *Ressort-Reglement*) was signed by the king, who had hitherto kept in the background. This document represented a compromise – strange and archaic in view of

Prussian absolutism – between Estate and state administration and illustrates how varied and flexible administrative practices of the period could be. The independence of the Aurich *Kammer*, equal in status to the *Regierung*, was confirmed. In Harlingerland and on the islands (which had always been exempted from the privileges of the Estates) the Chamber was to enjoy authority similar to that of the War and Domains chambers in the other Prussian provinces; and in general hunting, fisheries and forestry were placed within its competence. Police affairs were, 'for the time being', to come under the *Regierung*, but 'if any specific changes have to be made, and in all cases where something has to be regulated concerning trade and transport, the *Regierung* must consult with the War and Domains Chamber'. The staffing of the Chamber was at this time being completed. Councillor Peter Colomb, born at Neustadt on the Dosse twenty-six years earlier of a Huguenot refugee family, was transferred from Minden to Aurich where he was to remain for half a century, becoming president of the Chamber in 1768. Departmental regulations could not, however, eradicate East Friesland's administrative problems.

In February 1747 the Estates sent Kettler, as *Landsyndicus* (judicial adviser to a *Landtag*), to Berlin bearing a sheaf of complaints about Bügel. The East Friesland Estates, ignorant of the *esprit de corps* and working methods of Prussia's central authorities, assumed that presents of linen, cheese, tea and salmon, and the distribution of considerable sums of money, would win them support. Their attempt to bribe officialdom was doomed to failure. In the meantime, Bügel had won adherents among those officials of the principality's previous regime who had lost their posts during the Prussian take-over in 1744. These men, anxious to regain their positions, were familiar with the financial chicanery and sharp practices of the Estates, a fact which proved of great advantage to the General Directory. The Estates became aware of the writing on the wall with the appointment of *Regierungsrat* Backmeister to the post of inspector at the Estates *Kollegium* on 16 August 1748. A native of East Friesland, Backmeister (who had four years earlier been imprisoned for anti-Prussian intrigues) was instructed 'to introduce and maintain good order in all matters'; he and the *Kollegium* were enjoined to observe punctuality on duty, supervise the book-keeping, introduce a strict budget, and sanction extraordinary expenditure only with the prior permission of the General Directory. By attempting to put East Friesland's administration 'on a Prussian footing', Frederick was aiming at the professional standards which had by this time become part of the natural order of things in the older provinces.

Bügel died suddenly on 28 April 1748, leaving behind the memory of an official 'honest and skilled in the king's service'. He was succeeded as director of the East Friesland Chamber by Daniel Lentz, a native of the Altmark, whose administrative experience had been gained in the Gumbinnen Chamber. Lentz's instructions were to end 'the utterly evil management of the Estates there' (i.e. in East Friesland). The king left the execution of these instructions to Lentz, 'for I am too far away to judge, having never seen that land, nor am I familiar with its circumstances'. Lentz called the *Landtag* for 16 January 1749 and achieved the transfer of the Estates Treasury (the *Landkasten*) from Emden to Aurich, where it would be under the supervision of the Chamber. The *Landtag* also agreed that the supervision of the Emden municipal administration should be transferred to the Prussian authorities, party divisions within the *Landtag* having been skilfully used to promote central authority. The old *Regierung* was left the task of regulating taxes and debts with the *Landtag*: this took fourteen years to complete. In Emden as elsewhere in Prussia the supervision of municipal finances became the responsibility of a *commissarius loci* (a *Steuerrat*). The emasculation of the power of patrician East Friesland was generally welcomed in town and country, and Lentz, made president of the Chamber, ruled without opposition in Aurich.

In June 1751 Frederick, accompanied by his three brothers, journeyed via Brunswick from Magdeburg to Emden and stayed in the town from 13 to 16 June. The king was enthusiastically received, with triumphal arches and odes of homage in High and Low German, and took a yacht trip on the Dollart. On 16 June he inspected the Chamber in Aurich and on the following day attended a meeting of the Asiatic Trading Company of Emden before setting out for Wesel. A second royal visit to Emden took place on 14 to 16 June 1755 when Frederick watched the launching of a large sea-going ship before travelling on to Utrecht and Amsterdam.

By this time Frederick's relationship with East Friesland had become friendly, even warm. Exports had risen to almost 300,000 talers a year: butter accounted for 30,000, cheese for 125,000, and horses for 120,000. The needs of the English market made the growing of oats a lucrative business, and fen cultivation had gained in importance. New roads had been built and existing ones had been improved to the benefit of trade and the postal service. The town of Emden had charge of the Amsterdam post while royal Prussian stage coaches covered communications between Aurich and Oldenburg, Bremen and Minden. Lentz tried to organize a second postal service through Leer, Lingen and

Tecklenburg to Bielefeld, but the obstruction of the archbishop of Cologne-Münster prevented this. At first the domains were in charge of East Friesland's internal postal service, but after 1756 the General Post Office in Berlin took over and managed to raise the annual profits from 3,000 to 12,000 talers. During the French occupation in 1757 and the Austrian invasion in 1761 the East Friesland authorities – with few exceptions – behaved correctly; and groups of peasants offered sporadic resistance to the invaders. On 31 March 1758 Frederick praised the faithfulness of the province: in a cabinet order of 23 April 1758 he instructed his East Friesland officials to assure 'my faithful and trusty tenants as well as the burghers and peasants in the province of my gracious satisfaction that despite all the threats of our enemies they have never wavered in their faithfulness and devotion'. Lentz, despite the war, raised the revenues as he had in peacetime and sent them in full to the General Directory. After 1757 he had difficulties with Homfeld who did not get on with Christoph Friedrich Derschau, the poetically-inclined East Prussian president-in-chief of the East Friesland *Regierung*, recently transferred from Cleves to Aurich. In 1759, as a result of friction between these two, all judicial matters and lawsuits came under the control of Derschau, while all other authority remained with the chancellor. Homfeld's many and ingenious protests had no effect; by the time of his death on 20 May 1761 at the age of seventy-three his importance had long since disappeared.

From 1768 the president of the East Friesland Chamber was Peter Colomb, the most gifted – with the exception of Domhardt in Königsberg – of the presidents. Wöllner, later minister of justice, said of him in 1788: 'He is, without doubt, the best and most experienced chamber president in the monarchy. He does much to improve his province.' Colomb was able to build on the solid foundations laid by Lentz's tireless industry. From 1751 a fixed annual sum had been set aside to protect the islands from the sea; in the same year Silesian mortgage regulations (with property registers) had been introduced into the province, as had regulations concerning deposits and bills of exchange and the criminal law of the Kurmark. 1754 had seen the state supervision of horse studs and the foundation of fire societies – first in the main towns, then in the larger market centres and the villages. Jhering in his turn introduced special fire regulations for mills, always a high fire-risk.

The Seven Years War brought setbacks to East Friesland's development; war taxes (the *Kontributionen*), billeting and staging duties burdened the already indebted province by almost 1·3 million talers. Nor was it spared the crop failures which in 1770-71 affected the whole of Central Europe: in this predominantly agrarian province royal depots had to relieve distress among the poor. The rains of 1785 were followed by catastrophic drought; and cattle epidemics, against which man seemed helpless in spite of the successes of inoculation, hit the province even harder. Between 1745 and 1761 more than 260,000 cattle perished; another 51,000 died in the years 1769-91; for 1774 the losses stood at 76,000. The king, in spite of other heavy demands on his assistance, helped with 50,000 talers in 1772. A plague of mice in 1773, and another in 1787, had disastrous effects on the harvests. Tidal waves engulfed the coastal lands. In the floods of 1775-76 the high-water mark was nine inches higher than in 1717, but the dykes held thanks to the new and effective inspection system. Even so the polders suffered 30,000 talers' worth of damage. The cost of the 1777 floods, particularly bad in Emden itself, amounted to more than 100,000 talers, of which the king paid 20,000. These setbacks did not discourage the Aurich Chamber. Great advances were made, from 1752 onwards, in the reclamation of land from the sea, the king contributing 45,000 talers towards the cost of this work. In 1758 North Sea storms drew from Frederick the resigned comment: 'I have today sanctioned money for the new reclamation project in East Friesland though I must say I am becoming a little tired of this Friesland polderization: one cannot sell them, so what is the point of it all?' Even so the king took a great interest in the development of the province and kept its chamber on its toes by a constant stream of new ideas and suggestions. On 12 October 1751 he wrote to president Lentz: 'The idea has just occurred to me that it might be possible to get workers for the production of the so-called bay salt in East Friesland, especially on the off-shore islands: such works have successfully been established for quite some time on the French coasts.' On 16 October he returned to the subject and on 13 November he explained how salt could be won from the sea by evaporation.

The most important aspect of the acquisition of East Friesland, from the commercial as from the political point of view, was that it afforded Prussia access to two seas. The significance of this dawned only very slowly on Frederick. His caution can be attributed to the lessons he had learned from the failure of the Emperor Charles VI's Ostend project. Yet the historical survey of the history of Brandenburg with which he occupied himself intensively towards the end of the 1740s made him ponder future possibilities. Ever a realist, Frederick, while given to speculation about minor matters, recoiled from the larger questions which probed the economic and political strength of his state. Cocceji, prosaic and cautious, wrote to Podewils from East Friesland in 1744: 'There are two quite respectable harbours in this territory – one at Emden, the other at Norden. The former, it is said, is better than the harbour at Amsterdam: His Majesty could keep a fleet there in times to come. . . . If ever a king of Prussia wanted to develop a maritime trade, Emden harbour could make him as feared at sea as he is on land.'

East Friesland did indeed offer prospects denied to the Great Elector. Chamber director Bügel, Prussia's second plenipotentiary in East Friesland, also realized the possibilities of the province's harbours: in 1748, when the Emden linen trade clashed with that of Bielefeld, he sent two ships flying the Prussian flag from Leer to France and sold the Emden goods at a fine profit. It was at this time that a retired French naval officer, the Chevalier Latouche, advised Frederick – intent on improving the trade of Stettin – to open trade with France via Emden. The king negotiated in 1750 with Latouche on the foundation of a trading company in Emden, though in the end, pressed by his Berlin financial experts, he gave preference to a Scot, Henry Thomas Stuart. The Aurich Chamber strongly favoured an Asiatic company to send Prussian ships to Canton once or twice a year. The first ship, the thirty-six gun *König von Preussen*, sailed from East Friesland in February 1752, followed in October by the *Burg von Emden*, both ships having been bought in England. Two further ships, acquired in Amsterdam – the *Prinz von Preussen* and the *Prinz Ferdinand* – left in 1753 and 1755 respectively. The return to Emden of the *König von Preussen* in July 1753 with a cargo of tea, porcelain and silk brought the company sole rights to market such merchandise. Among the purchasers of the cargo, sold at a quay-side auction, was the elector Clemens August of Cologne. The profits surpassed all expectations. President Derschau composed an ode in honour of the great day of the Emden Trading Company, when 'the Prussian state engaged in marriage with Thetis'.

Not so lucky was the less solidly based Bengal Company, founded in Emden in 1753 by another Scot, John Harris, which sent its first ship abroad in 1754. The Levant Company, set up in 1765 on the supposition that it could compete with Hamburg and the Dutch Republic, failed after a few years. The Seven Years War blasted the first shoots of Prussia's maritime trade, proving Frederick right in his belief that in wartime the Prussian merchant marine would be at the mercy of its enemies. After the war Colomb, the Chamber president, tried with the help of minister von Schulenburg-Kehnert to re-establish the Asiatic Trading Company. In 1781 *Der President*, named in honour of Colomb, set out for Batavia but got no further than the captain's home port of

Bremen, where he disposed of the ship's cargo destined for sale in the East. In 1782 another ship bought in Amsterdam – the *Asia* – sailed from Emden. The king had his doubts:

> All want to engage in trade with the Indies. This, however, is a dangerous business. Our ships are intended to trade with Poland and the Baltic, not with the Indies . . . However let these who wish to take the risk with this one ship do it. I must warn you however that if the ship is lost I will not pay them any compensation.

In December 1783 the *Prinz Friedrich Wilhelm* sailed for Batavia and the *Prinzessin von Preussen* went to Surinam in Dutch Guyana, returning with a cargo that proved profitable. The minute Prussian overseas trade was hit, however, by the money crisis and the surplus merchant tonnage which glutted the market after 1763, though the Emden coastal trade amassed profits. Frederick thought of initiating a regular cargo route to England but was led to believe that Emden was too unfavourably situated for such a plan to succeed. It must be admitted that Münster and Hanover cut Emden off from its natural hinterland; and – in spite of a promising start – the Emden overseas trading companies failed to develop because in times of crisis their lack of capital and consequent lack of staying power told against them. Prussia, with her small volume of overseas trade, could not attract partners and could not provide naval protection. For the same reasons Prussia's trade agreements with the maritime powers could not be exploited.

Nevertheless, under Frederick Prussia rediscovered her coast line. As early as October 1749 the king threw out the idea that 'the timber trade could be extended if Stettin and Königsberg entrepreneurs would build ships and sell them to foreigners'. By the end of Frederick's reign shipping had increased considerably. In 1783, 2,059 Prussian ships passed through the Sound, compared with 2,840 English and 2,470 Swedish ships, giving Prussia third place in the trade from the Baltic to the North Sea. The East Friesland Chamber tried to further shipping in many ways: by the foundation of a navigation school, improvement of piloting regulations, insistence on marine insurance, the setting up of commercial courts, and the building of lighthouses and buoys. Herring fisheries were of particular importance. Frederick at first proposed concentrating such fisheries in Pomerania and suggested the building of herring boats (*Buysen*) in Kolberg; but he was eventually convinced that Emden was more favourably situated and invited its merchants to found a herring fishing company. Lack of capital, as well as wars, delayed this venture until 1769. The enterprise then started suffered from under-capitalization, and the equipping and crewing of its fleets proved difficult: not till 1774 did the catch of the fleet of ten boats reach 5,000 tons. Frederick pressed for a fleet of at least eighty-four boats, but crews were not available for that number and the United Provinces, with its first-quality herrings, always maintained the upper hand. As long as the catch of the Emden boats remained insignificant, duties on Dutch imports and the building of additional ships were of little use. Basically the Emden venture was uneconomic and was encouraged mainly as a means of staunching the flow of Prussian money to other states. Even in the last year of his reign Frederick toyed with the idea of constructing twenty *Buysen* at his own expense so as to participate more fully in the fishing industry. In the end he turned his attention to whaling: 'Why are my subjects unable to take part in whaling? I cannot accept that we are less capable than other nations. The markets for blubber, whale oil and bone are so great that there is good business to be had.' The East Friesland whaling industry, operating from Borkum, seemed set for success; but the sinking of three boats and the later seizure by English privateers of other Emden boats in Dutch service brought total failure.

Strangely enough the impetus towards new overseas trade came from the Baltic. After their 1772 occupation of the Polish border areas both Russia and Austria stopped trading with Poland. Frederick, for his part, was eager to increase trade with Poland after the First Partition: he wished to import much sought-after Polish salt and to ship wax, timber and corn from Poland to Spain and South America. To facilitate such trade a state-controlled company, the Overseas Trading Company (*Seehandlungs Gesellschaft*), was formed as a joint-stock company on 14 October 1772; the general management was directed by the king. It was hoped that new markets could be opened up for Silesian linen and a company founded for that purpose in 1768, together with a trading house that had been opened in Cadiz, were now taken over by the Overseas Trading Company. The staple yard for Polish imports was the customs house near Fordon on the Vistula in West Prussia. The response expected from the merchant community did not, however, materialize: it proved wary of state competition. The first presidents of the company, ministers von der Horst and von Görne, were not experienced in the field and their mismanagement damaged the company's reputation. After 1782 privy finance councillor Karl August von Struensee, a superb organizer and an experienced cameralist who had studied science, became head of the enterprise; after his death, the post was taken over for a time by vom Stein. The Overseas Trading Company sent the tobacco and coffee designated for use in Prussia direct to the tobacco administration and the customs administration; thus the price of coffee could be stabilized. The company's original purpose, the trading in overseas goods by its own or chartered ships sailing under the Prussian flag, proved beyond its capabilities. Reorganized by the state, it split into two separate authorities, the Salt Administration and the Prussian State Bank.

STATE SETTLEMENTS

Frederick acquired one province, Silesia, by conquest; another, East Friesland, by inheritance; and a third, West Prussia, by negotiations which led to the first partition of Poland. Yet another was acquired – in the king's own words – 'through peaceful conquest'. Here Frederick referred, not to the appropriation of territory outside the state, but to the domestic settlement of uninhabited or previously uninhabitable lands. This was accomplished through state planning, backed by the resources of the *Gesamtstaat*; but there can be no doubt that the king was the driving force behind this development. Having launched the programme, he then gave it his constant attention. Throughout his reign he was helped in this work by a number of exceptionally able collaborators. Among them pride of place must go to Franz Balthasar Schönberg von Brenckenhoff, who from 1762 onwards sacrificed his fortune and his health to secure success for the 'settlement project'. The first extensive state-operated land reclamation scheme, the Oderbruch, was started in 1746. Frederick summed up the earlier achievement when the second phase began in 1763, after the depredations of the Seven Years' War. In his 'History of the Seven Years' War', written in 1763 (first printed in 1788), he wrote:

> From Swinemünde to Küstrin desolate swamps, uncultivated from time immemorial, extended along the banks of the Oder. A plan was drawn up for the reclamation of these lands. A channel dug from Küstrin to Wriezen drained the swamps and two thousand families were able to settle there. Similar work next progressed from Schwedt to Stettin and beyond. On this reclaimed land twelve hundred families have found a lucrative and comfortable living. Thus a new province came into existence, created by the victory of diligence over ignorance and laziness.

The Oderbruch venture had been discussed as early as 1736, but had to be postponed because of the great technical problems it presented. Ten years later these problems were solved by the Dutch engineer Simon Leonhard van Haerlem, who had entered Frederick William I's service

as an expert on dykes in the Kurmark Chamber, working in collaboration with the famous Swiss mathematician Leonhard Euler. Haerlem
cut a canal between Güstebiese and Hohensaathen with a steep enough
gradient to reduce the level of the Oder sufficiently to gain 44,200
Morgen of arable land protected by dykes. His labour force consisted
of eight hundred workmen and an equal number of soldiers under the
supervision of their engineer officers. In 1753 the land was ready for
settlement and the first of a projected number of 1,252 families arrived.
The Seven Years War did not interrupt the work. By 1761 over seven
hundred families had arrived and fifteen new villages had been built
to receive them, while old ones had been enlarged. Among the settlers
were lace-makers from the Erzgebirge, nail-makers from Gotha,
Palatines, Württembergers, Germans from Poland, and religious refugees from Austria. They found brickworks, poultry farms, churches and
schools already there, built at the initiative of Lieutenant-General Wolf
Friedrich von Retzow, who as state *Locator* was in charge of organizing
the settlements until his death in 1759. Settlement on the 20,000 *Morgen*
of land owned by the nobility – more than half of it belonging to
Margrave Karl von Schwedt – had not proceeded as smoothly; but by
1763 more than 2,250 settlers, most of them from Mecklenburg, Thuringia and Poland, were distributed over twenty-one villages.

Frederick continued his settlement policy after 1763, though not on so
vast a scale; by the time of his death the original plans had been exceeded
by three villages. Those who settled on noble-owned land were granted
exemption from taxes for a period of six to eight years and were given
free building timber, though they had to clear their own land and build
their own houses. Settlers on crown land were wholly exempt from
taxes for one year, and paid at a lower rate than normal for the next
three years; their houses were built for them, their land was handed over
to them already cleared, and they were granted exemption from labour
and military service. Tenancies were hereditable and settlers could
bring their belongings without paying customs duties. The cost of the
Oderbruch scheme, and its maintenance, was borne by the state. By
1763 the total cost, including repairs of flood damage, amounted to
about one million talers. Since the settlers paid low taxes this sum was
not recovered in Frederick's lifetime.

Plans for settlements in Pomerania had also been made in the reign
of Frederick William I, but they did not materialize till 1747. Then
Prince Moritz of Anhalt-Dessau, a lieutenant-general at Stargard and
son of the Old Dessauer, was put in charge. In collaboration with the
president of the Stettin Chamber, Georg Wilhelm von Aschersleben

and its director, Ernst Wilhelm von Schlabrendorff (later minister of
state for Silesia), Prince Moritz acquired land for settlement by having
forest cleared. To Frederick's annoyance no land could be bought from
noble landowners though they possessed much uncultivated farmland.
Scarcity of labour as well as finance for clearing the forests meant that
usually only a third of the new land was ready for immediate use; the
colonists themselves, who in any case worked the three field system, had
to clear their own strips for the second and third years. The settlements
were most successful on domain land. The domains of Friedrichswalde
(with fifteen new villages founded since 1747), Königsholland and
Kolbatz (with eleven each) led the field; next came the domains of
Lauenburg and Bütow and the municipal lands on the Krampe owned
by Stettin. Characteristically the names of the Pomeranian settlements
commemorated high officials of the General Directory. There was a
Bodenhagen, an Aschersleben and even a Coccejidorf; Moritzfelder was
named after the prince of Anhalt-Dessau; Schwerinstal and Möllendorf
after two generals, Amalienhof after Frederick's sister Amelia, and Constantinopel after the Pomeranian noblewoman, Countess Constantia von
Blumenthal. Before the Seven Years War 1,500 families, most of them
from Mecklenburg, Thuringia and Poland, had been provided for, 830
of them in fifty-five new villages. The war was particularly hard on
Pomerania; over 70,000 inhabitants lost their lives and 1,200 buildings
were consumed in flames. Brenckenhoff directed the post-1763 reconstruction with great success. He brought in free peasants, crofters and
cottagers, granting them from sixty to thirty *Morgen* of land in accordance with cabinet orders (the last of these of 29 July 1774); by 1775 the
population of the province was greater by 30,000 than it had been
before the war. There were in the total population more than 5,300
immigrant families living in over two hundred new settlements – in all
about 26,500 people.

The Chamber of the Neumark at Küstrin participated in the scheme
for the improvement of the Oder and its eastern tributaries. Brenckenhoff, as chairman of the *Immediatkommission* for the Neumark, showed
particular organizational skill. The province had lost a quarter of its
population, more than 57,000, in the war and almost 2,000 houses had
been reduced to rubble. Küstrin itself had been totally destroyed. It
was comparatively easy to entice settlers from neighbouring Polish
territories; mostly of German stock, they were keen to escape the increasingly uncertain conditions. Immigrants also came from Lausitz,
Mecklenburg, Erfurt and the Eichsfeld. After the war the fenlands from
Driesen to Sonnenburg through Landsberg, along the Netze and the

Warthe were drained and made arable. By 1775 Brenckenhoff, with a grant of 150,000 talers, had opened up the area and settled 800 families. He shouldered the responsibility for numerous setbacks and frequently paid the financial costs of getting languishing profits restarted. He was greatly helped by Isaak Jacob Petri, a lieutenant-colonel in the engineers, who had experience of the previous Oder project. Among the 15,000 who settled in Pomerania Germans from Poland outnumbered those from Saxony, next came those from Mecklenburg, the Palatinate and Württemberg: in all families from forty-one states participated. The full-time peasant farmers (*Vollbauern*) received thirty *Morgen* of land; cottagers settled on outfarms usually got ten *Morgen*. Reclamation and settlement projects were also carried out in other parts of the Neumark. Preparatory surveys took time, but when the projects took shape they came under the direct supervision of Frederick who kept a close check on costs. The amelioration scheme of 1776 was not completed till 1782. Its management was entrusted in 1780, on the death of Brenckenhoff, to chamber director Johann Friedrich Schütz. To encourage landed proprietors to participate the king was forced to spend large sums on 'gratifications' (*Gnadengeschenke*, literally 'gifts by the king's grace'). In 1777, for example, the state spent 200,000 talers to help settle 238 families on noble-owned land. By then the Neumark population was greater by 29,000 than in 1756; war losses had been made good and 152 new settlements had been founded. By 1780 almost 4,000 families (about 14,000 individuals) had entered the Neumark from places outside Prussia, bringing with them 500,000 talers in cash, 1,300 horses, 4,660 cattle, 16,000 sheep and 2,000 pigs.

The impressive river drainage schemes and the amelioration projects that went with them – technically in advance of their time – were not the only fruits of the colonization policy. Other provinces were engaged in similar improvements, and in Frederick's reign no province provided less than livelihoods for 1,000 new settlers. Colonization had, of course, to be concentrated at focal points so as to utilize most effectively the labour and money available. Primary consideration was initially given to the task of populating the underdeveloped areas of the central provinces and Pomerania. East Prussia, because of Frederick William's *rétablissement*, was far ahead in resettlement activities. The central provinces and Pomerania still suffered from the demographic decline of the Thirty Years War period: 120 years after that war the level of population had not yet reached that of 1620, and the Seven Years War brought new losses. Systematic settlement was facilitated by easier marriage regulations, family allowances, the creation of jobs in rural areas, and by the general encouragement of trade and industry in the towns. Above all, the state attempted to attract 'foreigners' to Prussia, not only to redistribute the population but to increase it. People migrated from one part of Germany to another for many different reasons: wars (as in Poland), religious persecution (as in Austria), overpopulation (as in southern Germany), economic decline (as in Mecklenburg), debasement of the currency and famine (as in Bohemia and Saxony); in the general hope of improving living standards all played their part. These migrations had started in the early seventeenth century when wars began to loosen people's roots. There were naturally adventurers and disreputable characters among those who accepted 'hand money' as colonists; but on the whole Prussian colonization policy was successful while emigration from Prussia was so low as to be statistically negligible. Many immigrants brought with them their own livestock and considerable sums of money. Settling into a different society, with its own peculiarities of climate, landscape and dialect, was not always easy; and the suspicious attitude of most of the natives did not help. But the advantages were enticing: legal freedom of the person, hereditable tenancies and exemption from cantonal obligations. Approximately 50 million talers was spent on colonization projects during Frederick's reign. He was not keen to rule over heath and marshes; he wanted his state to be a flourishing, cultivated, profitable, populated land 'so that not even a hand's breath of soil capable of being used in some way should remain idle' – as he informed the provincial minister for the Kurmark, Hans Ernst Dietrich von Werder, on 23 April 1786, four months before his own death.

The Kurmark was the most intensively colonized province during Frederick's reign. Up to 1756, when the Seven Years War broke out, some 50,000 settlers had been brought in, most of them in the towns. But war casualties in the province accounted for nearly the same number, so that post-war colonization had almost to start from scratch. Thanks to the zeal of Friedrich Wilhelm von Derschau, provincial minister for the Kurmark, another 50,000 immigrants were attracted to the province, again to the industries in the towns rather than to agricultural colonies. Between 1775 and 1778 66,000 *Morgen* of pasture-land – enough to feed 17,000 cattle – were reclaimed from the marshes along the rivers Rhin and Dosse. In a letter to the Kurmark Chamber, written on 12 April 1763, the king described his ideal colonization as numerous small farmsteads 'occupied by foreign Protestants holding hereditary leases'. Six new villages were built in the county of Cottbus; more than a hundred non-Prussian families were settled on farms;

and industry, mainly woollen mills, was attracted to the towns of Cottbus and Peitz. During Frederick's reign, 3,600 people migrated to Cottbus, though only 850 of these settled on the land.

Magdeburg-Halberstadt, the wealthiest and most heavily-populated
province in the monarchy, had little uncultivated land. It suffered,
however, from a perennial shortage of farm-labourers and it was hoped
that the immigration of cottagers would help to solve this problem:
this in large measure it did; and twelve new peasant villages were also
founded. During the first half of Frederick's reign 20,000 people settled
in the province; of these – before 1753 – some 2,800 came from Thuringia. The rate of colonization rose considerably after the Seven Years
War. One peculiarity of Magdeburg must be stressed: any foreigners
wanting to settle there were – following a royal edict of 1772 – permitted to remain under either French or Palatinate jurisdiction. The
privileges of the French and Palatinate courts had already been confirmed for Magdeburg in 1743 and from that date onwards there had
been an impressive increase in the number of French and Palatinate
colonies; by 1756 five villages of 'royal colonists' had been established.
The immigration to Prussia in 1769 of numerous settlers from the Upper
Rhine Circle brought a proposal from minister von Hagen that existing
peasant farms might be divided into smaller but still viable holdings.
This did not work for the Magdeburg region since both land and
building timber were scarce and the majority of the would-be settlers
were without capital. Colonization of waste lands on the domains was
promoted, with tax relief for a period of three to four years; but in the
meantime poor immigrant families from Swabia and Bavaria became
a burden on the Chamber treasury. In 1770 164 families were settled
and a further 1,000 families were supposed to receive holdings in the
following five years. Famine struck, however, before the 1769 arrivals had
time to settle in properly, and this brought the programme of selecting
applicants to a temporary halt. Not till the 1772–77 period were a further
690 families admitted, among them exiles from Anhalt-Bernburg.
Support for the colonization policy came from Magdeburg's richly
endowed religious houses and from some private individuals as well as
from the domain leaseholders. The reclamation between 1777 and 1784
of the Finow-Bruch, the Trübenbruch and the fenlands along the
Stremme and the Tanger considerably enlarged and improved lands
belonging to existing villages; it also provided holdings for fifty-five
new cottager families, preference being given to disabled soldiers.
Dairy farms on the Dutch pattern (*Holländereien*) were established at
Königshorst, and a model farm with a cowshed was built for 100 at

Falkenstein near Parchen. In all Magdeburg absorbed almost 4,500 new families, most of them on good flat farmland; about half of these immigrants were 'foreigners'.

Rural settlements in Silesia were affected by the fundamental differences which distinguished that province from the rest of the monarchy. Between 1746 and 1749 settler permits were preferentially given to manufacturers and craftsmen, especially weavers. By 1756 some 6,500 immigrants had settled in Silesian towns. Settlement in rural areas was confined to underdeveloped domains, since the Silesian nobility displayed little interest in colonization. An enquiry of 1763 showed that the province was short of peasants, gardeners and landless labourers: jobs equivalent to livelihoods for about 18,000 individuals were vacant. The Charter for Foreigners of 1763 (the *Ausländerpatent*) had some effect; although the provincial minister was strongly prejudiced against amelioration schemes, at least twenty-nine villages, containing 700 families, were established in Upper Silesia by 1768. Two years later Frederick urged minister von Hoym to do more:

> the population in Upper Silesia, between Oppeln and Ratibor, is so thinly spread that whole villages can be built there. We must raise the common people from their stupidity and savagery; to do so we need to attract more foreign colonists of the sensible and civilized type.

Work was now speeded up and 174 new villages, housing 2,537 inhabitants, were founded by 1776, most of them in Upper Silesia. Less successful was Hoym's distribution between 1770 and 1773 of very poor land between the rivers Stober and Malapane in Upper Silesia as gardener settlements of 8–20 *Morgen*: these holdings soon became notorious as 'starvation settlements'. More successful were the so-called Hussite villages of Hussinetz, Podiebrad, Gross-Tabor and Friedrichsgrätz and the peasant settlements in *Amt* Herrnstadt. The king's declaration of 28 August 1773 on colonization is Silesia strongly urged the mixing of nationalities: 'It is our express wish that in the areas which have been completely Polish up to now, only Germans should be settled; conversely, Polish people can be settled in German areas.' By 1785 Silesia had about 47,500 urban and 30,000 rural settlers, which was near the optimum density of desirable settlement. If one subtracts the Saxon estimate (possibly too high) of the 2,000 young men of Silesia who migrated to Saxony to avoid military service, a total remains of 65,000 immigrants during Frederick's reign – a small percentage of the province's total population of 1·3 million.

We find a different picture in East Prussia. This large province, administered by two chambers, had since the *rétablissement* of Frederick William's reign been successful in attracting settlers. With more than 700,000 inhabitants it was, after Silesia, the most populous province in the monarchy. It had, moreover, space and opportunities for more village settlements and amelioration schemes. Peasant farms were large, of two and sometimes even four *Hufen*,* so that there was plenty of unused land. Outfarms could also be turned into villages. On the extensive royal domains – as elsewhere in Prussia – new settlements were more easily organized than on the noble-owned estates. During the 1750s 2,000 families were settled in the province, and many more after the Seven Years' War. Altogether 73 new outfarms were created (67 of them on noble-owned land), 94 villages were established (13 of them on noble-owned land) on former outfarms, and 293 villages (22 of them on noble-owned land) were built on newly-cleared ground: 2,366 families were thus settled, 374 of them on manorial land. A further 2,588 families were settled on farms which had by 1740 become waste land (162 families on such land owned by nobles); superfluous land, the so-called 'second farms' (*2.Hufe*), were distributed to 4,549 families (30 of these farms were in noble ownership), while 5,383 families were settled individually in various villages (54 through noble initiative). In all not less than 14,866 families, that is at least 70,000 individuals, were settled in East Prussia (not counting the county of Rastenburg, which was omitted from the survey) during Frederick's reign. The province has the distinction of having admitted more rural settlers in two consecutive reigns than any other Prussian province, and there is no justification for the contention that East Prussia was treated worse by Frederick II than the other provinces. Until the end of his life Frederick was much concerned with East Prussian affairs. In connection with the cultivation of the Grosse Moosbruch, west of Tilsit, he wrote to Chamber president von der Goltz at Königsberg:

> The peasants who are to be settled there must hold their land in full ownership, for they are not to be slaves. And would it not be possible that all peasants in the domains under my Chamber could be released from bondage and be settled on their land as owners? I await your opinion as to the difficulties such a course of action could bring.

As rural colonization in West Prussia could not start until after 1772, it naturally lagged behind the other provinces in Frederick's lifetime. About 12,000 people were settled during his reign, mostly immigrants from Württemberg, the Palatinate, Saxony, and Germans from Poland.

* 1 East Prussian *Huf* = approx. 40·9 modern acres.

At first Frederick had intended to settle individual German families in villages where the majority of the inhabitants were either Cashubian or Poles, in order 'to teach them better ideas and habits', but later he decided on new closed settlements: 'Whole villages and colonies must be established among the rough and backward people, forming their own communities, working and trading for their living, so that the local population can all the better see and grasp their way of life.' On 2 May 1781 Frederick informed minister of state von Gaudi of his plan for 'settling each year about 1,000 families in West Prussia', estimating that some 14,000 families in all could be established there; but this idea was not followed up.

Colonization in Prussia's western provinces progressed more slowly than it did in the others, since here the state did not provide the finance. On 30 January 1772 Frederick told minister von der Schulenburg that he preferred one colonist on the eastern side of the Weser to a dozen on the other bank. This typically Frederician comment was not intended as a reflection on the quality of available colonists, but as a pertinent statement about an actual situation. The inhabitants of the western provinces had become more mobile than the population of the central and eastern territories. Breaking new land and working on amelioration projects and colonization of land had little appeal for its young people; they were more inerested in trying their luck in the weaving industry and in other non-rural jobs. With no state support the western provinces had to provide their own settlement schemes. *Amt* Limberg in Minden-Ravensberg established only fifteen new farmsteads after 1740; and even after the Seven Years War, when the wave of immigration reached the western provinces, *Amt* Sparenberg on 14 June 1769 reported to the Minden Chamber that it could provide no land and should not be deprived of pasturage by confiscation of common lands, while Schildesche claimed that there was not 'at present a square foot of land available for the settlement of colonists'. In the Vlotho area a few holdings for settlers were provided at Seebruch and other places; and in 1771 eighty families were settled in Minden-Ravensberg though after that the number sank to about eight a year. On the Lower Rhine, in Cleves and Moers, rural settlements were more important. During the first half of Frederick's reign immigration to these regions – and to the county of Mark – was mainly to the urban areas; in 1753–54 57 Dutch families came to towns as compared with the 111 families (511 persons, of whom 464 were natives of the province) who settled on the land in 1752–53.

The population, here as elsewhere, fell during the Seven Years

War and did not regain its pre-war numbers till 1776. Many young people emigrated. In 1766 141 families and 54 individuals left; there was a shortfall in that year of 56 peasants and 113 craftsmen, and 234 houses and farms stood empty. After some early disappointments with immigrants from the Palatinate some 2,500 newcomers were settled in 1770 both in the towns and on the land, in all about one-tenth of the 4,940 settler families in the western provinces as a whole. Between 1771 and 1776 Cleves accepted 106 and the county of Mark 169 foreign families; but as most of these arrived without any money it was difficult to provide homes for them since the province had no building fund. The settlement of disabled soldiers, which was desired, was under these circumstances unfeasible. The number of colonists in Tecklenburg-Lingen, Ravensberg and Gelderland was higher; and in East Friesland 571 families were settled in the early 1770s.

The following table shows the complete number of rural settlements in Prussia during Frederick's reign:

Province	New Villages and *Vorwerke*	No. of families settled thereon
Kurmark	217	10,740
Neumark	152	3,643
Pomerania	100	5,312
Magdeburg-Halberstadt	20	2,805
Cleves-Mark ⎫ Tecklenburg-Lingen ⎬ East Friesland ⎭		4,940
East Prussia	460 (incomplete)	14,886 (incomplete)
West Prussia	50	1,119
Silesia	?	14,050
	999 (?) excluding Silesia	57,475 families
	at least 1,500 including Silesia	c. 250,000 persons

This shows that of the 4·75 million living in Prussia at the end of Frederick's reign a quarter of a million had entered the country as settlers or, expressed otherwise, that around 1780 one person in twenty was an immigrant rural settler. Enormous sums had been spent to achieve this increase in the population. Frederick's policy has been criticized, but the imputation that the king was solely concerned to acquire more tax payers and soldiers is too simplistic. A better populated country enjoyed more trade and a higher standard of living; it was not only an important producer of goods but also a consumer, offering opportunities for developing industries. In addition every newly-founded village brought trade and crafts to the rural areas.

The number of colonists fell below the king's expectations, but it would be unfair to compare Prussia's achievements in domestic colonization with the much larger Austria and Russia. The very fact that such comparisons have been made concedes the point that domestic colonization was in tune with the spirit of the age and thus justified. The great philosopher Leibniz had laid down, *Vera regni potestas in hominum numero consistit*. Frederick found confirmation of this dictum in the writings of the French philosophers and included it in his 'Anti-Machiavel': 'On this point there is but one opinion: the strength of a state depends not on the length of its frontiers but on the size of its population.' He repeated this sentence almost word for word in his political testament of 1768: 'The first principle, the most general and true, is that the real strength of a state is based on the high number of its inhabitants.' Economic and arithmetical considerations were, however, not the only fundaments of domestic colonization. Frederick as crown prince had – as we have seen in his letter to Voltaire in 1739 – been deeply moved by his father's work for East Prussia. The historian will extend this praise to Frederick II for the whole of his Prussian achievement.

IV

Safeguarding Prussia's Existence

WARTIME ADMINISTRATION

Frederick II's axiom that 'the burgher should not be aware that the
soldier is at war' held good, in some measure at least, for the two
Silesian wars of 1740–48; but with the overwhelming superiority of
Prussia's enemies in the Seven Years War it quickly lost any validity
it may have had. 'The military' (the *Wehrstand*) and 'the commercial
sector' (the *Nährstand*) remained distinct, and the burgher engaged in
trade or industry belonged to the ranks of the latter. The production of
commodities, low at the time, and of the limited number of goods
destined for export had to be maintained during the war with as little
interruption as possible (and preferably none): the idea of the 'nation in
arms' was alien to the eighteenth-century mind. Trade and industry
provided the state with revenues; manufacture even of luxury goods
had to be kept up lest the markets laboriously secured were lost. Yet
not one of Prussia's provinces emerged unscathed from the Seven Years
War. Manpower losses rose alarmingly. Death, deportation and plague
all took their toll and many of those who survived took advantage of
the general confusion to flee the country: the growth in Prussia's
population and economy achieved during the first half of the century
was now put in jeopardy.

By the summer of 1756 Frederick knew that neither negotiations nor
non-resistance could save his state from certain destruction. Only the
ultima ratio regis remained to him: nothing but war, fought along interior
lines and with sudden thrusts against the opposing coalition, could
reduce his enemies to the extent that the coalition would fall asunder.
Tenacity and endurance were demanded not only of the king but of all
subjects. For the administration the acceptance of additional and extraordinary responsibilities under abnormal conditions became part and
parcel of its wartime routine. Moreover it had to perform its duties
without that direction by Frederick to which it had become accustomed,

for during the earlier wars the king had been able to make fairly frequent visits to his *Residenz*. But in the Seven Years War, from the time he left Potsdam on 28 August 1756 until his return to Berlin on 30 March 1763, Frederick paid only one brief visit (4–13 January 1757) with his brother Henry to Berlin and Potsdam. Throughout the long and difficult war years the head of state was far removed from his ministries. For seven years Frederick constituted an itinerant army-state, preoccupied with problems of strategy and forage, entrenchment and shortages, wandering between Bohemia, Saxony, Silesia and the Lausitz, enduring long marches, extremes of weather and sudden enemy attacks. Yet during this time the state was expected not to notice that the king had become an army commander.

Only very slowly did the ministries learn to adapt themselves to the new situation and to exercise their authority with confidence, promptitude and decision. Wherever possible procedures were simplified. For the duration of the war the reports of the *Regierungen* were discontinued. In the western provinces *Landtage* were suspended, and complaints from the Estates concerning the infringement of their rights were prohibited. Documents dealt with or considered non-essential were disposed of to render the authorities more flexible and prompt in their decisions. By royal decree 'worthless old folios' from the Cleves *Regierung* were in December 1756 removed to the fortress at Wesel to be used as cartridge paper. During the removal and disposal of documents – often carelessly carried out – many of them fell into the hands of hawkers, necessitating a search for their recovery before orders could be carried out. In March 1757 the General Directory advised the War and Domains chambers to cut down on building projects, repairs, surveys and the work on dykes: only road bridges were to be kept in repair. As early as January 1757 Frederick had called a halt to the Potsdam building scheme for the duration of the war.

The activities of the royal cabinet, operating in the field under the most primitive conditions, had to be drastically curtailed. From early 1759 the king signed only the letters-patent of captains, staff officers and higher ranks; ensigns and lieutenants were appointed by the War Chancery (the *Kriegskanzlei*) in Berlin. When, in September 1757, a shortlist of three names for the vacant general-superintendancy at Stettin was put before Frederick, he approved the list with a laconic 'good, Fch.'; but he left the actual choice to the dumbfounded Supreme Consistory. Some time previously the Kurmark Chamber had received permission to lease domains; for the king 'cannot devote his attention to such matters at present, being fully occupied with affairs of much greater moment'. Schlabrendorff, the bustling president-in-chief of the Silesian chambers, was asked to spare Frederick the reading of reports until more settled times, unless they were of the greatest importance: 'my present occupation does not permit my being distracted by such matters.' In June 1759 a sharper rebuke was administered to the General Directory: the king was 'not to be annoyed in the current confused wartime situation with reports and enquiries more appropriate to times of peace'. Reports made directly to the king (*Immediatberichte*) were to be kept short and to the point. From 1757 onwards the General Directory at times sounded privy councillor Eichel, the king's cabinet secretary, to discover in a roundabout way the king's opinion on administrative problems.

Frederick believed that his stringent prohibition against any changes in matters affecting trade would suffice to make the General Directory preserve manufactures at their pre-war level. During the whole course of the war the Fifth Department received only four directives from the king; there was, therefore, no royal interference with commercial policy. But for the rest Frederick regarded the highest administrative authorities solely as executive organs, above all in matters relating to the fulfilment of essential deliveries to the army. When in the spring of 1758 grain transports to Silesia were delayed, the General Directory received orders to dispatch them immediately, 'without the slightest further argument or delay . . . for let it be understood that I shall know how to enforce obedience to my instructions'. The commandant of Berlin, Lieutenant-General von Rochow, was simultaneously ordered to have the grain boats moved by troops if, after three days, the General Directory had not got the transport started. That the administration did not function smoothly can be deduced from the General Directory's circular to subordinate officials requesting that applications should be correctly addressed to the appropriate departments so as to avoid confusion and delay; this order was reiterated in June 1763.

When news of the heavy defeat at Kunersdorf, east of Frankfurt on the Oder, reached Berlin on 13 August 1759 some of the chief officials left the capital, Frederick having designated Magdeburg as a meeting place. Ministers Happe and Boden obeyed but the vice-president of the General Directory and director of the Kurmark *Landschaft* (Estates), Count Heinrich IX Reuss, continued the work of the General Directory in Berlin, ignoring the protests of the ministers in Magdeburg. On 4 September 1759 the Magdeburg contingent were ordered by the king to return to Berlin. Continuous over-work made officials tired and irritable and sapped initiative. Numerous posts remained vacant. The

Third Department excused this in March 1760 with the argument that most of the provinces within its administration were in enemy hands. In April of the same year a cabinet order sharply reprimanded the General Directory for its lethargy, again over delays in transport: as a result of their 'criminal indolence', 'unbelievable laziness' and 'sordid bickering', urgent salt deliveries to Silesia had failed to arrive on time. The president of the Magdeburg Chamber was instructed to cooperate with the commandant of Berlin in getting the salt transports moving. To improve matters the king in October 1761 sanctioned the temporary transfer of his cabinet secretary to the General Directory.

Subordinate authorities, especially the Silesian chambers and the colleges of justice, ensured thorough and conscientious performance of duties by strict discipline and control without Frederick's help. Occasionally they created unnecessary problems for themselves. Thus the confessional question unexpectedly became an issue after Catholic tax collectors in September 1756 had been transferred from the Silesian border areas into the interior lest they be tempted to collaborate with the Austrians. Two years later when an enquiry into the composition of the bench of magistrates in the Silesian *Mediat-Städte* (towns owned by individual landlords) showed that the Catholic element was favoured, the Chamber proposed that each municipal administration should have at least two Protestant members – proportionately more in Protestant towns. Frederick doubted the wisdom of introducing such propositions in wartime and refused his consent: the quiet, 'unnoticed' admission of Protestant magistrates seemed to him a more sensible course. Another issue, the long-smouldering conflict between the endowed abbey (the *Stiftsabtie*) of Quedlinburg, whose abbess was the king's sister Amelia, and the royal *Stiftshauptmann* (layman who supervised the temporal affairs of the abbey), who had fiscal authority over the abbey, was settled with some difficulty by the cooperation of the Department of External Affairs and without the king's knowledge.

Chamber and country authorities enforced general regulations, such as maximum bread prices, decrees against emigration without permission, and prohibitions against export of grain and the production of spirits from grain. Numerous regional and temporary measures had to be enforced as had the supervision of the horse-relay service for military transports. That this service – usually promptly paid for – had to be controlled down to the prompt return of horses and wagons indicates the breakdown in efficiency in some areas: dawdling on the return journey until fodder, bread and money had been used (or sold or squandered) could put the service out of action for days at a time. A cabinet order of 1762 emphasized the necessity of keeping the postal service in operation and prohibited the use of postilions and post-horses (supplied by the peasants) for war transports and flour deliveries; the rural commissioners were in their capacity as *Marschkommissare* (commissaries for the march) responsible for the latter.

Generally speaking chamber presidents took sharp action against negligence in the performance of duties, piling up debts or official misdemeanours. Conduct reports testify to the high standards demanded. Officials were expected to prepare their work at home; the study, *oculo fugitivo*, of a case during chamber sittings earned a reprimand. In Glogau three war tribunal councillors (of indifferent reputation) were obliged to reimburse the costs of a pleasure trip disguised as an inspection journey to a forge. Economy in the use of porterage, relay services and express postage of letters was demanded of all higher officials.

Fairly typical of the workload carried by a government department of three higher and seven middle grade civil servants was that of the War and Domains Chamber at Glogau. After its reorganization in 1761, the first director of the chamber presided over the *Collegium* and was responsible for the chancery, the registry, the drafting of documents and letters, the revision of drafts and the dispatch of correspondence. The second chamber director supervised the treasury and prepared the yearly budget and the accounts; he also dealt with court summonses and directed the first senate of justice. The general fiscal prepared the cases for the first senate of justice and the *Collegium medicum*; he handled taxation matters and provincial inspections; he also had control of regulations for servants and matters affecting hospitals and the poor. The first war councillor saw to the marching of troops, the artillery and their horses and drivers, relay services, salt, and to the affairs of disabled soldiers. The second councillor controlled the war-chest and its finances, forage, provisions and magazines, forests and the chase, assessments, inspection of county treasuries, fire societies in rural areas, three rural counties, six domains and eight towns. The third councillor was responsible for brewing regulations, the toleration of Jews, stamped paper, the *Chargenkasse* (appointments-tax fund), four rural counties and nine towns. The fourth councillor supervised building matters and building accounts, surveys, inspection of domains accounts, colonists' affairs, fire societies in the towns, three counties, two domains and ten towns. The fifth councillor was in charge of customs matters and the inspection of its accounts and fines, grain imports, posts and roads, services, enrolment and recruitment, three counties, five domains and five towns. The sixth councillor had for his share the excise and its accounts and fines, the daily reports of the gendarmes, commercial affairs, matters concerning factories, wool and silk manufactures, mines, coinage, three counties and twelve towns. The seventh and last councillor was responsible for affairs touching on territorial sovereignty, the second senate of justice, enquiries submitted for judicial decision, legal fees, church and school affairs, crafts and guilds, plague and cattle diseases, inspection of old records, and the publication of royal edicts. Through the *Korreferat* system (in which officials were appointed to check the work of other officials) the war councillors could deputize for each other and help with one other's work.

The even tempo of bureaucratic life was increasingly disturbed by enemy raids into Prussian territory. Such emergencies were supposedly covered by the regulations of 20 May 1748 but experience soon exposed their inadequacy. In the late summer of 1756 the Upper Silesian authorities withdrew from Oppeln to Brieg. Panic flights among officials in the western provinces brought on 2 October 1756 strict instructions forbidding them on pain of dismissal to quit their posts, though preparations were made for the orderly transfer of the Cleves *Regierung* to the fortress of Wesel in the event of an enemy raid. When French and Austrian troops approached the Weser in the spring of 1757 the documents and treasuries of the Minden War and Domains Chamber were transferred to Bremen, whose neutrality was respected by both France and Austria. The president of the Minden Chamber issued an instruction at the end of July 1757 to the administration in the French-occupied zones with the aim of uniting, temporarily, Prussia's western possessions, Cleves-Mark, Tecklenburg-Lingen and Minden-Ravensberg, into one comprehensive authority to avoid confusion: the duty of administering the territories must not be neglected even if the enemy was in the land. The Magdeburg Chamber reacted in much the same way when in August 1757 French troops moved close to the county of Saale and Halberstadt; documents and treasuries were taken to the fortress of Magdeburg for safety.

In East Friesland Maria Theresa's patent of occupation was issued in the summer of 1757; in August the Cleves-Mark authorities were permitted to return to their posts on giving a written declaration that they would cooperate with the Austrian administration. When the members of the Breslau *Oberamtsregierung* did the same a year later – though without a written promise – the Prussian authorities had them incarcerated in fortresses. All Prussian subjects were warned against helping the enemy in any way or leaving their homes during enemy occupation. In March 1759 the *Kabinettsministerium* asked the General Directory to reassess the practicability of the existing regulation which insisted on rural commissioners taking their documents, treasuries and land registers to the nearest fortress in the event of enemy occupation. The cabinet ministry now considered it more sensible for the commissioners to remain within their own districts under enemy occupation to help maintain order, and in May 1761 a decree to this effect was signed by the king. The wisdom of this later course was disputed at the time as occasionally (e.g. in Silesia in 1758 and Quedlinburg in 1759) high officials were taken as hostages and released only after long years of negotiations. The discussions of the East Friesland *Regierung* on whether to set up a regional committee (a *Landes-Deputation*) during the enemy occupation presupposed the improbable simultaneous dissolution by the occupation authorities of the *Regierung*, the chamber and the administration *Kollegium*, and for this reason no change was made. Thus a tendency towards continuing the normal tasks of administration during enemy occupation gained ground, even though at the end of August 1759 (after the defeat at Kunersdorf) the supreme tribunal of Berlin was of the opinion that 'the administration of justice must be totally discontinued on enemy occupation'. Here, as in the *Kammergericht*, resignation was seen to be the only possible alternative to the unreasonable act of paying homage to the enemy. In the following year the Kurmark Chamber reminded its officials of the correct procedure in the event of enemy occupation: the *Kreise* authorities were not to issue the enemy permits for forage nor were they to authorize the use of transport for lengthy periods of time. The Stettin *Gouvernement* also exhorted people to remain faithful to their king.

The province of East Prussia was a special case. Here the *Gouverneur* Field-Marshal Lehwaldt, whose force of 24,000 men could provide only a temporary defence against a strong Russian army, had to wield executive authority as soon as the imperilment of communications with Berlin and the General Directory made it impossible to control the province from the centre. The *Regierung* at Königsberg doubted the wisdom of evacuating frontier areas on the approach of the Russians in the spring of 1757: if the villages were emptied, the fields would remain unharvested and famine would result. Yet the Gumbinnen Chamber with the single exception of its chamber director moved to Königsberg. Soon the authorities reported that the inhabitants of the frontier countries were 'forcibly removed in droves by the Cossacks'. Memel fell in July. Only with reluctance did the officials of the Lithuanian Chamber accede to the demand of the Russian governor of

Memel to return to their posts, for they lacked clear directives. Lehwaldt answered the Russian propaganda advising the inhabitants to emigrate with a counter-manifesto encouraging them to stay. When after the battle of Gross Jägersdorf Lehwaldt withdrew with his army, the Königsberg *Regierung* left for Danzig. This proved a premature move since the Russians themselves unexpectedly withdrew their forces from the province. At the end of September therefore the administration returned to Königsberg. Almost simultaneously all Prussian troops were pulled back to Pomerania. A portion of the Chamber and *Regierung* archives had been taken via Pomerania to Küstrin, to be returned only in July 1763. When the Russians again marched into the now defenceless province in January 1758 the militia – contrary to the king's instructions – made no attempt to defend Königsberg, and on 22 January the city was occupied. The treasuries and the valuable collection of amber had already been removed to Stettin by the ministers of state, and cash deposits and money held on behalf of wards of court were now taken to Danzig. From Breslau Frederick issued an order to preserve the province as much as possible. But on his birthday, 24 January, the tsaritsa Elizabeth demanded (as the previous year in the border areas) an oath of allegiance from the authorities. Later this was demanded from all East Prussia's inhabitants, though in their case the expression 'faithful and obedient servant' was deliberately omitted.

Frederick did not hold it against East Prussia (any more than he held it against East Friesland, Cleves and Silesia in a similar situation) that homage was paid to the invader. At the end of that unhappy year, 1758, he ordered the vice-president of the General Directory, Adam Ludwig von Blumenthal, to report on the East Prussian situation only in respect of the movements of the Russian troops: on anything else it 'would be too painful, the superiority of my enemies allowing me no opportunity to help my faithful subjects there or to hurry with worthwhile assistance to their aid'. On the conclusion of peace with Russia a cabinet order of 27 May 1762 to the Prussian minister of state stated categorically that he and those who served under him must 'treat with much kindness and moderation all those who had recently administered the province in the name of the court of St Petersburg and by its order, and to avoid all disputes and chicanery with them'. Johann Friedrich Domhardt, president of the Gumbinnen Chamber, who enjoyed the king's special trust, was placed at the head of the administration in East Prussia; on 27 May 1762, he was quite exceptionally also named president of the Königsberg Chamber as a reward for his loyal perseverance under foreign rule.

In 1756, as in the earlier wars, war zone commissariats (*Feldkriegs-kommissariate*) were set up for Saxony, Silesia and Pomerania, all three under the control of a War Zone Directory (*Feldkriegs-Direktorium*) headed by Friedrich Wilhelm von Borcke, the leading minister of the General Directory. This organization proved unlucky, both in its management and in the staff assigned to it. A Saxon, excise councillor Schimmelmann, had been commissioned to buy army supplies for Prussia in Saxony, but his measures and those of the War Zone Directory often clashed; many frauds and embezzlements were also committed by the staff of the Directory; the whole organization was difficult to supervise. After Saxony became a battleground, with foraging and *Brandschätze** exacted by troops of all belligerents marching back and forth across its territory, the War Zone Directory could do little systematic work. In the autumn of 1759 Borcke was recalled and the War Zone Directory merged with the Saxon War Commissariat under finance councillor Zinnow who died in 1760.

By the time the Prussian financial administration of Saxony ended on 10 February 1763 Frederick had extracted more than 48 million *Reichstaler* from that unfortunate land. Quite apart from this sum, state and private property in Saxony had been mercilessly squeezed either to exert pressure or as reprisals for Austrian and Russian outrages. Restraint had been exercised in Silesia in 1757 and Austrian-owned estates had not been sequestered until Vienna had begun to take over Prussian properties; but in 1760 orders were given that Prussian ministers of state should seek compensation for unpaid salaries by sequestering the estates of the Saxon minister Count Heinrich von Brühl. This they refused to do. Revenge was, however, taken on Brühl in other ways, and much damage was caused to property by billeted troops and general indifference even where no cause for revenge existed – as in 1761 when the Saxon hunting lodge at Hubertusburg was destroyed by Prussian irregular troops.

Heavy demands on the occupied territories made possible lesser calls on Prussian resources. Here a careful balance had to be held: excessive enforced labour services would necessarily bring diminished agricultural production, but total suspension of peasants' duties to furnish horses and wagons for transport would spell empty army magazines and catastrophe. The General Directory's instructions of March 1758 to the Kurmark and Magdeburg chambers not to ask more from 'the king's subjects, suffering from the many hardships of the war, than they in their present

---

* *Brandschatz* (pl. *Brandschätze*): a sum of money paid by the inhabitants of a town in order to ensure that it would not be burned down.

situation are able to do', hit the right note. To protect subjects against unjustified demands, the Silesian ministry of state compiled a catalogue of complaints that required action: the extortion of too large deliveries and too frequent transport services, the irregular acquisition of peasant land by unnecessary evacuation of villages, the prevention of marriages and other measures which aimed at lessening the number of inhabitants in the care of the province. That the *Kabinettsministerium* was willing to act on complaints is shown by the case (in spring 1761) of the Lebus tenant who had forced war wounded Ackerburgers to render transport services five days every week: this was reduced to two days. The investigation of the Lebus case by Eichel, the king's cabinet secretary, indicates the limitation of the royal field-chancery's registry resources: Eichel apologized for troubling minister von Blumenthal 'as nobody here knows which department of the Royal General Directory administers the town and *Amt* of Lebus and the villages belonging to it'. A cabinet order of November 1760 called for leniency in the levying of taxes in the war-ravaged parts of Silesia. Measures for the reconstruction of Küstrin, the Neumark and Pomerania began in the autumn of 1758. An estimate of that year of damages in the area administered by the Magdeburg Chamber amounted to more than 70,000 *Reichstaler*; in October 1760 it was not yet possible to estimate how much money, cattle and grain had been seized and farms destroyed by the Russian invasion of the Kurmark. In 1761 50,000 *Reichstaler* were spent on immediate relief in the Neumark. War damages in East Friesland (including debts) alone amounted to 650,000 *Reichstaler*. In April 1762 a commission headed by chamber president Franz Balthasar Schönberg von Brenckenhoff, a native of Anhalt-Dessau, was sent to Pomerania and the Neumark to determine the exact extent of the war damage and to draw up plans for reconstruction. To replace burnt-down dwellings a first rebuilding programme provided for 6,000 new houses in Pomerania and the Neumark and 3,100 in Silesia.

The cost of the reconstruction programmes had to be defrayed from extraordinary funds, and the extent to which these were available depended on the general financial situation of the state, a topic which will be dealt with later. Our present concern is with the special burdens and problems which the Seven Years War posed for the administration of financial affairs. As early as January 1757 Frederick realized that the war would be a long one. Despite the considerable state treasure (*Staatsschatz*), the contributions levied in Saxony and the British subsidies, Prussia's resources were stretched to the limit. Loans amounting to

4 million talers were granted by the Estates and provinces in the year following the melting down of the royal table-silver. In September 1757, after the defeat at Kolin, a drastic decision had to be taken: all civilian salaries and pensions were credited to the general war chest (the *Generalkriegskasse*) and in lieu of salaries vouchers, redeemable at a later date, were issued. This measure put the lower grades of civil servants who had no other income – and indeed were not permitted to have any – into desperate straits. To objections and warnings of the resignations, staff shortages, moonlighting and temptations of dishonesty that would follow the king had one laconic answer: 'I know all this myself, but I have no money.' Occasionally it was possible to make some payment in cash by ingenious juggling with the finances but not till June 1759 were salaries and pensions paid in full to those earning up to 400 *Reichstaler*; those above this limit still had a quarter of their salaries paid in vouchers. From June 1762 civilian salaries had to be stopped once more; but the peace with Russia eased the financial pressure and at least half of the salaries owed were paid. From 15 February 1762 – exactly a year before the Peace of Hubertusburg – the redemption of vouchers and the payment in full of all salaries was decreed and carried out. Up to that time it had been impossible to pay Prussian officials who had come, mostly on official business, from the occupied territories, since there was not enough money to pay the salaries for the unoccupied provinces. The Estates had been warned that they must not count on full compensation for deliveries of forage during the war; the payment of a first instalment on the forage-debt was authorized in the spring of 1760 but more than a year passed before the money could be found. That the Prussian administrative apparatus survived years of interruption in the payment of salaries (normally paid with proverbial punctuality) without collapsing or suffering lasting damage demonstrates the willingness to make sacrifices, the restraint, the sense of duty and the *esprit de corps* of officials and their families. *Travailler pour le roi de Prusse* had become a point of honour which in times of want passed the severest tests.

The administration of Prussia's enemy-occupied provinces was, under difficult conditions, carried out by the Prussian officials who did not leave. The General Directory, although without much opportunity for taking action, kept itself informed of developments. In October 1757 in the province of Magdeburg, the Duc de Richelieu, commander-in-chief of the French invasion force, levied, in accordance with the then rules of war, 33,333 *Reichstaler* as *Sauvegarde* money in lieu of services up to 1 May 1758. The provinces of the Altmark, Prignitz and the

Uckermark had to raise an equal amount, while Mansfeld paid 10,000 *Reichstaler*. On top of the *Sauvegarde* money came smaller levies, gratifications and enforced gifts (*douceurs*). The neutralization of the county of Mark in January 1759 cost a sum of 21,000 *Reichstaler* paid to the French army; and in February 1760 compulsory loans were necessary in Cleves and Mark to furnish their share of the *Sauvegarde* money. One break in the clouds was the payment of a small surplus to the Prussian treasury by the Minden Chamber in 1759, despite the drain on the province by war and occupation.

Frederick was adamant that the civilian treasuries, which were in any case overburdened, should be free from military interference. In January 1761 the commandant of the fortress at Schweidnitz was sharply reprimanded for causing a treasurer to make arrangements that enabled the general to avail himself of a royal treasury. The debasement of the coinage towards the end of the war created special problems; as a result the Breslau Chamber had to forbid its treasurers to exchange coins in their keeping even within the treasuries. Only with the coming of peace did such departmental difficulties and other problems unravel themselves; yet settlement dragged on for years, partly because of strict book-keeping regulations and audits, partly because the commencement of the reconstruction programme brought the administration great new tasks.

The king, normally almost the sole driving power in all departments of state, made only a few of his characteristically sharp sorties into the administration during the war. The army was for the duration the essence of the state and the king's presence with it was essential. The Pyrrhic victory at Prague followed by the defeat at Kolin (for which the king must bear responsibility) had destroyed hopes of an early peace, though the victories of Rossbach and Leuthen put an end to the immediate threat to Prussia's survival. The enormous losses sustained in warding off the Russians at Zorndorf and the negligence displayed at Hochkirch severely strained the very structure of the army: Frederick's miserable tactical and strategic leadership before and during the battle of Kunersdorf in 1759 showed this clearly enough. Here was the nadir of Prussia's fortune in the Seven Years' War. In the evening of the day of the battle Frederick wrote to the minister for external affairs, Count Finck von Finckenstein:

> Our losses are very considerable. Of an army of 48,000 I have, as I write, less than 3,000 men left. All flee and I am no longer master of my men. Berlin must look to its own safety. This is a terrible mishap and I shall not survive it. Its results will be worse than the event itself. I have no more reserves and to tell the truth, I believe all is lost.

This paragraph is not, as often alleged in our own time, the manifestation of a nervous breakdown but the clear presentation of irrefutable facts. It is certainly to the king's credit that, after Kunersdorf, he systematically and with great tenacity tapped new resources and rebuilt his army. Both in politics and war he showed a rare maturity during the following years: the victories of Liegnitz, Torgau and Burkersdorf were the fruits of his sharp insight, tireless energy and firm leadership. But Frederick's ability to surmount the crisis was not due to his merit alone; the disunity of his adversaries, the death of the tsaritsa Elizabeth in January 1762, Britain's tying down of France in an exhausting worldwide maritime and colonial war – all these, alongside the great accomplishments of the Prussian army, administration and population, combined to work the *miracle de la maison de Brandenbourg*.

Part of the miracle was Frederick's survival. All his life he suffered frequent illness. Colic, stomach cramps, skin-rashes, gout in hands and feet, cramps, fits of choking, chest pains, fever and piles consecutively or simultaneously assaulted his delicate frame. He was now thin and pale and his teeth had fallen out. He habitually wore a blue coat several sizes too large for him, torn by bullet holes and roughly mended with white thread. Though generally in control of himself, Frederick was at times either irritable or tearful. He could also be bitingly sarcastic. His cutting comments and harsh measures, seemingly so enigmatic, are explained by his shifting moods. These also provide the key to many of his mistakes and omissions. After the withdrawal from Bohemia in 1757 he entrusted, though not without qualms, his brother and heir presumptive, Augustus William, with an army corps. When the prince showed himself unfitted for the task Frederick, deeply disappointed, publicly and contemptuously relieved him of his command. Further mental stress followed. Hard on the heels of the defeat at Kolin came news of his mother's death. In the evening of the catastrophe at Hochkirch – where he almost lost his own life – his adored sister Wilhelmina, always closest to him, died. A few weeks earlier, Augustus William had died before any reconciliation between the brothers had taken place. His eldest son, Frederick William, at the age of fifteen now became heir presumptive, and after Kunersdorf Frederick briefly pondered whether homage ought to be paid to the boy to ensure the succession. Prince Henry, one of Frederick's younger brothers, an experienced if over-cautious strategist, was indispensable to him throughout the war. Henry criticized bitterly, and justifiably, the king's military dilettantism in 1759; yet he remained absolutely loyal and dependable, a man of integrity and significance, inspired by the concept of service and convinced of the necessity of subordinating himself to the interests of the state. During the war years Frederick found his thoughts turning to his father. On three occasions – in April and May 1758 and in July 1760 – he told his reader, Henri de Catt, that his father had appeared to him in dreams that made a deep impression on him and even obsessed him. Twice the spirit of Frederick William had reproached him 'because he had not loved his father enough'; in the third dream he found himself in Charlottenburg in the presence of his father and the Old Dessauer: 'Have I done well?' I asked the Old Dessauer. 'Very well', he said. 'That pleases me. Your approval and that of my father flatter me more than that of the whole world.' Talking to de Catt about his father Frederick confessed that 'only by his care, his untiring work, his scrupulously just policies, his great and admirable thriftiness and the strict discipline he introduced into the army which he himself had created, made possible the achievements I have so far accomplished.'

Even in the turmoil of camp-life Frederick never escaped a depressing feeling of great loneliness. He did what he had to do from a sense of duty, not from inclination. His self-analysis in a letter of December 1758 to Marquis d'Argens is revealing and convincing:

> Although I and the troops have endured unimaginable hardships we do not deserve any praise. I am heartily tired of life. Everything I have loved and respected on this earth I have lost; I am surrounded by unfortunates whom in their present needs I am unable to help. I am still completely crushed by the devastation of our loveliest provinces. Overburdened with cares and trouble I am a poor, god-forsaken man, condemned to battle till the end of time and to sink under my burden of work.

In the battle of Prague Field-Marshal Kurt Cristoph von Schwerin had fallen; during the skirmishes that followed Kolin Adjutant-General Hans Karl von Winterfeldt was mortally wounded; at Hochkirch Field-Marshal Jacob Keith met his death. These three capable officers had been particularly close to the king and professionally they were irreplaceable. In the summer of 1759, before the disastrous battle of Kunersdorf, Frederick's reader, de Catt, noted down how the king spent his time in the camp and recorded conversations with him:

> The king read much. He busied himself with Tacitus, Sallust and Cornelius Nepos and he talked to me about them in the afternoons. He also corrected several pieces of poetry. 'You see me', he often said, 'very busy reading and writing. I need this diversion from the gloomy thoughts that agitate me. I know that the clouds are gathering and that a heavy storm will soon break. God knows where it will wreak its havoc. I would not be quite so worried

if the orders which I give or cause to be given were at least carried out. . . .
One can never be happy in any position in life where one has to deal with a
great many people; how much less can one be happy in a position like mine!'
To play the flute, to compose verse, to write letters, and now and then
pass an hour in the evening talking to his reader – such were the scanty
hours of relaxation which the king allowed himself in his field headquarters. This was not a flight from reality but entry into a second,
equally real, world. 'Some get drunk', Frederick once explained, 'I
relax by versifying.' Quite a few of his epistles and odes date from the
years 1757–62. Frederick's lucid, sharp intellect always remained awake
and active; he had forced himself to become scrupulously objective
before demanding objectivity from others.

During the period of greatest danger after Kunersdorf thoughts of
Charles XII of Sweden, naturally enough, preoccupied him. From the
situation of 1759 sympathy for Charles XII flowered. Frederick felt
that only now did he really understand him and he rushed to correct
Voltaire's dilettante portrait of the Swedish king. 'His perseverance,
which raised him above his fate, his wonderful energy and his heroic
courage were undoubtedly his most prominent qualities.' Audible notes
of self-criticism can be heard in his assessment of Charles: 'Our hero
might have been more economical with human blood . . . Commanders
who want to give battle because they do not know what else to do' –
here the stinging nettles of Prague and Kunersdorf are conjured up,
waiting to be grasped. Frederick realized this: 'Have you, great critic,
followed the advice you so freely give? Alas, no! My only defence is
that we notice the mistakes of others, but we ignore our own.' In the
event Frederick was luckier than Charles. Russia's withdrawal from the
war on 5 May 1762 gave him a chance to settle with his remaining
enemies. On 22 May 1762 the Peace of Hamburg was concluded with
Sweden. On 24 November 1762 Austria agreed to an armistice for
Upper and Lower Silesia, after Britain had forced France to conclude
a preliminary peace of 3 November 1762 at Fontainebleau. On
15 February 1763, five days after the signing of the Peace of Paris
between Britain and France, Austria and Saxony came to terms with
Prussia at Hubertusburg. The treaties of Berlin and Dresden were
renewed, and the Peace of Westphalia confirmed. During the winter of
1763–64 the Empire was included in the peace by the conclusion at
Regensburg of treaties of neutrality with Prussia by the electorates of
Bavaria, the Palatinate and Cologne, and the duchy of Württemberg.
Until the Peace of Tilsit in 1807, a period of forty-four years, the
Prussian state was free from external dangers. The seven years of cease-

less strain from 1756 to 1763 had also generated the internal cohesion necessary for the creation of a Prussian *Gesamtstaat*.

ARMY ADMINISTRATION

Prussian eighteenth-century army administration was of the imperfectly bureaucratized kind which we described for the administration in general. Many traditional practices had survived into the Age of Reason, in spite of numerous innovations. Personal relations still strongly determined the work of the executive, above all the king's right to interfere whenever and wherever he liked. Frederick had need of many collaborators; he often changed their functions, and their duties always corresponded to the king's assessment of their abilities and his own requirements.

Despite the use of some modern-sounding titles Frederician Prussia had neither a real 'minister of war' (*Kriegsminister*) nor a 'general staff' (*Generalstab*), as these are understood today. The king's orders to his military administration were issued through his cabinet secretary, a civilian. The Secret War Chancery (the *Geheime Kriegskanzlei*), the eight members of which were subordinate to the *Generalauditeur* (the army's chief judicial official), did not deal with ministerial duties. Its main function was the compilation of the handwritten monthly army list. After 1758 the number of adjutants-general was reduced from seven to one, a kind of 'higher adjutant', but as he at times played an important part in the drawing up of operational plans he can also be designated as chief of the general staff. The most clearly functional department was that of the quartermaster-general, responsible for plotting marching routes and fixing camp sites.

The General Directory, as in the days of Frederick William I, remained responsible for the actual administration of the army. Its Second Department provisioned and equipped the army, and took care of marching and billeting expenses and 'service money' (*Servisgelder*), the tax levied in lieu of billeting obligations. Experiences gained in the first two Silesian wars caused Frederick to found on 25 February 1746 a Sixth Department of the General Directory to which these duties were transferred. After 1749 it also administered the Potsdam military orphanage. Heinrich Christoph von Katte, a civilian and former president of the Magdeburg Chamber, was put in charge of the new department. During the Seven Years War the overworked civilian personnel of the General Directory, understaffed and in financial straits, proved itself incapable of anticipating the king's needs and too slow and inflexible in responding to them.

On 27 January 1761 Frederick appointed Lieutenant-General Karl Heinrich von Wedell as minister of war, though the Second Department of the General Directory continued to deal with matters relating to the General War Treasury (the *Generalkriegskasse*) and the Third with the affairs of disabled soldiers. Cantonal affairs remained, as before, the responsibility of the provincial departments. A clear dividing line between the command and the administration now emerged. The inspector-general of artillery, the head of the engineer corps and the fortresses, the commissary-general and the quartermaster-general were directly responsible to the king. The commander in East Prussia held the rank of field-marshal and had regional authority over all troops and fortresses in the province; a similar arrangement operated in Silesia.

The most important task of the many different but necessarily connected branches of the army administration was the organization, formation and provisioning of the standing army. On 1 June 1740 the Prussian army consisted of thirty-two infantry regiments in sixty-six battalions (with a company of grenadiers attached to each battalion), twelve regiments of cuirassiers in sixty squadrons, six regiments of hussars in nine squadrons, one battalion of field artillery and another of garrison artillery, four battalions of garrison troops and four regiments of militia, stationed in Berlin, Königsberg, Magdeburg and Stettin respectively. Some 26,000 of the total of about 80,000 troops were foreigners. The infantrymen were mainly musketeers. The fusiliers (from regiment no. 28 onwards) were distinguished by caps with a mitre-shaped metal shield instead of the more traditional hat; similar caps were also worn by the grenadiers (originally equipped with grenades), elite units which Frederick II organized into battalions.

The army of Frederick William I, the Soldier King, was regarded in Europe as being excessively large for a state with Prussia's small population. Yet Frederick II, immediately after his accession, added sixteen battalions and twenty-three squadrons to the army. Some of these troops were raised by Duke Karl of Brunswick, Duke Wilhelm Heinrich of Sachsen-Eisenach, Margrave Karl of Ansbach, Duke Friedrich of Sachsen-Gotha and Prince Friedrich August of Holstein-Gottorp. The new formations had not become fully operational by the time the First Silesian War broke out. During the winter of 1741–42 Brunswick-Bevern supplied a new regiment; another was raised for the margrave of Brandenburg-Schwedt; and the king formed two more, one at Breslau and another at Wesel. A regiment of dragoons was taken over from Duchess Maria Auguste of Württemberg and kept for a time its red Württemberg uniforms, but Saxony refused to allow Prussia to

The royal title gained: Frederick I, 'king in Prussia', on his way to
ceremonial anointment

Frederick's mother, Sophia Dorothea

3 Frederick's father, Frederick William I

4 The brothers in youth; Frederick on the left. Next to him, Ferdinand, Augustus William and Henry

5, 6, 7 Three of the sisters grown up: Wilhelmina, margravine of Bayreuth, the famous memoir writer and, as the eldest, especially trusted by Frederick; (Louise) Ulrica, who became queen of Sweden and was active in the peace negotiation of the Seven Years War; Amelia, who became abbess of Quedlinburg

8 The education of a crown
prince. The castle of
Küstrin where he learnt
his *métier*

9 Self-education at Sans
Souci: Frederick as a
writer

OEUVRES
DU PHILOSOPHE
DE
SANS-SOUCI.
SECONDE EDITION.

FRIDERICUS
REX.

A POTZDAM.

M. DCC. LX.

10 A clock from
Frederick's
collection

11 Frederick's tabatière
decorated with allegorical
reliefs, set with diamonds
and adorned with his
portrait in miniature

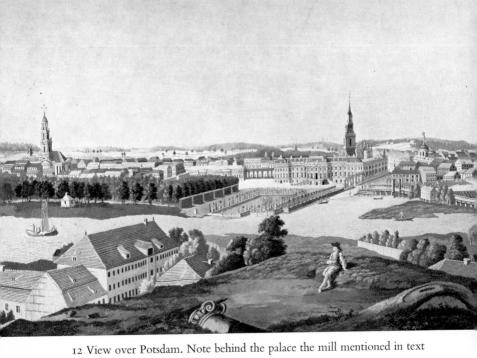

12 View over Potsdam. Note behind the palace the mill mentioned in text on p.211

13 South façade of Sans Souci palace

14 The Gendarmen Markt (Friedrichstadt square) with the German and the French cathedrals

15 Berlin, Unter den Linden showing, to the right the arsenal and beyond the palace of Prince Henry

16 The Silesian Estates do homage to Frederick in the town hall of Breslau in 1741

17 Frederick meets the villagers of Güstebiese on the Oder (near Küstrin) before the battle of Zorndorf in the Seven Years War

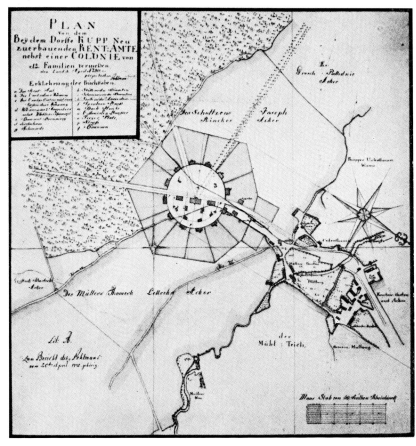

18 A Frederician settlement at Kupp in Upper Silesia. Contemporary plan

19 The same area photographed from the air in the present century

20 Merchant ship *König von Preussen* (purchased in England) which sailed in February 1752 to Canton for the newly-founded Prussian-Asiatic Trading Company

21 Warehouse of the Prussian-Asiatic Trading Company founded 1750 in Emden

22 Frederician granary in West Prussia

23 Textile factory in Brandenburg

4-28 Prussian
administrators. Domhardt
(above left): with much
experience of the War
and Domain chambers,
specially those of West
Prussia. Brenckenhoff
(above right): active in
finance and in the
melioration projects.
Stein in old age (centre):
transmitter of the

Frederician administrative
tradition; visited England
in connection with his
work for the Prussian
mining industry. Heinitz
(below left): in his
uniform as minister in
charge of the Silesian
mines. Podewils (below
right): war and cabinet
minister, expert in
foreign affairs

29 Frederick visiting officials and experts in charge of a domestic colonization project in Mark Brandenburg

30 Silver medal commemorating the homage given to Frederick by the West Prussian Estates in 1772

31 Samuel von Cocceji, Prussian jurist and statesman active in law reform

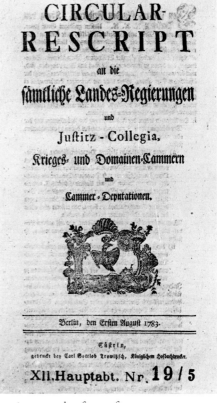

CIRCULAR-
RESCRIPT
an die
sämtliche Landes-Regierungen
und
Justitz - Collegia,
Krieges- und Domainen-Cammern
und
Cammer-Deputationen.

Berlin, den Ersten August 1783.

Cüstrin,
gedruckt bey Carl Gottlob Trowitzsch, Königlichem Hofbuchdrucker.

XII. Hauptabt. Nr. 19/5

33 An example of one of many Frederician decrees, from which the Prussian General Law was compiled

32 Karl Gottlieb Svarez, Prussian judge who completed the Prussian General Law

34 Frederick discussing building plans, c.1788

35 Frederick on his journeys: the mayor hands him a drink

Serviteur · Herr Landrath
Votre serviteur Mr le Conseil Provincial

Aned IW Hp 43

36 Frederick, to the left, lifting his hat, takes leave of a rural commissioner

37 A rare engraving showing Frederick and his queen, Elisabeth Christina, born Brunswick-Wolfenbüttel

38 The last sentence with date and signature, of Frederick's last will and testament. Note the mention of the reigning duke Charles de Bronswic (i.e. Brunswick)

39 Frederick visits the weavers. This is not a contemporary engraving, but is of much historical interest since it was made by the draughtsman and painter Adolph von Menzel (1815-1905), who had made a particular study of Frederick the Great and his reign

40 Frederick II of Prussia. Wedgwood cameo portrait by Tassie, *c.*1780-1800

raise an Uhlan regiment in Poland. From Silesian volunteers and Austrian prisoners of war the Black and the Brown Hussars were formed. The fortresses were manned by seven garrison regiments and the field artillery corps was doubled by the addition of Silesian volunteers. In Upper Silesia a pioneer regiment with sappers and pontooners was raised. Shortly before the outbreak of the Second Silesian War four more infantry regiments were formed, including two from Württemberg and Holstein; one dragoon regiment and two hussar regiments under their Hungarian commanders were taken on; the garrison battalions were also increased. Squadrons of lancers were now raised, Prussian 'Bosnians' in colourful uniforms, but they did not live up to the king's high expectations: 'The Uhlans are not worth their keep.' With all the new units the army reached a total strength of 132,000 men. The Prussian army's extremely detailed regulations, enforced with especial strictness during reviews and manoeuvres, were essential because of the varied origins of the troops. Common wartime experiences meant that a certain *esprit de corps* was formed within individual regiments; this helps to explain the astounding coherence maintained even in the worst period of the Seven Years War. Punctual pay and regular, ample rations also contributed to the high morale of the troops.

Feeding the army was the responsibility of the *Magazinverwaltung* (stores administration) which the king established in 1746, based on his experiences in the Silesian wars. In fortresses and regional depots 44,000 *Wispel* of rye was stored, two-thirds of it ground into flour. For immediate needs there were *Fouragemagazine* (forage stores). Keeping the depots and stores stocked was the duty of the General Supply Office (the *Generalproviantamt*). Requisitioning of the stores was carried out by the War Zone Commissariats; supply depots distributed food to the troops and flour to the field-bakeries. Provision wagons, flour carts and mobile field-ovens followed the troops into the field, while battalion hand mills were used for grinding flour acquired *en marche*. According to Captain Johann Wilhelm von Archenholtz, who fought in the Seven Years War and wrote its history, 'the Prussian army was never without pay, never without bread or forage, very rarely without vegetables and even more rarely without meat.' This was quite an achievement, the result of Frederick's foresight, and the vigilance and adaptability of the army administration. Equally well-organized was the provision of fodder for the horses of the cavalry regiments. The general efficiency reached a level which the Prussian army could not emulate in the Revolutionary and Napoleonic periods.

Army commissary General von Massow and his staff supplied

uniforms, equipment, ammunition and replacements for weapons and horses throughout the Seven Years War, though extraordinary efforts were needed after the great losses at Hochkirch and Kunersdorf. The small-arms manufactories at Potsdam and Spandau could produce only 1,200 weapons a month, and domestic casting of cannon did not suffice to meet wartime needs. Arms therefore had to be imported from abroad. The elaborate uniforms were worn by the troops at all times, even for battle formations, though they wore out quickly. Watching his troops march along a muddy road in an autumn downpour Frederick once commented: 'My chaps look like scarecrows but they bite.' Almost all the colours behind which they marched had to be replaced during the course of the war. Frederick William I's motto had been *Non Soli cedit*; the new colours carried the words *Pro Gloria et Patria* and the initials 'Fr.'.

In June 1756 the Prussian army, after further minor additions, consisted of 95 battalions, 211 squadrons and 23 garrison battalions: on mobilization 29 extra grenadier and 12 garrison battalions were added as well as 4 *Landregimente* in the old provinces. The entire army numbered 158,000 men, of whom 127,000 were combat troops. The Silesian contingent, to the number of 35,000 men, formed part of this total. Frederick, anxious to avoid trouble with his new subjects, had initially been content to accept service money only from Silesia, but by edicts of 15 August 1742 and 16 August 1743 recruitment cantons for thirteen regiments had been established in the province. Breslau and the six mountain *Kreise* had been exempted as industrial areas on agreeing to provide sixty recruits a year and to bear the cost of their equipment, victuals, transport and bounty, an obligation which was found too onerous and from which they were freed during the years 1764–70. Despite Silesia's reluctance to assume military responsibilities the province's contingent played a glorious part in Frederick's campaigns: from it were formed such famous regiments as the Seydlitz Cuirassiers, the Jung-Platen Dragoons, the White and Brown Hussars, the Margrave of Schwedt Fusiliers and the Jung-Zieten Fusiliers.

The four *Landregimente*, formed from retired soldiers who had agreed to take up arms if the need arose, were intended for regional defence. The threat of enemy invasion produced a cabinet order of 1757 that asked the General Directory 'in the present precarious situation' to raise a militia in the Kurmark, the Neumark, Magdeburg, Halberstadt, Pomerania and East Prussia: 'All young men who can carry a musket are to be called up, irrespective of whether they are in the musterbook or have been rejected, or neither.' Towns, too, were expected to raise their fair share of men for the militia, 'so that the entire burden does not fall on the rural areas'. In East Prussia, the Königsberg *Regierung* ordered the town magistrates to enlist even exempt categories for defence of the province. In this way 5,580 territorials were enlisted in Pomerania, 823 in the Uckermark, 1,700 in the Neumark, 3,300 in Magdeburg-Halberstadt, 3,000 in the Kurmark and 2,200 in East Prussia. The provinces were expected to bear the bulk of their own defence costs, but the long drawn-out war made the burden a heavier one than some of them could carry: in 1761 Pomerania and the Uckermark were exempted from further payments and an annual sum of 306,000 *Reichstaler* was allotted by the *Generalkriegskasse*. By the autumn of 1757, twenty-one territorial infantry battalions and six squadrons of hussars, a total of 16,000 men, were part of Prussia's armed forces; but by the end of the war, the number had shrunk to about 9,000 as war casualties and the difficulty of running the substitute system exerted their toll. It had been estimated that Silesia's exempt industrial *Kreise* would need a militia of twenty companies, but only a few of them materialized. This was due in part to faults of organization (the terms of pay, provisions and officers' commissions had been left too vague),* but in part also to the fact that 'volunteers' did not come forward: it was generally believed that enlistment in the militia would be converted into life service in the regular army. In the Second Silesian War peasants from *Kreis* Hirschberg fought a guerrilla war of their own against Austrian raiding forces. In the rest of Silesia and in the western provinces no militia was raised during the Seven Years War, though 'free' regiments and battalions were raised for the duration, mainly by foreign officers with the king's permission. Altogether twenty-three units of light infantry and cavalry were thus formed but their indiscipline made them feared by friend and foe, and on the whole they harmed the reputation of the Prussian army. Only a small number of the free-corps officers were taken into the regular army; one of these was Guillaume L'Homme de Courbière, who became a field-marshal and distinguished himself in 1807 as the defender of Graudenz. To enlarge the Prussian army considerably at one fell swoop, ten Saxon infantry regiments were newly raised in the winter of 1756–57. This experiment proved a failure: seven regiments were disbanded in 1757 on account of mutiny and desertion, and by the end of the war only two regiments were still up to full strength.

The enlistment of foreigners, not infrequently by the use of force or near force, brought many ruffianly and anti-social elements into the

* Plans were formulated to remedy these faults but were dropped when the end of the war seemed in sight.

Frederician army; but it had the advantage of providing men who served for life. After the Seven Years War at least 25 per cent of the Prussian army were 'foreigners', though it must be remembered that this category contained not only non-Germans but all non-Prussian Germans as well, including natives of Kurland, Alsace, Transylvania and even all supernumerary Prussian cantonists or those coming from other districts: for a Prussian regiment 'abroad' began at the borders of the canton (A. Skalweit). The sons of foreign soldiers were also liable to life-long service; in 1777 there were nearly 20,000 foreign soldier-families in Prussia. As a rule regiments got their replacements through the cantonal recruiting offices, not through conscription. Mustering recruits was the responsibility of the local regimental commander, helped by the rural commissioner and the tax inspector. The following categories were exempt from cantonal obligations: the nobility, officials and their sons, owners of peasant farms and their eldest sons, all colonists and their sons, craftsmen and members of certain professional groups, merchants, manufacturers and seamen. Whole regions were also exempt, as in East Friesland, the Rhine-Westphalian provinces, and the mountain counties in Silesia; so were individual cities, for instance Berlin and Breslau. Army service thus fell largely on the rural population, but only one able-bodied cantonist in 200 was called-up in peacetime. Height was the main consideration in choosing recruits (this was so till the beginning of the nineteenth century). Officers came from the cadet corps, though others joined the regiment as ensigns. The officer corps was not exclusively aristocratic: former non-commissioned officers and men of bourgeois stock became officers and a number of these were later ennobled. The nobility did, however, take precedence. Frederick wanted a closed officer caste with uniform concepts of honour and duty. The higher bourgeoisie consisted at this time almost solely of officials, and these the king wished to reserve for the civil service. Here family tradition also played an important part. But family tradition alone was not enough in either civil or military service. In June 1786 Frederick informed a petitioner that

> The son of Major-General Count von Lottum must first serve for a year as a volunteer corporal before he can become an officer. You must understand that the father's title does not count. Even in England the king's son must begin his naval career at the bottom of the ladder.

Hardly any new army units were formed during the Seven Years War. Indeed, it was only by the transfer of garrison troops, the merging of regiments, and the exchange of prisoners-of-war that Frederick was able to maintain the strength of the army at about 100,000 men. When the war ended there were 219,000 men under arms, including garrison troops and reserve units. On the conclusion of peace 42,000 native Prussians were demobilized and 37,000 horses released so that the rehabilitation work might prosper. The army, reduced to 151,000 in 1763, had increased to 195,000 by the end of Frederick's reign. This made it the third largest army in Europe after Austria (297,000) and Russia (224,000), followed closely by France (182,000). In the year of Frederick's death the Prussian army consisted of 55 regiments in 110 battalions, 20 garrison battalions, 25 battalions of grenadiers, 7 battalions of garrison grenadiers, 4 *Landregimente*, a *Feldjäger* corps (chasseurs, or sharp-shooters), 13 cuirassier, 12 dragoon and 10 hussar regiments – in all 234 squadrons; four regiments of field artillery, garrison artillery, sappers, pontooners and a corp of engineers.

In his instruction of 20 December 1722 to the General Directory Frederick William I had laid down rules for the maintenance of soldiers invalided out of the army or retired from it with honour. In that year the military orphanage in Potsdam had also been founded. Frederick continued and extended his father's work. Originally those no longer fit for service had been kept with their regiments, formed into special companies assigned to light barrack duties. In 1742 they were formed into twelve companies of the New Garrison Regiment destined for service in the small fortresses of Regenstein, Peitz, Küstrin, Greetsiel, Moers, Stettin, Tempelburg, Spandau and Charlottenburg. Discharged soldiers unable to earn a living in civilian life were helped by the *Invalidenkasse* (the disabled soldiers' fund). This fund was financed by disciplinary fines imposed for such offences as absence without leave, negligence in the performance of sentry duty and getting into debt, and also by voluntary contributions made by soldiers on receiving promotion. By 1 June 1748 some 4,685 needy ex-soldiers were being fed and clothed from the *Invalidenkasse*.

In 1730 Frederick William I had established a hospital at Werder near Potsdam for guards declared unfit for service. After the Second Silesian War Frederick built the *Invalidenhaus* opposite the Oranienburg Gate in Berlin. This great building housed 600 ex-soldiers; they were divided into three companies, and received free uniforms, accommodation, light and heat and army pay appropriate to their rank. Old soldiers capable of earning some sort of living outside the hospital had their earnings supplemented by state benefits. Retired officers **were** given pensions or positions as directors of domains, as postmasters and *Landräte*. Some were retained in the service as commanders of garrisons, fortresses or *Landregimente*, others were appointed to positions in the *Kriegskom-missariat* (provisioning service) or were made *Platzmajore*, charged with the upkeep of town fortifications. Each individual case was reviewed by the king whose decisions were influenced by considerations of merit, need, and good rather than long service. Pensions for officers came from the *Generalkriegskasse*. Before being appointed to posts as rural commissioners, tax inspectors or domains councillors officers had to sit an examination set by the Civil Service Commission (*Ober-Examination-kommission*) of the General Directory. Officers retiring from service in free or garrison regiments did not, in general, receive financial or other support.

In 1746 Frederick reprimanded the War and Domains chambers for not employing enough retired soldiers and followed this up on 13 March 1747 with a circular rescript (repeated in 1758) to the chambers. A list was compiled of 391 soldiers able to read, write and calculate who were considered eligible for posts as police riders, chancery messengers and for vacancies in the salt and postal services. The appointment of disabled or retired non-commissioned officers as village schoolmasters caused a stir, but only seventy-nine, all of whom had passed the General Directory's examination, were thus employed. In 1763 Colonel von Billerbeck was appointed inspector for the affairs of disabled soldiers. He excluded from the *Invalidenhaus* all those able to fend for themselves; recipients of the *Gnadentaler* (literally, 'the taler of grace', a kind of pension) were subjected to a means test. The Neumark Chamber alone decided that 268 of the 431 men in receipt of such benefits had no need of them. In 1758 the maintenance of disabled or retired *Feldjäger* in the forestry service was decreed. Some of them were transferred to East Prussia in 1762 when the evacuation of Russian troops took place. In 1761 the Magdeburg Chamber agreed to the employment of 'foreign' (that is non-Magdeburg) disabled or retired soldiers provided new permanent posts were created for them. With the establishment of the new tax administration, the *Regie*, most posts for tax collectors, auditors weights and measure inspectors, toll-masters and bridge guards were, by 1772, filled by former non-commissioned officers.

The coffee-*Regie* alone employed 200 ex-soldiers as supervisors, the so-called 'Coffee-Sniffers'. Other ex-soldiers were employed as stall-holders, wood keepers, night-watchmen, shepherds and rangers of woods, fields and meadows. In the Kurmark 3,000 ex-soldiers were settled as military colonists. Other provinces, especially Pomerania, also took some of them, as did the Neumark and East Prussia. Of almost 200,000 officers and men wounded or otherwise disabled during the

Seven Years War about 10,000 were taken care of by the state. In 1785 5,900 ex-officers and men were still unprovided for; a year later this number had risen to almost 6,500. Soldiers of all ranks served to the age-limit: in 1787 the Borcke Dragoons had still 134 men between the ages of fifty to sixty who had fought in the Seven Years War, some of them even in the Second Silesian War.

Widows and orphans could not claim pensions but remained dependent on welfare. A provincial pension fund was established at Breslau in 1769 for poor widows and orphans from the nobility; and the king donated 100,000 talers to the Silesian Credit Bank, the interest of which was to be used for orphans of officers. Similar institutions existed for the *Ritterschaft* of Pomerania and the Neumark. In 1775 a Widows' Providential Fund (a *Witwen-Verpflegungsanstalt*) was set up for the aid of all classes, though it was active only in peacetime. Generally speaking, provision for poor or disabled soldiers did not advance much beyond the standard laid down by Frederick William I. Considering the large number of war victims the state aid authorized by Frederick II seems meagre. Quite apart from the scarcity of money and the many tasks which competed for funds, the idea of a welfare state was yet remote; the belief that people should in the first place try to help themselves was generally held. The absence of norms for determining degrees of need doubtless resulted in unintentional injustices. Within the army the attitude was prevalent that the old, retired or disabled soldier should be helped, as long as he behaved himself; and much help was given to old comrades. The provision of free medicines from the field dispensaries – a practice dating back to the reign of Frederick William I – was continued. From small beginnings medical care had developed so far that mobile field infirmaries and the service of apothecaries were available in sufficient numbers. Dr Cothenius, the general staff physician, reckoned that during the Seven Years War field infirmaries had nursed 220,000 men back to health. The efforts of *Generalchirurg* (chief surgeon) Schmucker to maintain the fighting strength of soldiers for periods of two weeks at a stretch by feeding them a concentrated nutritive powder could not succeed, however, at the then stage of knowledge of nutritional chemistry. Finally it must be mentioned that, apart from the chaplaincy – a theme that will be treated elsewhere – the institution of the field post contributed most to the psychological welfare of the troops, and that in Frederick the Great's army we also find the beginnings of mobile regimental libraries.

Between the Peace of Hubertusburg and the death of Frederick II few radical changes were made in army administration. To help concentrate the attention of company and squadron commanders on their military duties the recruitment of 'foreigners' was completely taken out of their hands, and their influence over questions of leave and the granting of exemptions was greatly reduced. The War Department assumed responsibility for all recruitment and the supply of uniforms and fodder for the whole army, thus bringing to an end the era of 'company management' (*Kompaniewirtschaft*) which had flourished since the Thirty Years War and allowed officers to profit handsomely from their entrepreneurial skills. Frederick further established an inspectorate whose duties included the introduction of uniform equipment and the improvement and standardization of training methods. Six inspectors of infantry and five of cavalry, all reliable officers, were appointed on a provincial basis. The king himself took a close interest in the army, particularly in matters concerning levies, training methods and provisioning. On 1 March 1765 he founded the *Académie des Nobles* in Berlin for the specialized training of about twenty future officers and diplomats. In works such as *Pensées et règles générales pour la guerre* and *Eléments de castramétrie et de tactique*, and in numerous essays on the use of all types of weapons, he condensed his experiences and his thinking on the art of war. After the Seven Years War he resumed his provincial tours of inspection. In 1763 and again in 1768 he visited the western provinces. The unrest in Poland caused by the succession struggle made him cancel a visit to Königsberg planned for 1764; but after the acquisition of West Prussia he held a review of his troops almost every year at Mockrau near Graudenz. He also resumed his visits to Silesia to review the troops there, combining this military duty with a thorough inspection of the civil administration right down to *Kreis* level. His last visit was in 1785, when he was seventy-three years old. Towards the end of his life Frederick gave much thought to the formation of light infantry battalions, the increase in horse artillery, and the improvement and enlargement (by buying from Sweden) of gun-parks. From his troops he demanded the highest possible degree of mobility and the most rigid discipline, and from his generals a mental agility capable of outwitting the enemy. In this he was only partially successful. Prussian tactics remained, on the whole, formal and derivative and although troop movements were executed with precision they were both slow and awkward; the Prussian army's performance in the War of the Bavarian Succession (1778–79) brought unpleasant surprises in respect of mobilization, marching and the strategic exploitation of early successes. The king faced painful self-analysis; the troops felt little confidence in Frederick's strategy and Prince Henry's military career came to an end: the military demonstration had been unnecessary for the achievement of diplomatic success. Yet the presence of a large army was indispensable. Prussia needed it to maintain a balance of power in Europe and in Germany favourable to itself.

The maintenance of a standing army of 190,000 troops was a heavy burden on the Prussian economy. The Austrian army was stronger by a third, but Prussia raised twice as many troops in proportion to the number of inhabitants. To preserve the population and work force half the troops were recruited from abroad. To promote the economy native and foreign soldiers were assigned to industrial work during their army leave, and exemptions from military service were granted to those engaged in industry. Sixty men of each company were generally on leave for periods of ten months annually, working mainly in agriculture. Apart from the months of training and manoeuvres, therefore, 70,000 soldiers were on leave while an additional 13,000 foreign, off-duty troops were engaged as temporary labourers in the garrisons. That such compromises had a bad effect on discipline and battle-readiness was understood and allowed for; but only in this way was it possible for Prussia, with its small population, to maintain a large standing army and to develop the economy.

FINANCES

For Frederick William I the state treasure (the *Staatsschatz*) was – in contemporary cameralist parlance – the *nervus rerum gerendarum*, a phrase that presupposed complete royal control over its disposal. The freedom of action of absolute rulers rose and fell with the efficiency of their budgetary system; and the well-known financial shrewdness of the Hohenzollerns had, over the generations, matured into a thrifty mastery of investment planning. Frederick William was the first to set up a 'treasure' that was completely at his own disposal, kept separate from the state's other financial resources and reserved for extraordinary purposes. By the year of his death he had accumulated 10 million *Reichstaler* in gold coin, stored in barrels in the vaults of the Berlin Schloss. Two-thirds of this sum was used by Frederick to pay the costs of the First Silesian War, but by 1745 the reserve had once more grown to almost 6 million talers, having been replenished from the central funds, by money from Silesia and a loan from the *kurmärkische Landschaft* (the Kurmark's credit institute). All of it – and another 6 million *Reichstaler* – was consumed in the Second Silesian War; yet, by 1756 war reparations and surpluses from current revenues had enabled Frederick to put aside almost 20 million *Reichstaler*.

The value of this treasure depended on its buying power, subject to frequent fluctuations. Efforts to establish a uniform currency within the Empire had failed and the German money market was dominated by the French *louis d'or* and the Dutch florin. The silver coins which circulated inside the Empire had become debased; this was one reason why Prussia had hesitated overlong to mint its own silver coinage, the common world currency. During the First Silesian War Frederick had large numbers of small silver coins minted in Berlin in two-groschen and half-groschen pieces; once peace was restored he began to work for a more permanent solution of the Prussian coinage problem. In January 1750 he appointed Johann Philipp Graumann, Master of Trade and Coinage to the duke of Brunswick, noted for revolutionary theories on currency matters, to the post of General Director of the Prussian Mint. Graumann was under the authority of the General Directory and was thus not an independent entrepreneur. The Mint Law of 14 July 1750 created the 'Friedrichsdor' worth 5 talers, with a gold content of six grams; it was based on a ratio of 14 talers to one mark* silver. The Friedrichsdor was so sought after that all those minted were speedily drawn out of Prussia. Since Prussia did not yet engage in world trade the coins rarely returned, with the result that the revenue expected from the enterprise failed to materialize. The mints set up at Aurich, Berlin, Breslau, Cleves, Königsberg, Magdeburg and Stettin were indeed forced to close and eventually only those at Breslau and Königsberg operated at a profit. In 1754 Graumann was given indefinite leave of absence though he retained his title of *Generalmünzdirektor* until his death in 1762. In spite of the disappointment as to the profitability of the venture, the most important mint reform within the Empire for centuries had been effected, bringing the real value of the coinage into line with its nominal worth. This principle, and the ratio of 14 talers to one mark of fine silver, was eventually adopted by most of the German states. Not till 1764, at the instigation of minister von Schlabrendorff, was the Friedrichsdor revalued by 5 per cent; it then stabilized at 5 *Reichstaler* and 8 groschen. In 1750 the salaries of the mint masters had been raised, because of their responsibilities, from 300 talers to 1,000 – half that of a minister. They were, however, strictly forbidden to accept outside work, a condition which needed several sharp royal orders before it was enforced. Former officers were appointed as co-directors, jointly responsible for methodical business management,

* 1 mark = 234 grams.

especially after Graumann's departure when the mints were leased to Jewish commercial companies: in 1754 to Herz Moses Gumperts and Moses Fränckel and then, in 1758, to Veitel Ephraim. Frederick was advised by Peter Lorenz Knöffel, director of the Old Mint in Berlin, and Graumann's place was taken by the General War Commissioner and General Superintendent Lieutenant-General Wolf Friedrich von Retzow. Unfortunately Retzow in his ignorance of technical matters was unable to prevent the Cleves Mint from striking an excess of poor small coin, which caused a 25 per cent depreciation of the Cleves *Stüber* (stiver). It was also the Cleves Mint which, in the summer of 1756, began coining large numbers of six-*Kreuzer* silver pieces meant for circulation in the Empire and Poland. Thus the deviation of the coinage from the established standard, that is, its devaluation, had already started, at a ratio of 18 talers instead of 14 to a mark of fine silver, before the Seven Years War broke out. In 1758, after only two years of war, the *Staatsschatz* was completely exhausted. In that year the Prussian, Dresden and Leipzig mints were ordered to produce 3 million talers in brass coinage; in December Ephraim was authorized to mint Friedrichsdor in Berlin at a ratio of 19¾ *Reichstaler* (the *Mittelfriedrichsdor*, with some copper content) since the Dresden and Magdeburg mints had already from April been turning out eight-groschen pieces at that ratio. Soon all silver coinage was being treated in the same way. In the following years the silver content was reduced first to a ratio of 30, then 35 and (in 1761) 40 *Reichstaler* to one mark of fine silver – a devaluation of almost two-thirds compared with the pre-war Graumann period. Vast numbers of small 'light' coins were also minted, mainly for circulation in Poland. The *Dritteltaler*, one third of a taler (called the 'Ephraimite' after the mint entrepreneur), and the 'Tympfe'* (an 18-groschen piece), both minted in Saxony, were of little value. In July 1758 the payment in gold of Britain's subsidy (£670,000 annually) began, and by the beginning of 1761 the equivalent of 2 million *Reichstaler* had been paid. Half of these were minted as *Mittelfriedrichsdor*, the rest, at the Saxon mints, as 2 million *Augustdor* with a high copper content, the ugliest gold coin of modern times. Three million *Augustdor* in all were coined up to 1762.

With Prussia fighting for her existence during the Seven Years War the king tried every possible means to raise money. Retzow's successor at the Mint Directory – with control of the Breslau Mint and the administration in general – was Lieutenant-General Friedrich Bogislaw von Tauentzien, but actual day-to-day business was carried out by privy

* Named after a seventeenth-century Polish mint master Andreas Tympf. The Polish taler contained 90 groschen, the Prussian (high value) 24.

councillor Friedrich Gotthold Köppen, treasurer of the General War Chest. For the dubious practices sometimes engaged in the king alone was responsible. Once the state's meagre internal credits had been exhausted, the only possible expedient open to him was the much criticized debasement of the Prussian coinage. Frederick, however, went further than this: he authorized state forgery when he copied and at the same time debased foreign currencies. These 'light' coinages were not valid in Prussia, but were sent into the territories of Frederick's enemies. Austria, financially exhausted by heavy interest rates on many loans, became in 1762 the first German state to issue paper currency; her copper coinage was so debased that Prussia's debased silver war-coinage was used in preference by the whole Austrian army.

Frederick had been restocking the state treasure (*Staatsschatz*) throughout the war, leaving not only his enemies but also his own administration completely in the dark about his cash reserves. Only privy cabinet secretary Eichel and war paymaster Köppen in the General Directory were aware of the numerous and various reserves and funds which the king had at his disposal. These were, for the most part, kept separate: the *Staatsschatz* with its subsidiary treasuries (for mobilization, horses, uniforms and iron rations), the general domains treasury, the general war chest, the Breslau military chest of the Silesian provincial administration, the field war chests of the field-war commissariat in Silesia, Pomerania and Saxony, the royal *Dispositionskasse* (the reserve treasury to which the king alone had access) and the *Zentral-Dispositionsfond* ('Köppen's big chest'), which comprised the *Kontributionen* (wartime levies), the profits from the mints, and the British subsidies. From 1758 to 1761 Britain paid Prussia about 27·5 million *Reichstaler*, a smaller sum than Saxony had been forced to contribute. At the end of 1763 the *Staatsschatz* amounted once more to some 14·5 million *Reichstaler*, collected from the surpluses of the various *Kassen*, the *Kontributionen*, the profits from the mints and the balance of the subsidies. This was a considerable reserve if we take into account that the war had cost Prussia 140 million *Reichstaler*. While Austria remained burdened by state debts for decades to come, Prussia emerged from the war with a not inconsiderable *Dispositionsfond*: the victor was he who had the last taler in his pocket. There had always been sufficient precious metal in reserve to have commemorative medals struck immediately after Frederick's victories at Lobositz, Prague, Rossbach, Leuthen (its reverse proudly copied from the Austrian medal issued after Kolin), Liegnitz and Torgau, all bearing the inscription *Fridericus Magnus*.

Immediately after the war Prussia began the reform of her currency.

The taler ratio of 19¾ to one mark of fine silver was restored in 1763 and in 1764 the Graumann ratio of 14 talers to the mark was re-established. A Mint edict of 29 March 1764, the work of Martin Kröncke, director-general of the Mint since the end of 1763, provided for the reduction of the amount of coinage in circulation and its enforced exchange (*Reduktion und Einwechslung*). This calling in and melting down of coins, as well as new and necessary regulations for the payment of debts, hit both the state and private individuals hard: the early post-war years were economically the hardest of the whole reign. The abrupt end to war speculations led to the collapse of numerous Amsterdam and Hamburg banks, which affected the Berlin merchant community adversely. But Frederick was unwilling to shift the financial burden to the future. He wanted to create, as quickly as possible, a financially secure base for a state capable of action. This he achieved. Once Prussia had got over the catastrophic harvests at the beginning of the 1770s, a favourable balance of trade was obtained, thanks to her stable currency.

The acquisition of precious metals for the minting of full-value gold and silver coins presented Prussia with difficulties. In 1783–84 4 million talers' worth of English guineas were bought and recoined. The purchase of gold through Amsterdam made essential the foundation of a Prussian State Bank, planned by Frederick as early as the winter of 1762–63. An Italian, Anton Maria Calzabigi, knowledgeable in finance and the operation of lotteries, had been in touch with the king since a Leipzig meeting in December 1762. Plans for the foundation of a Prussian joint-stock bank on English lines, capitalized at 25 million *Reichstaler* – an enormous sum for Prussia – were worked out in more detail between the autumn of 1764 and the spring of 1765. Frederick realized that because of the differences between English and Prussian conditions he could not count on the public buying shares in the venture, especially at a time of economic difficulties. It was only with the greatest effort and the strong participation of Prussia's administrators and officials that 622,500 talers were raised. The Prussian State Bank was founded on 20 July 1765 and the Dutch financier, Philipp Clement, whose Emden-based Levant Company had foundered, was appointed co-director. The original plan had been modified, the joint-stock aspect had been dropped and not more than 321,000 talers were allotted to the bank which was to be supervised by the General Directory. Minister Ludwig Philipp von Hagen, busy in many affairs, was most active in the bank's direction. Initial teething troubles, attributable to inexperience, the employment of unsatisfactory staff and unprofessional conduct, were slowly overcome; the bank, although engaged in business unfamiliar to Prussian merchants,

won increasing trust. Its growth was promoted by the 1768 royal directive to the law courts ordering the deposit in the bank of all monies
belonging to wards of court at an interest rate of 2 to 3 per cent. Of the
numerous tasks which Calzabigi had proposed for the bank the maintenance of the rate of exchange by discounting bills and the granting of
loans against security were undertaken. The bank increasingly became a
deposit-bank, however, and the clearing-house business was discontinued
as early as 1768. The fact that the bank had little capital of its own was no
real drawback as the *Staatsschatz* provided adequate cover. But this
presupposed the continuance of peace, for only peace could keep the
state reserves in being. As a concession to Silesia a state bank was founded
in Breslau, but this was soon absorbed by the main bank in Berlin.
Branches were also opened at Königsberg, Stettin, Kolberg, Frankfurt
on the Oder, Magdeburg, Minden, Emden and Cleves. The Kolberg
branch was later closed, but bank offices were opened at Memel in 1774
and at Elbing in 1777; and in 1786 the sum on deposit in the head office
in Berlin amounted to 8·6 million talers. The bank thus fulfilled the king's
aim of being useful to the community, though Frederick refused to let it
engage in the mortgage business because of its uncertainty. Almost all the
trade in precious metals, which supplied the mint and in which the
Overseas Trading Company (the *Seehandlung*) coöperated, was transacted through the bank. Its annual profits amounted to some 100,000
Reichstaler, and rose to 200,000 after 1784. The king was well content:
Prussia had successfully embarked on the road towards becoming an
industrial and commercial state in the field of banking.

From Frederick William's reign the state's regular revenues were
derived from the rural *Kontribution* and the urban excise duty (*Akzise*).
In Silesia, and in West Prussia after 1772, the general land tax (the
Generalhufenschoss) was based on the yield of arable land, though at a
lower rate for free peasants and *Kölmer** whose tax level was the lowest in
Europe, amounting only to 33·3 per cent of ascertainable net yield. No
further changes were made either in the method or extent of direct
taxation of land during Frederick's reign; in fact, the general land tax
produced a little more than expected. The indirect urban tax, the
Akzise, however, which had been quite progressive during Frederick
William's reign, proved to be badly in need of re-examination. Its
origins went back to four different tax systems: the *Ziesen* (originally an
excise duty on beer, later extended to other goods) of the sixteenth

---

* *Kölmer*: free landowning peasants whose name derives from the privileges
granted them under the Culmic Law of 1233 for the Prussian territories of the
Teutonic Knights. These privileges continued into the nineteenth century.

century, the *Licenten* (licences) of the seventeenth century, the *Akzise* itself and the new transit duties. These had to be coordinated and brought within the general framework of the state economy; for in the matter of taxation each town worked independently of all the rest and without consideration for the interests of the state as a whole. The General Directory on its own could not bring about the necessary readjustment as four different departments, in addition to the War and Domains chambers, were involved in fiscal administration. Between 1763/4 and 1764/5 the net yield of the *Akzise* fell from 17·3 million to 11·8 million talers. This drop in revenue must be attributed mainly to the financial consequences of the war and the shortage of money consequent on the currency reforms; but it cried out for swift counter-measures. France's fiscal administration was the most developed in Europe and Frederick decided to utilize French experience. He did not wish to copy the French tax system, which would have been unsuitable for Prussia; but in 1766 he took five French taxation experts into his service and instructed them to devise an effective tax administration to eliminate, as far as possible, smuggling and embezzlement, to standardize and simplify working methods, and to normalize tariff-rates. Staff for the offices and the frontier posts was fixed at two thousand, and two hundred of these were obtained from France.

The new *Administration générale des accises et des péages*, usually called the *Regie*, was established by an edict of 9 April 1766; its work began in the same year when contracts for six years were signed with five French chief superintendents (*Generalregisseure*). At the head of this central financial administration, which nominally came under the General Directory, Frederick placed Freiherr Julius August Friedrich von der Horst, till then president of the Kurmark Chamber and now promoted minister of state. The king, with the help of Horst and head of department Ludwig Philipp von Hagen, laid down the fundamental principles of commercial and taxation policies; in charge of the execution of these policies was the French taxation specialist de la Haye de Launay, an experienced, reliable and honourable man. Most of his French colleagues, the other chief superintendents, the provincial directors (all Frenchmen), and the greater number of the two hundred who worked in the *Regie*, were of similar character. The administration of the *Kassen* remained entirely in the hands of Prussian officials. It was not intended that the French experts of the *Regie* should push the Prussians aside; on the contrary, young Prussian officials were trained for the higher ranks of the *Regie* and most subordinate posts were held by Prussians from the start.

When the chief superintendents' contracts expired in 1772, the king, on de Launay's advice, modified the organization to take into account experience gained. In place of the *Kollegium*, which had been without responsibility, a central board (the *Aufgabenstellung*) was set up which did have responsibility. Four chief superintendents were dismissed, leaving de Launay to head the *Regie* assisted by two French and two German deputy-superintendents, each of whom was given charge of a largish tax district: (1) the Kurmark and Neumark; (2) Prussian Lithuania and Pomerania; (3) Silesia; (4) Magdeburg, Halberstadt and Westphalia. In 1774 West Prussia was given its own deputy-superintendent, a Frenchman. De Launay administered the *Generalkasse* of the *Regie* with the help of the general collector (the *Generaleinnehmer*) of the Kurmark. A special accounts bureau audited the accounts for accuracy and accordance with budgetary regulations. Within the provincial and local administration there remained a great number of controllers, supervisors, collectors, inspectors and auditors, a cumbersome bureaucratic apparatus although it had been set up to increase and facilitate trade and commerce. The tollman at the town gate, as for centuries past, collected small imposts on the spot since it proved impossible to expedite the movement of goods via the excise offices. It was not desired that the *Regie* should become a *Rechtsbezirk*, that is, have its own court; but to prevent extortion and embezzlement (which certainly took place) the excise jurisdiction was in 1772 modified so that in the higher courts an independent bench of judges replaced the single judge. Real progress was also made in the tightening of frontier controls. In all provinces excise officers on foot and on horseback – the so-called 'Brigades' – were responsible for the supervision of border and transit traffic. Only by changing from inland tolls to external customs duties was Prussia able to unite all her territories into a unified customs area.

The Prussian public strongly resented the *Regie*. Probably no other measure of Frederick's after the Seven Years War so strained his relationship with his subjects as the frenchified administration of the tax. Yet the *Regie*, while responsible for the collection and administration had no influence in laying down excise rates. It was, however, the method of collecting the tax – the strictness, and even extortion meted out to the public while irregularities committed by officials went undiscovered and unpunished – and the abstract fiscalism of the system which made the *Regie* so detested. Moreover, the *Regie* was equally alien to the regular bureaucracy which disliked its administrative style and its innumerable and dubious encroachments on the preserves of other authorities. The provincial chambers and the General Directory expressed reservations and reported transgressions; but when a frank and critical report of the *Regie* was presented to Frederick in the autumn of 1766 he curtly refused to accept it and condemned privy finance councillor Erhard Ursinus, who had compiled it, to a year in a fortress. Frederick, however, was not blind to the weaknesses of its administration; Heinitz had demonstrated that it was run uneconomically and that in other respects also the results of its endeavours fell behind expectations. In 1783 the king cut its budget so heavily that most of the unpopular supervisors from its middle and lower grades had to depart. At the end of the reign the *Regie* produced a surplus of 23 million talers, but the administrative costs had been high.

Between 1766 and 1768 the imposition of the new *Akzise* brought Frederick into conflict with Neuchâtel (Neuenburg), a dynastic possession (since 1707) which had enjoyed a quiet existence with considerable autonomy, untouched by the great political events of the age. Situated in the foothills of the Swiss Jura, this region, mainly inhabited by French-speaking farmers, had some significance as a reservoir of settlers for Prussia. Military protection of Neuchâtel and responsibility for its judicial affairs had been given to Berne, and it was this fact which decided the struggle over an increase in the Neuchâtel taxes in Prussia's disfavour. Riots broke out and on 24 April 1768 advocate-general Gaudot was murdered. Lieutenant-General Joseph Cäsar Freiherr von Lentulus, a Bernese by birth who had entered the Prussian service in 1757, was appointed governor of Neuchâtel by Frederick and, ably helped by the president of the Gelderland-Moers Chamber, Friedrich Wilhelm von Derschau, who was sent as a special envoy, he restored order once the people had been guaranteed their ancient rights. The king had to reconcile himself to this outcome in much the same way as he had to accept defeat in a matter that touched him more deeply, his failure to have asylum granted to Jean Jacques Rousseau in Neuchâtel.

The *Regie* could not be worked in all Prussian territories. In West-phalia it had to be abolished in 1772, as the local peasants, harassed by *Regie* officials, either stopped visiting the town markets or took their produce to the nearest non-Prussian market. The *Regie* also lost the important state prerogative of the Post after three years, when it was given to a Prussian postmaster general. The king's rigid adherence to a centralized financial administration shows that he was, above all, pursuing social aims in his taxation policy; in addition to increasing the revenue he was trying to shift the burden of taxation. The strictly protectionist policy, designed to profit the state's own trade, was comple-mented by regulations that show that Frederick wished to spare as much as possible the poor sections of the population. The *Akzise* on flour and malt was completely removed, thereby lowering the price of bread; and while the tax on pork was maintained at a constant level the tax on the rarer kinds of meat was increased. Steep import duties were levied on luxury goods, especially on tobacco and coffee, 'a delicacy that is very injurious to the state, for it drains much money abroad to pay for it'. The *General-Tabaks-Pachtungs-Gesellschaft* (General Tobacco Leasehold Company), founded in 1765, had already lost its share capital by 1766, thanks to the unfortunate management of Calzabigi; after temporary control by the *Regie*, a state-owned General Tobacco Administration was established, the profits of which were to benefit the Royal *Dispositionskasse*. The General Tobacco Administration eventually produced earnings of 1·2 million talers a year. In 1781 coffee also became a monopoly under *Regie* administration, with sole rights to the sale of roasted and ground coffee. To ensure that the *Regie*'s privileges were observed 200 (later 400) state controllers (the 'Coffee-Sniffers') were employed, but their intrusion into private households was widely resented. In spite of the reduction in the price of coffee and its increased consumption, the *Regie* was never able to produce a surplus of more than 96,000 talers a year.

Could the General Directory have administered the taxation policy better or cheaper than the *Regie*? Frederick often pondered this question, but this would have necessitated comprehensive reforms: the 'old fogeys' (in German *die Alten Perücken*, literally 'old wigs') in the department chambers were not yet accustomed to modern fiscal techniques. There is no doubt that the *Regie*, despite its many unpleasant aspects, assisted the growth of state centralism in Prussia. The general administration of the finances was retained by the old authorities and successfully developed by them. The *Ober-Rechnungskammer* (Chief Bureau of Accounts), established in the seventeenth century on the Dutch model, was exemplary. In 1745 Frederick transferred it from the Town Palace to the Marstall; it worked under the king's eyes and the confidential nature of its activities was constantly emphasized. Frederick in 1750 criticized its irresponsible carelessness in the auditing of the Halle salt treasury, but expressed satisfaction with its work in 1768; in 1784 it participated in the revision of the Berlin public funds. It is noteworthy that of seven presidents of the bureau during Frederick's reign six were of bourgeois origin and, of these, five were later ennobled. Against the wishes of the General Directory the king considerably strengthened the *Oberrechnungshof* (Chief Accounts Court), 'the ruler's eye': it was not there to provide sinecures for senile councillors. Its membership was small: four privy finance councillors with small salaries but high reputations laboured under its president.

At the end of his reign Frederick had more than 51 million talers in the *Staatsschatz* and its associated funds. With this amount of money he could have waged six campaigns without raising taxes or incurring debts. The Prussian state had, for the first time in its history, become encumbered with public debts when the annexation of Silesia meant that Prussia had to take over that province's debts to the tune of 11·3 million Rhenish gulden. These were quickly paid off, in part from the British subsidies of the Seven Years War. Apart from two compulsory loans during that war – and the war loans of 1745 – Frederick kept almost obsessively free of debt. This gave him almost unlimited possibilities in the use of his own financial means and resources. His reserves never reached the rumoured 100 million talers but – given the basic poverty of the country – Prussia's financial accomplishments during his reign are astonishing. They are a testimonial to the energy of its population and the financial management of its ruler. In his memoirs Frederick wrote:

> Government must not limit itself to one function. Advantage alone must not be the sole impetus to action. The public welfare, which includes so many branches, presents a wealth of tasks to which it must dedicate itself. A financial system, handed over by father to son and constantly improved, can change a government's position. From being originally poor it can make a government so rich that it can throw its grain into the scales of the balance between the European great powers.

V

The Second Rétablissement

Administrative Reform

Life-long admiration for his father's administrative achievements, which he regarded as a model of their kind, made Frederick reluctant to tamper with existing institutions. The *rétablissement* of East Prussia had led to the organization of the *Gesamtstaat*, and Frederick hoped to leave it at that. But it could not be denied that, forty years after Frederick William's death, the state had changed: its territory had expanded, the population had increased and with this had come the need for more arable land; domains and manufactures, towns and trade had grown; and after long and destructive wars reconstruction work was urgently needed. It was this work that brought with it modernization of the Prussian administration. Neither could be achieved through isolated decrees; a whole series of coordinated measures, which together developed into a second great *rétablissement*, were necessary.

Prussia had lost almost 400,000 inhabitants in the Seven Years War, more than 10 per cent of the total population of 1756, and almost 20 per cent of the estimated population of 1740. Given Prussia's circumstances and the low density of population, this was an enormous loss. East Prussia, with 90,410 dead or deported, had suffered most, followed by Pomerania (72,216), the Neumark (57,028), the Kurmark (56,993), Silesia (46,088) and Magdeburg-Mansfeld (7,186). The remaining 65,000 had been lost from the western provinces, where a fluctuating population made the gathering of exact returns difficult. These figures, collected by the War and Domains chambers, laid the groundwork for statistical studies and valuations, even if uncertainty about the methods used in their compilation made them, at first, unreliable for comparative analysis.

In the scientific plotting of population movements a useful supplementary aid was the ordnance survey, necessitated by the compilation of an assessment roll (*Kataster*). By its exact measurements the pro-

ductivity of farms could be determined more closely, the extent of the
domains and the precise position of the frontiers ascertained. Plans of
towns and fortresses were made and land improvement schemes and
settlements were prepared. Many fundamental innovations and simpli-
fications were introduced in this field during the Frederician period
with the aim – as elsewhere – of standardizing the various traditional
peculiarities. No less than twelve different ways of measuring length
were in current use, varying from the old Oletzkoschian *Rute* of 4·172 m
to the great Neumark *Rut* of 5·021 m. The Rhenish *Rute*, 4·666 m in
length, was on 28 October 1773 declared the standard Prussian *Rute*. The
Brandenburg mile of the eighteenth century corresponds to the modern
figure of 7,407·41 m, the Silesian mile to 6,479·024 m and the Breslau
Rute to 4,319 m. A first instruction for surveyors, worked out by the
War and Domains chambers of Königsberg and Gumbinnen, was
issued on 20 November 1755 and became the standard for the other
Prussian territories. In 1766 a surveyor's table with telescope and
hydrostatic balance, improved by the Augsburg mechanic Brander, was
introduced. The training of the engineer corps was carried out in
accordance with principles established in Electoral Saxony. Surveying,
which for economic reasons had mainly been carried out by army
personnel, was gradually taken over by civilians, for example, those
serving in the chambers and in the forestry department. In 1776, at
the instigation of the General Directory and minister of justice von
Zedlitz, a training school for cartography and topography was set
up in the Berlin Schloss, and the French professor Marsson was put
in charge. The king contributed to the development of cartography;
he drew topographical sketches and made suggestions for others.
Interest was shown in all provinces, and impressive results were at
times achieved.

Apart from setting up the Fifth Department Frederick had left the
central authorities, above all the General Directory, unchanged. By the
end of the Seven Years War that generation of leading ministers which
he had taken over from his father had disappeared: Friedrich von Görne
in the First Department, Franz Wilhelm von Happe in the Second,
August Friedrich von Boden in the Third and Adam Otto von Viereck
in the Fourth. Görne died in 1745 at the age of seventy-five, Viereck in
1758 aged seventy-four, Happe in 1760 at the age of seventy-six, and
Boden in 1762 at seventy-nine. Although towards the end Frederick was
not satisfied with their performances under the stress of war, he left them
in office as he feared harming the Directory by making changes in
personnel. Görne's successor, Adam Ludwig von Blumenthal, president

of the Gumbinnen Chamber and a trusted collaborator of Frederick
William I, died in 1761 aged seventy.

In an attempt to match ministerial functions to personal abilities
Frederick had in 1747 transferred the weakest of the departmental heads,
Happe (who had come from the diplomatic service), to the Fourth
Department, put Viereck in the Third, and given Boden the most
important department, the Second. In March 1759 – the year of his
worst crises – Frederick reprimanded this man, the best qualified and
most experienced of his officials, in a harsh and offensive manner because
he had presented a document at an inopportune moment. Boden
answered, 'For over fifty years I have honestly served the Royal House
and despite my seventy-six years and all the persecution meted out to me
I shall continue to serve for the remainder of my life. . . . As long as I
have my faculties and while it pleases Your Majesty, I shall not cease to
work faithfully and conscientiously, without any thought of self.' This
dignified reply shamed Frederick, though he retained his ingrained
suspicions of red tape and laziness – suspicions which were quite unjustified in Boden's case.

The king's wartime experiences and the deaths of the older generation
of administrators led him, after 1763, not only to appoint younger men
to top posts but also to refashion the General Directory. His instruction
of 1748 had aimed at prompter dispatch of routine business for which, in
the king's opinion, three hours each morning should suffice: 'If they pass
the time gossiping and reading newspapers then the whole day is not long
enough.' He was also keen to delimit and coordinate the work of the
various departments. This proved difficult, however, since the duties of
the departments increased and intertwined so that an overall view proved
nearly impossible and *ad hoc* decisions had to be taken. Three ministerial
colleges, or boards, existed side by side: the Department of Justice, which
met daily at the State Council (the *Staatsrat*); the Department of External
Affairs, which formed a separate authority under the direction of the
king; and the General Directory, the original function of which had
been the administration of the finances. In 1766 this task became the
responsibility of the Fourth Department, the Customs and Excise
Administration (the *Zoll- und Akzise-Verwaltung*) – the *Regie* – only
nominally subordinate to the General Directory. At the same time, the
Regie was relieved of all other duties of the Fourth Department, and
especially of its territorial responsibilities for Halberstadt with Hohenstein, Minden, Ravensberg, Tecklenburg and Lingen. These, together
with the administration of currency matters and also, from 1771,
Magdeburg with Mansfeld, were transferred to the Third Department,

which became responsible for all the western provinces, for stamp duties and for the affairs of disabled and retired soldiers. Between 1747 and 1769 the Third Department, for its part, handed over control of the post and the salt administrations to the Second Department, though both later acquired greater independence when the General Salt Administration and the General Post Office were established. Provisioning had been put under the Sixth Department at an earlier date. Finally, the 'Prusso-Lithuanian Department', formerly part of the First Department, was made independent in 1769; within its jurisdiction lay the Königsberg and Gumbinnen chambers and, from 1774, the province of West Prussia and the administration of the affairs of the treasuries in general. The provinces of Pomerania and the Neumark, the *Tresor* (Exchequer) and currency matters (originally controlled by the Third Department) remained under the control of the First. A decree of April 1769 ordered that all departments were in future to be identified – like army regiments – by the names of their managing ministers of state rather than by their numbers or functions; but in practice this did not happen.

From the establishment of the Fifth and Sixth departments of the General Directory Prussian administrative practice developed along lines ever more alien to Frederick William I's system. The separation of the Customs and Excise Department from the rest of the administration and the establishment of new departments for Mining and Metallurgy (1768) and Forestry (1770) continued this trend. If one adds to these the administration of justice, the diplomatic service, the Supreme Building Authority (*Ober-Bau-Departement*), the church and school administrations, and the independent Chief Bureau of Accounts (*Ober-Rechnungskammer*) one can distinguish a continuous development of the old and still regionally orientated General Directory into separate functional departments. This rather drastic transformation was possible and feasible only because the king had developed into a virtuoso in the art of administration, confidently assuming administrative burdens far removed from the normal demands of an organically-structured state. The highly flexible and astonishingly small government apparatus was, indeed, something of a miracle, but one which worked only under the immediate and continuous presence of its activating force. The absence of any supreme coordinating authority, superior to the several functional ministries, allowed the cabinet – the working methods of which were devised to suit Frederick's personality – to imprint its character on the administration during the later years of the reign.

Such a development was far in the future when in 1748 Frederick issued a document unique in the history of Prussian administration: the new Instruction of 20 May 1748 for the General Directory. Here was an attempt to create a comprehensive constitution for the Directory, the success of which was to depend more on the conformity of ministers to its aims than on a literal observation of its rules. In assuming the presidency of the General Directory the king took on the never-ending task of settling the inevitable departmental squabbles and jurisdictional disputes. Prussia, like other states, was to discover that rules and regulations were not necessarily the most effective lubricants for the administrative machine. While Frederick William I's few home-made rules certainly needed amplification and modification, Frederick II's cabinet secretaries could not imagine the king departing from his father's system. Yet in the summer of 1748 he devoted much work to a clause by clause revision and modernization of the Instructions of 1722. For years Frederick had been in the habit of castigating the General Directory for its negligence and inefficiency, particularly in its management of the treasuries. Many irregularities had, indeed, been uncovered; the most alarming was the embezzlement, from 1746 onwards, of 40,000 talers by the Pomeranian war councillor Liebeherr (whom the king had at first protected against the timely warnings of the General Directory). In the preface to the Instruction of 1748 the introduction of a new version of the service regulations was defended by the need

> to awaken the General Directory which had, in the course of time, often fallen into slovenliness and to persuade it to mend its ways through honest, hard work and once again place duty in first place. This *Collegium* is one of the largest and foremost in the country and the welfare of the state, the country and the people depends in large measure on its industry, conscientiousness and activity. The more important the office, the greater and more constant the vigilance, diligence and incorruptibility it demands.

In thirty-seven main articles duties were defined and responsibilities distributed. Ministers were allowed to propose their collaborators. The utmost promptitude was inculcated as was the constant inspection of towns, domains and villages, regular and punctual meetings, more systematic compilation of statistics and stricter supervision of the treasuries and the chancery personnel. Detailed instructions were laid down for dealing with incoming documents and for appointing substitutes during absence or illness. The king's own experiences were responsible for article II, clause 5, one of the eighty-four changes and additions made by the king himself to the Instruction of 1722: it laid down that ministers 'were not to waste time over *particularia* and the settling of rarified disputes; if within six minutes any dispute remained unsettled a *relatio ad regem* was to be drawn up immediately'. Conflicts between departments, therefore, were not seen from a fundamental or theoretical point of view, but solely in relation to their practical consequences and as capable of being resolved. The Instruction abounds in illustrations of this and shows that the king's approach to the problems of state administration was empirical rather than theoretical. The aim and essence of his work was not the creation of an ideal constitution, but the formation of a functional state machine with all the rough edges, anomalies and frictions that this implied.

While the General Directory's sphere of activities, its structure and its responsibilities later underwent changes, the internal service regulations remained in force until long after Frederick the Great's death. This was even more true for the provincial administrations for which the 'Revised Instruction for the General-Chief-Finance-War-and-Domains Directory' of 20 May 1748 established clear-cut guidelines. This royal instruction, marked highly secret, was sent the next day to the ministers of the General Directory to serve as a framework for special instructions designed for the provincial chambers. These were ready within four weeks, regional peculiarities having been taken into account. This achievement is highly characteristic of the Prussian absolutist period: royal initiative followed by speedy action. The regulations for East Prussia, Lithuania, Pomerania and the Neumark were worded alike; but those for the other provinces – especially the western ones – show, at times, sharp regional variations, mainly in the form of supplementary or special instructions. Silesia, which did not come under the authority of the General Directory, was not covered. Frederick approved his ministers' proposals with only a small number of changes. Throughout the exercise the king had asked for advice from his administrative experts, and had collaborated with them.

The result was an improved set of business-like regulations which in the following years were amended as needs arose. They give us unique insights into the daily workings of the Prussian administration of Frederick II's later reign; they also lead to the conclusion that Frederick William I's Instruction was not fundamentally altered by his son.

The reconstruction that took place after the Seven Years War was decided on when impatient instructions and frequent admonitions had failed to achieve the quick results Frederick desired. But even during the reconstruction the king took the utmost care to reorganize the administration cautiously and by degrees. Except with the *Regie*, what is most striking are the half-measures. Frederick avoided ministerial changes throughout his reign; his dismissal in 1740 of Eckart, an official with special responsibilities, had been an exceptional though popular move. The most spectacular dismissal in later years came with the imprisonment at Spandau in January 1782 of Friedrich Christoph von Görne (son of the old minister) for large-scale embezzlement. His career had been dazzling: head of the Fourth and Fifth departments since 1774 (when von der Hort retired because of illness), and Director of the Overseas Trading Company and the Salt Company. He was succeeded in both departments by the Prussian envoy in Copenhagen, the thirty-two-year-old August Wilhelm von Bismarck. After Bismarck's death in 1783 his duties were handed over to Heinitz, already responsible for the Mining and Metallurgy Department (the Seventh); but professional disputes within the Fourth and Fifth departments caused Heinitz' resignation from both. He remained at the Mining Department, brought its administration to the highest pitch of efficiency, and kept, on the whole, Frederick's confidence. Heinitz' strong attack on the *Regie* in 1783 decisively hastened the king's disenchantment with the French system, but even Heinitz could not make Frederick break completely with de Launay. Heinitz himself suffered periods of near disgrace with dignity and Christian fortitude; while remembering his place, he gave the king tit for tat in argument, generally making his point and always justifying the measures he himself had taken. Heinitz managed all along to make Frederick spend large sums on behalf of the Seventh Department; no mean feat, for Frederick – as Heinitz himself noted in his diary – 'looked after the income of the state as if he might be held accountable for it each and every day'.

Heinitz was correct in his analysis of the extreme interdependence between customs, excise, manufacture, commerce and industry; and it was on these grounds that he refused to carry out mere supervisory duties in the General Directory while the *Regie* functioned independently and without regard for the economy of the state as a whole. Obstructive measures by *Regie* officials, for example, had badly hit the fair at Frankfurt; it could not flourish in the *Regie* climate. Heinitz succeeded in preventing the taxation of home-produced goods that the *Regie* had planned to compensate for tax remissions on exports. He failed, however, to achieve a projected advantageous customs convention with Poland as the *Regie* succeeded in sabotaging his plan; nor was he able to persuade the king to lower any of the formidable customs barriers which surrounded Prussia.

The fundamental reason for this was that the state was not yet an organic political economy. Regional and general tasks were still inextricably interwoven in the organization of the old General Directory, and the increasing trend towards functional departments was bound to lead to demarcation disputes between them, making cooperation difficult. Emanuel Fäsch, the experienced Swiss merchant, who from 1750 was the real head of the Fifth Department (though without the title of minister), was so alarmed at the growth of an almost sovereign finance and tax administration that in January 1766 he defined the borders of the Fifth Department (the department most threatened by the new development) as he saw them. His concern was in line with the programme initiated by Frederick in 1740; on his list were the general improvement of trade, the establishment of new branches of industry, improvements in the manufacture of luxury goods such as silk and velvet, and such high-quality products as, for example, type-faces, printed cottons, knives and scissors, and the recruitment of suitable workmen. But he also claimed the fairs of Leipzig, Brunswick and Frankfurt on the Oder, the 'extraordinaries' such as banking and insurance, the overseas trading companies, the timber trade and the tobacco monopoly – all matters which were soon, to a greater or lesser extent, removed from the General Directory. The ponderous expedient of informing other departments or the royal cabinet of these 'extraordinaries' to obtain their comments and their help was attempted, but clear directives could scarcely be expected from such a procedure. The king's policy was clear: he wanted a flexibility that would permit change and experiment and, above all, supreme control. A *marginalia* of the spring of 1766 laid down that 'the gentlemen [i.e. the ministers] are employed to carry out my orders, not to interfere. ... they must obediently let themselves be governed, and must not take over the government.' Fäsch was fighting a losing battle. By the end of 1766 the Fourth Department, under minister von der Horst, secured priority in dealing with incoming matters of the Fifth Department; soon afterwards he was formally granted equal say in commercial and industrial matters; a year later it was decreed that the affairs of the Fifth Department were not to be placed before the plenum of the General Directory but pass, 'without further enquiries', directly to the king via Horst; and until Frederick's death the Fourth and Fifth departments remained in the control of one and the same man. The functions of the Fifth Department were extended by the inclusion of a *Manufacturkommission*, established in 1767, which carried out bi-weekly inspections of the silk factories and maintained the stipulated quality and quantity of the merchandise. Dodo Heinrich Freiherr von Knyphausen, formerly envoy in London, joined the ministry in 1765 as *Commissaire général de Commerce*, distinguishing himself through numerous statistical reports and the revival of the regular bulletins of the chambers on economic development. On Horst's resignation, because of illness, in 1774 the younger Görne was appointed to his post as head of the Fourth and Fifth departments. His overbearing manner caused Knyphausen's resignation early in 1775; he was succeded by another ex-diplomat, Adrian Heinrich von Borcke, Prussian envoy in Dresden. In March 1777 Fäsch took his leave, after twenty-seven years of futile waiting for a ministerial post. Following Görne's arrest in 1782, Heinitz administered the Fourth and Fifth departments for a year. At the beginning of 1784 Hans Ernst Dietrich Freiherr von Werder, former army officer and later rural commissioner of Ziesar, took over both departments, as well as the Salt Department and the General Post-mastership (up to then within the sphere of the Second Department).

The Sixth Department (the war department) also depended on cooperation with the other departments of the General Directory; since its foundation in 1746 methods had evolved for this though no special regulations had been laid down. But Frederick's participation in the work of the Sixth Department in reality took it out of the sphere of the General Directory and moved it into the close proximity of the royal cabinet and the adjutant-general. Its other main link was, through the *Generalauditeur*, with the Justice Department. The Seventh Department (Mines and Metallurgy) was equally independent, having acquired on its very foundation in 1768 the privilege of conducting its own business without having to wait for the weekly meeting of the General Directory. This position, won by Hagen, proved extremely useful to Heinitz in his long and successful career. The newest department – the Eighth – which dealt with forestry, was also set up by Hagen. In 1772 it was taken over by Schulenburg, who was also in charge of the Third Department and of banking. He put *Landjägermeister* von Lüderitz in charge of the forestry service, but got rid of him in 1775 on the grounds that it was to the detriment of that service to be separated from other sections of the financial administration. The factual accuracy of this could not be denied; here too the disadvantages and dangers resulting from administrative division made themselves felt. While metallurgy, being still in its infancy, needed a steady, even-paced growth, timber was Prussia's most important raw material and an essential part of her economy. All the same, Lüderitz' energetic and wide-ranging activities had ensured the orderly development of forestry administration in East and West Prussia and in Pomerania. In 1770 the indefatigable Hagen had set up the Supreme Building Department (*Ober-Bau-Departement*) as a collegiate authority of the General Directory with Gottfried Konrad Wilhelm Struve at its head. Instructions assigned the following duties to the experts of the department: public buildings, the revision of all estimates of costs, the checking of timber-permits (*Deputatholzanforderungen*), the construction of dykes, harbours and locks, the testing of machinery and materials, the supervision of chemical laboratories and of the teaching of higher mathematics. The work begun by Knobelsdorff had thus, thirty years later, developed into a scientific department with an important workload.

The General Directory, as we have seen, was responsible for supervising the administrative work of the War and Domains chambers which constituted the actual provincial governments. The king never lost sight of their role as the true executive authority in the provinces, and detailed reports from his distant territories provided him with as much information as his tours of inspection in the Kurmark, Neumark and Silesia. The nine chambers created by the great administrative Instruction of 1722 had, fifty years later, become twelve: the Kurmark, the Neumark, Pomerania, East Prussia (Königsberg), Lithuania (Gumbinnen), West Prussia (Marienwerder), Magdeburg (with Halberstadt-Hohenstein), Minden, Cleves-Mark (with Moers and Gelderland), East Friesland, Breslau and Glogau. On 13 April 1772 Moers and Gelderland, previously independent chambers, were united into one *Kammerdeputation*, sitting at Moers and subordinate to the War and Domains Chamber in Cleves. Other provinces also experienced major structural changes. A *Kammerdeputation* in Lingen for Tecklenburg-Lingen, subordinate to the Chamber in Minden, helped in 1769 to create better demarcation lines in the scattered and structurally varied western provinces. Frederick had meant to create an independent chamber for the county of Mark, and on 6 November 1766 signed an order to this effect; but the next year – probably because of staffing problems – this plan was transformed so that a *Kammerdeputation*, subordinate to the Chamber of Cleves, was set up in Hamm. On 10 November 1763 the establishment of a *Kammerdeputation* at Köslin, subordinate to the Chamber at Stettin was made responsible for the administration of an area stretching from the eastern borders of Further Pomerania to the Persante, as the territory was too remote to be effectively administered from Stettin. In 1769 minister of state von Derschau suggested the establishment of a separate War and Domains Chamber for the Altmark, because of the straggling nature of the Kurmark and the consequent burden of administration. Frederick largely accepted his argument and, on 8 February 1770, authorized not an independent chamber, but a *Kammerdeputation* at Stendal for the Altmark-Prignitz area, subordinate to the Kurmark Chamber in Berlin. Related changes took place in Halberstadt-Hohenstein where the Chamber was dissolved on 13 February 1770, to be replaced by two Chamber-committees, one for Halberstadt and the other for Hohenstein (sitting at Ellrich), both subordinate to the Chamber at Magdeburg. Prussia's oldest *Kammerdeputation*, that for the Saal district (sitting at Halle), was already under the Magdeburg Chamber, which was thus in charge of no less than three subordinate and quite distinct departments. At Marien-werder, in 1772, the West Prussian War and Domains Chamber was established with a *Kammerdeputation* for the Netze district (sitting at Bromberg). On two separate occasions Frederick took up his father's plan for the establishment of a *Kammerdeputation* for the Oberland at Neidenburg. He failed, partly because of the cost involved, but mainly because of the stubborn resistance of the Königsberg Chamber, which, since the Gumbinnen *Deputation* had become an independent chamber, feared that Masuria might follow that pattern. Minister of state von Blumenthal, who carried out an on-the-spot investigation for the king, effected as a compromise solution a re-distribution of *Kreise* between the two East Prussian chambers. Domhardt, the first effective president-in-chief of the province, had a chance to clear up the anomalies left by Blumenthal in the period of chamber adjustments in the 1770s but was unable to use the opportunity. His imaginative, but expensive, Johannis-burg timber-logging canal had cost a great deal more money than expected; he was in no position to assume additional obligations, nor could he expect the General Directory to help him. Thus, in contrast to the general rationalization of the chamber administration achieved in Frederick's reign, one anachronism remained in East Prussia, which became more of a disadvantage as the nineteenth century progressed. From 1779 until Frederick II's death there were in the whole monarchy twelve War and Domains chambers along with nine subordinate chamber-committees.

The establishment of the numerous chamber-committees did not ease the pressure of work on the chambers. The General Directory feared that the subordinate institutions would duplicate work and waste time, since they lacked the power of independent decision and also the authority wielded by a chamber president, equal in standing to the Assembly of Estates. Frederick did not wish to increase the chambers in numbers; he argued that there were already too many and pointed to the fact that in Austria much larger territories were administered by bodies similar to the chambers. He held that chamber-committees could deal better and quicker with administrative problems on the spot and that therefore small War and Domains chambers should be abolished and – if necessary

– replaced by chamber-committees. This was done and the smaller authorities proved better suited than the larger conformist administrative bodies to cope with the regional peculiarities that still survived. That Prussia was far from being a fully centralized administrative state is demonstrated by what happened in the principality of Moers and the duchy of Gelderland (Upper Quarter). Not till 1763 were these western territories, insufficiently supervised and financially neglected, brought together in a common War and Domains Chamber with its seat at Moers, the *Kammerdeputation* of Moers having ceased to exist in 1756. During the process of dissolving small chambers the *Kammerdeputation* of Moers was reinstated to be supervised by the Cleves Chamber. The Estates in Gelderland succeeded, after tough negotiations with the General Directory and against the objection of the *Regie*, in having it replaced by a '*Geldrische Landes-Administrations-Collegium*', set up at Guelders. This institution, unique within the Frederician administration (approved by the king on 13 March 1770), came directly under the Third Department of the General Directory. Administratively it enjoyed equal status with a War and Domains chamber, but it was a mixed *Kollegium* under the chairmanship of a royal councillor; it consisted of three royal councillors and three representatives of the Estates. From 1779 Moers had only a *deputatus* in the Cleves Chamber.

What was allowed in Gelderland, however, had already been denied to the Pomeranian Estates, without the king having to intervene, in an attempt to curb separatist tendencies. As early as 1752 the *Ritterschaft* and Estates of Lauenburg-Bütow had protested because the Estates *Oberhauptmann* had to take orders from the War and Domains Chamber at Stettin. The king refused their protest: he did not want to see re-established the old Estates constitution which 'gets everything into a turmoil'. After the Seven Years War they tried again, making the acceptance of the post of *Oberhauptmann* conditional on having their grievance remedied. The Stettin Chamber countered by withholding that official's salary. *Grosskanzler* von Fürst had to have recourse to the law-courts to settle the issue – not without a sigh that 'Lauenburg and Bütow make more trouble than many a large province'. In the summer of 1771 the Estates revived the quarrel. The former War and Domains councillor von Woedtke had become *Oberhauptmann* and demanded that the Stettin Chamber should write to him *per modum litterarum* and not order him *in stylo curiae*. The *Ritterschaft* and Estates had asserted that they took orders only from the General Directory, not from the Chamber 'with which the country has nothing directly to do'. The Chamber, for its part, complained bitterly that 'the Estates were once more pretending that their *Oberhauptmann* was the equivalent of a *Kammer-Collegium*, while his rank was in reality that of a rural commissioner'. The General Directory's decision that the *Landtag* should be convened not oftener than at six-monthly intervals eventually succeeded in dampening down Lauenburg's desire for self-government. Von Fürst admitted that 'these districts [i.e. Lauenburg-Bütow], because of their constitution and privileges, cannot be treated like other provinces'. By this time, however, Prussia no longer paid much attention to the articles of the 1657 Bromberg Convention, which made provision for the cession of Lauenburg and Bütow to Poland should the House of Hohenzollern become extinct, nor to the article which obliged the House to receive them as a fief from the hands of each newly-crowned king of Poland. In effect, on 18 September 1773 Poland surrendered these rights.

Silesia remained outside the jurisdiction of the General Directory. The province succeeded in retaining a certain independence and was permitted to keep something of the Estates tradition. West Prussia also succeeded briefly in maintaining an exceptional position, but in the third year after its annexation it was put under the General Directory. The Kurmark, as the first of Prussia's provinces, aspired to a special rank without ever really attaining it: having the most important royal residences and all the central authorities within its borders meant that it was constantly under the king's eyes, and that all decisions and reforms affected it immediately. In the Kurmark therefore the War and Domains Chamber maintained its position as the sole competent administrative authority, if under the shadow of the General Directory, while Königsberg, the East Prussian capital with the ancient title of 'Royal Seat of the Kingdom of Prussia', boasted a *Regierung* that had survived from its ducal past. There, despite the reforms of 1751, the *Regierung* competed with the War and Domains chambers of Königsberg and Gumbinnen for authority over feudal services and *Kassen*, as also in the fight against epidemics, supreme supervision over ecclesiastical affairs, frontier questions, vassal lists, the college of wards, affairs of the academy and the libraries, the auditing of hospital and church finances, publication of edicts and numerous other matters of lesser importance. The administration of justice had, however, been taken decisively out of the hands of the *Regierung*. It is significant that this reform had become necessary three years after the Instruction for the Prussian Chamber (of 1748) to help establish the new system; after the elucidation of the judicial position a further decree (of 1752) was necessary to provide the chancery with regulations of its own. The real unification of the East Prussian provincial administration did not take place till Domhardt's appointment in 1762; the extensive 'Revised Instruction for the Royal Prussian Government' of 30 July 1774 was passed to make a formal end to old practices. It would therefore be true to say that nowhere within the Prussian administrative system did Frederician absolutism rule 'with the stroke of a royal pen'.

During a conference with his ministers of state on 24 December 1769 Frederick frankly admitted to Hagen and von Derschau that his hesitation in reforming the larger administrative bodies sprang from the fact that 'there was a great scarcity of capable people and one would not know how to go about finding presidents and others'. Only very rarely and in pressing cases did the king change ministers, though he frequently dismissed chamber presidents. One of Frederick's early plans was the opening of 'training sections' for higher civil servants – a *pepinière* (literally 'a plant nursery') – since the establishment of an administrative academy was considered too expensive and elaborate for the small number of officials involved. Because theoretical training was of much less value than practical experience, the excellently-run Silesian chambers were highly regarded as *pepinières*. From 1769 onwards potential chamber presidents and directors spent some months working in the General Directory before being appointed to leading positions. Only 'qualified nobles' could be appointed chamber presidents, though 'outstandingly intelligent burghers' could, with the king's express permission, become chamber directors. Eight promising civil servants were chosen by Hagen for the first 'training semester', which lasted from Easter to Michaelmas 1770. On completion of the course they were transferred to the General Directory and within a year three of them had become presidents or directors. Another semester was held in 1771. Officials were, of course, expected to continue to educate themselves and to keep informed on the latest principles of administration: the General Directory pointed out that it had bought Mylius' collection of edicts, the *Novum Corpus Constitutionum*, published by the Prussian Academy, from its own funds, but had been encouraged to hope for a grant towards the purchase.

In view of the high standard demanded the selection of suitable candidates, usually proposed by the General Directory to the king, was a difficult task. Few of the more intelligent young aristocrats were prepared to commit themselves to so strict, exhausting and ill-paid a service. A university education was almost obligatory, especially for younger sons, though Frederick placed a higher value on practice than on theory, especially when it came to selection of chamber presidents. Officials with only theoretical training in cameralism were increasingly less preferred for presidential posts and rural commissioners, men used to acting on their own initiative, were appointed. In order to eliminate as far as possible indigenous rights, promotions, even when made *in loco* – because familiarity with regional conditions was important – went to men not originally natives of the province. Only four of Frederick's forty chamber presidents came from the officer corps, so that the appointment of military men to this office was exceptional. No less than 25 per cent of all appointees eventually failed to come up to expectations. The reasons for premature dismissal were not, of course, always professional or just, but royal displeasure became dangerous only after a lengthy period and many complaints. The onset of old age, or increasing incompetence, were not normally considered valid criteria for dismissal; neither factor was held against the once-respected von Lesgewang, president of the Königsberg Chamber, despite the increasing inefficiency and chaos of his administration. At Minden Rochow's carelessness and indifference was such that he regarded his dismissal as a release: at last he could devote himself to his estates. At Stettin Grumbkow let the reins go completely and quarrelled with his staff. Only the dissolution of the Moers Chamber ended Werder's long reign of inaction. 'Fat Bredow', who had advised against his own promotion at Königsberg, did not escape the presidential office. Both Aschersleben in Pomerania and von der Groeben in the Kurmark did not live up to their respective tasks during the Seven Years War; only a timely resignation enabled Ribbeck in Halberstadt to escape the threatening storm. Dacheröden showed himself as little able to administer Minden as Wegnern was to administer East Friesland, or Below West Prussia; all three had to be promptly replaced. So had *Landrat* von Luck (to whom Frederick was well disposed), whose responsibilities in the Cleves Chamber put him into a state of deep depression. Apathy and inaction brought about Winckel's dismissal from his post at Magdeburg.

Every provincial administration in the state experienced such and similar changes in personnel. No doubt the *marginalia* with which the king adorned chamber reports and petitions were partly responsible for undermining the confidence of weak personalities or causing them to seek refuge in resignation. A handwritten postscript, admittedly exceptionally severe, addressed to the West Prussian War and Domains Chamber on 26 April 1780, throws light on the methods by which 'fear of the master' was inculcated: 'You are a thorough-going pack of scoundrels, not worth the bread you eat. The whole lot of you deserve to be given the boot. Just wait till I come to Prussia.' Similar, though less harshly expressed sentiments can be found in the rescript of the General Directory: 'Only an effort is needed but nobody thinks of that! Everything is neglected.' The *Dienstmechanismus* (excessive attachment to bureaucratic routine) which Freiherr vom Stein criticized time and time again was not 'Frederician' in origin: it had been continuously and sharply condemned by the king throughout his reign.

In spite of the examples cited above there is no doubt that the majority of presidents conducted themselves ably in their office. Exceptionally gifted administrators served Frederick, men such as Caspar Wichard von Platen at Magdeburg and Domhardt, president-in-chief in East and West Prussia and thus in control of three War and Domains chambers and a *Kammerdeputation*. Others, as for example Lentz and Colomb at Aurich, Breitenbauch at Minden, Buggenhagen at Cleves and Schöning at Stettin, administered their provinces so efficiently that – to their personal disadvantage – they became irreplaceable. Eleven of Frederick's chamber presidents became ministers of finance; and von der Horst, von Derschau and von der Schulenburg-Kehnert (a former officer and already a minister at twenty-eight) must be numbered among eighteenth-century Germany's most distinguished administrators. Training and a rigorous selection procedure made the post of a Prussian chamber president one of great prestige, which in time created its own traditions; three of Frederick's officials – Breitenbauch, Buggenhagen and Stein – later became presidents-in-chief. Perfecting the administrative system was, of course, a slow process: ever alert, generally ruthless and sarcastic, Frederick maintained a continuous pressure on his officials to obtain lucid, professional, methodical and constructive reports; regular and increasing tax yields; and improvements in the trade of their provinces. The methods by which these objectives were to be achieved were laid down by detailed royal oral and written instructions and the initiative of a chamber president was confined within tight limits. Yet in this position only an individual capable of combining detailed knowledge with farsightedness and perspective was of any use to Frederick. Ability and intuition were equally essential in interpreting the king's intentions and reconciling these with the necessities of their own province. The chamber presidents had to walk the tight rope between Frederick's strict orders, the cameralism of their day and their own experience. Just as ministers such as Hagen, von der Horst, Derschau and Schulenburg made the king see to it that instructions they thought necessary were sent out, so the chamber presidents – via the General Directory – were often able to secure royal backing for their arguments. They could not, however, behave as independently as minor princes; an essential element of success was the ability not to forget their positions as assistants to the king. In Frederick's own words they had to be 'faithful, resourceful and experienced people' who 'put aside all considerations, even those of their families, keeping in mind only my service and the welfare of the country'. A similar definition of the duties of civil servants, though with emphasis on allegiance to the state rather than to the person of the ruler was expressed by the reformers of the early nineteenth century. 'The civil servant must give his time and energy to the state. He cannot predict if he will have a surplus left over for other pursuits, but even such a surplus should be spent on further studies that he may make himself more perfect for the service.' These are the words of the municipal reformer Johann Gottfried Frey, written from Königsberg in 1808. He had completed his university law studies in Frederick's own lifetime and his link with the Frederician tradition is strong: Frederick had put state above king in his philosophy of government. During Frederick's reign the War and Domains councillors began their careers as secretaries and their legal training had to be acquired in practice; after examination their first posts were in the chancery. There was as yet no structured promotion procedure. Frederick had decreed examinations and practical training for civil servants in 1743 and 1745 and the Instruction for the Kurmark Chamber in 1748 laid down that 'as the best people are, generally speaking, those who begin their careers at the bottom of the ladder, His Royal Majesty is not disinclined to fill the posts of war councillors and tax inspectors from the ranks of secretaries.' A decree of 1746 had strictly forbidden the employment of 'lackeys' in state service, thus ridding it of patronage and clientage. Well-educated sons of officials were, however, always given preferential consideration. The administrative reforms of 1770 introduced a state examination system run by the institution, proposed by Hagen, of a *Ober-Examinationskommission* (Higher Examination Commission). Officials of the justice department, actuaries and elected rural commissioners were also obliged to undergo examination. No less important was the constant supervision of personnel and the influence of chamber presidents and directors on their assistants and junior staff. Schlabrendorff's example in Silesia strongly impressed other high civil servants; his chamber had earned the reputation as an exemplary administrative body and his disciplinary measures (e.g. against running into debt) were widely adopted.

As part of the post-war administrative reforms an attempt was made to standardize the office of *Landrat* throughout the Prussian provinces. This office had first developed in the Kurmark where the official, part Estates-representative and part state servant, also acted as *Marschkommissar.*

Frederick William I established rural commissioners on this pattern in Magdeburg, Halberstadt, Minden and Ravensberg and also in Hither Pomerania, though here the *Landrat* was appointed by co-option, and not by a vote of the Estates. In his county the *Landrat* was both executive officer of the War and Domains chamber and its overseer; apart from the functions of a *Marschkommissar* he exercised police authority in a wide sense though without judicial power. Frederick continued his father's practice of confirming one of the three names for the office of *Landrat* on a short-list proposed to the War and Domains chamber by the district Estates. In 1741 Silesia was divided into counties and the office of *Landrat* introduced. Soon, however, Frederick began to appoint rural commissioners in Upper Silesia. He did not trust the local Estates but he did not formally abolish their rights in the matter. The county of Glatz, which from 1747 had a *Kammer Deputatus* as a 'justice commission' under Breslau, was a special case insofar as the *Landrat* there held (until 1751) judicial power delegated by the *Oberamtsregierung*; this *Landrat* held the rank of a War and Domains councillor and was subordinated to the Breslau Chamber. Because these functions could not be regarded as subsidiary duties the *Landrat* in Glatz was always a non-native, a trained official appointed by the chamber. In Silesia every county had two deputies chosen by the Estates who assisted the *Landrat*; this innovation was later introduced into the central provinces beginning with the Kurmark in 1753. In 1756 the *Jus praestandi* was confirmed or given for the first time to the Estates in a number of provinces. The Instruction of 1748 had defined the rural commissioner's place within the organizational framework, but on 30 April 1766 Frederick laid down the guidelines for the working out of new instructions for the offices of both *Landrat* and *Steuerrat*. Separate instructions were soon drawn up for Cleves-Mark, the Neumark, East and West Prussia, the Kurmark, Magdeburg, Minden-Ravensberg and Tecklenburg-Lingen; but Pomerania's instructions were not ready until 1779. Gelderland and Moers had neither rural commissioners nor tax inspectors, and none were introduced by Frederick; chamber officials performed their functions. The General Directory, in close partnership with the chambers, incorporated the fruits of observations and experiences gathered by the king on his tours of inspection into a comprehensive system which made allowances for regional peculiarities. The Instructions of 1766 for rural commissioners and tax inspectors brought together all the haphazard directives previously issued. The *Landrat* was to report on the villages in his *Kreis*, including the number of inhabitants and the mean yield of the farmed land; he had to take timely measures to prevent the dispossession of peasants and the spread of epidemics, to encourage the farmers to plant fruit trees and keep bees, to see to the repair and reconstruction of buildings and the implementation of school regulations. The *Steuerrat* was responsible for the economic life of the towns; he must inspect weights and measures, supervise health inspectors, examine the condition of buildings, foster the planting and increase in mulberry trees, and prevent excessive charges in inns and taverns. The regulations laid down for the Neumark were the most comprehensive and instructions were modelled on these as much as regional peculiarities permitted. Hagen's memoir of 31 October 1769 on the desired improvement in the education of civil servants noted that the *Landrat* needed to master the geographical conditions of his county, and all the regulations pertaining to it, if he wished to serve king and Estates well. He must further encourage the inhabitants of his district to work hard, 'for these people have to earn all the provincial, local and service taxes with the sweat of their brow and they must also provide for the state's necessities'. Taxes and impositions had to be raised and paid in full. It was essential to find good men for the office of the *Landrat*, 'since for supervision and protection of the state's interest, the country and the chambers can depend on nobody but the *Landrat*'. Frederick William I had granted the rural commissioners of the Neumark the right (confirmed by Frederick II in a cabinet order of 2 November 1743) to participate – and vote – in the work of the War and Domains chambers. Few of them ever exercised this right, however, since they could not afford to leave their counties unattended for six to eight weeks each year when travel and subsistence allowances were not available. In practice, therefore, their participation in government did not come to much. Nor was much use made of the examination system set up in 1770; like many another Frederician reform lack of time, money and interest postponed its implementation.

The Instruction of 1766 rounded off development in the *Landrat* office in Frederick's reign. East Prussia and Cleves-Mark, the last two provinces in which an older representative system had survived, now changed to the *Landrat* system on the Kurmark pattern. In East Prussia the *Landtag* Recess of 1612 had established a college of four *Amtshauptleuten* (leading district officials) and eight *Landtag* deputies appointed for life and salaried by the ruler: these twelve, called *Landräte*, together with the *Oberräte*, were responsible for legislation. As the East Prussian *Landtag* had lapsed in 1704 only a few *Landräte* paid homage at the *Landtag* of 1713. Twelve *Landräte* were appointed *ad interim*, though without duties, confirmation or salaries, for the homage of 1740; when they petitioned for these Frederick answered that this would only be done if the Kurmark pattern were adopted. East Prussia had since 1722 three salaried *Kreisräte* (district councillors) for the Oberland, Natangen and Samland. They supervised the local *Steuerkassen* (tax chests), made tours of inspection of their *Ämter*, and sent reports and annual audited accounts to the central government. The Instruction of 1748 specifically listed these duties and added one for mustering artillery horses in case of war. All other, less important, fiscal matters were the responsibility of the *Amtshauptmann*. This office was, however, misused as a sinecure, and for this reason the *Landrat* institution on the Kurmark pattern was introduced into East Prussia on 22 August 1752. Königsberg's chamber president von Massow amalgamated several *Amtshauptmannschaften* into ten large *Kreise* (Schaaken, Tapiau, Brandenburg, Rastenburg, Mohrungen, Neidenburg, Marienwerder, Insterburg, Seehesten and Oletzko). The three existing *Kreisräte*, each of whom administered two of the new *Kreise*, were supported by four newly appointed *Landräte*. One of these came from the justice department, while the other three were retired army officers. In contrast to the Kurmark the East Prussian *Landrat* was clearly a *Kreis* official – as was the *Kreis* excise collector and the *Kreis* gendarme. Since East Prussia had neither *Landtag* nor lesser assemblies *Kreis* deputies were not needed. The Estates' privilege of putting forward proposals for *Landräte* was, however, granted.

One year later the *Landrat* system was also introduced in Cleves, the last Prussian province in which the Estates still had some influence. With the abolition of the office of *Drost* in 1724 judicial and administrative powers had been transferred to the rivals of the *Droste*, the judges. The domains remained, however, a mixture of state and locally administered areas. Taxes were collected annually during the *Amtstag* and the *Erbentag* by 107 tax collectors. Assessment of taxation rates provided opportunities for all kinds of deals and evasions, especially as jurisdiction largely remained in the hands of the nobility. Investigation into judicial procedures in 1749 uncovered these irregularities and caused the king to introduce rural commissioners on the Kurmark pattern. This was not, in accordance with Frederick's custom, imposed by decree. The king instructed the Third Department of the General Directory – the responsible authority – to consult with the Cleves-Mark Chamber on the proposed reform. Characteristically the comments and suggestion which came from Cleves-Mark raised doubts within the Directory – ever reluctant to interfere with the privileges of the local Estates and to restrict the jurisdiction of the nobility – as to the legality and feasibility of the reform. On 24 August 1749 minister of state von Viereck confided his fears to great chancellor von Cocceji: 'The installation of *Landräte* will, initially anyhow, bring all kinds of difficulties to the surface. The gentlemen of Cleves are opposed to all innovations, looking upon them as inapplicable to their province. They like to leave everything in the hands of nepotists and court clerks and they will certainly put all kinds of obstructions in our way.' The best solution in his opinion was the appointment of local nobles as rural commissioners. Three new *Kreise* were formed in Cleves (Cleves, Emmerich and Wesel), and four more in the county of Mark (Hamm with the independent town of Soest, Hörde, Altena and Wetter); on 6 February 1753 the office of *Landrat* was officially established in Cleves-Mark by cabinet order and shortly thereafter given its instruction by the General Directory. The Estates in Cleves proved, as expected, mistrustful and uncooperative and progress was relatively slow. In February 1764 minister of state von Hagen, discussing necessary improvement, urged that the Cleves *Landräte* ought to be familiar with the constitution of the province, its agriculture and its tax system, and that they should be called, every two or three months, to conferences with the chamber director. He particularly stressed that the county clerks should not be permitted to encroach on the powers of the *Landrat*, nor be allowed 'to play the role of petty tyrants over the hardworking peasants'. His proposals and detailed regulations for office work and inspection tours were included in the Instruction for the *Landräte* of Cleves-Mark of 23 September 1764; a revised instruction of 1766 in the main confirmed that of 1764. The Estates persisted in their opposition but since they failed to put forward positive proposals they played no positive role. The *Ritterschaft* of Cleves-Mark was not divided into counties but acted for the whole province; this served the nobility as a pretext to avoid taking on the burdensome *Landrat* office. An efficient provincial administration was, however, essential to ensure a just spread of the burden of taxation and its punctual payment, and to prevent waste of the resources of the province and the enrichment by fraudulent means of individual subjects.

In the Frederician use of the *Landrat* office we find no 'mechanical concept of the state'. Wide scope was allowed for local divergences, as long as these did not thwart the general interests of the state. Against the wishes of his central administrators, who wanted to get rid of the provincial Estates and the county deputies, Frederick continued to keep those institutions alive, seeing in them a useful counterweight to his own bureaucracy. It is for this reason that the Estates maintained a place in the Frederician system of government. The large-scale, hitherto little known, administration reforms of the post-1763 years give ample proof of the king's intentions, and his success, in this respect.

REFORM OF THE DOMAINS AND OF AGRICULTURE

Frederick regarded an efficient administrative system not as an end in itself but as the means whereby the state's productivity could be increased. He expected that large and constant increases in revenues would be more likely to come from industry than from agriculture: 'Industry makes the real profits.' Yet his administrative activities and reforms were mainly devoted to agriculture, especially after the widespread devastations of the Seven Years War; the increasing needs of the Prussian industrial worker for cheap bread and clothes had to be satisfied within the state. Simultaneously the new methods which had been developed in England to increase and improve agricultural products challenged the king to embark on a reform programme. This was implemented by the War and Domains chambers, working through the royal domains officials and the rural commissioners.

Increased agricultural production, particularly for grain, could in some measure be obtained by land improvement schemes, especially by the drainage of fens and the irrigation of dry wasteland. The rural labour force, if properly organized, could cope with the work involved in such 'amelioration' projects, but the projects needed considerable financial support. The king planned on the supposition that private landlords would contribute part of their profits, as the royal domains did and, to a lesser extent, the provincial chambers. Larger projects were only feasible when the state gave help from central funds. As an example we may mention the Kurmark amelioration project which gave 36,000 *Morgen* of agricultural land at a cost of 142,000 *Reichstaler*. Seventy-seven families were settled and 2,500 cows and 500 sheep grazed on the reclaimed land. An increase in the number of farm animals was an indispensable prerequisite for increases in agricultural production, since this depended on the provision of regular and adequate supplies of manure. Winter stall-feeding of cattle in its turn depended on increased production of feeding stuffs, which could best be achieved by the cultivation, on the English model, of lupins, sainfoin and other high-grade fodder crops. Successful growing of such crops, supervised by English agronomists on the Mühlenbeck domain in the Kurmark, eventually led to general cultivation of the fodder crops. Crop-rotation, however, was not introduced at this time. It is possible that its usefulness was not yet recognized, though a cabinet order of 29 March 1782 instructed minister von Werder 'to plant a field with fodder crops for as many years as anything will grow there and then to sow corn in it'. Cattle-raising, previously possible only on the great grazing grounds along the river lowlands from Tilsit to Wesel, could be both extended and improved. Agriculturalists with experience in animal husbandry were appointed by the chambers as advisers to demonstrate the possibilities open to graziers. Progress in hygiene had already checked the catastrophic cattle epidemics. In 1773 Prussia had 2·5 million cattle, more than one fifth in East Prussia and Lithuania, provinces which were surpassed only by Silesia. East Prussia and Lithuania had the most horses (350,000, more than one-third of the total number in the state) of the highest quality. Silesia, the Kurmark and Pomerania were the leading provinces in sheep-farming. In pig-rearing East Prussia was in the lead; it was also the state's leading producer of potatoes, followed by Lithuania, Silesia, the Kurmark and Pomerania (where potatoes for human consumption had first been grown in Germany). In 1763 von der Horst, on instructions from the king, had set about finding suitable sites for planting potatoes in the Kurmark; the next year the king reminded him 'to make sure that the rural inhabitants were kept busy planting potatoes'. The scarcity of flour during the famine of 1771 furthered a more general use of potatoes. Numerous edicts and instructions encouraged the cultivation of other root crops and the planting of fruit trees, quite apart from the famous mulberry trees. In 1770 in the Kurmark minister of state von Derschau employed forty gardeners to demonstrate the correct method of tending fruit trees. Magdeburg had the largest number of fruit trees per square mile (12,743 as against Silesia's 4,800 and the national average of 2,700), but Silesia grew the highest number of any province. Despite the large increase in planting more could have been achieved:

> As in other branches of agriculture the king's attempts to introduce a general fruit culture eventually failed because of the apathy and reluctance of the masses, who shied away from an undertaking from which they could expect a profit only in years to come.*

Frederick's interest was also aroused, by English example, in enclosure and the consolidation of the scattered strips of arable land whose cultivation had always involved the peasantry in enormous wastage of time and energy; and though reform was not completed till the mid-nineteenth century, beginnings were made. The *Allmende*, the communally-owned land, whether arable, pasturage or commonage, had, since nobody was responsible for it, been neglected. It was now decided to distribute it for intensive cultivation. Frederick broached the topic in his annual 'Review of ministers' on 11 June 1765. The General Directory

* O. Behre, p. 242.

was ordered to consult the ministry of justice on the legal problems
involved, for the Kurmark in the first instance. The legal experts were
not enthusiastic; after long deliberations they prophesied protracted
legal proceedings and even miscarriages of justice. They admitted the
benefits which on the English evidence would follow, but suggested
that the scheme should be tried out on the domains. Disputes arose as to
the amount of land that should be enclosed; a *Publikandum* was necessary,
and commissioners versed in the law had to be appointed in the *Kreise* as
expert advisers. While waiting for the report of the ministry of justice
(which was ready in December 1765), Hagen drew up a list of suggestions
which were – with minor changes – incorporated in the 'Circular on the
Partition and Distribution of Commonage and Pasturage' submitted for
the king's signature on 22 April 1766. Addressed to all colleges of justice
and all War and Domains chambers it was extended to Silesia on 15
May 1766: thus it was one of the earliest decrees valid throughout the
whole monarchy. Communal hunting, fishing and timber rights, and
herdings in woods and on heaths were excluded from its provisions,
since its main purpose was the improvement in tillage land and meadows.
Hereditable communal lands were also outside its provisions. It was
expressly stated that the reform would not bring increased taxation or
levies, and *Lassbauern* were permitted to take advantage of its opportunities. A commission to supervise the enclosures *in loco* was decreed and
instructed to report within four weeks. At this stage doubts expressed by
the officials of the ministry of justice made Frederick more cautious, in
spite of encouraging reports from Switzerland of its successful *Allmende*
distribution. No further progress was made until October 1769 when
Hagen came to an understanding with the former president of the
Supreme Court (*Kammergericht*), Ernst Friedemann Freiherr von
Münchhausen, now head of the Department for Ecclesiastical Affairs,
on the immediate issuance of instructions for the commissioners and the
speeding-up of the enclosure project at the College of Justice. On 24
October 1769, after more than four years of legal preparations, the
enclosure decree was issued by the king, who emphasized that force and
injustice should not be tolerated. Frederick avoided, however, personal
commitment in the phraseology; the long delay had annoyed him and
cooled his interest. Enclosures were first effected in *Amt* Nauen, where
fewest difficulties were expected, and enlarged pasture to feed more
cattle was obtained. In the spring of 1770 reports of successes reached
Frederick: a total of 105 enclosures had been effected across the monarchy
with a further 31 in the county of Mark by the enclosure of village
common land, and 14 by the buying up of land in Gelderland and Moers.

By the end of 1770 a further 124 enclosures had been carried out and in 1771 there were 380 more (98 of them in the duchy of Magdeburg). Only the scarcity of surveyors prevented speedier progress. On 14 April 1771 a special *Reglement* abolishing communal herdings in Silesia was issued. Thus Germany's first great agrarian reform got under way.

During Frederick William I's reign the nobility had (not without pressure from the king) accepted the place allocated them within the Prussian scheme of things. Although continuing to occupy this under Frederick II, they were expected to subordinate their privileges and class interests to the greater good of the state. Frederick guaranteed them their power base – their landed estates – but he demanded from them in the way of taxes even more than his father. They also preserved their privileges in respect of civil service preference at the level of cabinet minister and chamber president; and the officer corps, which from the eighteenth to the twentieth century helped to typecast them more than any other profession in Prussia, was almost exclusively their preserve. The nobility responded by devoting themselves with remarkable class solidarity to the idea of service, civil as well as military. Eighteenth-century Prussia was no breeding-ground for aristocratic *frondeurs*, and the bravura with which the nobility gave their lives for king and country on the battlefields of Bohemia sealed their compact with the monarchy. Frederick was less successful with the Silesian nobility, whom he tried to tempt into Prussian service throughout his reign. In 1768 he made them a *Gnadengeschenk* (a gift of grace) of 300,000 *Reichstaler* for the work of reconstruction. Eighty-three families received assistance, preference being given to those with sons in the army; the money was distributed, according to need, by Carmer, then president of the Breslau *Oberamts-regierung*. Similar 'rebuilding grants' were made available to the *Ritter-schaft* in some of the other provinces. The foundation in 1770 of the *Landschaftliche Kreditinstitut* (provincial credit bank) of the Silesian landed nobility was another example of royal aid to this class. These agricultural credit banks (*Bodenkreditanstalten*) were also set up in the Kurmark, Pomerania and East and West Prussia, but these provinces had to find most of the money themselves. Yet Frederick failed to establish that close personal relationship with the Silesian nobility as a class which he had succeeded in forming with that of the Kurmark and the Neumark: invitations to Silesia's feudal magnates to attend the wedding of Frederick William, prince of Prussia, were nearly all declined – an indication that, despite appointments as chamberlains and the bestowal of other honours, the Silesian nobility rejected the king's attempts to orientate them towards Berlin. His hope that they would flock around him was never fulfilled. Indifference, a deliberate effort to maintain their distance, the dislike of the yoke of royal service, lack of money and the sheer inconvenience involved in playing the role the king had cast them for were all contributory factors. Most important was the fact that the Silesian nobility could not see the point of the exercise: why did not the king continue to visit them in Silesia rather than try to make them come to Berlin? During these same years Schlabrendorff, the president-in-chief of the Silesian chambers, formulated the privileges of the Silesian nobility in respect of former noble land in the Frederician phraseology:

> At the first indication that non-noble owners of noble estates have maltreated their dependents or have imposed additional burdens on them, they are to be compelled to sell their states to nobles; for their behaviour shows that they have neither the intelligence nor the necessary qualities to govern dependents equitably.

This paragraph not only attributes quasi-aristocratic qualities to commoners who show that they 'can exercise authority in a just manner', but simultaneously warns noble estate-owners not to forget the moral basis of their privileged status. The freedom to purchase noble estates – possible at this period, though not legally guaranteed until the edict of October 1807 – contained two contradictory tendencies. The first stirrings of the movement towards fundamental equality were already present in Frederician Prussia. Frederick William I had introduced the *Generalhufenschoss* in East Prussia as a uniform land tax, payable alike by nobility, free peasants and hereditable peasants, based on the land assessment rolls and the productivity of the soil. Frederick introduced a similar tax to Silesia in 1740 and to West Prussia in 1772, and continued the cash commutation of the *Rossdienst* (service in war with own horse) owed by the nobility of Magdeburg and the Kurmark for their tax-exempt *Hufen*. At this period the attitude to taxation was undergoing a general change; the obligation to pay tax was no longer conceived as deriving from the ruler's alleged ultimate right to dispose of the property of his subjects but from an agreement between ruler and citizen. According to the *Allgemeine Landrecht* (II 14 §2) those 'who enjoy the state's protection in their persons, possessions or trade' were liable to taxation.

Around 1770, at the time of the administrative and agrarian reforms, there were 13,132 peasant farms within the jurisdiction of the Minden-Ravensberg War and Domains Chamber. Of these 3,843 were owned either by nobles or religious foundations; another 5,035, of which 3,828 were freehold, belonged to royal colonists. Although few in number the royal domain officials were the torchbearers of agricultural progress. The financial shrewdness of the *Fiscus* enabled the Chamber to experiment in a way that was impossible either for the perennially undercapitalized landed nobility or for individual peasants. The leading role played in rural areas by the domains is shown by a pamphlet written by Johann Ernst Tiemann, a domain official from Brackwede in Ravensberg. This tract, published at Bielefeld in 1785, was distributed by the thousands, even in neighbouring, non-Prussian territories. The title is characteristic: *An Attempt to make profitable Farming more popular among the local Inhabitants of the royal Prussian Amt of Brackwede in the county of Ravensberg or Proposals on how the Inhabitants of the Amt of Brackwede can become rich within a few Years; committed to paper during the leisurely Christmas holidays.* By the second half of the eighteenth century domainal leaseholders had become a wealthy and quite self-confident class, experienced in land amelioration and settlements. They were, however, handicapped by short leases (with the consequent fear of non-renewal) and threatened by competition which was not only financially strong but *au fait* with the latest agricultural innovations. But though the domainal leaseholders were strictly supervised, their leases were renewed by the chambers time and again. Their familiarity with land and labour, their experience of soil conditions and yields made their retention preferable to the uncertainty which might follow while a new leaseholder became acclimatized. The old leasehold families also helped to keep each other in office in the *Amt*. The king distrusted them and criticized them, probably unjustly. Domhardt and Schön were not the only sons of domainal leaseholders to reach high office within the state service. Honesty and ability, scientific knowledge combined with a practical approach to agriculture, these were the qualities which made numerous *Amtsmänner* into exemplars for their rural localities and reliable collaborators of the provincial chambers.

The great period of domainal development had passed its peak before Frederick's accession. In the old provinces the number and extent of the domains were declining, with many of the outfarms being converted into farmsteads. The king did not wish to compete with the nobility when it came to possession of land. Neither Silesia nor East Friesland brought many crown estates to Prussia. In West Prussia former crown lands and church-owned estates were in part redistributed as peasant farms and hereditable leaseholds; and in other instances land, e.g. the episcopal lands of the bishopric of Ermland, were taken into cultivation by the state without becoming state property. Agrarian reform touched the domains only in the sense that their cultivation was rationalized and intensified. At mid-century half of Prussia's revenues came from the domains, but by the end of Frederick's reign this had dropped to one-third, despite the addition of the three new provinces. Yet the total income from the domains in 1786 was considerably higher than it had been in 1740. It was possible for the chambers to reduce their expenditure on the domains and to increase the price of leases, not by profit-hunting or 'by other people's misfortune' but by the application of cameralist principles in the pursuit of 'the real solid plus' which Article XVIII of the Instruction for the General Directory of 1748 had recommended. In this respect the domains were in a satisfactory condition around 1770. In Magdeburg only one or two days *Spanndienst* (provision of a horse and man) were demanded weekly and in many cases service money had been substituted. All farms were in peasant ownership. The Kurmark soon followed Magdeburg's example; unlimited service survived for any length of time only in Pomerania. *Scharwerk* (labour service) for the domains was fixed at sixty days annually in East Prussia, but it was paid for according to fixed rates. The Balga domain was the first to introduce the idea of substituting piece-work for the more usual time-work. The king's desire (first expressed in 1755) of commuting domainal service to a fixed service payment throughout Prussia proved impossible to realize because of the acute shortage of ready money in the agrarian world. The intensification of the domain economy did, however, represent an important saving to the state treasury.

The declining domainal system was partly reformed by two moves of the central authorities: the review of domain leases in 1768 and the investigations into the surreptitious enlargement of some of the domains in 1777. In June 1768 minister of state von Hagen persuaded the king to compare domain yields with the leases paid. Investigations were to be carried out in East Prussia, Pomerania, the Neumark and, later, in Silesia. As the First Department – within whose competence these matters lay – had not been consulted in the early stages there were unfortunate delays before the work could get under way. Eventually Blumenthal gave his agreement, and already by the beginning of 1769 the commission had been able to raise an extra 50,000 talers in the two East Prussian chambers with another 3,400 talers from higher rents for mills. That the leaseholders were able to pay the higher rents without much difficulty shows how stable the agricultural economy was at this period. A second change in the domainal system came with the appointment of Leopold Otto von Gaudi as leading minister of the General Directory. From 1775 he was in charge of the administration of the East Prussian, Lithuanian and West Prussian chambers; after two years to familiarize himself with the records, he sent a commission to his territory and himself spent three months on its thorough inspection. Investigations showed that the domains officials, contrary to their instructions, but with the connivance of the chambers, had practised a policy of land consolidation. Nobody had complained and as apparently no other interests had been infringed the General Directory, despite Gaudi's disapproving report, saw no reason for interfering. The cultivation of wastelands was, in any case, government policy and there was still an abundance of land available. The investigation did, however, provide an opportunity for abolishing the prohibition against the acquisition of land by the domains; at the same time the lot of the domain peasants was eased and beneficial alterations in the *Scharwerk* regulations were made. On 3 December 1778 the Königsberg Chamber was told by the General Directory that:

> As a systematic *Scharwerk* is being introduced throughout our province, the *Dispositions-Tage* [days on which peasants had to be available if required] will be abolished and the *Bitte-Dienst* [boon work] forbidden on pain of punishment. Castle-service, the transport of wood and grain are to be fixed by rescript in such a way as to discourage the abuse of service obligations. We have resolved to allow leaseholders to purchase waste lands within their *Amt* and establish themselves there; also to allow them the opportunity to buy by auction outfarms to be held in hereditary ownership wherever possible.

This reform did not help to preserve the domainal system, for the trend was towards wider land ownership and the creation of medium-sized farms for free peasants, leading to increasing redistribution of domainal land.

The most important aim of Frederick's agrarian reform was to protect the peasantry, improve the productivity of their land and free them from the most burdensome services. That this was not fully achieved can be attributed to the existing structure of the state (which could not be altered without great risk), the limitations on the enforcement of state authority, and the economic and legal considerations involved. Characteristic of Frederick's reforms in general is the fact that he, being much more circumspect in his approach to reform than Joseph II or Struensee, limited himself to what was attainable; he recognized the obstacles and accepted that with his limited resources he had to expend much energy to obtain small but lasting results. Article VII of the fundamental Instruction of 1748 for the General Directory deals with the position of the peasants. Its aim was to free domain and *Amt* peasants as much as possible and to limit the labour services of the *Untertanen* (literally 'subjects', but at this period meaning serfs) on town-owned and noble estates to three or four days each week for manual work (*Handdienst*) and *Spanndienst* (work with a horse, provided by the peasant): 'At first this will cause something of an outcry but . . . it must be enforced and it is to be hoped that all reasonable landowners will adapt themselves to it.' During an inspection tour of the Kurmark in 1749 the king noticed domain officials striking peasants with sticks. This crime was now made punishable by six years fortress imprisonment, no matter who the culprit was. The Kurmark Chamber was repeatedly urged to protect the peasantry from the tyranny of domain officials. *Landräte* were obliged by their *Reglement* of 1766 to report to the chambers every case of oppression of peasants in their counties. That improvements were not always immediate can be seen from the fact that in 1750, two years after the promulgation of the great administrative instruction which all provinces received to lower labour services, the Hither Pomeranian Estates complained of the *Codex Fridericianus* and demanded the maintenance of their right to unlimited services from their peasants. The introduction of uniform peasant legislation for the Prussian state was difficult because of existing privileges and variations in the legal position from one province to another. East Prussia's *Kölmer* were free peasants; other eastern provinces had *Lassiten*, personally free but with restricted legal rights; both were under certain conditions hereditable (*bedingt*) and they were bound to the soil. Colonists were, from the first, given more rights than 'free people' as regards tax. The situation in the western provinces was quite different. In Minden the Chamber distinguished in 1753 between three classes of peasants: *Leibfreien*, free *Zinsbauern* exempt from labour services; the *Erbmeierstättschen*, peasants tied to the soil by local custom; and the *Leibeigenen*, the serfs. In Cleves-Mark the distinction between serfs belonging to the royal domains and serfs owned by individuals was unknown; as royal domains comprising whole villages did not exist there, domains were limited to individual estates.

Thanks to the vigilance of the authorities serious incidents arising from dissatisfaction with labour services were avoided. Rioting and general peasant unrest was limited to the border areas of Prussian Lithuania, the Johannisburger Heide and Upper Silesia. During the 1749 harvest the domain peasants of the Prökuls and Heydekrug refused, with the encouragement of some soldiers, to perform their labour services. The trouble was speedily crushed by a squadron of hussars, but the chamber complained that Major-General Friedrich von Stosch, commander of the dragoon regiment stationed at Ragnit, had, by entering into negotiation with the peasants interfered with the normal course of justice. In 1766 Schlabrendorff had a nobleman, notorious for tyrannizing the peasants, imprisoned and his estates compulsorily sold. In *Kreis* Ratibor in Upper Silesia in the spring of 1766 the peasants on the estates of Count August

Wilhelm Leopold Gesler zu Odersch refused excessive labour demands. Provincial minister von Schlabrendorff persuaded the exasperated nobility to remain calm, but the strike spread to *Kreis* Leobschütz and threatened to spread to the counties of Beuthen, Tost and Pless. Refusing to heed the assurances of the *Oberamtsregierung* and the *Landräte* that their grievances would be scrupulously examined and justice done, the peasants took refuge in the forests and within a short time many villages stood empty. Agitators from outside the area, among them a tailor's journeyman who claimed to be the bearer of an instruction from the king at Potsdam, announced that all compulsory labour services (*Fronarbeit*) were abolished, and thus helped to fan the flames. The Breslau Chamber feared that the spring sowing would not be done – to the detriment both of province and people – and Schlabrendorff, who had no means whereby order would be restored, asked the king for military assistance. Lieutenant-General Friedrich Wilhelm von Seydlitz, inspector of cavalry in Silesia and famous as a cavalry commander in the Seven Years War, carried out this delicate task with remarkable impartiality and restraint: the peasants were brought back on to the estates without the use of force except in the case of a few ringleaders. Schlabrendorff pleaded even for these in a letter to the great chancellor 'so that not too many peasants are taken from their place of work unless it is necessary'. This had been a strike, lasting two weeks, not a revolt against the administration or the king. The provincial *Regierung*, already on bad terms with the Estates of Upper Silesia, threatened prompt legal proceedings against anyone who took revenge on the strikers. Riots of armed peasants in the neighbouring Austrian duchy of Teschen at this time point to social rather than political motives behind the strike. Such extreme expressions of dissatisfaction remained rare and had no influence on the king's plans to complete the protection of the peasantry by liberating them.

In a cabinet order of 16 April 1754 the king observed to Cocceji, the minister of justice, that 'the slavery of serfdom still customary in Pomerania seems to me to be so cruel and to have such a bad effect on the whole country that I really would like to have it completely abolished.' This was a theme to which Frederick returned time and again after the Seven Years War. On 22 May 1763, in an instruction to the Pomeranian War and Domains Chamber, he decreed that 'first of all serfdom in villages owned by the crown, the nobility and the towns is to be completely abolished as from this hour'. Another instruction, issued to the Kurmark Chamber some days later, provided for the abolition of serfs in the domains. Everything went well for a time. Brenckenhoff obtained the agreement of the Pomeranian Estates at Stettin in December of the same year. Hoym's instruction – when he became Silesian provincial minister in 1770 – made it obligatory to proceed with the abolition of serfdom in Upper Silesia. He gave an undertaking that this had already been done in that no serf could any longer be sold, though one had yet to achieve 'that they should own their farms and possessions so that the territorial domains [*Grundherrschaften*] cannot do what they like with them'. Hoym was not the man to push through the policies of the 'peasant protector', Schlabrendorff, who for his pains had, like his predecessor, to endure the vituperation of many of the Silesian nobility. The promising developments towards abolition in Silesia were not cut short. Hoym withheld from publication, with the consent of the Silesian minister of justice von Danckelmann, a cabinet order of 3 May 1786 which decreed a minimum of two days' service a week where no agreement on labour services could be reached – so as not to annoy the nobility by publicizing the idea that two days' service might suffice.

In no other field of Frederician administrative reform was the path from the royal initiative through the cabinet order, via the instructions to the General Directory and the chambers, down to the implementation of the royal orders by the *Landräte* and domain officials so long, laborious and full of divergences as in the field of agriculture. That written instructions are not synonymous with implementation is, of course, the experience of every administration at all times; the longer the chain of command the odder the metamorphoses suffered en route. In the emancipation of the serfs the selfishness of the Estates could affect the issue, but even legal decisions in favour of the people meant to benefit could have a detrimental effect. An excess of zeal, impatience, inappropriate reactions, personal considerations and changes of personnel – all of these could at times hamper the work of reform.

Some results were, however, achieved. Labour services were limited in accordance with the circular to the Silesian *Landräte* of 15 May 1763; the Instruction of 12 July 1764 protected peasant land throughout the entire state; all farmsteads in Silesia were made hereditable, from the beginning of 1770, by a decree of 14 September 1769; and *Leibeigenschaft* (serfdom) was changed into hereditary subjection. In Silesia a further step was made with the edict of 10 December 1748 which released the serf from subjection to the soil: no landowner could deny this freedom except for certain carefully defined reasons. The Pomeranian peasant decree of 30 December 1764 confirmed the tying of the peasant to the soil since without it no large estate could survive. The next step was the abolition of serfdom in East and West Prussia by the patent of notification of 28 September 1773 and the ordinance of 8 November 1773. No longer could 'slaves' in bondage be bought and sold or even given away, and emancipation on the Silesian pattern was simultaneously decreed. During the drafting of this ordinance, as also in the General Directory's ruling of the same year on the obligatory five-year period for domestic service, some regional peculiarities were overlooked. In East and West Prussia there was a free farming class, the *Kölmer*, who were not subjected to the manor; the *Gesindedienstzwang* (compulsory domestic service) had already in 1763 been abolished for the East Prussian domain peasants; moreover, Frederick William I had freed them from their bond to the estates. They were bound only by a personal promise to remain, and were thus already free men with no hereditary bondage. The final expression of this long process of development is given in the *Allgemeine Landrecht* of the Prussian states, in the section on personal duties and rights of serfs (II 7 §147 ff., 520ff., 547ff.); this is based on the cabinet orders and individual ordinances on peasant reform of Frederick II's reign, condensed and made applicable to all provinces. This was as far as the Frederician state could progress in peasant reform. The serfs in Westphalia were in a worse situation at that time as far as their personal position, services and obligations were concerned. A later attempt by the king, in an edict of 11 September 1784, to change unlimited service into limited service was only partly realized. Frederick's optimistic expectations, in tune with the Enlightenment, that the reduction in labour services would encourage the peasant to work with more interest and enthusiasm was countered by some estate owners, who maintained that the peasant had become lazier and more slipshod in his ways.

Frederick's agrarian policy is seen in the many decrees issued with the object of making human beings more independent and more industrious, but there were few signs that his ideals were widely shared. The king once described agriculture as 'the first of the arts, without which there would be no merchants, kings, poets and philosophers'. The limitations of state-enforced agrarian reforms soon became clear. Frederick's own experience is described in a short essay he wrote in 1777, in which he also deals with the *Schollengebundenheit*, the legal obligation binding the peasant to the soil:

> Of all conditions this is the most unhappy and must stir human feeling most deeply. Surely no human being can be born to be the slave of his equals. One rightly despises this abuse and thinks that only will power is necessary to abolish this barbaric custom. But this proves not to be so. Custom is based on old agreements between the lord of the manor and the settler. The tilling of the soil is part of the peasant's labour service [*Frondienst*]. If one tried to

abolish this loathsome custom at one stroke, one would cause upheavals throughout all agriculture and the nobility would have to be compensated for the financial losses sustained by them.

WEST PRUSSIA

West Prussia, acquired in 1772, benefited from the administrative experiences and reforms previously introduced throughout the Prussian state, and within a short period of time it caught up with the other provinces. Being almost equal in size to East Prussia, though with a smaller population (520,000 including the inhabitants of Ermland and the Netze district), the new territory took its place among the larger provinces of the Prussian *Gesamtstaat*.

Ruled after 1309 by Teutonic Knights, by whom it was settled and cultivated, Western Prussia was ceded in 1466 to the Polish crown which granted autonomy to 'the Royal part', i.e. the duchy of Prussia. In 1698 Elbing was mortgaged to the elector of Brandenburg and in 1703 the territory of Elbing was finally annexed, though without the town of the same name; at the frontier posts the Prussian Black Eagle was displayed. It was administered as a dependent territory (a *Dominium*) under the control of an intendant. When the rent assessments of the Prussian domain lands were raised in 1768, the Elbing territory had to pay an extra 6,000 talers annually and was obviously well able to afford it. During the Seven Years War the towns of Elbing, Marienburg, Dirschau, Graudenz and Thorn served as Russian bases. The threat of East Prussia's being cut off from the rest of the monarchy (should Russia annex Poland which was fast sinking into anarchy), the economic importance of the Vistula, and the prospect of joining up his central and eastern provinces were reasons why Frederick coveted West Prussia. In his Political Testament of 1752 he wrote: 'I do not find it opportune to acquire this province by force of arms. . . . acquisitions by the pen are always preferable to those gained by the sword.'

The opportune moment came during the Polish civil wars. In 1769 Austria occupied the thirteen towns of the Zips, a strip of ancient Hungarian territory mortgaged to Poland, and in the summer of 1770 part of the Carpathian foothills was annexed to the Austrian *Gesamtstaat* as *terrae recuperatae*. In October 1770 Prussian troops formed a thin *cordon sanitaire* against the plague then raging in Poland, from Teschen and the Neumark via Crossen-Tuchel and Marienwerder around East Prussia, so as to maintain the flow of trade and traffic by way of Danzig. Frederick hesitated to put forward any far-reaching claims, but Prince

Henry of Prussia, on his own initiative during his visit to St Petersburg in the winter of 1770–71, suggested to Catherine II that Prussia should acquire Ermland and Pomerelia. Having received Catherine's consent to this in January 1771, Henry convinced Frederick that the time was ripe for negotiations with Russia on territorial adjustments in Poland. The treaty of partition was signed by Russia and Prussia at St Petersberg on 15 January 1772 and joined by Austria on 5 August. By this Prussia acquired the territory of Polish Prussia, comprising the voivodeships of Marienburg, Kulm (excepting the town and district of Thorn), Pomerelia (excepting the town and district of Danzig), the Netze district, the town and district of Elbing, besides the bishoprics of Kulm and Ermland – a total area of about 36,000 sq. km. Most of the population of 500,000 was German, the rest Polish and Casubian. After Silesia, West Prussia was the second Prussian province to have a majority of Catholics. Possession was taken of the new province on 13 September 1772; a fortnight later at Marienburg the inhabitants of the bishoprics of Ermland and Kulm, the voivodeship of Kulm, Marienburg and Pomerelia, and the Netze district paid homage to the king's representatives, minister of state von Rohd and General von Stutterheim. On a suggestion made by minister von Hertzberg in October 1772 the two parts of Prussia were – by a cabinet order of 31 January 1773 – designated East Prussia (in accordance with its old name of *Prussia orientalis*) and West Prussia. The War and Domains chamber for the new province was established at Marienwerder, but the bishopric of Ermland was assigned to the Königsberg Chamber, thereby becoming, for administrative purposes, part of East Prussia.

The ceremony of homage was held on what was called Unification Day. In his address Rohd explained how 'this land, once torn from the Prussian eagle, has again been taken under its wing' and the commemorative medal struck for the occasion showed a topographical view and the inscription *Regno Redintegrato*. The claim was valid – leaving aside the Netze district – and in 1793 Danzig and Thorn and their hinterlands were also returned to Prussia.

The southern frontier of Polish Prussia, as fixed by the Treaty of St Petersburg, extended beyond the former lands of the Teutonic Knights into old Polish territory. Prussia was in very general terms granted possession of the Netze district, including both banks of the river from the Neumark to the Vistula near Schulitz. This gave her the regions and towns of Deutsch Krone, Camin, Bromberg and Inowrazlaw (Hohensalza). All of these towns had been under Magdeburg law since the thirteenth or fourteenth centuries; the territories whose western parts

had, at one time or another, belonged to the Neumark had been strongly
penetrated by medieval German settlers in the *Drang nach Osten*. Privy
finance councillor Franz Balthasar Schönberg von Brenckenhoff,
deservedly respected for his work on the Oder reclamation scheme, was
given the task of determining the actual frontier and of taking possession.
For hydrographic reasons he believed that the Netze flood-lands should be
included in Prussian territory, and the local population – including some
Polish magnates – also asked that the region should be absorbed into
Prussia. Thus the towns of Filehne, Czarnikau, Usch and Bartschin were
also annexed. The change-over in authority which began on 13 September was completed by the end of October 1772.

Frederick, despite hesitations, had allowed himself to be carried away
by the surveys and his zealous officials. Soon, however, the general
consequences of what was being done in his name made him pause.
Officials, expecting praise for their zeal, were confounded when the king
began to have second thoughts on the state's ability to defend the
proposed new frontier. Frederick now reverted to the original border,
which Poland approved after having turned down the Prussian offer of
the lordships of Tauroggen and Serrey in exchange for the Netze
region. In the Prussian-Polish border agreement of 22 August 1776
Prussia agreed to evacuate all lands on the left bank of the Netze, apart
from those belonging to estates on the right bank and villages directly
on the left of the river. Polish enclaves within Prussian territory were left
to Prussia. Various other unsettled points were eventually decided on
28 July 1777 through the intervention of the Russian plenipotentiary
von Stackelberg. As finally settled, Prussia's southern border in the
Netze district was extended to include Filehne, Radolin, Budsin,
Margonin, Exin, Znin, Gonsawa, Mogilno, Gembitz, Stelno and
Gniewkowo. Two hundred and forty-six villages, estates, domains and
Catholic ecclesiastical lands were returned to Poland after five years
under Prussian sovereignty. Frederick always sought clear rights to his
acquisitions, his objective being stability and durability.

Following the annexation of the new province, Prussian administrative
authorities were immediately introduced. With both parts of Prussia
united under one sceptre the title 'King of Prussia' was first used in the
patent of annexation of 13 September 1772 – replacing the title 'King in
Prussia' which had been its official designation since the coronation day
of Frederick I, 18 January 1701. The new title was generally considered
more fitting to the royal rank of the state.

In June 1772 the king ordered chamber director Karl Gottlieb Vorhoff
to set up a War and Domains Chamber at Marienwerder. With Johann

Friedrich von Domhardt as president-in-chief this West Prussian chamber was responsible for the new territories of Elbing, Marienburg, Kulmerland and Pomerelia, the old Prussian domains of Marienwerder and Riesenburg and the hereditary domains of Schonberg and Deutsch Eylau. To compensate for these transfers Ermland was put under the Königsberg Chamber. At first the Netze district was designated an independent administrative region, called the province of Little Prussia, to be administered independently by Brenckenhoff. To support Domhardt, Karl Friedrich Ludwig von Gaudi was appointed chamber director at Marienwerder in 1773. When Brenckenhoff became ill, Gaudi established a *Kammerkommission* at Bromberg for the Netze district. This was changed into a *Kammerdeputation* – dependent on Marienwerder – on 1 June 1775, though its functions were similar to those of a War and Domains chamber. Here Frederick followed the methods used by his father in the early days of the Gumbinnen Chamber. He retained the West Prussian chamber under his own direct control until 23 January 1774, when it was placed under the General Directory. For a period of five years the Netze district was treated as a special area till the king decided it was ready to be treated on the same footing as the rest of the monarchy. In 1777 the division of the region of the Bromberg *Kammerdeputation* into four counties, each with its own commissioner, and eighteen domains was concluded.

The annexation of West Prussia gave Frederick an opportunity to emulate his father in the *rétablissement* of a province, a field of activity in which his father's success had impressed him deeply as crown prince. Frequently-quoted reports of the Prussian Annexation Commission paint an unforgettable picture of the pitiful conditions of the towns and the low productivity of the land:

> Some towns were more like heaps of rubble than human settlements. To find the pavement in the street one had to dig through several feet of filth and rubbish. Numerous villages had altogether ceased to exist and occasionally one found traces of them in the middle of dense forests. The countryside was empty and neglected; the cattle underfed and of poor breeds; the farm implements of the most primitive kind down to the bladeless plough; the fields exhausted, full of weeds and stones; the meadows waterlogged; and the woods carelessly felled and thinned to sell as much timber as possible. The old fortified towns, called castles, lay in ruins and rubble, just like most of the smaller towns and villages. Most existing dwellings seemed scarcely suitable as shelter for human beings – miserable hovels of straw and clay, of the roughest sort, built with the poorest materials and in the most slap-dash manner. This land has been demoralized and depopulated by the endless wars and quarrels of past centuries, by fires and epidemics and poor administration.

The justice was as bad as the administration. The peasantry is debauched, the bourgeoisie non–existent; forests and swamps encroach on the towns, which – to judge from the old German graveyards – were at one time well-populated.

Only indirectly can the Polish state be blamed for this situation. From the period of the Swedish-Polish war of the previous century every generation had seen the country ravaged by terrible wars and incursions, billeting and plundering. The Great Northern War and the Seven Years War were followed by devastating epidemics that killed all hope of successful recovery; finally there was the confusion of the succession war and the confederate civil war. The members of the Prussian survey commission, despite their dismal findings cited above, praised the quality of the soil, especially in the Netze district. Unlike East Prussia and the Oderbruch area, West Prussia under Polish rule had never received state aid for the encouragement of immigrants, peasants or trade; the natives had had to rely on themselves, without incentives and without guidance on more up-to-date agricultural methods.

The West Prussian *rétablissement* began with a magnificent effort to bring the province into line with the other regions, and an experienced and efficient provincial administration was speedily got together. Yet it cannot be said that Frederick hurried on the reconstruction. That was not his way of doing things; deliberation and a sense of proportion were always characteristic of his methods. At his side were Domhardt and Brenckenhoff, untiring, inventive, immersed in the work; also privy finance councillor Franz Rembert Roden, president of the *Ober-Rechnungskammer* (Chief Bureau of Accounts), in charge of the land survey for the assessment rolls and of the assessment of the property tax. From the estate of the *starosti* (the Polish king's representative at district level) 79 domain *Ämter* were formed and their owners compensated with state pensions. Large ecclesiastical estates were also taken over and their clergy similarly compensated. Serfdom was abolished in 1772, though manorial and domain peasants remained in hereditable service until the reform edicts of 1803 and 1807 respectively.

In his determination to have the land settled by experienced German farmers the king allowed middle-class Germans to acquire sequestered Polish estates, preferring German businessmen to Polish aristocrats who would take their money to Poland and live in Warsaw. But the break-up of manorial estates into farmlands for colonists did not proceed beyond the planning stage, since there was a shortage both of settlers and money. Just over 50 per cent of the province's population at the time of its annexation was German, and the provincial administration was

under orders to raise the Casubian and Polish inhabitants to the German
level of efficiency. German colonists were, therefore, distributed
throughout the province as free leaseholders on hereditable holdings.
The king held that the surest way of teaching the indigenous inhabitants
'better methods and habits will always be to mix them in time with
Germans, who from the beginning should number two or three in each
village'. In practice, however, compact colonies proved more suitable:
in the Netze district, for example, fifty new villages were founded,
colonized by immigrants from Mecklenburg, the Lausitz, the Palatinate,
Thuringia and Saxony. Almost a third of all settlers came from Württemberg, and these maintained in their colonies their own dialect and
customs. During Frederick's reign 12,000 settlers at the most were
brought into West Prussia, scarcely more than two per cent of the
province's population. To settle the territory more densely the king
contemplated bringing in Tartars and was willing to build mosques for
them. One cannot therefore talk of a policy of Germanization, any more
than one can talk of a self-assertive Polish nationalist element. The
ready cooperation of all classes and sections of the population, appreci-
ative of their unambiguous legal status and their increasing wealth,
facilitated the execution of the government's enlightened measures.

A programme, adapted to existing conditions, was also developed to
aid the towns. Elbing and Marienburg could help themselves, and were
made to do so. In Kulm, Konitz and Schönlanke the state gave support
to the dyeing, tanning and weaving industries. Graudenz was made
into a strong fortress, and many privileges were given to Kulm,
Graudenz, Mewe and especially to Bromberg. About 1,000 artisans and
their families moved into workshops and dwellings built specially for
them. The most important melioration project, however, was the
systematic opening of the numerous waterways. Within sixteen months
Brenckenhoff, with a work force of 6,000, built the Bromberg canal to
connect the Vistula to the Oder. Through the control that this gave over
the water levels of the Netze, Vistula and Nogat it was possible to lower
the Vistula so that the Nogat became the main stream, in the hope of
diverting Danzig's trade to Elbing and Bromberg. In this there was
partial success. All Frederick's projects in West Prussia were firmly based
on practical reasoning. Nothing was done for show. Pleas for the restoration of the great rectory at the Marienburg were turned down: the
building was needed for a weaving-shed and a granary, and the rest was
used as barracks.

The province's security, especially against Polish partisans in the south,
was not neglected. In 1773 four new fusilier regiments were raised,

cantoned at Marienburg, Preussisch Holland, Braunsberg and Kulm-Graudenz. The following year a fifth fusilier regiment, with quarters at Mewe, Dirschau and Preussisch Stargard, was raised, a regiment of infantry was transferred to Elbing, and a garrison regiment was stationed in the suburbs of Danzig. Strasburg, Soldau, Köbau and Neumark each acquired a regiment of hussars, while another was distributed among ten towns of the Netze district from Schneidemöhl via Nakel to Usch. A dragoon regiment was stationed at Marienwerder and four other Pomeranian towns. While the influx of soldiers brought extra money to the towns, the shortage of houses made the duty of billeting troops particularly onerous. In time, however, barracks were built as well as quarters. From 1773 onwards, with the exception of 1778–79, Frederick held an annual review of the troops and received the reports of the higher officials at Mockrau near Graudenz, where he had a simple half-timbered house with a thatched roof built for himself. Numerous cabinet orders bear, therefore, the West Prussian name of Mockrau as their place of origin. Important for the development of a flourishing province was the institution of a prompt and reliable postal service. In the time of the Teutonic Knights there had been a good service, but no trace of that remained in 1772. From 1 October 1772 East Prussia was once again connected by post with the Kurmark, through Pomerania. A new wide-ranging network with 600 horses was set up by the Fehrbellin postmaster Uhl, appointed West Prussian chief postal director; within ten weeks he had assembled the necessary personnel and material. In Ermland the old episcopal postal service with its mounted and foot post was replaced by three larger post-coach routes and ten post offices.

Aristocracy and clergy, hitherto the important classes in the provinces, were soon superseded by the administrators; but the Catholic Church was treated with consideration. Although its property was taken over by the state, the Church was not secularized. Protestants had to pay their usual contributions to the Catholic priests (with the exception of the surplice-fees). This considerably hampered the building of Protestant churches and caused much unrest in Protestant communities in the province, especially since Frederick – as in Silesia – had been greeted as a liberator from the theological dogmatism of Catholicism. As in Silesia, he also refused to return to the Protestants those churches which had been confiscated by the Catholic bishops before the Prussian annexation. The province had 560 Catholic churches; but only twelve new Protestant churches, all in the simplest style, were built. Some Protestant churches were also attached to livings. The Mennonites were allowed to commute army service into cash payments, but they were forbidden to acquire more property so as not to diminish the cantonal catchment areas. In principle no distinction was made between creeds. The Chamber at Marienwerder kept a watch on the buying and selling of ecclesiastical estates. Only two bishoprics, Ermland and Kulm, were entirely within West Prussia's ecclesiastical administration; part of four other dioceses (Gnesen, Plock, Posen and Kujawien) lay within the province. Following previous practice in Silesia, officials were appointed to act as observers of ecclesiastical jurisdiction and the visitations of Polish bishops within West Prussia. The benevolent attitude of the Prussian administration towards the Catholic clergy was an important element in the peaceful incorporation of West Prussia into the Prussian state. Count Karl von Hohenzollern, coadjutor (1777) and later bishop of Kulm (1785), abbot of Pelplin and later prince-bishop of Ermland, warmly identified himself with this policy.

The supervision of schools remained the responsibility of the clergy who were obliged to teach three model lessons each week in the presence of the schoolmaster, 'so that he might be able, at the same time, to improve his own teaching'. In 1776 a school fund was set up for West Prussia and regulations on education issued. The number of schools within the area administered by the Marienwerder Chamber was almost doubled, 187 being added to the existing 194. There was much room for improvement in the Netze district where only nineteen Catholic and thirteen Lutheran schoolmasters were appointed up to 1778, mainly on the initiative of the local population. The Lutheran teachers often came from the orphanage at Halle. The eight Jesuit colleges in West Prussia and Ermland were changed, with the approval of the majority of the staff, into grammar schools. A cadet college with places for sixty pupils was opened at Kulm in 1776.

Carmer and Svarez, the great Prussian jurists, were responsible for the establishment of judicial institutions in the new province and founded the provincial superior court at Bromberg. All judicial institutions had in 1772 been put on the same basis as elsewhere in the Prussian state, a necessary prerequisite for the great administrative changes ahead. The legal and administrative changes all have a familiar ring: taxation of nobility and clergy, hereditary tenure on the domains, and the settlement of colonists on the domain *Vorwerke*. Payments from the province's domains and customs duties to the Domains *Kasse*, and from *Kontri-butionen* and *Akzise* to the War *Kasse* mounted in the last years of the reign to 400,000 talers annually after the costs of the army stationed in the province had been paid. Yet the West Prussian Chamber was a whole year in arrears, a fact which it did not dare confess to Frederick. State contributions to the province were not inconsiderable: 460,000 talers were spent in setting up new royal domains and purchasing estates; from the profits of these estates and domains teachers' salaries were paid. Leaseholders and peasants who were in financial difficulties were granted tax remissions. The towns received grants towards the improvement of trade and contributions (the so-called 'competence money') at a rate of 22,000 talers (later reduced to 18,000 talers) annually. Duties always remained below the estimates as merchants invariably avoided Prussia with its high tariff walls. The rate of the *Kontribution* favoured the peasants by leaving profits above the assessed rate free of tax, a point not at first understood and therefore not fully exploited. In the years 1774–86 the state contributed more than 6·7 million talers to the economy of West Prussia, a high amount for the period. This money financed town improvements, ameliorations, colonization, waterways, fortresses and factories. The development of industry was very important if the province was to be made self-supporting in the future, able to export goods such as high-quality cloth to neighbouring countries.

Considering the demands made on Frederick by the state as a whole he devoted much time, energy, money and personal attention to the affairs of West Prussia. Without wishing to belittle the achievements of Domhardt and his aides, it should be stressed that the king was, in his own lifetime, referred to as the actual president-in-chief of West Prussia. His aim was to turn those who lived there into 'human beings and useful members of the state' in the full sense of these words as understood in the age of the Enlightenment, so that – as he wrote to Voltaire in 1772 – 'a land which brought forth a Copernicus is no longer bogged down in a kind of barbarism to which the tyranny of the magnates has reduced it'.

VI

The Old King

CHURCH AND SCHOOL ADMINISTRATION

Frederick William I had failed to inculcate in his successor that belief in Pietism which coloured his own approach to the problems of government. Frederick II was a freethinker, a deist, a freemason, a *philosophe* without metaphysical depth. Contemporary French literature offered no significant insights into the mysteries of Christianity; what Frederick searched for, anyhow, in the writings of the Enlightenment were 'rational' solutions. His personal rejection of Christian beliefs did not affect his public attitude. He took seriously his role as *summus episcopus* of the Lutheran Church in Prussia, denying himself as king – and everybody else – liberty to mock religion publicly though he did so in private. Religion in Frederick's reign had its allotted place in the structure of the Prussian state.

The young king's maxim that all religions were equally worthy of toleration so long as they tolerated one another shows how little he feared the temper of intolerance. The era of the religious wars had passed: if players on the European chessboard were still identifiable as white or black, Frederick presumed that he had the approval of the enlightened world if he ignored such distinctions. It was, of course, an easy attitude to adopt, for at his accession Prussia's population was almost exclusively Protestant. Only in the western provinces were Catholics in a majority: Gelderland with 49 Catholic churches and 16 religious houses, was entirely Catholic; Lingen, 97 per cent Catholic, had 14 Catholic churches; Cleves, with 83 Catholic churches and 40 religious houses, was 60 per cent Catholic. In the eastern provinces, less than 10 per cent of the population of Lauenburg and Bütow were Catholics; while the Catholics numbered less than 5 per cent in the rest of the Prussian state and less than 1 per cent in Brandenburg, Pomerania and the Neumark. Of the total population of 2·3 million 90 per cent were Lutheran, 3 per cent Calvinist and 7 per cent Catholic. A first survey of church and school buildings showed that the state was responsible for the upkeep of 1,611 Lutheran churches which were in the gift of the crown. Yet another survey revealed the considerable wealth of the Catholic Church in Prussia.

Even before any changes were made in traditional church organization the outcome of the First Silesian War presented Prussia with a hitherto unfamiliar confessional situation. For the first time a large and contiguous province with a Catholic majority was annexed to the state. Frederick set out to woo not just his new Protestant subjects but the whole population of Silesia; he made no attempt to wean the Catholics from their faith nor did he rob them of the preferential rights they had possessed under the Habsburgs. All the rights enjoyed by the Catholic Church in the province were confirmed in full and its administration remained in Catholic hands, at least temporarily. The Lutheran population continued to pay tithes to the Catholic clergy, who contributed nothing towards the modest churches which the Lutherans were now allowed to build. The initial jubilation of the Silesian Lutherans at the Prussian annexation was dampened by the feeling of injustice at the double burden of having to support their own and the Catholic churches: they found it as difficult as their Catholic neighbours to accept that state interests took priority over confessional matters. In 1742 the Lutheran Church in Silesia was divided into two Supreme Consistories with seats at Breslau and Glogau; in 1744 another Lutheran ecclesiastical administrative unit was created in Upper Silesia with offices at Oppeln. In 1756 Silesia had 212 Lutheran parishes, some communities of Bohemian Moravian Exultants and of the Union of Brothers, and a few Calvinist flocks. The ordinance for the inspection of Lutheran and Calvinist administrative districts in Silesia (*Evangelisch-lutherische Inspektions- und Presbyterialordnung für das Herzogtum Schlesien*) issued in 1742 organized inspection districts and regulated external organization; this was followed in 1748 by an ordinance on visitations and in 1750 by another dealing with surplice fees. Prussia's relationship with the Catholic Church in Silesia did not proceed smoothly. Frederick carefully prevented Protestant encroachment, appeared friendly and willing to maintain the *status quo*, and accepted the homage of the Catholic clergy without question. But the bishopric of Breslau was subordinate to the archbishopric of Gnesen; other parts of Silesia (Hultschin, Katscher and Leobschütz) were part of the archbishopric of Olmütz; while the vicariate of Glatz formed part of the archbishopric of Prague. That these church connections permitted Austria also to maintain other ties with Silesia was obvious. The papal right of appointment to the bishopric of Breslau was repugnant to Frederick's conception of sovereignty; he had yet to learn how to deal with the Roman curia. After it had thwarted his plan to make the bishop of Breslau, Cardinal von Sinzendorf, vicar-general for all Prussia, Frederick set up a synodal college of judges – formed from members of Breslau's cathedral chapter – as an ecclesiastical court of the second and third instance. On Sinzendorf's death in 1747 the king had Count Philip Gotthard von Schaffgotsch, the most debauched of the Breslau canons, elected bishop of that see and by various subterfuges obtained papal approval for the appointment. His intention of using Schaffgotsch as his mouthpiece in dealing with the Silesian Catholics was, however, frustrated by the bishop's defection to the Austrians in 1756, upon which the cathedral chapter elected his suffragan, Count Strachwitz, to succeed him. The king's attempt to nominate to ecclesiastical benefices caused further trouble with the Catholic Church. State interests and Protestant tradition prompted Frederick to claim the right of appointment from a short-list of three candidates, but the curia – for fundamental reasons – refused the exercise of this right to a Protestant king. Frederick was all the same often able to influence appointments to livings indirectly through various state administrative bodies, not only in Silesia and in Lingen but later also in West Prussia. The king was motivated by considerations of state: he regarded Catholics as being divided in their allegiance and tried to steer them away from state service. He certainly mistrusted the Silesian clergy, suspecting them of pro-Austrian sentiment and of harbouring deserters; and he therefore severely restricted their freedom of movement. Since it proved impossible to re-draw diocesan boundaries along provincial lines, Frederick arranged to have a number of religious houses, some in Upper Silesia and (later) others in West Prussia, including the abbey of Rehwalde, made independent of affiliated houses in Austrian territory. That the purpose of this action was political rather than religious or racial is shown by the fact that the Franciscans were allowed to retain a connection with the Polish friaries of their order: the king's real motive was to prevent Austrian ecclesiastical and political influence in Silesia. Cocceji proposed as early as 1742 that benefices in the Catholic Church should be restricted to native-born Silesians, but the scarcity of suitable candidates frequently made this impracticable. Inevitably the visitation of Prussian parishes by foreign prelates was construed as interference in the internal affairs of the state. When the archbishop of Olmütz made his Silesian visitations in 1756 and 1764 he was accompanied by Prussian commissaries; so was the archbishop of Gnesen and the bishop of Kujawien in West Prussia in 1775 and 1777. Prussia's high taxation rates were a novel experience for the hitherto privileged Silesian Catholic clergy. The property of defunct religious houses was confiscated by the state; the Catholic Church was forbidden to acquire new property, nor could it privately dispose of that which it already possessed – a measure in part intended as a discouragement to land speculators. To increase productivity the king abolished some of the numerous Catholic and Protestant feast days, but fierce opposition by all Silesians forced him to moderate this policy. While religious tolerance was maintained in Silesia, Frederick frequently interfered with the previously sacrosanct constitution of the Catholic Church or imposed changes contrary to canon law. Such apparent contradictions were not motivated by deceitfulness or arrogance, or even by 'Protestant' bigotry on the king's part, but by vigilant concern for the interest of the state as a whole.

Those Silesian and West Prussian Protestants who complained that Frederick did little for them overlooked the fact that they were in a minority in their provinces and that the king had neither the power nor the desire to alter the relative positions of the two faiths. The virtue of tolerance had to be learned by both confessions: the Catholics were made to realize that the Protestants enjoyed equal rights with themselves, and the Protestants had to accept that church buildings which earlier had been taken away from them could not now be restored by the king. The Protestant confessions for their part also had to show tolerance among themselves. Only in 1748 did East Friesland allow Lutherans to practise their faith. Emden's first Lutheran church was not built until 1774; about this time Leer's Lutheran church was permitted to erect a tower. The state presented the former garrison church to Aurich's Calvinist minority. Sects were tolerated and churches built for them, as long as they made no claim to a special position within the state. In the interests of religious peace controversial sermons and any form of heresy hunting were forbidden. The ultimate purpose of all state regulations on religious matters was the preservation of state unity. The state claimed and obtained supremacy over the churches.

The laying of the foundation stone of the Catholic St Hedwig's Cathedral in Berlin in 1747 – the *Residenzstadt* of the king of the Protestants – caused a sensation throughout Europe. Frederick, who directly and indirectly contributed much to its building, was extravagantly praised by the pope. When the sums available proved insufficient, the king in 1754 arranged for a church-building lottery to be held – outside Prussia, of course. The Seven Years War interrupted work on the site and it was not until 1 November 1773 that the cathedral was consecrated.

The ceremony was to have taken place on 15 October, the Feast of St Hedwig, but was postponed because the bishop of Ermland, the officiating prelate, was unable to attend. Among the Catholic clergy it was believed that 1 November was deliberately chosen because it was the anniversary of the suppression of Catholicism in Brandenburg by Elector Joachim II in 1539. In a letter to Voltaire the king justified his interest in the building of the cathedral: 'You accuse me of excessive tolerance. I am proud of this failing. Would that it were the only failing of which princes could be accused.'

Religious toleration did not, however, mean that the separation of church and state had already been achieved. Indeed the connection between church and state was strongly emphasized. This was especially true of the Lutheran Church, where appointments were controlled by the king. But the Catholic Church also acquired official status in Prussia, e.g. in its keeping of church records, in matters relating to the *Kassen*, and in the administration of estates and villages on ecclesiastical land. Church involvement in state affairs was sometimes attacked by the Protestant confessions: the reading from the pulpit of numerous edicts from the king, the chamber and the domain took much time during services, though not at the expense of long sermons. The chambers or special ministerial commissions inspected church accounts, even those of noble patrons. As patron-in-chief of the Church the king was also concerned with appointments and stipends. The great Instruction to the General Directory of 20 May 1748 dealt, in Article XIX, 5, with all the king's responsibilities for maintaining the fabric of churches, parsonages and school-houses. Clerics with previous service as chaplains in the army, hospitals or orphanages were to be given preference in appointments to vacant parishes. In 1775 the churchwardens of Ragnit proposed that parochial clergy should be paid fixed salaries instead of being dependent upon an uncertain living from glebe lands and payments in kind. The king considered this a 'good idea' and ordered an enquiry. In 1750 a general visitation of the Kurmark was decreed on the lines of that already held in Pomerania and East Prussia. These visitations were connected with royal plans for changes in the upper reaches of church administration.

A departmental regulation of 1749 gave Cocceji, the minister of justice, authority to examine the ecclesiastical department of the privy council set up by Frederick William. The head of this department, minister of state Christian von Brandt, had died in March 1749. Cocceji put Johann Peter Süssmilch, a consistorial councillor and dean of Berlin cathedral, in charge of the preparatory work. Süssmilch, who had a well-deserved reputation for organizational skill and statistical analysis, found this a time-consuming and difficult task: ecclesiastical jurisdiction had been transferred to lay judicial authorities on 10 May and this caused many problems. An unfortunate rivalry developed between him and Nathanael Baumgarten, preacher at the Friedrichswerder and Dorotheenstädtischen church in Berlin – who had been asked to provide an alternative proposal – and with the army's chief chaplain, Johann Christoph Decker, court and garrison preacher in Potsdam who examined and ordained preachers for the orphanages. The first step towards the foundation of a ministry of ecclesiastical affairs was the formation on 4 October of the Lutheran Supreme Consistory, a body consisting of two presidents and seven principal consistorial councillors. Although their competence was confined to the Lutheran Church, the first president and three of the seven councillors were Calvinists. The Supreme Consistory was the state's highest ecclesiastical body with authority over all provincial consistories (with the exception of those in Silesia and Guelders); but it was at the same time the Kurmark's own provincial consistory and had its own provincial chancery. As the Supreme Consistory was part of the privy council, of which body the first president was a member, all its documents went through the secret Chancery. Among the functions of the Supreme Consistory was the employment and supervision of preachers, the theological examination of the Kurmark's ordinands, the inspections of the religious foundations independent of the provincial consistories, and the provision of references for candidates for chairs of theology at the universities of Halle and Königsberg. Performing similar functions for Prussia's Calvinist communities was the long-established Reformed Church Directory; for the Huguenot parishes, founded in large numbers throughout Prussia at the time of the Huguenot settlements, there was the French Supreme Directory. Some judicial powers were returned to the Lutheran Supreme Consistory on 16 May 1760: erring clergymen could be punished by being relieved of their offices for periods up to three months and fined up to thirty talers; all other offences and legal quarrels were to be dealt with by the ordinary law courts. The Pomeranian consistory at Saalfeld, which had evolved from the bishopric of Riesenburg and exercised ecclesiastical supervision over southern East Prussia, was dissolved on 12 July 1751 at Cocceji's suggestion. Its ecclesiastical powers were given to the Samland consistory at Königsberg, the only consistory now remaining in East Prussia, and its three civilian councillors were transferred to the main office at Marienwerder. The dissolution of the Saalfeld consistory had serious consequences for Prussian church policy since the Elbing clergy, who had previously been ordained by it, now claimed the right of ordination for themselves though the bishop of Ermland. The Polish crown made strong legal objections. It is clear that neither Frederick nor Cocceji had realized the political implications of changes in Prussian ecclesiastical administration and that the General Directory had not been consulted on Cocceji's proposed dissolution of the Saalfeld consistory: neither had stopped to consider what responsibility, if any, Prussia might have for the Elbing clergy.

The next phase in the administrative reform came in the autumn of 1763 on the retirement of Karl Ludolph Freiherr von Danckelmann from the presidency of the Ecclesiastical Department. This was now completely separated from the Department of Justice and all church and school affairs were brought together in one department. This was a sensible step; but it was (for reasons of faith) opposed by the Calvinists who did not wish to relinquish their dominant influence in these fields. Philipp Joseph Pandin de Jariges, the minister of justice and himself a Calvinist, sought a suitable head for the new department from among his co-religionists in the other German states, but the number of wealthy Calvinist noblemen qualified for the post was necessarily limited. Von Dörnberg, the president of the Hessian *Regierung*, showed an interest in the position but pitched his demands so high as to make him unacceptable to Frederick. Conversely, as one Prussian agent concerned in these negotiations complained, 'the prejudices current abroad about the Prussian service, although without foundation, are sufficiently strong to keep many from entering it.' Jariges' failure to have his fellow Calvinist and favourite, Johann Ludwig von Dorville, a director of the French High Court in Prussia, appointed to the post gave rise to a scheme for dividing the responsibilities of the new department between two presidents of similar rank and title, one in charge of the Lutheran section, the other of the Calvinist. On 15 June 1764 the king approved this arrangement. Ernst Friedemann Freiherr von Münchhausen, first president of the *Kammergericht* (the Supreme Court), who had left the Saxon service for the Prussian in 1750, was appointed first minister. While retaining responsibility for the Silesian Department of Justice and for the preparation of all criminal cases he took control of Lutheran churches, religious foundations and schools. He became president of the Supreme Consistory and of the Directory for the Revenues of the Kurmark Ecclesiastical domains (*die kurmärkische Amtskirchen-Revenuen-Direktion*); he was curator of the Dreifaltigkeits church and head of the Directory for the Poor (*Armendirektorium*), director of the Royal Library, the Art Collection, the Cabinet of Medals and the Library Fund. Dorville was appointed minister of the Ecclesiastical Department and took over the presidency of the *Kammergericht* from Münchhausen. Within the department Dorville assumed control of Calvinist churches and schools, became president of the Directory of the Reformed Church, the French Department and the French Supreme Consistory; director of the Joachimstaler School, the School Foundation Fund (*Montis Pietatis*) and the Potsdam Home for Widows. This division of staff and responsibilities undermined whatever influence the department might have been expected to wield in the church and school reforms which were just beginning. It was indeed regrettable that the king, at this time totally absorbed in the work of the *rétablissement*, should have been so ill-advised by Jariges. The death of Dorville in December 1770 did not affect this bisected structure of the department and the Calvinists retained their ministry within it. They were determined to win Freiherr Ferdinand von Dörnberg for their cause and did so: in May 1771 he took over Dorville's responsibilities, including the presidency of the three senates of the *Kammergericht*. Münchhausen left the Ecclesiastical Department in January, to be succeeded by the minister for justice Karl Abraham Freiherr von Zedlitz. As Münchhausen retained control over the Silesian Department of Justice, and Zedlitz's only outside responsibility was for criminal proceedings and the affairs of the colonists from the Palatinate, the latter was able to devote himself to the work of his new department. But not for long. His élan and zest won him Frederick's full confidence and in 1772 the king gave him, in addition to his other duties, the difficult post of head of the Supreme Court for Customs and Excise (*Ober-Akzise- und Zoll-Gericht*), 'so as to give both authority and activity to the court'. Here is another instance of the way in which a few specially-qualified and exceptionally able officials were overburdened with work. Only in 1788, under Johann Christoph von Wöllner, did the Ecclesiastical Department become a purely functional ministry.

Despite the existence of centralized administrative bodies regional differences surviving from earlier periods had still to be reckoned with. There was no question of a central direction of church affairs, though the provincial consistories had lost their semi-autonomous position. Even the attempt to introduce a common hymn book in some provinces failed. The king did not insist; he took the line that as far as he was concerned every member of the congregation could sing from whichever hymn book he liked. In Cleves-Mark the synodal constitution remained in force, binding Lutherans as well as Calvinists. Each Calvinist church was administered by a presbytery; several presbyteries formed a 'class' which each year came together in a 'class conventicle' to elect moderators as collegial leaders of the district synod. The Cleves synod was formed from three classes, that for the Mark from four. Every third year these two joined with the provincial synod from neighbouring Jülich and Berg to hold a general synod. The Lutherans were also organized into classes though they did not join with groups from neighbouring territories. Soest and the Soest plain had their own urban and suburban conventicles. Until the formation of the Supreme Consistory in 1752 all these churches were self-governing, without any supervision from the state. This also affected Cleves-Mark, for though it had no consistory of its own, the *Regierung* was made responsible to the Supreme Consistory in Berlin for religious affairs. On 18 January 1771 the Ecclesiastical Department had responsibility for Protestant religious matters transferred to the provincial administrative college established at Guelders in 1770. A sub-consistory was established at Köslin in East Pomerania in 1747, at the same time as the chamber committee was set up. Lauenburg, which had a sub-consistory since 1695, was – with Bütow – transferred to the West Prussian consistory after its foundation at Marienwerder in 1772. West Prussia at this time had 68 Lutheran parishes and 70 churches, but any increases in their number was unlikely, as Article VIII of the Polish-Prussian Treaty of 18 September 1772 guaranteed the integrity of the Catholic position in West Prussia. East Pomerania also had Catholic churches in areas where all the inhabitants were Lutheran; in Draheim alone eleven village churches stood empty, unwanted by the Catholics, but forbidden for Lutheran use.

One of the biggest surprises sprung on his contemporaries by the Philosopher of Sans Souci was his toleration of the Society of Jesus, considered the very symbol of sinister reaction, and the protection he offered the Jesuits in his own dominions. The papal brief of 1773 which abolished the order was not published in Prussia, and Bishop Strachwitz of Breslau was instructed to extend his protection to the Jesuits in the exercise of all their religious functions. Their scientific and pedagogical approach to teaching made them irreplaceable in Silesia and West Prussia; even the education of Catholic seminarians would have suffered had their services been withdrawn. The numerous Jesuit-run gymnasia were not closed. Tolerance and *raison d'état* mingled in the royal decree of 1776 ordering the Jesuits to change their name to that of 'Members of the Royal School Institute'. From 1781 all Jesuit schools in Silesia, West Prussia and Ermland were turned into academic gymnasia.

In the many new rural settlements different religions had to live side by side. Although Catholic colonists had been ejected from the council of a Pomeranian town, the authorities saw to it that they remained in the province; soon they had their own priests and chapels. The arrival of Calvinist settlers in Lauenburg in 1754 provoked communal riots, but strict measures were taken to prevent the interruption of their religious services. Legal action as well as social integration helped to quell intolerance, until the issue of mixed marriages arose to cause friction throughout the nineteenth century.

The army insisted on the different religious denominations serving together without friction. Difficulties did arise, however, since soldiers and their families were grouped in military communities with their own pastors, quite separate from the civil church administration. The military communities were subordinate to the *Kriegskonsistorium* (the War Consistory), whose president was the auditor-general, the army's most senior legal official. The members of the consistory were the deputy auditor-general, the chief chaplain of the army, the war councillors and chief auditors stationed in Berlin, and the padre of the Berlin garrison. Two staff officers attended if military matters had to be debated. Chaplains were strictly forbidden to use their privileged position for proselytizing. The Revised Military Consistorial Reglement and Church Ordinance (*Renovierte Militär-Konsistorial-Reglement und Kirchenordnung*) of 3 August 1750, compiled by chief chaplain Johann Christoph Decker, passed by the consistory and approved by the king, contained the relevant regulations which remained in force, with various revisions, until 1811. Each regiment had its chaplain, appointed by the regimental commander after examination and ordination by the chief chaplain, who was the chaplain's superior in ecclesiastical matters. To him the chaplain submitted an annual report on his community and the army school, and a written sermon. The soldiers of the regiment, their families and servants, were part of the military community, regardless of religious persuasions: religion came second to the indissoluble unity of the regiment. This emphasis on regimental *esprit de corps*, as well as the prescribed toleration, helped to dilute confessional differences, but the internal cohesion was naturally greatest where individual differences were least. In peacetime all chaplains were Lutheran; only in wartime were Catholic and Calvinist chaplains appointed to care for their co-religionists. Catholic military chaplains were not permitted to form military congregations in peacetime. Their numbers were always low; in the Seven Years War, ninety Lutheran and four Catholic chaplains were (with their assistants) thought sufficient for some 100,000 troops of many nationalities and creeds. Only regularly appointed Lutheran chaplains were allowed to perform the priestly offices of baptismal, marriage and funeral services. Protests from the archbishop of Cologne and the bishops of Roermond and Ermland against this breach of religious liberty were rejected. The chief chaplain seemed unaware of the fact that according to Catholic canon law the Tridentine decree *Tametsi*, though not operative in Potsdam, invalidated baptisms and marriages conducted by a Lutheran minister in the town of Wesel. Only after 1774 were Catholic priests allowed to officiate within the military communities, though the surplice fee was still paid to the Lutheran chaplains.

In the military communities nobody was forced to attend Lutheran services; soldiers were perfectly free to attend Catholic or other churches. A complaint from the garrison at Stettin that the children of Catholic soldiers were being forced to adopt Lutheranism caused Frederick to demand a reason why the regiment 'acts so harshly towards Catholic soldiers, which is contrary to my will and to justice'. The first Catholic military chaplain appointed at the beginning of the king's reign was Fr Dominikus Torck who came from the Dominican friary at Halberstadt, which continued to supply Catholic chaplains to the army. On campaign religious discipline was stricter: the regiment met twice daily for prayer and Holy Communion was held every other week. Hymns were popular throughout the army. On the evening of the victory at Leuthen 'Now thank we all our God' was sung spontaneously on the battlefield itself and has since been known as the Leuthen Chorale. The singing of hymns on many other occasions is well documented: in the reports of officers, clergy, neutral witnesses, even enemies. Before leaving camp in the morning the regiment sang a hymn and the Prussian poet, Major Ewald von Kleist, who died in the Seven Years War, noted that 'mornings on the march, before the soldiers strike up songs about the king of Prussia, they sing hymns'. No other army of the period permitted freedom of religion while at war. The supra-confessional Prussian military communities, with at least formal concessions to different religious groups, are the rare fruit of practical tolerance in the age of Enlightenment. Frederick held, and repeatedly stressed, that it was 'sensible' and 'essential' that within the army all men should be treated equally, in matters of religion as well. The pastor of the Marienkirche and Nicolaikirche in Berlin, Johann Joachim Spalding, in 1772 wrote also of the 'usefulness of the office of pastor' in civilian life. Churches everywhere experienced a difficult crisis in the second half of the eighteenth century and were badly shaken by intellectual and moral decline. Frederick, however, never questioned the church's institutional role; the work done during his reign to maintain and stabilize its relations with the state helped the church over the critical phase until it found ways and means to get its message across to a new generation.

Frederician church policy, with its enlightened tolerance, did not ignore Prussia's scattered but religious and culturally strongly unified Jewish communities. The king's comments on the Jews in general, as on other denominations, are often ambiguous, changeable and even contradictory: he cared more for individual cases which aroused his concern for justice and humanity. State interests, as in other fields, tended to dictate policy. Every Jew who was able to serve the state was given its aid and protection; energetic entrepreneurs and merchants with capital at their disposal were especially welcome in Prussia. But towards those who only thought of their own or their company's profits Frederick proved ruthless. He suffered some disappointments and disillusionment which provoked harsh comments and generalized criticism; and, to assess his Jewish policy, we should look not to these but to documents which show what action was taken with his approval. The administrative records show that the General Directory favoured granting the Jews greater protection and, as Frederick never tolerated the implementation of a policy of which he personally disapproved, we can deduce that he was of the same opinion. He may, however, have had to be convinced of its desirability: he was always open to practical arguments based on facts, and officials who shared his ambitions for the state expected a hearing and to be able to influence him to a greater or lesser extent. The poet Gotthold Ephraim Lessing, the most famous Prussian bureaucrat of his generation and the freest from anti-Semitic prejudices, expressed his own views in the dramatic poem *Nathan der Weise* (1779). From 1760 to 1765 Lessing was secretary to the governor of Breslau, General von Tauentzien, and had personal experience of the Silesian monetary system in the war years and the busy immediate post-war period. He had some unpleasant experiences with Jewish business men, but his behaviour towards them was, in the words of his literary rival Friedrich Nicolai, 'extremely just and wise, as everybody familiar with the circumstances knows'. Prussia was as far removed from emancipation and complete integration of the Jews as any other state of the *ancien régime*; but the intensity of its public and inter-departmental debate on the Jewish issue indicates a movement away from traditional prejudices towards greater tolerance. Its legislation for the Jews was in various ways more liberal than that of the rest of Europe and did at least provide binding rules for contracting parties. Exclusion, persecution or expulsion of Jews did not happen in Frederician Prussia; on the contrary, the future equality of the Jews was brought closer.

There was room for conflicting views on the legal status of Jewish communities and the powers of their religious leaders. When the consistories were shorn of some of their judicial powers, the minister of justice pressed for similar limitations in respect of the Jews. From this followed a full scale review of all legislation affecting Jews, and a comprehensive 'Revised General Privilege and Regulation for the Jews in the Kingdom of Prussia' was issued on 17 April 1750, valid for all provinces except Silesia and East Friesland. Rabbis were confirmed in their religious jurisdiction and their competence to settle problems of inheritance and marriage within their own communities: as the General Directory pointed out, 'Jews can be tried only in accordance with the tenets of their own Mosaic law, and as long as they enjoy toleration in the lands of His Prussian Majesty everything should be done in accordance with their law.' The minister of justice, who had recently taken matrimonial jurisdiction away from the Christian consistories, argued against this; but the king decided that the requisite powers 'should remain with the Jews in accordance with their privileges, on the grounds that this matter is of special importance to them, and nobody is harmed by their keeping these powers; and, if anyone thinks he is, he can appeal to our courts'. This cabinet order of 25 May 1750 was central to Frederick's conception of the position of the Jews in Prussia. The General Privilege, which remained in force until 1812, was later – with some changes – introduced into Silesia (where the Austrian regulations in respect of Jews had hitherto remained in force) and East Friesland and, on 28 February 1772, also into West Prussia. The elders of the Jewish communities had to compile monthly lists of numbers of Jews to be sent to the chambers. Recognition as a protected Jew (*Schutzjude*) cost 1,000 talers. Communal responsibility for crimes committed by members of the community, an exceptionally oppressive piece of legislation, was relaxed only in 1776 after an embittered legal struggle. The other 32 paragraphs of the General Privilege dealt with the trades which Jews were allowed to pursue, the election of rabbis, religious toleration and the conditions under which conversion was permitted.

The separation of trade from legal status transferred large areas of Jewish affairs from the Fourth to the Fifth Department. Until 1772 West Prussia was a free, though unprivileged, area for Jews and protection under the General Privilege was only slowly extended to this province. The king had demanded that all poor and unemployed Jews should leave West Prussia, but the administration rejected this as being impracticable. Within a year the Marienwerder Chamber had found work for most of the Jews within its jurisdiction, though some 7,000 Jews had to be settled in other parts of West Prussia and in the Netze district. Others were moved from rural areas into the towns but were allowed to stay in the province; the only ones to be deported were those who had arrived without permission from Poland after 1772. Quite a number of Jews found work in Stolzenberg, the new independent town formed from the Prussian suburbs of Danzig, at the fair at Altschottland, in the sea trade at Neufahrwasser, and in the new factories. The Jews who lived in the *Residenzstädte*, especially Berlin, were much better off. Those with money to invest received special privileges, the top range of which gave them a status similar to that of Christian merchants. But here, too, state interest rather than personal influence was decisive. The answer given by the Breslau *Oberamtsregierung* in 1777 to complaints of Christian merchants show official awareness of what was at stake: 'Not only do the principles of law and order demand that we protect the Privileged Jews; but the common good, especially as manifested in the preservation and development of industries, do so as well.'

The General Privilege of 1750 guaranteed the Jews undisturbed possession of their schools, synagogues and cemeteries at Königsberg, Berlin, Halberstadt, Halle and Frankfurt on the Oder. West Prussia was in 1772 found to have a considerable number of Jewish rural schools and these were supervised in the same way as those of Christians.

The clergy was officially empowered to supervise schools. The supervision of the clergy was the responsibility of the Supreme Consistory and the Ecclesiastical Department. Until the Seven Years' War Prussian primary education had changed little since the beginning of Frederick William's reign: the 'Royal Prussian Ordinance for Lutheran and Calvinist gymnasia and other Schools', issued on 24 October 1713, was still in force in all provinces except Cleves-Mark and Ravensberg; similar regulations, though of a more-or-less provisional nature, had been introduced into Silesia and East Friesland. Numerous supplementary directives were, of course, issued during Frederick's reign, e.g. the necessary warning (dated 29 October 1741) to estate owners that the proper maintenance of school furniture was their responsibility. Procedural changes were facilitated when in 1750 the newly-founded Supreme Consistory was made responsible for the supervision of teachers. Common educational standards were not established. Variations in local conditions in patronage (which could be state or manorial), in the number and ability of teachers, in the time which the pupils could spend at school (depending on the seasons) and, not least, in the teaching aids available – all militated against uniformity. The development of a wider network of schools was in itself an important step forward. Most children now received some schooling, fairly regularly in the winter, less regularly during the summer when farmwork had the prior call on them.

The majority of youngsters were educated by teachers whose qualifications were meagre. A systematic start was, however, made with teacher training. It began, characteristically, with state encouragement for private initiative. Motivated by Pietism Johann Julius Hecker, a student of August Hermann Francke at Halle and experienced in the running of schools for the poor, established in 1747, when a pastor at the Dreifaltigkeits Church in Berlin, the *Ökonomisch-Mathematische Realschule*. This vocational school ran an 'Institute', a training course for teachers. Hecker's collaborator at this Institute was Johann Friedrich Hähn, a *Realschule* inspector, who developed new and progressive teaching methods. An Instruction of 25 September 1752 gave preference to students of the Institute in the selection of schoolteachers. In 1753 the state assumed responsibility for the Institute and renamed it the Kurmark Training College for Rural Schoolteachers. Hecker himself, an authority on pedagogy, was often called upon by Frederick for advice on educational matters. When the Minden War and Domains Chamber in 1753 submitted to the king a draft proposal of twenty-four paragraphs for a general school ordinance, it was immediately sent to Hecker who revised it in cooperation with the General Directory. Issues of general significance were now considered. How could the state persuade patrons and estate owners to help the rural primary schools reach a set standard in the teaching of reading, catechism and, if possible, writing and arithmetic to male and female children? How could the schools be kept open throughout the year without interfering too much with regional customs which, for instance, used children to herd cattle. Educational propaganda in the countryside would be necessary to awaken interest in reform. The Minden draft, revised and supplemented, was confirmed in April 1754; but the Seven Years War interrupted work on a model school ordinance for Minden's Latin school.

On 8 February 1763, a week before the signing of the peace treaty, Frederick committed the Prussian state to an extensive and intensive drive for primary education, to run alongside the effort to promote the economic development of the state. By a cabinet order, dated 1 April 1763, the king told the minister of the Ecclesiastical Department 'that rural schooling was to be improved and better organized throughout my provinces'. A *Reglement* was to be prepared, and superintendents were instructed to send to the Supreme Consistory full reports on the condition of rural, urban and noble schools and teachers. A decree was read from all the pulpits in the land that from now on no schoolmaster would be appointed who had not passed Hecker's examination. Within a few weeks Hecker submitted a comprehensive draft, based on work done on the Minden proposals of 1754, which (after consultations with interested departments) was published on 12 August 1763. This was the famous *General-Landschul-Reglement*, valid for all the territories of the monarchy without exception. In accordance with pietistic principles singing, prayers, the reading of the scriptures and the learning of the catechism were stipulated as essential; regulations as to hours of teaching, syllabuses and textbooks were next laid down, and the 'New Berlin ABC for Spelling and Reading' published in 3 parts between 1758 and 1761 by Johann Friedrich Hähn (general superintendent for Altmark-Prignitz) was specially recommended. Each child was to have his own copy of books; fees were graduated according to age and poor children had their fees paid from money collected in church. If children missed school parents and guardians would be fined. Three hours of lessons were to be held each day during the summer months; child herders had to attend school at least three times weekly, and would be replaced in their non-school tasks by herders employed by the village community. The clerical supervisors of the schools should in their annual reports cover the conduct of the teachers. A companion Instruction to the *General-Landschul-Reglement*, issued by the Supreme Consistory on 1 March 1764, laid down regulations for the annual visitations of churches and schools. Noble patrons were warned against contravening the school *Reglement*: the state's rights over children of school age were declared to be greater than those of the owners of the estates on which they lived, and absence from school would mean punishment of the patron.

The enactment of these decrees, necessary as they were after the long years of war, did not guarantee their execution. Estate owners and farmers resisted summer schooling; the teachers also disliked it and demanded higher salaries. During the early post-war years it was not possible to improve teachers' pay. Each profession had to manage as best it could, and most teachers kept going by extra work in gardening, cattle raising or trade. As teaching posts were occasionally bought, they must have been desirable positions. School fees were irregularly paid, however, and in many instances the teachers' qualifications remained inadequate. The royal decree which recommended suitable candidates among disabled or retired soldiers as teachers had little effect. Those who, after passing their examinations, were appointed made good teachers since the army had brought together men of varied earlier careers. But since so few did pass the examination the widespread assumption that the Prussian corporal ended up a village schoolmaster has now been proved false.*

In spite of much reluctance, protests and secret resistance the *Reglement* was put into effect, the chambers being particularly active in this field. General superintendent Hähn, inspector of schools in the duchy of Magdeburg, in his report of 12 December 1764, noted an improvement: the old habit of the children sitting 'idle, talking noisily' was gone. Inspections were subject to considerable delays and much expense, of which the staging services fell on reluctant village communities. The rationalist bureaucrats in the Supreme Consistory thought to remedy matters by getting the teachers themselves to compile *Schulkataloge* (school catalogues) describing the state of their own schools. Precise regulations laid down that these reports were to be written on four sheets of paper and forwarded twice yearly – in quadruplicate – to the consistories and inspectors. This was not a good solution and no substitute for independent inspection. Hähn calculated that the duchy of Magdeburg over a period of three years produced 14,000 *Schulkataloge* on 57,600 sheets of paper, and this at a time when the whole of Prussia had some 600,000 children of school-going age. Eventually (in 1771) the authorities, inundated with documents of which nobody took any notice, produced a simplified annual form.

Outside Berlin and Halle training courses for teachers were given at Kloster Berge near Magdeburg. This was quite inadequate to meet current needs, but as the state could not afford generous financial support the provinces had to rely on private initiative. In 1772 war councillor Balthasar Philipp Genge established a state-approved teacher training college (and an orphanage) on the outfarm of Loelken at Klein Dexen (*Kreis* Preussisch Eylau). The curriculum included nature study, hygiene and husbandry, and fifty-five teachers had been trained there by 1780. The last teacher training college to be set up during Frederick's reign was at Halberstadt, established in 1776 by consistorial councillor Christian Gottfried Struensee, a product of Kloster Berge and Hähn's inspectorate. Hähn, who had been transferred to East Friesland, held regular meetings

* In answer to a query the War Ministry reported on 16 September 1779 that they could recommend only 74 disabled soldiers out of a total of 3,443 for school-masters' posts (a later report made this 79 out of 4,258). Of these, 10 were trans-ferred to the consistory at Stettin in September 1779 for examination, but not one of them passed. In 1780 the West Prussian Chamber found only one applicant whom it could employ. Of 15 applicants, Königsberg picked 5 as suitable and employed 3. In the county of Ravensberg in 1761 there were 9 successful ex-soldier teachers. See F. Vollmer, pp. 218–32; H. Notbohm, pp. 152 ff., 210 f.

with the teachers of his area on teaching methods in accordance with
paragraphs 24–26 of the *Landschul-Reglement*, which required the pastor to
pay a weekly visit to the local school and the superintendent to hold a
monthly conference on educational matters with the teachers of his
district. It also insisted on the superintendent keeping his school inspections separate from his church visitations. The uselessness of the *Schulkataloge* as instruments of improvement was shown by the tenacity of
regional variations and customs. In Cleves no *Konduitenlisten* (conduct
reports) were drawn up, hardly any schools remained open during the
summer and schooling was, generally speaking, very backward. In
Lingen the opposition of the Calvinists proved too strong for the Catholic
teachers in their fight for equality. In Reckahn in the Kurmark, the land
owner Friedrich Eberhard von Rochow, dean of Halberstadt cathedral,
worked hard to improve rural conditions: he wrote on education and
founded a model village school. During his final reform phase, at the
beginning of the seventies, Frederick had more money available for
primary education. He gave most help to the central provinces of the
Kurmark, the Neumark, Pomerania and West Prussia, where he improved teachers' salaries, set up charity schools (the so-called *Gnaden-
schulen*, literally 'schools by grace'), and built a great number of simple
but adequate school-houses.

The *General-Landschul-Reglement* applied also to Silesia, yet the
province remained exceptional because of its Catholic majority. An
excellent set of regulations had been drawn up by the abbot of Sagan,
Johann Ignaz von Felbiger, for his own school district. Hecker brought
these to Schlabrendorff's attention and the minister proposed that they
should be extended to the whole province. The tolerance practised in
Frederician Prussia is exemplified by the fact that Felbiger discussed his
ideas at length with Hecker in Berlin and Hähn at Kloster Berge and
that his draft regulations (with hardly a change), approved by Frederick,
were issued on 3 November 1765 as the 'Royal Prussian General Reglement for Roman Catholic Rural Schools in the Towns and Villages of
the Sovereign Duchy of Silesia and the County of Glatz'. This document
of seventy-three paragraphs corresponded closely to the *Landschul-
Reglement* of 1763. It adopted Hähn's teaching methods; and responsibility for the supervision of schools was, as in the rest of the monarchy,
given to the clergy. Schlabrendorff opened a central training college for
Catholic teachers at Breslau in 1765, and a further eleven colleges and
251 schools were established in Silesia during the remaining years of
Frederick's reign.

The Silesian Reglement was superior to that for Prussia in general in that its regulations were binding also for urban schools. This had not been possible in the old provinces as the town magistrates jealously defended their right to supervision of schools against the central bureaucracy. With the exception of some of the schools in Berlin, Halle and Königsberg, town schools, though numerous, were of a mediocre quality. By means of the edict of 26 November 1764, which made the employment of urban teachers subject to their acceptability to the Supreme Consistory, Münchhausen (the minister of the Ecclesiastical Department) found an opportunity to introduce necessary reforms. The state claimed the right to supervise and standardize schools, but reform in content of teaching could hardly be expected from the central administrators who differed in their ideas on education. It should also be noted that the higher schools were not solely orientated towards university entrance. The Latin schools and the grammar schools had almost all 'middle forms' (*mittlere Klassen*) which prepared pupils for trade and practical professions; only the upper forms focused on academic studies. The academies for the nobility and the Junkers as, for instance, those at Brandenburg an der Havel and Liegnitz, taught their pupils logic, German and French, ancient history, geography and mathematics, a curriculum similar to that of the Cadet School in Berlin. Great emphasis was put on the acquisition of *esprit de corps*, fluency and clarity in speech, a clear style in writing, and the development of good judgment. The *Académie des Nobles*, founded by the king at Berlin as a nursery for the higher civil service and the army, had similar aids. Numerous un-controlled but not necessarily inferior schools flourished: the 'back-yard' or private schools (*Winkelschule*), the poor or charity schools (*Armenschule*) and the garrison schools where those born teachers, the drill masters, conscientious clergymen and pensioned staff-trumpeters usually formed the corps. Thus in the towns many types of teaching of varying quality coexisted, and the life of the eighteenth-century urban school was on the whole more chequered than that of the rural school with its more placid tempo.

To formulate purposeful educational theories was a task well suited to the spirit of the Enlightenment. But the Prussian school administration, working to a long-term plan, fought shy of experiment; reality rather than *desiderata* dictated its policy. Saxon educational practice was much admired, but to copy it, or even to bring in Saxon schoolmasters, was soon proved impracticable. In any case it would have needed much more money than could be spared at that time for the Prussian rural schools. The exercise of economy – mainly by making use of what was to hand – had to be practised in education as in all other branches of Frederician

Prussia. In his Letter on Education (15 December 1769) the king blamed some of the most reputable schools in the state for teaching aims he thought defective:

> There are several of them, such as the Joachimstaler Gymnasium, the new *Académie des Nobles*, the Cathedral School at Brandenburg and the Kloster Berge at Magdeburg. They have capable teachers. The only thing one can possibly reproach them with is that they stuff the heads of their pupils full of information instead of training them to think for themselves; they do not form their judgment early enough and they neglect to instil them with ambition or noble and virtuous principles.

The king sent his essay of 1769 to Münchhausen 'because some of the reflections in it might be of use to the universities': he had planned a complete educational system (which included the education of girls) and now sent it to the authority responsible for teaching to provide guidelines for future reform of the spirit of education. Independence as the purpose of education is his theme and here the experience of the absolute monarch, aware that independent leadership is in short supply, is nudging the enlightened philosopher. A few years later Frederick, when listing the most important educational Prussian establishments (the *Fredericianum* at Königsberg, the *Marienstifts-Gymnasium* at Stettin, the *Pädagogium Unser Lieben Frauen* at Magdeburg and the *Elisabeth-Schule* at Breslau), turned his attention to the specific educational content he desired. Rhetoric, logic and Latin were essential ('I do not depart from this'); so was religious instruction ('that the people do not turn Catholic'); but philosophy was 'not to be taught by clerics'. Regular attendance at school was necessary and boarding schools would be ideal. Education was not to be misused to undermine the natural order of society: teaching ought to be slanted towards specific occupations and young people should learn 'what they needed without encouraging them to run away from their villages to become pen pushers'. Schlabrendorff, the minister for Silesia, had been even more outspoken as early as 1765: the state was, in his opinion, better served by people who earned their living with their hands than by 'half-baked scholars swarming all over the place'. Frederick's instruction of 5 September 1779 to the minister Karl Abraham Freiherr von Zedlitz-Leipe (who from 1771 energetically pursued the reform of higher education) was essentially on the same wavelength.

When Zedlitz-Leipe took over the Ecclesiastical Department, the teaching profession had largely reached the standards of loyalty and conscientiousness aimed at during the early reform period. What he wished to develop was a sharper sense of responsibility in a profession freeing itself, if slowly, from the domination of the clergy. Zedlitz, though he did not succeed in introducing a general *Reglement* for all higher schools, made the *Ritterakademie* at Liegnitz into an elite institution, reformed Hamm's *Gymnasium*, at the request of the school's own governors and, in time, breathed new life into all the schools criticized by the king. His most important innovations were the foundation of provincial high school colleges (*Ober-Schulkollegien*) and the introduction of the *Abitur* as the obligatory entrance qualifications for the university. These did not come till after Frederick's death, though they can be found among reforms planned by him before 1786.

In the very first year of his reign Frederick had begun university reform. Johann Gustav Reinbeck, the dean of Berlin-Cölln, was given the task of reshaping the philosophical and theological faculties of the university of Halle along lines recommended by Wolff. He drew up detailed plans, but his sudden death in the summer of 1741 meant they were not put into immediate effect although Frederick appointed a commission to do so. This still functioned in 1747 but had achieved nothing positive. The Prussian universities enjoyed considerable autonomy and changes in their status would have unleashed unending and damaging quarrels. The amount of state supervision necessary to effect reform was disputed, and it would have been in the universities' own interest to initiate reform from within. This did not happen and, though the universities escaped attention when the Ecclesiastical Department was divided in 1764, they were in 1771 expressly subordinated to Zedlitz by the establishment of a university department within the ministry. Its effect varied: it had no noticeable effect on the venerable *Academia Viadrina* of Frankfurt on the Oder (1506), the *Academia Albertina* of Königsberg (1544), the *Academia Fredericiana* of Halle on the Saale (1694), the Cleves provincial university at Duisburg (1655) or the Leopoldina at Breslau (1702). On the other hand, the Prussian Academy of Sciences at Berlin,* founded by Elector Frederick III (later King Frederick I) in 1700, was reorganized in the spirit of the Enlightenment by Frederick and acquired a high reputation. The king not only attended its sessions but occasionally lectured there.

Frederick's church, school and educational policy did not introduce fundamental changes, but kept in step with the development of the state and the times. The king had at his side a number of highly talented educational experts. Limited means hampered the administration in

---

* It was not state directed, though numerous links were forged with the universities and with the departmental authorities in respect of legal, medical and botanical research.

enforcing the instructions assigned to them. Certainly education was not one of the overriding priorities in Frederician Prussia, but that is not to say that its development lagged behind that in the neighbouring states. At times practical experience rather than abstract theology or educational philosophy laid down guidelines for individuals, and the fund of experience in its turn enriched educational and even religious theories.

THE REFORM OF JUSTICE

One of the most popular anecdotes told about Frederick the Great is the story of the windmill at Sans Souci, the constant rattling of which got so much on the king's nerves that he ordered it to be demolished, only to be told by the miller, 'Your Majesty, there are still judges in Prussia': the king obeyed Prussian laws, and the mill at Sans Souci stands to this day. What really happened is a different story; but what is worth stressing is that the folk tales grown up round the memory of Old Fritz are imbued with a belief that in Potsdam there was 'justice for all'. And in fact efforts to improve the law constituted the greater part of Frederick's administrative activity; numerous letters, edicts, cabinet orders and marginal notes give proof of his search for impartial justice. Such lofty ideas and such deep concern for humanitarian ideals – couched in well-turned phrases – are also found in Frederick's two Political Testaments, in his essay on law, and in his other writings. They culminate in the theory that the proper function of the monarch was not to lay down law, but to protect and support it.

At Frederick's accession the administration of justice appeared to be in a healthy state, though the unwieldy mass of Imperial law pressed upon it and much mindless routine consumed time. The young king first applied his drive to the abolition of torture (already in part achieved under his father), and here he both sought and found support. Next the hold of Imperial law was loosened by the extension, on 31 May 1746, of the *Privilegium de non appellando* to those Prussian provinces still subject to it; in 1750 this *Privilegium* was made applicable also to East Friesland. Prussia was now, for the first time, independent and sovereign in the field of law. In the same year the cumbrous and time-consuming practice of consultation, and the collection of evidence and counter-evidence, inside and outside Prussia was stopped; from now on Prussian law-courts had to reach their verdicts independently and stick to them. Comprehensive reform of the legal system thus became possible. The administration of justice had hitherto been part of the work of the Secret State Council; now, while continuing to remain nominally part of that body, an increasingly separate functional ministry developed.

Legal reform, initiated by a cabinet order of 27 August 1746, was carried out by the minister of justice Samuel Freiherr von Cocceji. He came of a Bremen family originally called Koch and was the son of Heinrich von Cocceji, professor of political science at the university of Frankfurt on the Oder. The younger Cocceji, made president of the Supreme Court (the *Kammergericht*) in 1723, was appointed Chief Justice in 1738 and Great Chancellor (*Grosskanzler*) in 1747; at the same time the king invested him with the order of the Black Eagle. Cocceji had thus achieved first rank among Prussia's ministers of justice who between them dealt also with the Silesian ministry of justice, the Department of Ecclesiastical Affairs, judicial matters in the Department of External Affairs, and acted as president of the Superior Court of Appeal (*Oberappellationsgericht*). There was no hard and fast division of duties among the ministers of justice: a change of minister led to internal negotiations during which duties were reassigned according to ability, knowledge and experience, taking into account also the funds available for salaries. The aim was to standardize all the courts under the supervision of the state so that one law, valid for the whole monarchy, could be administered. Cocceji carefully selected a small reform commission to help him in his task. He was convinced that court procedure would become speedier if the monetary interest of the advocates were removed. States measures to impose fixed legal costs, the demotion of the numerous junior lawyers to posts as assistants to judges and clerks of the court, the limitation of legal processes to three instances and a maximum duration of one year, the persuasion of litigants to settle their cases, and the speedy dealing (often rough and ready) with the back-log of old cases – all helped to free the authorities for a flexible handling of current cases. A prerequisite for a good system was a professional bench of judges with respect for their calling and a well-developed sense of honour. It was essential that the administration of justice should remain independent and it was realized that a few well-paid judges were better than an army of fee-hunters. The Estates' prerogative of having half of all judgeships reserved for the nobility now ceased: suitability for the post and performance were alone taken into account in appointing judges. The king, usually susceptible to the claims of the nobility, agreed to this. Patrimonial jurisdiction was restricted in that it became obligatory for estate-owners, as well as for domain leaseholders, to have legal matters in their courts dealt with by qualified lawyers. Several domains, following the example of Halberstadt, were placed under the supervision of an office of justice, while in Cleves-Mark, East Prussia and West Prussia 'district colleges of justice' (*Landvogteigerichte*) were formed to look after domains or counties. In Silesia a *Kreis* justice councillor and three commissaries was installed to control the lower courts. Appointments to honorary positions and sinecures within the judicial administration were abolished. Cocceji and his commission journeyed from Pomerania in the autumn of 1746 (having settled 400 lawsuits in three months) to Brandenburg, Magdeburg, Halberstadt, Cleves-Mark, Minden, Silesia, East Prussia and East Friesland. Five years of reorganization completed the reform: precise professional regulations had been laid down and considerable changes in personnel had been effected. In 1745 11,500 lawsuits were still pending throughout the monarchy and 7,200 of these were settled within a year.*

Cocceji did not succeed in completely unifying Prussian justice. Silesia was not the only exception. While in Stettin, Cleves-Mark and East Friesland the manorial courts had without fuss or further enquiry been joined to the *Regierung*, this could not be done in East Prussia. Here the provincial superior court (*Hofgericht*) at Königsberg and at Insterburg survived as did the East Prussian *Oberappellationsgericht* (the *Tribunal*) – the only one outside Berlin. This shows the residuary power of Königsberg as a subsidiary *Residenz*; but as the *Tribunal* and the *Hofgericht* at Königsberg were given a common president, the Berlin *Oberappellationsgericht* actually acted as a third instance to decide issues with Königsberg as its executive organ. Ravensberg lost its own *Oberappellation* in 1750, and in Gelderland four *Revisoren* of the *Regierung* functioned as a regional superior court of appeal. It proved a much more difficult matter for the Justice Department in Berlin to superintend and supervise the provincial chambers. A paragraph, added at Cocceji's suggestion to the *Reglement* of 1748 on demarcation of judicial circuits, did not achieve much. The justice commissariats (*Justiz-Kommissariate*) of the chambers had been established by Frederick William I to see that centralized royal justice prevailed over the provincial judges of the Estates. The legal powers of the chamber thus represented centralized justice and could scarcely be abolished without furthering the judicial powers of the Estates. The disadvantage of this system was that in lawsuits against domains and towns the chamber appeared in the guise of both advocate and judge. The maxim *in dubio pro fisco* no longer had any place. The chambers for their part doubted, with some justification, whether

---

* Pomerania with 1,500 lawsuits had by far the largest number while the Neumark with 450 had the smallest.

centralized justice could take account of the regional peculiarities of provincial constitutions. Cocceji in impassioned direct reports to Frederick tried to save the subjects from the injustices of the chambers and the 'tyranny of the departmental councillors and the tax inspectors', but in the end the provincial chambers were left with the following judicial functions: disputes of royal domains with towns and of towns with one another; disputes of domain leaseholders with officials in respect of the allocation of farms, taxation and similar problems; reconciliation between magistrates and burghers; interpretation of guild privileges; exercise of brewing rights; offences against military, police and tax regulations; offences against the timber laws; and, finally, disciplinary proceedings against officials. The Estates in East Friesland protested against even this much legal power for the chamber, arguing that their privileges, renewed in 1744, would be infringed. The chamber at first refused to discuss the matter, relying on royal privilege; but the king stepped in and arranged, through Cocceji, an amicable agreement with the Estates on condition that procedures were to be carried on in accordance with the normal rules that lawsuits were to be completed within a year.

Cocceji had drafted a tentative set of court rules in his *Codicis Fridericiani Pomeranici* of 1747 and the *Codicis Fridericiani Marchici* of 1748. The final rules embodied in the *Codex Fridericianus* were then published in all provinces, lastly in East Friesland in 1749. Progress had been excellent, and in 1748 Frederick had a commemorative medal struck depicting the figure of *Justitia* with the circumscription *Emendato jure*. In the same year the Berlin *Oberappellationsgericht* was joined with the French *Obergericht* (for the Huguenot colonies in Prussia) and the *Kammergericht* into a supreme court of law. Cocceji called this the *Grosses Friedrichs-Kolleg*, but the old title of *Kammergericht* was generally used and was indeed better from the descriptive point of view. This was the highest court of appeal over the *Hofgerichten*. Royal councillors sat on it, responsible not only for the Kurmark but, as the Fourth Senate, for the whole monarchy. Its president held the position and rank of a minister of justice as did the heads of the other three senates; all were subordinate to the Great Chancellor. At the end of December 1749 the Secret Justice Council, the judicial authority which dealt with suits in which members of the royal house were involved, was merged with the *Kammergericht*, as was the Ravensberg *Appellationsgericht*. The reform was extended to personal and commercial law, but these parts of the Cocceji's manuscript were lost in transit. The parts he had already completed, the main body of the work, were published in 1749 and 1751 under the title 'Project of the *Corpus Juris Fridericiani*, that is the Common Law, based by His Prussian

Majesty on common sense and the constitution'. Cocceji believed that
he had reached his goal in creating a *jus certum et universale*. Commentaries were forbidden so as not to introduce uncertainty or endanger
what had already been achieved. On 20 April 1754, however, a visitation
regulation was decreed, by which all colleges of justice were to be
inspected, or 'revised', every three years. This regulation laid down brief
but clear rules for a commissary during a visitation. General instructions
were also given. The following are worth noting: 'Refendars [legal
trainees] should be taken along for training purposes. No commissary
should stay or take a meal with a member of a college during a revision.
Unsuitable young men were to be told to move to another profession.
Checks were to be made if the consistory kept adequate watch on the
teachings and behaviour of the clergy and whether the church accounts
were audited annually. Clashes between *Regierung* and chamber must be
avoided and efforts be made to settle differences amicably.' Reform of
the criminal law came to an end when Cocceji died in 1754; he had been
attacked by his colleagues during his lifetime as the 'Justice Dictator' but
Frederick had trusted him completely.

His successor as Great Chancellor was Philipp Joseph Pandin de
Jariges, president of the *Kammergericht*, a member of Berlin's Huguenot
community who had collaborated closely with Cocceji. A continuation
and completion of Cocceji's reforms was hindered not only by the Seven
Years War but also by the new Great Chancellor's disinclination for the
work. The Justice Commission, set up in 1756 to deal with disputes about
competences and to suggest further reform of the administration of
justice, produced a handwritten *Codex revisus* in four folio volumes with
appendices. The *Collegia Medica*, the post, the lottery, the excise and
customs, besides mining and trade affairs, thus kept, if only to a limited
extent, their own legal powers. During the post-war *rétablissement*
minister von Hagen, in the spring of 1769, took over from the General
Directory the improvement of justice in the provincial chambers. This
was successful as far as the establishment of justice *Ämter* for the supervision of the domains; but the death of Great Chancellor Jariges towards
the end of 1770 interrupted the work. His successor, minister of state
Carl Joseph Maximilian von Fürst, was full of praise for Jariges 'who had
untiringly served His Prussian Majesty and the state', but he did not
encourage Hagen's reform work. Hagen himself died in 1771. The
General Directory now had to take the initiative and Hagen's colleague
and successor, Derschau, submitted a draft for further reform which the
king signed on 12 August 1772. A new authority, the *Ober-Revisions-
Collegium*, was set up, a court of arbitration of the second instance for

disputed questions of justice within the War and Domains chambers. It was at the same time a kind of supervisory authority in matters of justice, but as it was not an independent court it could only work in an advisory capacity.

Fürst had taken an active part in introducing the Prussian judicial system into West Prussia and had perfectly expressed Frederick's point of view on 28 September 1772: 'We ourselves or our state ministry can give no decisions which have the force of a judicial ruling.' The investigation of court verdicts by visitations did not satisfy the perenially mistrustful Frederick that all was well in the realm of justice. Various matters came to his notice which caused him in 1774 to send a circular through the General Directory to all chambers to stress that the legal protection of the subject as against the administration was insufficiently guaranteed: subjects complained that they 'are not listened to or given enough help, while, conversely, the officials are highly favoured'. The next year Frederick rebuked the General Directory: 'It seems to me as if justice begins, once more, to fall asleep.' Similar rebukes followed, mostly on trivial grounds, up to the end of 1779. Ever since 1776 Frederick had been thinking of changing the *chef de justice*: he had his eye on the Silesian minister of justice von Carmer, the youngest of Cocceji's colleagues, whose career he had followed with interest. Disaster struck not only the Great Chancellor but the whole administration of justice. Frederick, who had repeatedly emphasized that he was against peremptory royal orders, took it into his head that a miscarriage of justice necessitated his intervention. A miller, Arnold, from *Kreis* Züllichau, had petitioned him asking for legal protection against the Neumark Chamber, claiming that the *Landrat* had diverted water from his mill by digging a carp pond with the result that, unable to pay his rent, he had been dispossessed. Frederick sent a colonel and a *Regierungsrat* from the Neumark to investigate. Experts were also brought in. Opinions differed; the chamber refuted the miller's assertions and the *Kammergericht* gave judgment accordingly. Frederick then intervened in person. Fürst was interrogated by the king and dismissed on 11 December 1779. He kept his seat and vote as a minister in the Secret Council of State, but was not expected to make use of either and did not do so. The president of the Küstrin Chamber was also dismissed, and a new *Landrat* was appointed in contravention of the *Ritterschaft's* right of nomination. Finally, six councillors of the *Kammergericht* and the Neumark *Regierung* were, despite minister of justice von Zedlitz' appeal, sentenced to nine months imprisonment. Officials had, at that time, no legal protection. The dismissals were therefore in accordance with the law, and so was

the sovereign's alteration of a verdict by his fiat. But the conviction of
the judges was not, in any sense, right or justifiable: though wanting to
create justice Frederick had practised injustice. Immediately after his
death the convictions were squashed and compensation paid to those
involved. This was not the first occasion on which Frederick had interfered with the due process of law, but it is the most notorious and the
last. Nor did Frederick restrain over-zealous judges who acted in
accordance with his wishes. The arrest of Justi was certainly unjustified;
errors were committed at Görne's trial; and the *Garde-du-Corps* officer,
Friedrich von der Trenck, was kept in strict confinement in the fortresses
of Glatz and Magdeburg, without court-martial, for high treason and an
alleged scandalous relationship with the king's sister Princess Amelia.
All the same there is overwhelming documentary evidence – in laws,
cabinet orders and marginal notes and other writings – that Frederick
had an earnest desire to act in an exemplary fashion in the administration
of justice. Characteristic also is his return of a proposal by the General
Directory for punishment by four weeks incarceration in a fortress:
'For eight days. Ministers who do not know what it is like to break stones
can hardly pass judgment. Four weeks is a lot. Eight days is enough for a
correction.' But this also shows that Frederick must have been fully
aware of what his nine months imprisonment of councillors of the
Kammergericht implied. Public reaction to his verdict of 12 December
1779 was sharply divided. Endless rows of carriages containing
prominent officials drove up to the house of the fallen minister, directly
opposite the Schloss, to condole with him. At the same time peasants
swarmed to the doors of the Schloss (where Frederick was confined
by an attack of gout) with petitions, and burghers illuminated their
houses at night to give thanks to the king who gave justice to his
people.

Frederick's next and last Great Chancellor was Johann Heinrich
Casimir von Carmer, a member of a Calvinist family from the Palatinate,
who since 1763 had headed the Breslau *Oberamtsregierung* and since 1768
the Silesian ministry of justice. Only three months after taking office
Carmer presented proposals for setting up more reliable colleges of
justice, for a new oral procedure in lawsuits, and for the compilation of a
general code of laws. Frederick pronounced his draft of April 1780
'admirable' and asked that the codification should also cover provincial
rights. By the memorable cabinet order of 14 April 1780 Carmer was
ordered to prepare a set of court rules and codification of the laws in
German. Law reform thus moved to the centre of the stage during the
last period of Frederician government. Reforms planned or started by

Cocceji were first implemented: a justice *Reglement* for East and West Prussia was introduced on 3 December 1781, and another for Kurmark and Neumark on 30 November 1782. The Königsberg *Hofgericht* and the *Tribunal* were joined with the *Oberburggrafenamt* under one president, the East Prussian *Regierung's Hof- und Halsgericht* (Criminal Court) and the *Pupillenkollegium* (Court of Minors) were transformed into two senates; in East as in West Prussia all special law courts were abolished. The Fourth Senate was now separated from the *Kammergericht* and became an *Obertribunal* for all provinces, and *Kreis* justice councillors on the Silesian pattern were appointed for the Marks. As chamber jurisdiction could not be abolished, a special *Justizdeputation* was established in every chamber; though its members remained part of the *Kammer*, the justice deputies were subordinate to the *chef de justice* from whom they took guidance. Thus two subordinate channels were created in judicial matters, the *Justizdeputation* being given an advisory function while the chamber was assigned an executive one. The *Reglement* of 1751, without being altered in any way, was re-interpreted. Decades later Stein concluded, from his experience as a chamber president and president-in-chief, that the division had been 'unsystematically and vaguely formulated' and asked the jurisdictional commission to comment on it to clarify the situation. New quarrels developed all the same, and not surprisingly if we take into account the small staffs of the chambers, who were inundated with new documents and varying problems in a period of rapid change. Yet too watertight regulations would have had a fossilizing effect and would have proved impracticable. In Frederician Prussia the central authorities were issued with instructions which presupposed a large degree of independence and participation, and friction was unavoidable within administrative units – so to speak part of the system. It should be stressed, however, that Carmer's court rules and his codification of the Common Law originated in a professional and legal corps to which sophisticated laws could be entrusted for interpretation and realization. And as for the 'justice deputations', they had been tested on an experimental basis from 1772 onwards in the chambers at Marienwerder and Bromberg.

New court and procedural rules became law on 26 April 1781, as a first part of the *Corpus Juris Fridericianum*. On 10 August 1783, the same year in which progressive rules on mortgages were promulgated, a revision commission was formed to supervise the codification project and supplement it where necessary. Carmer had left the practical work to his collaborator Carl Gottlieb Svarez (Schwarz) who, with an unsurpassed knowledge of detail and of superior drafting ability, made rapid

progress. Svarez had begun writing in 1780 and printed parts appeared
from 1784 to test public opinion. Frederick was very pleased with the
speed but shocked by the volume. 'It is very thick', he commented on
receiving the second part in 1785, 'and laws must be short and not
elaborate.' In this he echoed Montesquieu's *De l'esprit des lois* of 1748, the
principles of which he now used for guidance in his reform of justice.
It would be risky, however, to construe dependence on Montesquieu.
Montesquieu himself argued that every society creates its own judicial
system and therefore must have laws of its own. In Prussia much
preparatory work was done by others, but Frederick's inexhaustible
energy was necessary to get reform started and sustained, and to watch
constantly that the practical and useful aspects were not forgotten. He
was very much aware of the importance of the task. For that reason
foreign academic and practising jurists were asked for their opinions,
sometimes through competitions, both in the planning stages and
drafting. Fifty-two expert opinions and sixty-two commentaries, from
Copenhagen to Dresden and from Kassel to Königsberg, were received.
Stephen Ludwig Pütter, the famous expert on Imperial law, wrote in
1784 in the *Göttingische Gelehrte Anzeigen*: 'Does not every patriot
join with us in wishing that on this model legal codes will be compiled
for the other German states? Or, why not, for all Germany?' Frederick
did not live to see the publication of the whole code. Five years after his
death the drafts were coordinated and the resulting code was made law
on 20 March 1791. From 1 June 1794 the *Allgemeine Landrecht für die
Preussischen Staaten* (General Common Law for the Prussian States) was,
after bitter domestic disputes, enforced. It proved itself in practice and
achieved its aim.

In 1814 Achim von Arnim declared that the *Landrecht* had become 'the
document of our constitution'. The Frederician law code passed into the
age of constitutional struggles for which it was not intended. The
intended codification of provincial laws never took place, though East
and West Prussian provincial codes based on the General Common
Law were completed in 1801–2 and 1844 respectively. The *Landrecht* was
thus the creation of the eighteenth century and of Frederick the Great.
The jurist Hermann Conrad called the *Allgemeine Landrecht* of 1784 'the
basic law of the Frederician state'. As recently as 1970 the preface to a
new edition stressed that 'this code of law is easily the greatest codification of German legislation and also one of the most important monu-
ments of the Prussian Enlightenment.' Carl Gottlieb Svarez, who in
1791–92 taught the Prussian crown prince (later Frederick William III)
law and politics, summarized not only the fundamental principles of the

General Common Law but also the intentions which had brought
Frederick to undertake legal reforms for the benefit of the state:

> The most regular order in the whole constitution of the state; the strictest
> supervision of the prompt and impartial administration of justice; the ever-
> alert precaution against one estate or class of the nation impairing the rights
> of the others so that the poorer and lower is not oppressed by his rich and
> powerful fellow-citizens; the undiminished care for the foundation and
> support of public institutions whereby the prosperity of the individual is
> furthered and agriculture, manufactures and factories benefit; the regard for
> civil liberty, for the rights and the possessions of the subjects; and, finally,
> the most complete religious and intellectual freedom – these are the funda-
> mental pillars of the administration of the Prussian state.

CABINET GOVERNMENT

In Frederick's old age the style of his administration was increasingly
determined by his personal method of governing through written
directives from his desk rather than through sittings of the *Kollegium* of
ministers, though this was not a fundamental innovation. We must
distinguish between the small, highly flexible, executive staff at the head
of the state administration and the king's autocratic decrees issued via
cabinet secretaries for immediate implementation. We must also
discriminate between this kind of royal cabinet and the *Kabinettsministerium*, which, with the General Directory and the legal authority,
was concerned with Prussia's external affairs. In the normal course the
path from royal initiative to signed decree was a long one, paved with
the many obstacles thrown up by friction between the cabinet and the
administration. At the end of Frederick's reign the government of
Prussia was not schematically segmented and guided by mechanical
principles; nor was this intended. The diverse regions and the over-
lapping jurisdictions of official bodies demanded continuous decisions
from Frederick who wished to be consulted and to preserve a general
overall view. Early in the reign Frederick had felt unable to put limits to
his sovereignty or to delegate any of his powers. This was done, however, increasingly in the realm of justice and in such special fields as
mining and metallurgy where reliable and independent collaborators
did the real work. The *Allgemeine Landrecht*, Part II, section 13, ordained
that:

> All the rights and duties of the state towards her citizens and protected persons
> are embodied in its head. The most important duty of the head of state is the
> preservation of internal and external peace and safety and the protection of

each individual in his own possession against violence and disturbance. It is his duty to make such arrangements that the inhabitants may have opportunities to develop their abilities and powers and to use these to increase their prosperity. All the prerogatives and rights necessary for the attainment of this goal are therefore due to the head of state.

For the codifying of the *Allgemeine Landrecht* collections of earlier decisions were consulted, in so far as these were available. While the rescripts drawn up by the authorities used *Nomine Regis*, 'We Frederick by the Grace of God etc.' and the *stilus curiae* was expected for preambles, the cabinet decrees were informally written in the third person, in the manner of resolutions: as, for example, 'His Royal Majesty has, for the rectification of all the mistakes which, unfortunately, still persist in financial and cameral affairs etc.' Cabinet orders could also be written in the personal style of a handwritten letter: 'My dear Minister of State von Derschau etc.' Orders written on small quarto sheets needed no counter-signature. This type of document was not new, but under Frederick a uniform, short, matter-of-fact style emerged. From the few brief drafts of these cabinet orders it is impossible to reconstruct their origins and the deliberations that preceded them: the results and the final formulation of the instructions are all that we have. During the second half of his reign Frederick issued up to twelve cabinet orders each day, sometimes more; the total number of orders issued in the years 1728–95 amounts to between 300,000 and 400,000. Immediately after the writing down of an order, copies (wrongly called 'minutes') in the sense of drafts were entered chronologically in folio volumes (the copy-books). From 1741 onwards these were at regular intervals sent to the General Directory for storage in the secret archives. The central authorities immediately subordinate to the king were not the only recipients of cabinet orders; Frederick wanted, as a matter of principle, to reach every branch of the administration. In the 1770s some 170 cabinet orders were annually addressed to the presidents of the War and Domains chambers. Domhardt received most of them, but this can be explained by the fact that he was head of three chambers and one chamber deputation. Royal decisions were also issued in the form of marginal comments on incoming documents and papers, but these did not acquire validity unless re-styled into decrees or cabinet orders: in the process impulsive phraseology was smoothed out and abrasiveness tempered. The speed with which documents were circulated and administrative business expedited from one day to the next was unsurpassed for the period. This was in part due to the fact that administrative units were deliberately kept small and their procedural regulations examined time and again to see whether further rationalization was possible. The famous royal 'lapidary style' which assembled facts in short and pertinent form served as an example.

Frederick desired to be as well informed as possible on the contents of incoming documents so that, in the words of the Political Testament of 1752, only *bagatelles* should be left to the ministers. The king naturally informed himself on matters whenever he thought this necessary or handed documents to relevant departments for comment. Royal decisions from the cabinet were much rarer than often supposed. Frederick was extremely industrious and assiduous in the study of documents. Brief summaries and code signs beside the signature on incoming and outgoing documents helped him to master the contents. Reports had to be lucid, matter-of-fact and standardized. In 1773 Frederick complained that the president of the Cleves Chamber in a routine monthly report had used the term *Verfallzeit* instead of its synonym *Zahlungstermin* (time of payment). In the use of titles the second half of the eighteenth century is distinguished by professional position becoming more important than family status. On 20 June 1764 forms applicable to all Prussia's provinces were introduced, eliminating much bombast. West Prussia was the most progressive and from 1774 ceased to use curial phraseology in official documents.

The notion of an unlimited, absolute, governmental system was strengthened by the king's name being used at the head of all decrees. All royal directives had the force of law. By invoking the name of the king on official documents, in announcements from pulpits and in public proclamations, the authority of the state, conceived in the person of the king, was strengthened. To us it seems odd, however, when departments corresponded among themselves *Nomine Regis*. It was of the utmost importance that the king's comments, instructions and plans should remain confidential. They were, however, often noised abroad. Frederick complained bitterly to minister von Hagen from Potsdam on 13 May 1768 that cabinet orders, marginal notes on reports and even financial directives had, through the carelessness of the General Directory, 'often became known all over the town on the same evening or the following day'; even copies of the reports could be obtained and were objects of interest to collectors. Hagen, in his notes of that day, goes on:

> His Majesty the King does not prevent us from moving in society; but we should, as he only tells us and therefore makes us responsible, from now on keep secret all that pertains to business, especially cabinet orders. . . . He has written to us direct but does not wish that this should become common knowledge immediately.

Speculation focused on the origin of the 'leak'. It was not certain that it came from within the General Directory. Of the three cabinet secretaries whom Frederick had taken over from his father August Friedrich Eichel was most trusted. He was, indeed, far more than a secretary, his position approximating to that of a latter-day *chef de cabinet*. Eichel was certainly active in the formulation of cabinet orders and was indeed an adviser to the king. Ministers tried – not without success – to humour him to get what they wanted from Frederick. Eichel never left the king's side; in wartime he was taken prisoner at Soor but was later exchanged. His dependability had been tested and his discretion not found wanting; his death early in 1768 left a gap that could never be filled. None of the fifteen cabinet secretaries who served Frederick II ever attained such a position of trust; secretary Galster was in fact dismissed in 1774 for alleged breach of trust and for unlawfully enriching himself, and was confined in Spandau fortress for a year. All Berlin knew that the wife of secretary Stellter and her friend, 'Madame Privy Finance Councillor' Beyer, would have liked to be able to influence the appointment of ministers. But they did not succeed, Frederick being too careful in matters of appointment to depend on others. He was usually able to see through the manoeuvres of irresponsible advisers and dismissed them on principle. He differed from his successor, whose leadership of the state was practically non-existent and over whose ministers an almost omnipotent cabinet ruled. Frederick did recommend his cabinet secretaries to his successor in the Personal Testament of 8 January 1769: 'They have a good knowledge of affairs and they can, at the beginning of the reign, advise the king on many things of which they have knowledge and which are unknown even to the ministers.'

After the Seven Years War the centre of gravity in administrative activity shifted from the General Directory to the cabinet: the number of secretaries and cipher clerks rose from a total of three in 1740 to six after 1768. In February 1768, immediately after Eichel's death, cabinet business was divided into three sections – foreign, internal and military affairs. Incoming letters of a personal nature or those not fitting easily into one of the three categories were dealt with by the privy cabinet secretaries who formulated, on half a sheet of paper, a précis for presentation in the cabinet. This tendency towards functional specialization within the cabinet did not necessarily indicate a change in administrative procedures, though Frederick felt these to be inadequate to the strains of war. The central authorities, splintered still further since 1768, increasingly needed pulling together (*Zusammenfassung*) by a controlling hand. Frederick, however, during the period of the great reconstruction

could no longer keep abreast of the flood of matters calling for his
attention; the enlargement of the cabinet followed simply from his need
of more working staff. The thought that, with a larger cabinet staff, he
could all the better control rival ministries may have played a part, but
practical reasons were, it would seem, the deciding factor: at a time when
the drain on the finances of the state was greatest and income most
restricted, a reorganization of the ministries both on grounds of expense
and risk ruled itself out. Frederick was by now experienced and flexible
enough to utilize professionally the means at hand and the enlarged
cabinet proved a success. He could not, however, do without his
ministers of state. On their expertise and judgment he hoped 'to repose':
they were the experts, the reparative and executive organs of the
collegial General Directory, though they were not as yet
independent, responsible department heads in their own right. The
development in this direction could no longer be contained, and during
the last decade of his life Frederick contributed to this in practice if not in
theory. In 1775 the 'review of ministers', which up to then had taken
place at least once annually, was abolished; from that year onwards only
two department heads were at any one time 'reviewed' by the king. The
meetings of the *Staatsrat* had long ago lapsed and now the sole remaining
collegial contact, in itself minimal, was broken: the cabinet became the
one place from which it was possible to obtain a general view of the
whole state. Meanwhile the General Directory had grown and become
amorphous. In 1740 it had numbered only five ministers, nineteen privy
finance councillors and fifteen lower officials; forty years later there
were – not counting the Excise Administration and the new departments –
six ministers, twenty-four privy councillors and eighty secretaries: it had
thus tripled in size, while the business it handled had at the most doubled.
Cabinet control, exercised as before through written directives, now
developed in such a way that individual ministers were assigned special
tasks by the king – not always within their particular areas of competence; special deputies, some of them from outside the Directory, were
asked to carry out certain tasks within a specific period of time. An early
example of this was the special mandatory powers granted to Brenckenhoff; and it is symptomatic that 'exceptional conditions' could persist
for decades. Within narrower limits and with younger officials the king
carried out extraordinary inspections; in the winter of 1763–64, for
example, finance councillor von Hagen visited the nine western provinces
and was submitted over a period of 'three days in Potsdam [to] such a
searching examination by the king, province by province, that there can
be few such examples as this'. Four weeks later Hagen was appointed a

minister. Frederick had no intention, however, of damaging administrative unity as he saw it. He increasingly passed on responsibilities, especially in matters of personnel and in the field of justice. The jurisdiction of regimental commanders, which Frederick William I had tried to curtail, was thus again enlarged; and criminal proceedings under military law were shorter and more drastic than those in the civil courts. The *Generalauditeur*, as head of military jurisdiction, lost his direct access to the king and thus the opportunity of protesting decisions made or confirmed in the cabinet.

Frederick's dictum, written down as an exhortation to his successor, that the state should be as compact as a philosophical system seems to point to the individual decision as the best possible method of administration. It is, however, on the rhetorical side. The few sensational, truly absolutistic orders and the even fewer cabinet decisions based on fiats and arbitrary decisions (which, in any case, did not fit into Frederick's philosophical system) are outnumbered in their thousands by proceedings which show Frederick as bound by his own laws. Already under Frederick William I the state had been made independent of the sovereign: the 'King of Prussia' was a permanent institution above the king as a person. Indeed, the term 'sovereign' does not quite suit these two kings, however much they behaved as sovereign rulers: they served rather as the repositories of sovereign rights. Their power was limited by the goals set for the sake of the state, not for themselves as autocrats. What was desirable and possible was determined by *raison d'état*. As executors of the will of the state they performed duties in the service of the general public: they were 'the first servants of the state' rather than their own masters.

The counterpart to the written cabinet order was the *revue*, the inspection, the on-the-spot observation; while the mirror-image of the cabinet decision was – apart from the checking – the dependence on experts, on the effectiveness of the executive, on the dependability of collaborators. This also held good in the administration of the provinces, in the economy and in military affairs. The king's position in the cabinet was on an elevated platform which afforded a better view; but it was also in an open exposed position which brought isolation. In the later years of his reign Frederick was not fully informed of many things that happened or that should have happened. Only with effort and with the selfless concentration of his remaining powers could the enormous work load be mastered. In this last decade he was not always willingly obeyed: exhaustion, laziness and opposition were everywhere. Fear, wilfulness and lack of communication accounted for his being only partially in the picture. He was too intelligent not to notice and he reacted with fury, bitterness, harshness, greater personal effort and increased isolation. The table guests had long departed from Sans Souci. In his diary Heinitz refers to the seventy-one-year-old Frederick as 'a rod and a birch', though he admired the king who 'believes that through experience he is strong enough to rule without advice and to follow the plan he has made, to remain true to it and through it to give [the state] order and strength'.

Order and strength also held sway in the field of foreign policy to which Frederick was, through ability and inclination, as much attracted as he was to internal administration. Distinctions have been attempted between the talents of Frederick William I and Frederick II by depicting the father as Prussia's greatest king in domestic affairs while ascribing to the son a deeper inclination towards foreign affairs. Our analysis so far has shown that such a division can have only a limited validity. The Department of External Affairs, the adequate survey of which would require a separate volume, must here only be assessed briefly and in connection with the general administration. The foundations had been solidly laid by Frederick William I. The *Kabinettsministerium* together with the Secret Chancery and the cabinet – in its original sense – was responsible for the management of external affairs. At Frederick's accession in 1740 there were three *Kabinettsminister*: Adrian Bernhard von Borck, Wilhelm Heinrich von Thulemeier and Heinrich von Podewils. The first of these retired at the end of 1741 and was replaced by his nephew Caspar Wilhelm von Borck; the second had died in 1740 without being replaced. Podewils was by far the most important – careful, cautious and dependable – but he did not succeed in controlling the young Frederick II as he would have liked to have done. He made the best of the situation, however, and served the king to the best of his abilities until his death in 1760. His place was taken by Frederick's friend of his younger days, Count Karl Wilhelm von Finckenstein. Since 1749 he had replaced Axel von Mardeveld, who had himself replaced the younger Borck in 1747 as *Kabinettsminister*. In the years 1760–63 Fincken-stein was sole *Kabinettsminister* and proved fully capable of coping with Prussia's difficult position during the Seven Years War: experience gained as envoy in Copenhagen, London and St Petersburg helped him. He did not spare the king from frank comments and warnings. His high reputation and his long working life – outlasting Frederick's reign – lent great prestige to Prussia abroad, and he successfully mastered the crisis of the War of the Bavarian Succession. From 1763 onwards he was assisted by Ewald Friedrich von Hertzberg who had studied law at Halle.

Hertzberg, who also survived Frederick, helped to bring about the 1763 Peace of Hubertusburg; industry, capacity for work, and historical knowledge made him a valuable collaborator in German affairs. He differed, however, from Frederick on the aims of the *Fürstenbund*. While Hertzberg opposed this alliance, Frederick was elated at Prussia's success in 1785 in uniting under her leadership Saxony, Hanover, Brunswick, Mainz, Hesse-Kassel, Baden, Mecklenburg and the Thuringian princes and held this success to prove the correctness of his own policy: an equilibrium with Austria could now be achieved and the constitution of the Empire could be strengthened in the face of increasing external commotions and threats. A quarter of a century* after Frederick's first and only war of conquest he had become the protector of the Empire: he had not succumbed to the law of increasing expansion.

The business of the Department of Foreign Affairs was not very extensive and could be satisfactorily dealt with within the *Kabinettsministerium*. Among the privy cabinet councillors (the title of *Geheime Kabinettsrat* had been created in 1750) were the able jurist Johann Gotthilf Vockerodt, once a student of theology at Halle, and the professor of political science at the university of Frankfurt on the Oder, Schweikard Weinreich, both of whom had been appointed before 1740. Another was Rüdiger von Ilgen the younger, who as expediting secretary of the Secret Chancery and head of the royal house and cabinet archives served the king well in the preparation of memoirs and the formulation of Prussia's dynastic claims. External correspondence – with the exception of Imperial affairs – was, following the decree of 21 June 1740, conducted in French. The king was lucky in the selection of his diplomats. Carefully trained, with tact, dignity and reserve, they brought a new, contemporary style to the old-fashioned cabinet politics of enlightened Europe. Careful study and independent reports from personal agents enabled Frederick to check the dispatches of his envoys. As far as organization, personnel and effectiveness were concerned the Department of External Affairs was most efficient. As it was strictly separate from the other ministries and received instruction only from the king, Frederician cabinet government developed in its purest form in this department.

The ever-mounting volume of work demanded an ever more detailed arrangement of the king's timetable. The journeys to Silesia and to West Prussia to visit administrators and inspect troops had their fixed place in his annual programme alongside his reviews of the Potsdam garrison. Strict routine governed the course of his day. There had been room for

* Reckoned between 1743 and 1778.

music, fancy-dress balls and plays before the Seven Years War, but after 1763 there was no time for such entertainments. The flute concerts also ceased and the only leisure activity that remained was reading and conversation with his reader. Carl Hinrichs characterized Old Fritz's style of government thus: 'It was not a regard for rank and ceremony – as with those rulers who modelled themselves on Louis XIV – which made the king invisible, but work.' Contemporaries have described Frederick's daily programme. He rose at daybreak, at four o'clock or earlier in summer, around five o'clock in winter. A sealed envelope, containing letters that had arrived the previous evening were then brought to him. He sorted the letters and burned those that did not seem worth answering. In the ante-room he received the report of the adjutant of the Potsdam guard and dismissed him with instructions and messages. During breakfast he looked through the letters which had survived his initial sorting, gave instructions for dinner and sat down at his desk to await the reports of his cabinet councillors, each called in his turn. The one in charge of foreign affairs came first, followed by the chiefs of internal administration, justice and the department for ecclesiastical affairs. The king dressed in a threadbare uniform and high boots at all times, wore a large soft hat and was accompanied by his two whippets. After each report the king gave immediate, often very detailed, instructions and discussed these with the councillors who in their turn made proposals and comments. In the early afternoon answers and provisional decrees were presented in the form of cabinet orders, ready for signature. Instructions were similarly made ready in response to reports received from authorities, and heads of departments were informed of the king's intentions in writing. Next came a brief inspection of the Potsdam troops, reception of some foreigners and, though exceptional, of some petitioners. After dinner (which was often hurried) Frederick signed documents, orders and dispatches. The later afternoon and evenings were reserved for the reader, though Frederick usually fitted in some riding. He did not eat supper and went to bed before ten o'clock. Day after day passed according to routine. The king repeatedly held up the cabinet's efficient work methods as an example for the General Directory. Privy cabinet councillor Mencken, looking back on Frederick's workload, which he himself had shared, noted: 'It is clear that with such an unchanging routine much business could be transacted, but it is difficult to understand how the king was able to confine his great spirit so slavishly and tenaciously: in this he can really be regarded as exceptional.'

It is not surprising that Frederick's methods of governing, so successful in keeping his officials on their toes, should be the subject of many complaints and discussions. It is noteworthy that as a person Frederick was not denied respect, since everyone knew that he never spared himself. In 1777 the British envoy, Hugh Elliot, reported, on the occasion of the king's riding abroad, 'how much the people were pleased to see him on horseback; all the silly chat about a nation groaning under the weight of its burdens, and of a nation governed with a rod of iron vanished before the sincere acclamations of all ranks of the people, who joined in showing their enthusiasm for their great monarch'. Prussia gave Frederick the sobriquet of 'Great' in his own lifetime. A contemporary, Friedrich August Ludwig von der Marwitz, vividly described the king's return to Berlin from an inspection on 21 May 1785:

> The whole Rondell and the Wilhelmstrasse were crammed with people: all the windows full, all heads bare, everywhere the deepest silence and on all faces an expression of reverence and trust. The king, quite alone in the front, greeted people by continually taking off his hat. I am certain that between the Halle Gate and the Kochstrasse he took it off two hundred times. . . . The crowd stood still, bare-headed and silent, all eyes on the spot whence he had gone and it took some time before a person had collected himself and went quietly on his way. . . . Yet nothing had happened – an old man of seventy-three, shabbily dressed, covered in dust and returned from his day's work. But everybody knew that this old man was toiling for him, that he had devoted his entire life to that labour and that he had not missed a single day's work in forty-five years.

Epilogue

'I see death approaching', Frederick remarked to his reader, Marchese Girolamo Lucchesini, in February 1786, 'but I shall continue my work until he comes, and I shall die in harness.' On 17 August 1786 at about 2.20 a.m. the heart of the king ceased to beat and with it the state machine. His subjects were momentarily stunned, but when they got over the shock they felt as if they had been freed of a burden. Frederick's critics now came into their own; indolence triumphed, difficulties seemed to have disappeared. The essence of Frederick's statecraft, his concern for the state, his vigilance, his energy, his well-directed initiatives were no longer understood. In less than a decade his successor had needlessly squandered the *Staatsschatz* which Frederick had so painstakingly accumulated. In 1806 it was not Frederician Prussia that fell apart, but the arrogant and frivolous world of a later and less distinguished generation, only too eager to blame the wretchedness of their own age on the great Frederick and his 'system'.

Few, even among his contemporaries and admirers, really understood Frederick. Goethe appreciated his importance: 'We looked to the North whence Frederick bathed us in light; he was the Polar Star around which Germany, Europe, even the world, seemed to revolve.' The fixed star cannot fade. But what kind of epoch can be said to have passed with Frederick? And more importantly, what kind can be said to have followed him? The state reveals itself in changing forms, varying from age to age, but retaining, as long as men assemble for a common, political and creative purpose, an unvarying essential core. In Frederick the Great's purpose something of the state's immortality can be discerned. Those who have analysed the ideas of the Philosopher of Sans Souci have, variously, traced the guiding principles of his actions to Roman traditions, to Stoicism, to the French Enlightenment and to his own Brandenburg heritage, but they have not been able to 'explain' him fully. Even if we add his preoccupation with Machiavelli's ideas and his secret, and probably subconscious, obsession with crypto-pietism we shall not be able to plumb the depth of his being. He put three question marks above his last ode: '*Unde? Ubi? Quo?* Whence came I? Where am I? Where am I going? I do not know . . .'; but he gives us his own answer in a prose-sentence from his later years: 'It is not necessary that I live, but it is necessary that I perform my duty.' The guidelines of Frederician statecraft were not speculation but action, not plans but their accomplishment, not knowledge but experience. Frederick's thought processes led to goals which he pursued with vigilance, energy and perseverance; the process of thinking was for him not a goal in itself.

The results of Frederick's government can be expressed in a list of statistics as short as it is impressive. His state expanded from 119,000 sq. km. to 195,000 sq. km.; the population, in spite of heavy losses in the wars, rose from 2·2 millions to 5·8 millions. An enlightened philosopher who was also a king could be pleased at such progress if he had at the same time increased the happiness of his subjects. But happiness does not depend on external circumstances alone and, quite apart from any question of 'happiness', Frederick was well aware that to preserve his achievements would demand no less effort and sacrifice from Prussian subjects than had been needed to accomplish them. Such an attitude to future duties has been characterized as extravagant and in the long run untenable. But why should later generations be privileged to obtain more for less effort? The Frederician state had been able to help subjects hit by natural catastrophes. Thus when in 1784 the Rhine flooded its banks the king immediately provided 100,000 talers and later half as much again for relief; and after the Oder flood of the spring of 1785 one-thirtieth of the state's entire revenues for that year was used to repair the damage caused. 'What other ruler in the world', Frederick noted with pride, 'would have done that?' But Prussia was not a welfare state in the modern sense. The general good was the criterion of government, its goals that the state should be preserved from external and internal dangers and the population encouraged to be industrious and independent. Frederick had tried to put into practice, in an enlightened way, the motto which his grandfather had devised for the Order of the Black Eagle, *Suum Cuique*. It was not his ambition to rule over apathetic masses and barren wastes but to educate a civilized people in law and order; not to make them rich but to rescue them from wretchedness and make them competent, thrifty and reliable. The physiocratic theories current in the period discussed model states: what mattered in Prussia was feasibility; each man, each square metre, each taler counted.

Gustav Schmoller, in his academy address of 1892, demonstrated that in the Frederician state legal security and freedom of thought were as characteristic as obedience and subordination. Frederick also had to teach himself to be obedient and subordinate his own inclinations in order to set an example. Liberal, progressive legislation was not enough by itself. 'Human beings move if one drives them', the king wrote in his Political Testament of 1768, 'and stop the moment one ceases to urge them forward.' The state was not a toy in the hands of the monarch: to achieve success measures had to be earnestly and rigorously pursued at the cost of great effort. Again and again the king impressed on his ministers and chamber presidents that it was not enough to issue orders: one must also supervise their execution. He kept to this rule himself, and was always on the look out for collaborators who were independent enough to enforce the necessary measures with vigour and without constant prodding. Talent in his thinly-populated land was not inexhaustible and only a few – Heinitz, Hagen, Finckenstein, Domhardt, Winterfeldt and Seydlitz – grasped and shared the king's efforts fully. Frederick did not spurn those of average and mediocre intelligence; he encouraged them. Talent by itself was not sufficient to take on the burden of serving the Frederician state, as is shown in the careers of two gifted men who – though they were specially trusted by Frederick – yet left Prussia of their own free will. Friedrich Wilhelm von Steuben was an officer who served both in the Second Silesian War and the Seven Years War. He was picked by Frederick to be trained in the principles of strategy and before Schweidnitz he served as the king's personal adjutant. Yet he did not remain in Prussia; he took service first in Hohenzollern-Hechingen, then in Baden, and in 1777 gained fame and honour in North America. Friedrich Wilhelm von der Schulenburg-Kehnert was Frederick's youngest minister, entrusted with important assignments. He served the next two Prussian monarchs as well, but after Tilsit he became a minister of King Jerome, wanting to be on the winning side. That people of standing changed their masters was quite common in eighteenth-century Europe, but not in Prussia where the idea of the state and service to the state had been strongly developed. That men who had been close to Frederick should lapse in this way shows how little his conception of the state was really understood.

On the other hand many a servant of the state stayed even though he found Frederick a most difficult master. Rudeness to and cynical mockery of higher officials, ignoring of lower officials: these were unpleasant traits resented especially by those who were touchy and selfishly ambitious, unable to separate the royal office from the person of the king.

But to those able to take a more general view there was, in spite of Frederick's shortcomings, much that was rewarding in the service of the state. Prussia, often reviled, exercised a power of attraction the strength of which was greater because it was not consciously applied. When the young Nassau-born Reichsfreiherr vom Stein looked around in 1780 for a suitable administrative post, Potsdam became his goal. He felt a 'deep respect for Frederick the Great'; and this made him 'wish fervently to serve him and to train myself under him'. He was introduced to the king that same year and entered Heinitz' department. In his work as chamber president, president-in-chief and minister Stein adopted Frederician principles of administration, and in his history of his own times of 1807 he gave a well-balanced appreciation of Frederick's administrative accomplishment, based on his own experiences:

> Frederick earnestly desired to preserve the constitution of the Empire and as an old man he secured it with strength and wisdom by the Peace of Teschen and the German Fürstenbund. His administration of his own state was beneficient and moderate, he furthered internal prosperity, intellectual life and freedom of thought; he was economical in the use of public funds and his administration could serve as a model and as an example to be striven after by the rest of the German states, and especially by Austria. But everything was done by autocracy, there was no Estates constitution and no active state council to give unifying force; there were no institutions in which a community spirit, a comprehensive view and fixed administrative maxims could develop. Every activity awaited initiative from above, independence and self-confidence were lacking. . . . As long as a great man was at the head of the state, guiding it with spirit, strength and uniformity, the system produced good and brilliant results which hid from view much that was patched up and unfinished, as well as the general indifference of the north German masses. His example maintained thrifty, simple customs, stimulated intensive activity, frightened the bad, raised up the good, and forced the mediocre and weak to tread the narrow path of duty. How unexpectedly and quickly did all this change after the death of the great king. . . . One must have been a contemporary and an eye-witness to believe it.

When the great reformer of the nineteenth-century Prussian state here complains of a lack of 'community spirit' – in the sense of a shared responsibility for the state – in Frederician Prussia he was not blaming this on Frederick. Stein knew from his own experience how small the inclination towards independence and confidence in the state really was. He recognized the far-reaching effect and the exemplary influence Frederick had on future generations in calling up reserves of strength and concentrating these on the common good. In the person of the king Stein perceived a principle, the embodiment of the continuity of the state; in his activity the setting of standards for all time. Stein had grasped that Frederick conceived of himself as living in history and subject to secular judgment as far as his life's work was concerned. Because Frederick was part of a tradition of a kingship he was able to pass it on. No other testimony of Frederick the Great was more strongly imbued with enthusiasm than his Personal Testament of 1769 which looked to Prussia's future and to the legacy he himself hoped to leave behind: 'Until my last breath my wishes are for the happiness of the state. May it always be governed with justice, wisdom and strength. May it, as a state, by the mellowness of its law be the happiest, the best administered financially and, with an army that strives only for honour and noble fame, the best defended. May it flourish until the end of time.'

Over the last two centuries much has been written in many countries about Frederick the Great's idea of the state, about his personality, his wars and his victories, about the successes of his foreign policy. But little has, till now, been written about Frederick's administrative activities. Some of his helpers are well known: the merits and achievements of Zieten, Seydlitz and Schwerin have been recognized. But alongside them we should pay tribute to the many who served in the General Directory and in the royal cabinet, in chamber and county administration, in the departments of justice, religion and education. They influenced the king and he them, and the majority of them also exhausted their strength in the service of Prussia. In Frederick, with his devotion to duty and ability to get work done on time, they had a model for their own evolving profession as administrators. During Frederick's lifetime minister von Heinitz put into words what all of them, despite the king's many failings, admired in their master:

> that he looked upon his position as a profession and in so far as his mental and physical powers allowed, tried to accomplish as much as possible – this in chief makes him worthy to be honoured throughout the whole world.

GLOSSARY

Akzise = Accise: excise – the indirect tax payable in the towns.

Allgemeine Landrecht: the Prussian Code of Law, promulgated in 1794.

Amt, pl. *Ämter*: (1) office, (2) board, (3) administrative area. By the late Middle Ages the word *Amt* signified the area over which a lower court exercised jurisdiction. With the gradual acquisition of administrative functions by its leading official, the *Amtmann* (usual pl. *Amtsleute*), the *Amt* developed into the smallest administrative unit. A *Domänenamt* was a complex of state-owned estates, whose chief official was the *Amtshauptmann* (pl. *Amtshauptleute*).

Auditeur = Gerichtsschulze. Assigned to army units and fortresses, the *Auditeur*, a trained jurist, conducted investigations into infringements of military law and in court helped with legal advice. The army department to which he belonged was called the *Generalauditoriat*, at the head of which was the *Generalauditeur* – the Judge Advocate General.

Chargenkasse: Appointments-tax Fund. A fixed, graduated tax was payable on appointment to state offices and on promotion.

Commissarius loci = Steuerkommissar: the official responsible for the collection of the *Akzise* and, in general, for the promotion of trade and industry in the towns. Became known as the *Steuerrat* in the eighteenth century: local commissary.

Drost: in North West Germany – including East Friesland – an official whose duties originally corresponded to those of the *Amtmann*, though by the eighteenth century the office had become largely honorific and reserved for the local nobility.

Feldjäger: a member of the *Feldjäger Korps*, a mounted army unit drawn mainly from the sons of foresters. One of their duties was to act as couriers.

Fiscal, Fiscalat. The *Fiscal* was a royal agent, a member of the *Fiscalat*, whose duty it was to supervise the various state authorities in the interests of the king. Their access to accounts and records and their vigour in bringing to justice officials who had abused their office made them generally feared.

Generalhufenschoss: the East Prussian equivalent of the *Kontribution*, the general land tax.

Generalproviantamt: the General Supply Office, which administered the provision of supplies to the army and fortresses.

Gericht: court of justice. The *Hofgericht*, originally a princely household court, became, with the setting-up of *Hofgerichte* in the various provinces, a superior provincial court. Judicial matters reserved for the elector were decided in his chamber (*Kammer*), with the advice of councillors. The *Kammergericht*, the supreme court of Brandenburg, developed from this. For Prussian territories outside the Mark Brandenburg the Superior Court of Appeal was the *Oberappellationsgericht* which, in time, became the highest appeal court for all of Prussia. Usually referred to by its shorter name, the *Tribunal*.

Grafschaft: a state governed by a *Graf* (count).

Grundherrschaften: the forms of landownership in which the land is altogether or for the most part let out in small farms.

Kabinett: cabinet, i.e. the royal secretariat. Cabinet rule, in the Prussian sense, meant the king's personal rule through his cabinet secretaries.

Kammer: chamber. The *Kammer* (pl. *Kammern*) is the usual abbreviated designation of the *Kriegs- und Domänenkammer*, which was the provincial administrative authority directly subordinate to the General Directory. For the more efficient administration of remoter areas within a *Kammer's* jurisdiction a *Kammerdeputation*, i.e. a permanent sub-department responsible to the *Kammer*, might be set up, or a *Deputatus* (deputy) appointed to carry out the *Kammer's* instructions.

Kasse, pl. *Kassen*: treasury, chest or fund. Numerous *Kassen* existed and for a wide variety of purposes, from the *Dispositionskasse* in which the king kept his reserves and to which he alone had access, to such financial aids to industry as the *Wollmagazin-Kasse* (Wool Depot Fund) set up under Frederick William I to help finance the Kurmark's woollen manufacturers.

Kataster: assessment roll or land register.

Kreis, pl. *Kreise*: circle, the second level of provincial administration, roughly equivalent in extent to a county. Its Silesian counterpart, prior to the province's incorporation in Prussia, had been the *Weichbild*.

Landrat: the local commissioner who was responsible for the administration of the *Kreis*.

Lassbauer = *Lassit*: peasant who rented a farm in return for labour services and could not leave the farm until he had found someone else to work it.

Oberbergamt: the second level – above the *Bergamt* (Mining Office) – in the administration of mines.

Ober-Examinationskommission: the Civil Service Commission.

Oberrentkammer: Chief Treasury Board. This was the East Friesland equivalent (until 1744) of the War and Domains Chamber.

Oberrechenkammer: Chief Audit Office. Its older title was the *Ober-Rechnungskammer*.

Obersalzgraf: official in charge of the administration of the salt monopoly.

Rekrutenkasse: the recruiting chest, originally established by Frederick William I. Its main function was to provide for his giant guards. The source of the chest's finances was a tax payable by officials during their first year of service in a particular post, amounting to quarter or, sometimes, half their salary, in the reign of Frederick William I. Frederick II reduced this to one month's salary.

Regierung: originally a provincial government. Having lost most of its administrative functions when the War and Domains chambers were established it continued to operate mainly as the highest provincial court.

Steuerrat: a commissioner in charge of urban taxation.

Vorwerk: a subsidiary estate or farm, outfarm.

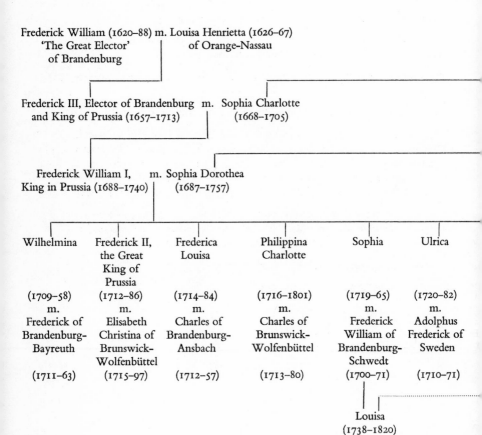

Frederick William (1620–88) m. Louisa Henrietta (1626–67)
   'The Great Elector'   of Orange-Nassau
    of Brandenburg

Frederick III, Elector of Brandenburg m. Sophia Charlotte
  and King of Prussia (1657–1713)   (1668–1705)

Frederick William I,   m. Sophia Dorothea
King in Prussia (1688–1740)   (1687–1757)

Wilhelmina	Frederick II, the Great King of Prussia	Frederica Louisa	Philippina Charlotte	Sophia	Ulrica
(1709–58)	(1712–86)	(1714–84)	(1716–1801)	(1719–65)	(1720–82)
m.	m.	m.	m.	m.	m.
Frederick of Brandenburg-Bayreuth	Elisabeth Christina of Brunswick-Wolfenbüttel	Charles of Brandenburg-Ansbach	Charles of Brunswick-Wolfenbüttel	Frederick William of Brandenburg-Schwedt	Adolphus Frederick of Sweden
(1711–63)	(1715–97)	(1712–57)	(1713–80)	(1700–71)	(1710–71)

Louisa
(1738–1820)

TABLE

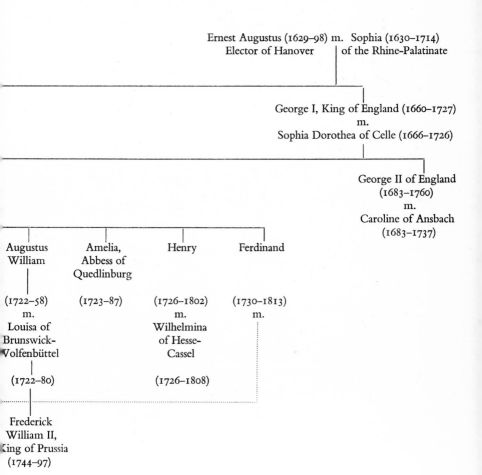

Ernest Augustus (1629–98) m. Sophia (1630–1714)
Elector of Hanover | of the Rhine-Palatinate

George I, King of England (1660–1727)
m.
Sophia Dorothea of Celle (1666–1726)

George II of England
(1683–1760)
m.
Caroline of Ansbach
(1683–1737)

Augustus William	Amelia, Abbess of Quedlinburg	Henry	Ferdinand
(1722–58) m. Louisa of Brunswick-Wolfenbüttel	(1723–87)	(1726–1802) m. Wilhelmina of Hesse-Cassel	(1730–1813) m.
(1722–80)		(1726–1808)	

Frederick
William II,
King of Prussia
(1744–97)

General Directory
(following *Acta Borussica*, Preuss, Klaproth-Cosmar, Rosenmöller et al.)

First Department [divided
into A and B in 1769]

Friedrich von Görne	1739–45
Adam L. von Blumenthal	1745–62
Joachim C. von Blumenthal [A only from 1769]	1763–98
Valentin von Massow [B only]	1769–75
Leopold Otto von Gaudi [B only]	1775–89

[A] Pomerania,
Neumark, treasury,
Mint [from 1769]
[B] East Prussia,
Lithuania, West
Prussia [since 1775],
'*Kassen*', frontier
matters, land
drainage and
amelioration

Second Department

Franz Wilhelm von Happe	1727–47
August F. von Boden	1747–62
Valentin von Massow	1763–69
Friedrich W. von Derschau	1769–79
Friedrich G. Michaelis	1779–81
H. E. Dietrich von Werder	1781–86

Kurmark
Magdeburg and
Mansfeld [1771 to
Third Dept.]
'*Mühlsteinregal*'
Maps and stamp
duties
Matters concerning the
General War *Kasse*

Marching and victual-
ling and quartering
troops [to Sixth
Dept. in 1746]
Salt monopoly [from
Third Dept. in 1747]
General Post Office
[from Third Dept.
in 1769]
[to Fifth Dept. in
1784]

Third Department

August Friedrich von Boden	1739–47
Adam Otto von Viereck	1747–54
Friedrich Wilhelm von Borcke	1754–64
Ludwig Philipp von Hagen	1764–70
Friedrich W. von der Schulenburg-Kehnert	1771–86

Cleves, Mark, Gelder-
land, Moers, East
Friesland
Neuchâtel, Montfort,
Turnhout, Minden,
Ravensberg [from
Fourth Dept. in 1766]
Halberstadt and
Hohenstein [from
Fourth Dept. in 1766]
Tecklenburg, Lingen
[from Fourth Dept.
in 1766]
Magdeburg with
Mansfeld [from
Second Dept. in 1771]
Mint [from 1747 to
1750]
Invalid affairs [from
1747 to 1770]
Mining and metallurgy
[until 1768]

Stamped papers [to
  Fourth Dept. in 1769]
Salt monopoly [to
  Second Dept. in
  1747]
Postal matters [to
  Second Dept. in
  1769]

Fourth Department

Adam Otto von Viereck	1731–47
F. Wilhelm von Happe	1747–60
(Friedrich W. von Borcke)	1760–64
Ludwig Philipp von Hagen	1764–70
J. A. Friedrich von der Horst	1766–74
Friedrich C. von Görne	1774–82
August Wilhelm von Bismarck	1782–83
Friedrich A. von Heinitz	1783–84
H. E. Dietrich von Werder	1786–91

Halberstadt and
  Hohenstein [to
  Third Dept. in 1766]
Minden, Ravensberg [to
  Third Dept. in 1766]
Tecklenburg, Lingen [to
  Third Dept. in 1766]
Mint [to First Dept. in
  1769]
Commercial enterprises
  and factories [to Fifth
  Dept. in 1740]
Trade statistics [from
  1766]
Customs and Excise
  (*Regie*) [from 1766]
Overseas Trade [to
  Third Dept. 1771]
State Bank [to Third
  Dept. 1771]
Invalid affairs [to Third
  Dept. 1747]

Fifth Department [1740]

Samuel von Marschall	1740–49
[Johann R. E. Fäsch interim]	1750–66
J. A. Friedrich von der Horst	1767–74
Friedrich Christoph von Görne	1774–82
Friedrich A. von Heinitz	1782
August Wilhelm von Bismarck	1782–83
Friedrich A. von Heinitz	1783–84
Hans Ernst D. von Werder	1784–86

Commercial enterprises
  and factories
Additionally, from
  1765, Commissaire
  général de
  Commerce;
Manufacture
  Commission incor-
  porated in 1767
Affairs of colonists

Sixth Department [1746]

Heinrich Christoph von Katte	1746–60
Carl Heinrich von Wedell	1761–77
Carl von der Osten-Sacken	1777–79
Levin R. von der Schulenburg	1779–88

Military affairs
  [*Kriegsministerium*]
Secret War Chancery
Marching, quartering
  and service matters
  [from Second Dept.]
General Commissariat
  and magazines
Saltpetre
Adjutant-General
Inspector-General of
  artillery

Chief of engineer corps
and fortresses
'*General-Auditeur*'
'*General-Intendant*'
Quartermaster-General
Military orphanage at
Potsdam
Invalid affairs from 1770
[from Third Dept.]

Seventh Department [1768]

Ludwig Philipp von Hagen	1768–70
Friedrich Wilhelm von der Schulenburg-Kehnert	1770–74
J. S. Waitz von Eschen	1774–76
Friedrich A. von Heinitz	1777–1802

Mining and metallurgy
(machinery matters)
[from Third Dept.]

Directly subordinate to
the General Directory:
'*Geldrisches Landes-
Administrations-
Collegium*' [from 1770]

*Chief War Office and
Domains Audit Office*

v. Piper	1744–52
Resen	1752–64
v. Tieffenbach	1764–76

Roden	1768–81
Hans Wilhelm Kummer	1781–86

Eighth Department [1770]

[Ob. Jäger-Meister Graf von Schlieben]	1748
Ludwig Philipp von Hagen	1770
Friedrich Wilhelm von der Schulenburg-Kehnert	1770–72
Friedrich Wilhelm von Lüderitz	1772–75
von der Schulenburg-Kehnert	1775–86

Forestry matters
(Timber Commission)
(Firewood Commission)

Postmaster General

Friedrich von Görne [I]	1719–45
Samuel von Marschall [V]	1745–49
Georg Dietloff von Arnim	1750–53
G. A. von Gotter	1753–62
Heinrich IX Graf von Reuss	1762–69
von Derschau *see* Second Dept.	1769–79
Michaelis *see* Second Dept.	1779–81
von Werder *see* Second Dept.	1781–1800

GOVERNMENTAL AUTHORITIES

Secret State Council

State Council of Justice
Great Chancellor:

Samuel von Cocceji	1747–55
Joseph Philipp Pandin de Jariges	1755–70
Carl Joseph M. von Fürst und Kupferberg	1770–79
Johann H. C. von Carmer	1779–98

Department of Justice

Samuel von Cocceji	1737–46
Levin F. von Bismarck	1746–63
C. J. M. von Fürst und Kupferberg	1763–70
Ernst F. von Münch-hausen	1771–80
Eberhard L. von der Reck	1794–1807

Department of Ecclesiastical Affairs
[subordinate to the Dept. of Justice
until 1764, thereafter independent]

Christian von Brandt	1738–49
Carl L. von Danckelmann	1749–64
LUTHERAN:	
Ernst F. von Münchhausen	1764–70
CALVINIST:	
J. L. von Dorville	1764–70
LUTHERAN:	
Carl A. von Zedlitz	1770–88
CALVINIST:	
Wolfgang F. von Dörnberg	1771–95

Justice Ministers for Silesia

Samuel von Cocceji	1742–43
Georg Dietloff von Arnim	1743–48
Carl L. von Danckelmann	1748–49
Hans Carl Fürst von Carolath	1750–63
Ernst F. von Münchhausen	1763–68
Johann H. Casimir von Carmer	1768–79
A. Leopold von Danckelmann	1780–93

Kabinettsministerium
(Department of External Affairs)

I Adrian B. von Borck	1740–41
Caspar W. von Borck	1741–47
Axel von Mardeveld	1747–49
Carl Wilhelm von Finckenstein	1749–60
Ewald Friedrich von Hertzberg	1763–91

II Heinrich von Podewils	1728–60
Carl W. von Finckenstein	1760–1800
III Wilhelm H. von Thulemeier	1740

Justice Ministers in the Department of External Affairs

Balthasar Konrad zum Broich	1731–45
W. F. von Danckelmann	1746
Ernst Wilhelm von Bredow	1746–56

War Consistory
[Its president was the Judge Advocate
General (*General-Auditeur*)]

Christian Otto Mylius	1739–52
Andr. F. W. von Pawlowsky	1752–65
Johann L. Reinecke	1765–73
Johann F. von Goldbeck	1773–87

Directly under the king were:
Provincial Ministers for Silesia

L. W. von Münchow	1741–53
Joachim E. von Massow	1753–55
Ernst W. von Schlabrendorff	1755–70
Carl Georg H. von Hoym	1770–1806

and *Heads of the Board of Works:*

Hans Georg W. von Knobelsdorff ('*Sur-Intendant*')	1740–53
Gottfried K. W. Struve	1770–

Prussian Provincial Administrations 1779
(War and Domains Chambers and Chamber-Deputations)

War and Domains Chamber	Seat	Subordinate Chamber-Deputation	Seat
East Prussia	Königsberg		
Lithuania	Gumbinnen		
West Prussia	Marienwerder	Netze District	Bromberg
Pomerania	Stettin	Further Pomerania	Köslin
Breslau	Breslau	(justice commission and deputatus)	Glatz
		Upper Silesia	Oppeln
Glogau	Glogau		
Kurmark	Berlin	Altmark-Prignitz	Stendal
Neumark	Küstrin		
Magdeburg	Magdeburg	Saalkreis with Mansfeld	Halle
		Halberstadt	Halberstadt
		Hohenstein	Ellrich
		Tecklenburg-Lingen	Lingen
Minden-Ravensberg	Minden		
East Friesland	Aurich		
Cleves-Mark	Cleves	Mark	Hamm
		Moers (only a deputatus from 1779)	Moers
		Gelderland Administrative-College (independent under the General Directory from 1770)	Guelders

1701	18 January	Elector Frederick III of Brandenburg crowns himself King in Prussia at Königsberg.
1712	24 January	Frederick II the Great of Prussia is born in Berlin.
1713–1740		Reign of Frederick William I of Prussia.
1713	24 October	*Königlich Preussische Evangelisch-reformierte Inspections-Presbyterial-Classical-Gymnasien und Schulordnung.*
1723	19 January	Establishment of the General Directory (the *General-Oberfinanz-Kriegs- und Domänen-Direktorium*) at Berlin.
1728	January–February	Crown Prince Frederick accompanies his father on a visit to the Saxon Court at Dresden.
1730	5 August	Crown Prince Frederick's attempted flight to England.
	20 November	Crown Prince Frederick begins his administrative apprenticeship as an *Auskultator* in the Neumark War and Domains Chamber at Küstrin.
1732	29 February	With the rank of colonel, Crown Prince Frederick assumes command of the Christoph Heinrich von der Goltz infantry regiment at Neuruppin.
1733	12 June	Marriage of Crown Prince Frederick to Princess Elizabeth Christina of Brunswick-Wolfenbüttel.
1734	July–September	Crown Prince Frederick at Prince Eugène's camp.
1735	September–October	Frederick, on his father's instructions, visits East Prussia.
1736	July–August	Frederick's second visit to East Prussia, this time accompanying his father.
	End of August	The crown prince and his wife take up residence at Rheinsberg.
1739	July–August	The crown prince's third visit to East Prussia, again accompanying his father.
1740	31 May	Death of Frederick William I. Frederick II takes over the government of the state.
	27 June	Formation of the Fifth Department of the General Directory (for commerce and factories).

1740	July–September	Frederick II's progress through the provinces for the ceremonies of homage.
	October	Military demonstration against Liège.
		Sale of Herstal.
	December to	First Silesian War. (Battles of Mollwitz and
1742	June	Chotusitz.)
	28 July	Peace of Berlin. Administrative organization of the duchy of Silesia and the county of Glatz.
1744	23 June	Homage of the East Friesland Estates, on Prussia's acquisition of the principality through inheritance.
	August–December	Second Silesian War. (Battles of Hohenfriedberg, Soor and Kesselsdorf.)
	25 December	Peace of Dresden.
1746	25 February	Formation of the Sixth Department (for military affairs) of the General Directory.
	27 August	Judicial reforms introduced by Cocceji.
1747	1 May	Completion of Sans Souci near Potsdam.
	Summer	Settlements in Pomerania (Prince Moritz von Anhalt-Dessau).
1748		Completion of the *Invalidenhaus*.
	20 May	Departmental *Reglement* for the General Directory and the War and Domains chambers.
1750	17 April	Revised General Privilege and *Reglement* for the Jews in the kingdom of Prussia.
	June	Frederick II's visit to East Prussia.
	14 July	Prussian Currency Law (Graumann Director-General of the Mint).
	3 August	Revised Military-Consistorial *Reglement* and Church Ordinance (Chief Chaplain Decker).
1751	June	Visit to Emden. Foundation of the Asiatic Trading Company in Emden.
1752	11 January	Frederick II's first Personal Testament.
	27 August	Frederick II's first Political Testament.
1753	June	Frederick II visits East Prussia.
	Summer	Work begins on the Oderbruch amelioration scheme.
1754	20 April	Judicial Inspection Edict issued as completion of first stage in reform of justice.
1755	June	Frederick II visits Emden and the United Provinces.
1756	August	Seven Years War. (Battles of Prague, Kolin,
1763	to February	Rossbach, Leuthen, Zorndorf, Hochkirch, Kunersdorf, Liegnitz, Torgau, Burkersdorf.) Occupation of Saxony.

	15 February	Peace of Hubertusburg.
		Royal Porcelain Manufactory in Berlin.
		Royal visit to Prussia's western provinces.
	12 August	*General-Landschul-Reglement.*
1764		Dispute over Polish succession causes cancellation of royal visit to East Prussia.
	15 June	Reorganization of the newly independent Department of Ecclesiastical Affairs.
	12 July	Edict issued on the protection of peasant lands.
		Instructions on the division of common lands.
1765	20 July	Foundation of the Prussian State Bank.
1766	9 April	Establishment of the Customs and Excise Administration – the *Regie.*
	30 April	Instruction for *Landräte* and *Steuerräte* issued.
1768	May	Formation of the Seventh Department of the General Directory (for Mines and Metallurgy). Hagen as director, later Heinitz.
	Summer	Frederick II visits the western provinces.
	7 November	Frederick II's second Political Testament.
1769	8 January	Second Personal Testament.
	25–28 August	Emperor Joseph II's visit to Frederick II at Neisse.
	Autumn	Herring Fishing Company founded at Emden.
	24 October	Edict on distribution of common land issued.
1770		Establishment of the Eighth Department of the General Directory (for Forestry) – von der Schulenburg in charge.
1771		Establishment of the Main Wood Administration.
1772		Incorporation, after treaties, of West Prussia, the Netze District and Ermland in Prussia.
		Foundation of the Overseas Trading Society.
1775		Beginning of settlements, after land reclamation, in the Netze and Warthe districts.
		Foundation of the Widows' Providential Fund.
1776	22 August	Frontier settlement between Prussia and Poland.
		Settlements in Upper Silesia.
1778–1779		War of the Bavarian Succession.
1779	13 May	Peace of Teschen.
	5 September	Cabinet decree on educational matters (Zedlitz).
1780	14 April	Directive on the codification of the law (unified law code, the *Allgemeines Landrecht* for the Prussian states; Carmer and Suarez).
1785	23 July	German Fürstenbund.
1786	17 August	Death of Frederick II the Great at Sans Souci.

GERMANY IN 1763

------- Boundary of the Holy Roman Empire

- - - - State and territorial boundaries

✗ Battle

⊙ Imperial city

0   100   200 Km

NORTH SEA

ENGLAND

SLESW

HOLST

EAST FRIESLAND
1744 Pr.

BREM
VERD

Bremen ●

UNITED

PROVINCES

Cleves

Dortmund

AUSTRIAN

Köln

Aachen

WESTPHALIA

HESSE

TRIER

NETHERLANDS

Frankfurt ⊙

MA

PALATINA

FRANCE

BAR-

Strasbourg

WÜRTTEMB

LORRAINE

Neuchâtel
Neuenburg
1707 Pr.

Bern
●

SWISS CANTONS

SAVOY

MILAN

PAR

PRUSSIA: administrative boundaries in 1779

★ Fortified place

◉ Administrative centre

——— Canal

0   100   200 Km

SWEDEN

DENMARK

NORTH SEA

SWEDISH POMERANIA

Greetsiel
Aurich
Emden EAST FRIESLAND

R. Ems

R. Weser

R. Elbe

R. Havel

UCKER

Rheinsberg
Neuruppin

ALTMARK
Stendal

Spandau
Berlin

Postdam

Lingen

MINDEN
Minden

Tecklenburg

Bielefeld
Ravensberg

Magdeburg

Cleves CLEVES
Wesel
Guelders
Moers
GELDERLAND

Hamm

R. Lippe

Soest

R. Ruhr

Halberstadt

Harz mountains
Ellrich
Hohenstein

Mansfeld
Wettin
Halle

Krefeld

MARK

Köln

R. Rhine

R. Saal

Erzgebirge mountains

Koblenz

R. Mosel

R. Main

NEUCHÂTEL
Neuenburg
1707 Pr.

Valangin

Neuchâtel

Frederick II has in the main been studied in a diplomatic or war context, though his musical gifts (which, incidentally, are frequently found in the Hohenzollern family) are usually mentioned as a pleasing aesthetic component of his personality. His talents as a military commander are undeniable, but often thought to have dominated him too exclusively: he is commonly compared to Charles XII of Sweden, 'the Northern Warrior King' of the early eighteenth century.* We owe it to an English historian, G. Peabody Gooch (1873–1968), who in 1947 published a biography entitled *Frederick the Great. The Ruler, The Writer, The Man*, that attention has been focused on other facets of Frederick's personality besides those of the warrior and the diplomat. Gooch, however, was not particularly interested in the politics of Frederick's time; for him Frederick the intellectual writer is the object of attention. We must be grateful that Gooch went against the conventional historical stream; but it must be admitted that one of Frederick's truly royal characteristics, that of a lifelong and great absorption in the administration of his state, is thereby obscured. A study of Frederick's administration is no easy task. It is necessary to find out what was attainable in the world of the eighteenth century, taking into account its presuppositions and its limitations. The talents Frederick brought to his office must be examined, his ability to grow into his responsibilities assessed, and the purposes which he sought to achieve discussed.

* For such comparisons see Thomas Carlyle, part IX, chapter 2 of his biography of Frederick and, more recently, Otto Hainz, *Karl XII* vol. I (sec. ed., Berlin 1958). Frederick himself, in letters, writings and political testaments, shows a strong interest in Charles and – as a counterblast to Voltaire's biography – wrote a study which, with hindsight gained from his own experience of war, gave due emphasis to the military talents of the Swede through showing his lack of political flexibility. For a modern important study showing that the Swedish king had interests beyond those of warfare, see R. M. Hatton, *Charles XII of Sweden* (London 1968).

SURVEY OF ARCHIVAL MATERIAL

Former *Preussisches Geheimes Staatsarchiv*:
now the Deutsches Zentralarchiv *Merseburg* [Remnants from the Brandenburg and Neumark sections now in the *Geheimes Staatsarchiv Berlin Dahlem* include, among other items, the documents of the crown prince's court martial, Küstrin; Mesures à prendre aus cas d'une guerre; Politiques 1763–64; Finances; Militaire; Budget of the royal court orchestra; Royal Household and forage budget; Exposé Du Gouvernement Prussien [1776]; Political Testament 1752 (clean draft in the king's hand); Frederick the Great's letters to Fredersdorf, his valet-de-chambre (the original letters), the Bromberg *Kammerdeputation*.]

Brandenburg-Preussisches Hausarchiv:
now Deutsches Zentralarchiv *Merseburg*

Former *Staatsarchiv Königsberg/Preussen*:
now in the State Archive Repository at Göttingen, Preussischer Kulturbesitz. (Contains, among other collections, the documents of the Königsberg and Gumbinnen War and Domains chambers.) Other individual sets are in the State Archives in Aurich, Düsseldorf, Koblenz, Magdeburg and Münster.
Former Staatsarchiv Stettin
Former Staatsarchiv Breslau
Former Staatsarchiv Danzig [War and Domains Chamber, Marienwerder]

Guides to the Archives:

Mitteilungen der Preussischen Archivverwaltung
Part 6 lists the contents in the Koblenz archive
Part 24 lists the contents in the Berlin-Dahlem I [now at Merseburg]
Part 25 lists the contents in the Berlin-Dahlem II–IX [now at Merseburg]
Part 26 lists the contents in the Berlin-Dahlem X–XI [now at Merseburg]
Part 27 lists the contents in the Brandenburg-Pr. Hausarchiv [now at Merseburg]
Part 21 lists the contents in the Danzig archive

Veröffentlichungen Niedersächsischen Archivverwaltung:
Part 3 The Preussisches Staatsarchiv in Königsberg [now Göttingen] (1955)

Übersicht über die Bestände des Geheimes Staatsarchivs Berlin-Dahlem:
Part I Provincial and local authorities (1966)
Part II Central authorities. Other institutions and collections (1967)

Übersicht des Brandenburgischen Landeshauptarchivs Potsdam (I. Weimar 1964)

POPULATION OF PRUSSIA 1776

(Prepared by the German Salt Fund for Frederick the Great. Printed by Gustav Schmoller, 'Studien über die wirtschaftliche Politik Friedrichs des Grossen. XII: Die wirtschaftlichen Zustände im Herzogtum Magdeburg: Die Industrie, hauptsächlich die Textilgewerbe und die Salinen', *Jahrbuch für Gesetzgebung, Verwaltung und Volkswirtschaft im Deutschen Reich.* 11 (1887) p. 872 f. – here completed.)

Province	Number of people
East Prussia	430,342
Lithuania	335,368
West Prussia (and Ermland)	416,233
Little Prussia (Netze District)	107,665
Pomerania	384,484
Neumark	233,354
Kurmark	618,463
Magdeburg, Saalkreis and Mansfeld	231,913
Halberstadt	78,146
Hohenstein	21,095
Minden and Ravensberg	124,812
Lingen and Tecklenburg	39,629
East Friesland	102,183
County of Mark	117,480
Cleves, Gelderland and Moers	146,598
	3,387,765
Silesia and Glatz*	1,372,754
Total number of inhabitants (1776)†	4,760,519

* according to Büsching, for 1776.
[Anton Friedrich Büsching, *Zuverlässige Beiträge zu der Regierungsgeschichte König Friedrichs II vornehmlich in Ansehung der Volksmenge, des Handels, der Finanzen und des Kriegsheeres* (Hamburg, 1790)]
Hoym's principal report for 1785 gives the Silesian population as 1,377,678 for the year 1777. E. Pfeiffer, *Die Revuereisen Friedrichs des Grossen* (Berlin, 1904), p. 108, n. 25, based on the former Staatsarchiv Breslau M.R.V., 9a.

† Not counting military personnel or their dependants.
See Reinhold Koser, 'Zur Bevölkerungsstatistik des preussischen Staates von 1756–1786', *Forschungen zur brandenburgischen und preussischen Geschichte*, XVI (1903), pp. 583–589. Also Koser, ibid. VII (1894), pp. 540–548.

General Bibliography

Œuvres de Frédéric le Grand, ed. J. D. E. Preuss (31 vols., Berlin 1846–57)
Die Werke Friedrichs des Grossen in deutsche Übersetzung, ed. G. B. Volz (10 vols., Berlin)
Briefe Friedrichs des Grossen, ed. M. Hein (2 vols., Berlin 1914)
Gespräche Friedrichs des Grossen, eds. F. von Oppeln-Bronikowski and G. B. Volz (3rd ed. Berlin 1926)
Politische Korrespondenz Friedrichs des Grossen, eds. G. B. Volz, et al. (46 vols., Berlin 1879–1939)
Friedrich der Grosse im Spiegel seiner Zeit, ed. G. B. Volz (3 vols., Berlin 1926–27)
Preussische Staatsschriften aus der Regierungszeit König Friedrichs II, eds. R. Koser and O. Krauske (3 vols., Berlin 1877–92)
A. Hildebrand, *Das Bildnis Friedrichs des Grossen. Zeitgenössische Darstellungen* (Berlin 1940; 2nd ed. 1942)
J. D. E. Preuss, *Friedrich der Grosse. Eine Lebensgeschichte* (4 vols., Berlin 1832–34)
L. von Ranke, *Zwölf Bücher Preussischer Geschichte*. Sämtliche Werke. Vols. XXV–XXIX (2nd ed. 1878–). Critical edition ed. G. Küntzel (3 vols., Berlin 1930)
T. Carlyle, *History of Friedrich II of Prussia, Called Frederick the Great* (6 vols., London 1858–65)
J. G. Droysen, *Geschichte der Preussischen Politik*, part V, 1–4 (Leipzig 1874–86)
M. Hein, *Friedrich der Grosse. Ein Bild seines Lebens und Schaffens* (n.d.)
R. Koser, *Geschichte Friedrichs des Grossen* (7th ed., 4 vols., Berlin 1921–25; new impression, Darmstadt 1963)
G. Ritter, *Frederick the Great: A Historical Profile*, trans., with an introduction, by P. Paret (Berkeley 1968)

G. P. Gooch, *Frederick the Great. The Ruler, The Writer, The Man* (London 1947)
W. Elze, *Friedrich der Grosse. Geistige Welt, Schicksal, Taten* (2nd ed. Berlin 1939)
W. Dilthey, 'Friedrich der Grosse und die deutsche Aufklärung', *Gesammelte Schriften* III (Berlin 1927)
E. Spranger, 'Der Philosoph von Sanssouci', *Abhandlungen der Preussische Akademie der Wissenschaften*, Philosophisch-historische Klasse 5 (1942; 2nd ed. 1962)
W. Hubatsch, *Das Problem der Staatsraison bei Friedrich dem Grossen* (Göttingen 1956)
G. Holmsten, *Friedrich II* (Hamburg 1969)
T. B. Macaulay, 'Frederick the Great', (to 1763) *Edinburgh Review* (April 1842). New German edition with introduction by Alexander von Hase (Berlin 1971)
P. Gaxotte, *Frederick the Great*, trans. from the French by R. A. Bell (London 1941)
D. B. Horn, *Frederick the Great and the Rise of Prussia* (London 1964)
W. F. Reddaway, *Frederick the Great and the Rise of Prussia* (London 1904)
Posthumous Works of Frederick II, King of Prussia, trans. by Thomas Holcroft (13 vols., London 1789)

Bibliographical Notes

I The Crown Prince

J. D. E. Preuss, *Friedrichs der Grossens Jugend und Thronbesteigung* (1840); E. Lavisse, *La Jeunesse du Grand Frédéric* (Paris 1891; 3rd ed. 1899; 4th ed. 1916); E. Lavisse, *Le Grand Frédéric avant l'avènemant* (Paris 1893); F. Arnheim, *Der Hof Friedrichs des Grossen*, Part 1: *Der Hof des Kronprinzen* (Berlin 1912); G. B. Volz, 'Die Krisis in der Jugend Friedrichs des Grossen', *Historische Zeitschrift* CXVIII (1917) [to 1734/35]; D. Rohmer, *Vom Werdegang Friedrichs des Grossen. Die politische Entwicklung des Kronprinzen* (Greifswald 1924); H. Droysen, 'Tageskalender Friedrichs des Grossen', Part 1: 1732-40, *Forschungen zur brandenburgischen und preussischen Geschichte* XXV (1913); Part 2: 1740-63 in XXIX (1916); R. Koser, ed., 'Tagebuch des Kronprinzen Friedrich 1734', *Forschungen zur brandenburgischen und preussischen Geschichte* IV (1891); R. Koser, *Friedrichs des Grossens Briefwechsel mit Grumbkow und Maupertuis 1731-1759* (Leipzig 1898). (Publikationen aus den Preussischen Staatsarchiven 72); R. Koser and H. Droysen, *Briefwechsel Friedrichs des Grossen mit Voltaire 1736-1778* (4 vols., Leipzig 1908-17). (Publikationen aus den Preussischen Staatsarchiven 81, 82, 86, 90); C. Hinrichs, *Der Kronprinzenprozess. Friedrich und Katte* (Hamburg 1936); *Mémoires de Frédérique Sophie Wilhelmine Margrave de Baireuth 1706-1742* (2nd ed. Brunswick 1845). Many editions since. See G. B. Volz in *Forschungen zur brandenburgischen und preussischen Geschichte* XXXVI (1924); G. B. Volz, ed., *Friedrich der Grosse und Wilhelmine von Bayreuth. Ihr Briefwechsel*, I: 1728-40; II: 1740-58. Trans. into German by F. von Oppeln-Bronikowski (2 vols., Leipzig 1924-26); *Denkwürdigkeiten zur Geschichte des Hauses Brandenburg*, ed. G. B. Volz (1913); Fiction: Jochen Klepper, *Der Vater* (1937. Various other editions).

PROVINCIAL ADMINISTRATION AT KÜSTRIN AND REGIMENTAL DUTIES

Hohenzollern-Jahrbuch (1908), p. 101; F. Förster, *Friedrich Wilhelm I*, 3 vols. with 2 vols of documents (5 vols., Potsdam 1834–35); 'Journal über die Anwesenheit des Königs von Preussen zu Dresden 1728', *Dresdner Geschichtsblätter* 1899 No. 1; H. Granier, 'Die kronprinzlichen Schulden Friedrichs des Grossen', *Forschungen zur brandenburgischen und preussischen Geschichte* VIII (1895); P. Becher, *Der Kronprinz Friedrich als Regimentschef in Neu-Ruppin 1732–1740* (Berlin 1892); E. Poseck, *Die Kronprinzessin Elisabeth Christine, Gemahlin Friedrichs des Grossen* (Berlin 1840; 2nd ed. Stuttgart 1952); B. Krieger, *Friedrich der Grosse und seine Bücher* (Berlin 1914); also in *Hohenzollern-Jahrbuch* (1911–1913).

EAST PRUSSIA AND RHEINSBERG

B. Schumacher, *Geschichte Ost- und Westpreussens* (2nd ed. 1957); F. Terveen, *Gesamtstaat und Retablissement. Der Wiederaufbau des nördlichen Ostpreussens unter Friedrich Wilhelm I. 1714–1740.* Göttinger Bausteine zur Geschichtswissenschaft 16 (1954); A. Skalweit, *Die ostpreussische Domänenverwaltung unter Friedrich Wilhelm I. und das Retablissement Litauens* (1906); W. Hubatsch, *Geschichte der evangelischen Kirche Ostpreussens* (3 vols., Göttingen 1968); *Briefe Friedrichs des Grossen in deutscher Übersetzung*, ed. M. Hein, vol. I (Berlin 1914); Knorr, 'Friedrich der Grosse als Freimaurer', *Hohenzollern-Jahrbuch* (1899); C. Hinrichs, *Der allgegenwärtige König. Friedrich der Grosse im Kabinett und auf Inspektionsreisen* (2nd ed. Berlin 1940); C. Hinrichs, *Preussentum und Pietismus* (1971); H. Iwanowius, 'Reisen König Friedrich Wilhelms I und des Kronprinzen Friedrich nach Preussen', *Sitzungsberichte des Vereins für Geschichte von Ost- und Westpreussen* IV (1900); R. Grieser, 'Friedrich Wilhelm I auf der Reise in Preussen', *Mitteilungen des Vereins für Geschichte von Ost- und Westpreussen* III (1928/29).

FREDERICK WILLIAM I'S HERITAGE

Friedrich der Grosse, Gespräche, eds. F. von Oppeln-Bronikowski und G. B. Volz (3rd ed. Berlin 1926). See also 'Podewils über die Unterredung König-Kronprinz am 28.5.1740', *Hohenzollern-Jahrbuch* (1904) pp. 23ff; H. de Catt, *Memoiren und Tagebücher. Unterhaltungen mit Friedrich des Grossen*, ed. R. Koser (Leipzig 1884). Publikationen aus den Preussischen Staatsarchiven 22. English edition: *Frederick the Great. The Memoirs of his Reader Henri de Catt (1758–1760)*, trans. by F. S. Flint with an introduction by Lord Rosebery (2 vols., London 1916) – see diary entries for 19.1.1760 and 26.1.1760; G. Küntzel and M. Hass, eds., *Die politischen Testamente der Hohenzollern* vol. I (2nd ed. Berlin 1919) – this contains Frederick William I's Instruction of 22 January–17 February 1722 for his successor and his last address to the crown prince; G. Schmoller, *Preussische Verfassungs-, Verwaltungs- und Finanzgeschichte* (Berlin 1921); *Acta Borussica. Denkmäler der preussischen Staatsverwaltung im 18. Jahrhundert. Behördenorganisation* vol. VI. 1, ed. O. Hintze (Berlin 1901); C. Jany, *Geschichte der Königlichen Preus-*

sichen Armee vol. I (Berlin 1928); C. A. L. Klaproth and C. W. Cosmar, *Der Königlich preussische und Kurfürstlich brandenburgische Geheime Staatsrat* (Berlin 1805) – indispensable for personal histories of leading officials.

II The Young King

Reinhold Koser, *Geschichte Friedrichs des Grossen* vol. I; Johann Gustav Droysen, *Geschichte der preussischen Politik V: Friedrich der Grosse* vol. I; Wilhelm Oncken, *Das Zeitalter Friedrichs des Grossen* (2 vols., Berlin 1871–82). 'Allgemeine Geschichte in Einzeldarstellungen' series, ed. W. Oncken; William Pierson, *Preussische Geschichte* vol. I (Berlin 1881); Ernst Berner, *Geschichte des preussischen Staates* (Berlin 1891); Leopold von Ranke, *Zwölf Bücher preussischer Geschichte.*

RESIDENCES

Friedrich Nicolai, *Beschreibung der königlichen Residenzstädte Berlin und Potsdam, aller daselbst befindlichen Merkwürdigkeiten und der umliegenden Gegend* (3rd ed., 3 vols., Berlin 1786; reprint Berlin 1968); Margarete Kühn, *Schloss Charlottenburg* (13th ed. Berlin 1966) – also available in English; Johann Daniel Friedrich Rumpf, *Beschreibung der äusseren und inneren Merkwürdigkeiten der Königlichen Schlösser in Berlin, Charlottenburg, Schönhausen, in den bei Potsdam* (Berlin 1794); Paul Seidel, 'Der neue Flügel Friedrichs des Grossen am Charlottenburger Schloss', *Hohenzollern-Jahrbuch* XVI (1912) pp. 86–94; Georg Holmsten, *Potsdam. Die Geschichte der Stadt, der Bürger und Regenten* (Berlin 1971); Hans Kania, *Potsdamer Baukunst* (2nd ed. Berlin 1926); Heinrich Ludwig Manger, *Baugeschichte von Potsdam, besonders unter der Regierung Friedrichs II* (2 vols., Berlin and Stettin 1789); Georg Sello, *Potsdam und Sans Souci. Forschungen und Quellen zur Geschichte von Burg, Stadt und Park* (Breslau 1888); Willy Kurth, *Sanssouci. Seine Schlösser und Gärten* (8th ed. Berlin 1968); Carl von Lorck, *Preussisches Rokoko* (Oldenburg 1964); Eduard Vehse, *Geschichte der deutschen Höfe seit der Reformation.* Section 1: *Geschichte des preussischen Hofes und Adels und der preussischen Diplomatie.* Parts 3 and 4, ch. V: *Friedrich II der Grosse* (Hamburg 1851); Anneliese Streichhan, *Knobelsdorff und das friderizianische Rokoko* (Magdeburg 1932).

On communications between Berlin and Potsdam: Nicolai, III, p. 1259f.; Vehse 3, 1, III, p. 225.

On gazettes: ibid. III, p. 227; Nicolai, II, p. 978; Preuss, *Friedrichs des Grossens Jugend und Thronbesteigung* (Berlin 1840) p. 486; E. Kaeber, 'Geistige Strömungen in Berlin unter Friedrichs des Grossen', *Forschungen zur brandenburgischen und preussischen Geschichte* LIV (1943); E. Consentius, 'Friedrich der Grosse und die Zeitungszensur', *Preussische Jahrbücher* CXV; Vehse 3, 1, III, p. 226f.; Bonn University Library has odd volumes of Haude & Spener's and Voss's newspaper from the reign of Frederick the Great; facsimiles of the *Journal de Berlin* and Haude & Spener's newspaper are to be found in Wilhelm Oncken, *Das Zeitalter*

Friedrichs des Grossen vol. I, p. 308f.; by cabinet order of 9 July 1743 the freedom of the press was again reduced on the grounds of 'abuse', the susceptibilities of foreign powers, the publication of confidential royal ordinances and the smirching of the honour and reputation of other people.

RECEIVING HOMAGE

Küntzel and Hass, *Politische Testamente der Hohenzollern* vol. I; Jany, II; Koser, *Geschichte Friedrichs des Grossen* I, p. 217ff.; ibid. IV, p. 34f. for other sources; Droysen, I, p. 48ff.; Oncken, I; Vehse 3, 1, III, ch. V. p. 228f.; Walter Mertineit, *Die friderizianische Verwaltung in Ostpreussen* (Heidelberg 1958) p. 39ff., 'Studien zur Geschichte Preussens' series, vol I.; Max Hein, ed., *Briefe Friedrichs des Grossen* vol. I (Berlin 1914); *Acta Borussica* IV-b, pp. 5ff., 21, 79, 110, 133, 141, 145, 150, 572–76; Johannes Schultze, *Die Mark Brandenburg* vol. V (Berlin 1969) p. 81ff.; Hermann Rothert, *Westfälische Geschichte* vol. III (3rd ed. Gütersloh 1964); Carl Hinrichs, *Der allgegenwärtige König* (2nd ed. Berlin 1940) pp. 80, 85, 108; W. Wiegand, 'Friedrich der Grosse in Strassburg', *Korrespondenzblatt des Gesamtvereins der deutschen Geschichts- und Alterumsvereine* (1899) pp. 122–29.

On torture: Ernst Berner, *Geschichte des preussischen Staates*, p. 330; *Acta Borussica* VI-2, 8–11; Koser, 'Die Abschaffung der Tortur durch Friedrich den Grossen', *Forschungen zur brandenburgischen und preussischen Geschichte* VI (1893) pp. 575ff.; Siegfried Isaacsohn, *Geschichte des preussischen Beamtentums vom Anfang des 15. Jahrhunderts bis auf die Gegenwart*. Vol. III, *Das Beamtentum unter Friedrich Wilhelm I und während der Anfänge Friedrichs des Grossen* (Berlin 1884).

On Frederick's interpretation of the capacity of princely power: compare his 'An Essay on Forms of Government and on the Duties of Sovereigns' (1777) *Œuvres* IX, p. 207ff., with his *Anti-Machiavel*. English trans. of both works by Holcroft, *Posthumous Works of Frederick II, King of Prussia* (13 vols., London 1789).

Fritz Gause, *Die Geschichte der Stadt Königsberg* vol. II (Cologne 1968); Edith Spiro, *Die Gravamina der ostpreussischen Stände auf den Huldigungslandtagen des 18. Jahrhunderts*, dissertation (Breslau 1929). Eckhart's undeniable ability as a cameralist is emphasized by August Skalweit, 'Die Entlassung des Plusmachers Eckhart', *Forschungen zur brandenburgischen und preussischen Geschichte* XXII(1909) p.274–82.

On Frederick II's marginal decrees: Georg Borchardt, *Herrschen und Dienen. Die Randbemerkungen Friedrichs des Grossen* (2 vols., Potsdam 1936–37). Newly edited by Erich Murawski under the title *Ihr Wintbeutel und Erzschäker. Die Randbemerkungen Friedrichs des Grossen* (Bad Nauheim 1963). See this volume for further reading on this topic.

On the journeys of homage: That the king travelled to East Prussia with a total of only three coaches, as Koser states, *Geschichte Friedrichs des Grossen* I, p. 217, is disproved by the royal rescript to the War and Domains Chamber at Königsberg dated Berlin, 25 June 1740; for such detailed relay arrangements would not then have been necessary, and the king took with him his personal cooks. Even with the smallest retinue there must have been a total of at least ten coaches. The three coaches mentioned in *Acta Borussica* VI-2, 43 contained only the personal attendants of the king's suite which, apart from the generals, included Borcke, Wartensleben, Jordan, Podewils and Buddenbrock. Koser's opinion of the regiments also needs to be corrected. The Neumarkers (Schulenburg's Dragoons) showed up badly while the Pomeranians were exceptionally good. Of the East Prussian regiments the Glaubitz regiment failed but Captain von Wobeser of the Flanss regiment was awarded the *Pour le mérite!* – see *Acta Borussica* VI-1, 43. On Katte, see von Natzmer in *Altpreussische Biographie* I, 327, where source material is listed. On garrisons, see Günther Gieraths, *Die Kampfhandlungen der brandenburgpreussischen Armee 1626–1807. Ein Quellenbuch* (Berlin 1964); an Army List of December 1740 is discussed in 'Zwei Ranglisten des Preussisches Heeres 1713– 1740', *Beiheft zum Militär-Wochenblatt* (1891) pp. 53–123. For church and university, see Walther Hubatsch, *Geschichte der evangelischen Kirche Ostpreussens* (3 vols., Göttingen 1968) I, p. 218ff. On the office of *Landrat*, see *Acta Borussica* VI-2, 58ff.; Otto Hintze, 'Die Wurzeln der Kreisverfassung in den Ländern des nordöstlichen Deutschland', *Staat und Verfassung: Gesammelte Abhandlungen*, ed. Fritz Hartung (Leipzig 1941). Compare Otto Hintze's article in *Sitzungsberichte der Preussischen Akademie der Wissenschaften*. Philosophisch-historische Klasse No. XXIII (1915) and that – on the office of *Landrat* in the Mark Brandenburg – in *Forschungen zur brandenburgischen und preussischen Geschichte* XXVIII (1915).

On the ceremony of homage in Berlin: Acta Borussica VI-2, 21ff., 66ff.; in Magdeburg – ibid. 79ff., 83ff.; in Halberstadt – ibid. 116; in Cleves – ibid. 14ff., 110, 133, 139; in Minden – ibid. 141; in Ravensberg – ibid. 145; in Lauenburg – ibid. 150; Wadzek and Wippel, *Geschichte der Erbhuldigungen der brandenburg-preussischen Regenten aus dem hohenzollernschen Hause* (Berlin 1798). On Frederick's visit to Strasburg, see W. Wiegand, 'Friedrich der Grosse in Strassburg', *Korrespondenzblatt des Gesamtvereins der deutschen Geschichts- und Altertumsvereine* XLVII (Berlin 1899) pp. 122–29. From Saxon sources Wiegand dates Frederick's arrival in Duisburg to the 30 August; according to Schmoller in *Acta Borussica* VI-2, 143 n., the king should already have been in Wesel on 29 August. But there is nothing there to indicate what the king was doing until 1 September. Wiegand's information, taking into account travelling time, seems therefore preferable. Compare with Hans Droysen, 'Tageskalender Friedrichs des Grossen 1740–63', *Forschungen zur brandenburgischen und preussischen Geschichte* XXIX (1916) p. 95ff.

PRUSSIAN CAMERALISM

Acta Borussica. Behördenorganisation VI-1, *passim*; Isaacsohn, *Beamtentum* III, 241ff.; Koser, *Geschichte Friedrichs des Grossen* I, 154ff.; Hugo Rachel, *Die Handels-, Zoll- und Akzisepolitik Preussens 1740–1786* (Berlin 1928). (*Acta Borussica. Die einzelnen Gebiete der Verwaltung* III. 1.2); Rachel, *Das Berliner Wirtschaftsleben im Zeitalter des Frühkapitalismus* (Berlin 1931); Rudolph Stadelmann, *Preussens Könige in ihrer Tatigkeit für die Landeskultur* vol. II (Leipzig 1882). Publikationen

262 *Frederick the Great*

aus den Preussischen Staatsarchiven 11). Compare also with vol. III (1887) p. 109; Gustav Schmoller, 'Studien über die wirtschaftliche Politik Friedrichs des Grossen und Preussens überhaupt von 1680–1786', *Jahrbuch für Gesetzgebung, Verwaltung und Volkswirtschaft im Deutschen Reich* N.F. 8.10.11 (1884–87), also separate in I–VII, VIII–XII; W. O. Henderson, *Studies in the Economic Policy of Frederick the Great* (London 1963;) Paul Rehfeld, 'Die preussische Rüstungsindustrie unter Friedrich dem Grossen', *Forschungen zur brandenburgischen und preussischen Geschichte* LV (1944) pp. 1–31.; B. Rosenmöller, *Schulenburg-Kehnert unter Friedrich dem Grossen* (1914). (Preussische Staatsmänner, vol. I); Otto Behre, *Geschichte der Statistik in Brandenburg-Preussen bis zur Gründung des Königlich Statistischen Büros* (Berlin 1905); L. Krug, *Topographisch-statistisch-geographisches Wörterbuch der sämtlichen preussischen Staaten* (13 parts, 1796–1803); L. Beutin, 'Die Wirkungen des Siebenjährigen Krieges auf die Volkswirtschaft in Preussen', *Vierteljahrschrift für Sozial- und Wirtschaftsgeschichte* XXII (1929) pp. 16–31; Hildegard Hoffmann, 'Die gewerbliche Produktion Preussens im Jahre 1769', dissertation (typescript). (East Berlin 1956); Conrad Matschoss, 'Friedrich der Grosse als Beförderer des Gewerbefleisses', *Festschrift des Vereins zur Beförderung des Gewerbefleisses* (Berlin 1912); A. Zottmann, 'Die Wirtschaftspolitik Friedrichs des Grossen', *Historische und politische Aufsätze* vol. II (Berlin 1908) p. 131ff.; O. Geissler, *Die Wirtschaftspolitik Friedrichs des Grossen und der Begriff der Planwirtschaft*, dissertation (Tübingen 1951); Carl Hinrichs, 'Das königliche Lagerhaus in Berlin', *Forschungen zur brandenburgischen und preussischen Geschichte* XLIV (1932) pp. 46–69; Helmuth Dehne, *Die Messe von Frankfurt an der Oder in der Zeit der merkantilistischen Wirtschaftspolitik Preussens im 18. Jahrhunderts*, dissertation (Frankfurt on Main 1923); Stephan Skalweit, *Die Berliner Wirtschaftskreise und ihre Hintergrunde*, dissertation (Frankfurt on Main 1937); Max Schulze-Briesen, *Der preussische Staatsbergbau im Wandel der Zeiten* vol. I (1933); C. Ergang, *Friedrich der Grosse in seiner Stellung zum Maschinenproblem* (1910) p. 78ff., 'Beiträge zur Geschichte der Technik und Industrie' series, ed. C. Matschoss, vol. II; O. Steinecke, 'Des Ministers von Heinitz "Mémoire sur ma gestion du 4e et 5e département"', *Forschungen zur brandenburgischen und preussischen Geschichte* XXII (1909) pp. 183–91; H. Stephan, *Geschichte der preussischen Post* (Berlin 1858); J. G. Krünitz, *Ökonomisch-technologische Encyklopädie* vol. XXIV (Berlin 1790), vols. CXLII–CXLIII (Berlin 1926); Kurt Hinze, *Die Arbeiterfrage in Brandenburg-Preussen zu Beginn des modernen Kapitalismus* (Berlin 1927; 2nd ed. Berlin 1963).

On the Fifth Department: *Acta Borussica. Die einzelnen Gebiete der Verwaltung, Handels-, Zoll- und Akzisepolitik 1740–1786*, compiled by Hugo Rachel, vol. III, parts 1 and 2 (Berlin 1928) – as an introduction to the above see H. Rachel, 'Der Merkantilismus in Brandenburg-Preussen', *Forschungen zur brandenburgischen und preussischen Geschichte* XL (1927) pp. 221–66; the Instruction of 27 June 1740 for the Fifth Department is in *Acta Borussica. Behördenorganisation* VI–2, 26–32; on Prussian economic policy see Otto Hintze in *Acta Borussica. Behördenorganisation* VI–1, 32f.; Isaacsohn, *Beamtentum* vol. III, 241ff.; W. O. Henderson, *Studies*; on the demarcation of the Fifth Department vis-à-vis the General Directory see

Acta Borussica VI–2, 35 (cabinet order of 12 July 1740), p. 182f. (protocol of the conference of leading ministers of 5 January 1741), p. 191 f. (cabinet order of 12 February 1741), ibid. for cabinet order of 16 March 1747; cabinet order of 16 March 1748 to the Kurmark Chamber refers to the spinning of flax by women and children; compare C. Matschoss, *Gewerbefleiss*; Behre, *Statistik*, pp. 212 f., 222, 272, 284, 289; Borgstede, *Statistisch-topographische Beschreibung der Kurmark Brandenburg* part I (Berlin 1788); Martin Wehrmann, *Von den Anfängen der Industrie in Pommern* (Veröffentlichung des Vereins der Industrie Pommern 16; 1907).

On the grain trade: *Acta Borussica. Getreidehandelspolitik* III and IV; ibid. for the depot policy. For the western provinces the investigation of the cultivation and consumption of corn in the territory of the Minden Chamber yielded the first exact information in 1767. See Behre, *Statistik*, p. 224. Friedrich Lampp, *Die Getreidehandelspolitik in der ehemaligen Graftschaft Mark während des 18. Jahrhunderts* (Münster 1912; Münstersche Beiträge zur Geschichtsforschung 40); Hildegard Lullies, *Zur Handelspolitik Friedrichs des Grossen*, dissertation (Königsberg 1926).

On the woollen industry: Carl Hinrichs, 'Das Königliche Lagerhaus in Berlin', *Forschungen zur brandenburgischen und preussischen Geschichte* XLIV (1931) pp. 46–69; Johannes Feig, 'Die Begründung der Luckenwalder Wollindustrie durch Preussens Könige im 18. Jahrhundert', *Forschungen zur brandenburgischen und preussischen Geschichte* XXIX (1916) pp. 407–56; F. Schmidt, *Die Entwicklung der Cottbuser Tuchindustrie* (1928); *Acta Borussica. Die einzelnen Gebiete der Verwaltung* III. 1 (1928) pp. 542–69; Anton Overmann, *Die Entwicklung der Leinen-, Woll- und Baumwollindustrie in der ehemaligen Grafschaft Mark unter der Regierung Brandenburg-Preussens besonders im 18. Jahrhundert* (1908; Münstersche Beiträge zur Geschichtsforschung 31); Hans Roemer, *Die Baumwollspinnerei in Schlesien bis zum preussischen Zolltarif von 1818*, dissertation (Tübingen 1914) – also in *Darstellungen und Quellen zur schlesischen Geschichte* XIX (Berlin 1914); Friedrich Freiherr von Schroetter, 'Die schlesische Wollindustrie im 18. Jahrhundert', *Forschungen zur brandenburgischen und preussischen Geschichte* X (1898), XI (1899), XII (1902) – this was originally intended for the *Acta Borussica*.

On the silk industry: *Acta Borussica. Die einzelnen Gebiete der Verwaltung. Die preussische Seidenindustrie im 18. Jahrhundert und ihre Begründung durch Friedrich den Grossen* 3 vols., compiled by Gustav Schmoller and Otto Hintze (Berlin 1892) – for a condensed account see Gustav Schmoller, *Umrisse und Untersuchungen zur Verfassungs-, Verwaltungs- und Wirtschaftsgeschichte* (Leipzig 1898) pp. 530–61; M. Mushacke, *Krefeld im friderizianischen Zeitalter unter besonderer Berücksichtigung der Seidenindustrie* (Krefeld 1899). On Gotskowski, see *Altpreussische Biographie* I, 224f.; Otto Hintze, 'Ein Berliner Kaufmann aus der Zeit Friedrichs des Grossen', *Schriften des Vereins für die Geschichte Berlins* XXX (1893) – also printed in *Historische und politische Aufsätze* vol. II (Berlin 1908).

On the manufacture of porcelain: *Acta Borussica. Die einzelnen Gebiete der Verwaltung, Handels-, Zoll- und Akzisepolitik* III, 1 (Berlin 1928) pp. 677–79; Paul Seidel,

264

Frederick the Great

'Friedrich der Grosse und seine Porzellan-Manufaktur', *Hohenzollern-Jahrbuch* VI (1902) pp. 175–206; G. Voss, 'Der grosse König und die Berliner Porzellan-Manufaktur', *Mitteilungen des Vereins für die Geschichte Berlins* (1912); A. D. Bensch, *Die Entwicklung der Berliner Porzellanindustrie unter Friedrich dem Grossen* (1928); Wolfgang Scheffler, *Jubiläumsausstellung des Kunstgewerbemuseums Berlin im Schloss Charlottenburg zum 200 jährigen Bestehen der Staatlichen Porzellanmanufaktur Berlin, 21.9. bis 17.11. 1963; Berliner Porzellan des 18. Jahrhunderts. Ausstellung zum 200 jährigen Jubiläum der Manufaktur 1963*, published by the Verwaltung der Staatlichen Schlösser und Gärten, Potsdam-Sanssouci, den Staatlichen Museen zu Berlin, dem Kunstgewerbemuseum (1963); Rachel, *Berliner Wirtschaftsleben*, p. 202f.

On mirror- and glassmaking: Acta Borussica. *Handels-, Zoll- und Akzisepolitik* III–1, 682f.; W. Hoff, *Die Glashütten in der Neumark, besonders in friderizianischer Zeit*, dissertation (Berlin 1940).

On communications: Stephan, *Post; Acta Borussica. Handels-, Zoll- und Akzisepolitik* III–1, 399–411.

On the timber industry: Stadelmann, *Landeskultur* vol. II; F. Mager, *Der Wald in Altpreussen als Wirtschaftsraum* vol. II (Cologne 1960). (Ostmitteleuropa in Vergangenheit und Gegenwart 7); Hermann Schorr, 'Die Hauptnutzholzadministration im friderizianischen Preussen', dissertation (Halle 1956) – typescript. Schorr determines that in the year 1770 the extent, in Magdeburger *Morgen*, of state-owned standing timber was as follows: Kurmark – 1,057,000; East Prussia and Lithuania – 1,000,000; Neumark – 542,000; Further Pomerania – 329,000; Hither Pomerania – 299,000; Magdeburg – 131,000. Silesia is not included in this list; in the western provinces the extent of state forests was insignificant. The ratio of state forest to private forest was 10:7.

On individual territories: Aloys Meister, 'Handel, Gewerbe, Industrie und Bergwesen bis zu Beginn des 19. Jahrhunderts', *Die Grafschaft Mark*. Festschrift zum Gedächtnis der 300 jährigen Vereinigung mit Brandenburg-Preussen vol. I (Detmold 1909) pp. 443–61; Gustav Schmoller, 'Studien über die wirtschaftliche Politik Friedrichs des Grossen. XII: Die wirtschaftlichen Zustände im Herzogtum Magdeburg', *Jahrbuch für Gesetzgebung, Verwaltung und Volkswirtschaft*, N. F. Jahrgang 11 (1887) p. 831ff.; *Acta Borussica, Handels-, Zoll- und Akzisepolitik* III–1, 669ff., 755ff.; Kurt Hinze, *Die Arbeiterfrage in Brandenburg-Preussen zu Beginn des modernen Kapitalismus* (Berlin 1927; 2nd ed. 1963); Hugo Rachel, *Das Berliner Wirtschaftsleben im Zeitalter des Frühkapitalismus* (Berlin 1931); Stephan Skalweit, *Die Berliner Wirtschaftskrise von 1763 und ihre Hintergründe*, dissertation (Frankfurt on Main 1937) – also printed in *Vierteljahrschrift für Sozial- und Wirtschaftsgeschichte* XXXIV (1937); Otto Wiedfeldt, *Statistiche Studien zur Entwicklungsgeschichte der Berliner Industrie von 1720 bis 1890* (Leipzig 1898), (Staats- und sozialwissenschaftliche Forschungen 16, part 2); Walter Mertineit, 'Ostpreussische Manufaktur- und Merkantilpolitik im 18. Jahrhundert. Ein Beitrag zur friderizianischen Verwaltungspraxis', *Zeitschrift für Ostforschung* IX

(1960) pp. 481–92; *Minden-Ravensberg unter der Herrschaft der Hohenzollern.* *Festschrift zur Erinnerung an die 300 jährige Zugehörigkeit der Grafschaft Ravensberg zum brandenburg-preussischen Staate*, ed. H. Tümpel (Bielefeld 1909) – see especially H. Tümpel, 'Politische Geschichte', section 2, 6, p. 37 ff.; O. Schulz, 'Entwicklung der Landwirtschaft', section 3, 2, p. 162; H. Potthoff, 'Geschichte von Gewerbe und Handel', section 2, 2, p. 193ff.; H. Blocks, 'Geschichte des Post- und Telegraphenwesens', section 1, p. 262f.; Aloys Meister, *Friedrich der Grosse und das preussische Westfalen* (1912); Otto Geisler, 'Die Wirtschaftspolitik Friedrichs des Grossen und der Begriff der Planwirtschaft', dissertation (Tübingen 1952) – typescript. On Frederick the Great's motivation for the protection of industry, see Conrad Matschoss, *Friedrich der Grosse als Beförderer des Gewerbefleisses* (Berlin 1912) p. 38 f.

III The New Provinces

SILESIA

Legal claims on Silesia: *Preussische Staatsschriften aus der Regierungszeit Friedrichs II*, ed. R. Koser, vol. I (Berlin 1877); C. Grünhagen and H. Markgraf, *Lehns- und Besitz-Urkunden Schlesiens im Mittelalter* (2 parts, Leipzig 1881–83); Fritz Wagner, *Kaiser Karl VII und die grossen Mächte* (1938).

On the Instructions for the period of Frederick's absence: Acta Borussica. Behördenorganisation VI-1, 178f.; duration of king's visits to Silesia in time of peace: July/August 1746; August/September 1747; September 1748; April/May 1749; September 1750; August/September 1751; September 1752; May and October/November 1753; September 1754; September 1755; Hans Droysen, 'Tageskalender Friedrichs des Grossen 1740–1763', *Forschungen zur brandenburgischen und preussischen Geschichte* XXIX (1916) pp. 113–39; Karl Ludwig von Klöber, *Von Schlesien vor und seit dem Jahr MDCCXXXX* vol. I (Freiburg 1785); vol. II (Freiburg 1786). The author, a native of the Palatinate, was from 1766 a councillor of the Berlin War and Domains Chamber. His book appeared anonymously, ostensibly as a translation from English. Heinrich Wuttke, *König Friedrichs des Grossen Besitzergreifung von Schlesien und die Entwicklung der öffentlichen Verhältnisse in diesem Lande bis zum Jahre 1740* vols. I and II (Leipzig 1842–43) – to 1740. Compare with this Otto Hintze in *Acta Borussica* VI-1, 507 n.2.

On Silesia before its incorporation in Prussia: Acta Borussica. Behördenorganisation VI-1, ed. Otto Hintze (Berlin 1901) pp. 493–556; Max Lehmann, 'Staat und Kirche in Schlesien vor der preussischen Besitzergreifung', *Historische Zeitschrift* L, 193ff. On administration: Colmar Grünhagen, *Schlesien unter Friedrich dem Grossen* (2 vols., Breslau 1890–92) – unsurpassed account, closely based on the sources, by the state archivist at Breslau. For further reading see the list at the end of ch. IV, vol. I; *Acta Borussica. Behördenorganisation* VI-2 (Akten zur preussischen Verwaltung in Schlesien) p. 205ff. – includes among other things the ceremony of homage at Breslau (pp. 223–33), the setting up of administrative bodies (pp.

236–326), the ceremony of homage at Glatz (p. 339f.), the administration of justice (pp. 341–50), the formation of the *Regierungen* at Breslau and Glogau (pp. 362–75, 380–400), the ceremony of homage at Neisse (p. 435), the building of Lutheran churches (p. 434f.), postal affairs (p. 453f.), the classification commission (pp. 455–68), the *Steurräte* (pp. 485–93), the *Instruktion* of 24 September 1742 for Münchow (pp. 498–502), report on Upper Silesia (pp. 508–13, 540f.), departmental divisions (pp. 551–61), homage ceremony in Upper Silesia (pp. 565–68), formation of the *Regierung* at Oppeln (pp. 627–33, 702–5, 734–38). For a comprehensive account see Isaacsohn, III, 206–30.

On the Field War Commission: Acta Borussica. Behördenorganisation VI–2, 188 n. 1. The original documents of this authority are not extant. Apart from the two heads and the *Generalproviantmeister*, War Councillor Köppen (who dealt with the *Kassen*) and several subordinate officials belonged to this body. Compare *Friedrich der Grosse, Werke* (German edition by Volz) VI, 15 and VII, 180f.; H. Helfritz, *Geschichte der preussischen Heeresverwaltung* (Berlin 1938) pp. 174–77; Fred Schädrich, *Das Generalfeldkriegskommissariat in Schlesien 1741* (Breslau 1913). (Historische Untersuchungen 2); Colmar Grünhagen, 'Die Entstehung des Schlesischen Sonderministeriums', *Forschungen zur brandenburgischen und preussischen Geschichte* XX (1907) p. 105ff. On the War and Domains chambers at Breslau and Glogau: for number of personnel – earliest list – see *Acta Borussica. Behördenorganisation* VI–2, 296–301. For Münchow's address on 2 January 1742 to the Glogau Chamber see *Acta Borussica. Behördenorganisation* VI–2, 296–301. On the turning down of Münchow's request to marry see ibid. p. 473. For the refusal of the gift made to him see ibid. p. 606 (cabinet order of 8 June 1743). On the *Oberamtsregierungen* in Breslau and Glogau see *Acta Borussica. Behördenorganisation* VI–2, 362ff.; for Oppeln see ibid. p. 627ff. A transfer from Oppeln to Ratibor or Kosel was envisaged but did not take place until the removal to Brieg in 1756. On Cocceji: E. Döhring in *Neue Deutsche Biographie* III (1957) where other sources are given. On his service instructions, see *Acta Borussica. Behördenorganisation* VI–2, 362–75 (especially p. 373 – note 1 lists the personnel of the *Oberamtsregierung* in Glogau as of 1742). On the revenue of the Domains *Kassen*, see Grünhagen, I, 387. On trade and industry: ibid. p. 490ff., ibid. II, p. 529ff. On the postal service see Stephan, pp. 205–11.

Hermann Fechner, *Wirtschaftsgeschichte der preussischen Provinz Schlesien in der Zeit ihrer provinziellen Selbständigkeit 1741–1806* (Breslau 1907) – this also contains Schlabrendorff's criticism of Frederick II's governmental system (p. 20). Friedrich Freiherr von Schrötter, 'Die schlesische Wollindustrie im 18. Jahrhundert', *Forschungen zur brandenburgischen und preussischen Geschichte* XI (1899); Alfred Zimmermann, *Blüte und Verfall des Leinengewerbes in Schlesien* (Breslau 1885); Ernst Pfeiffer, 'Die Revuereisen Friedrichs des Grossen besonders die schlesischen nach 1763 und der Zustand Schlesiens von 1763–1786', *Eberings Historische Studien* XLIV (Berlin 1904; new impression Vaduz 1965).

On Schlabrendorff: C. Grünhagen in the *Allgemeine Deutsche Biographie*.

On Hoym: compare H. Fechner in *Allgemeine Deutsche Biographie* with S. Skalweit in *Neue Deutsche Biographie* IX (1972). J. Ziekursch, *Beiträge zur Charakteristik der preussischen Verwaltungsbeamten in Schlesien bis zum Untergang des friderizianischen Staates* (Quellen und Darstellungen zur schlesischen Geschichte 4, 1904). J. Zierkursch, 'Zur Charakteristik der schlesischen Steuerräte (1742–1809)' *Zeitschrift des Vereins für Geschichte Schlesiens* XLIII (1909) 131–82.

On the Silesian mining industry: Hermann Fechner, 'Geschichte des schlesischen Berg- und Hüttenwesens 1741–1786', *Zeitschrift für Berg-, Hütten- und Salinenwesen im preussischen Staat* XLVIII–L (1900–02) – also separately in 1903. Karl Pflug, 'Zur Geschichte des Bergbaues im Waldenburger Berglande', *Zeitschrift des Vereins für Geschichte Schlesiens* XLIII (1909) pp. 75–98; Konrad Wutke, 'Die Wiederbelebung des schlesischen Bergbaues unter Friedrich dem Grossen, 1741–1776. Friedrich Anton Freiherr von Heinitz und sein Verdienst um den Aufschwung des schlesischen Berg- und Hüttenwesens', *Aus der Vergangenheit des schlesischen Berg- und Hüttenlebens* (Breslau 1913). (Der Bergbau im Osten des Königreichs Preussen. Festschrift zum 12. Allgemeinen Deutschen Bergmannstag, Breslau 1913, vol. V) pp. 1–90; Max Schulz-Briesen, *Der preussische Staatsbergbau von seinen Anfängen bis zum Ende des 19. Jahrhunderts* vol. I (Berlin 1933) pp. 1–71; K. Matschoss, 'Preussens Bergwirtschaft unter Friedrich dem Grossen', *Bergwirtschaftliche Mitteilungen* (1912) p. 221; E. Reimann, *Friedrich der Grosse und der Freiherr von Heinitz* (Gotha 1892) p. 124ff. (Abhandlungen zur Geschichte Friedrichs des Grossen); on J. von Justi see H. Rössler in *Biographisches Wörterbuch zur deutschen Geschichte* (Munich 1953); Ferdinand Frensdorff, 'Uber das Leben ... des Nationalöconomen J. H. G. von Justi', *Nachrichten der Akademie der Wissenschaften*, Göttingen. Philosophisch-historische Klasse, bk. 3 (1903) p. 448ff.; Hans Haussherr, 'J. H. G. von Justi', *Verwaltungseinheit und Ressorttrennung* (Berlin 1953) pp. 79–96; B. Rosenmöller, *Schulenburg-Kehnert unter Friedrich dem Grossen* (Berlin 1914); on Waitz-Eschen, see C. W. von Dohm, *Denkwürdigkeiten meiner Zeit oder Beiträge zur Geschichte des letzten Viertels des 18. und des Anfangs des 19. Jahrhunderts* vol. IV (Lemgo and Hanover 1819) p. 407; on Heinitz (Heynitz) see O. Steinecke in *Allgemeine Deutsche Biographie* LV (1910). *Nachträge* pp. 493–500; Ernst Opgenoorth, *'Ausländer' in Brandenburg-Preussen als leitende Beamte und Offiziere 1604–1871* (Würzburg 1967). (Beiheft 28 zum Jahrbuch der Albertus-Universität Königsberg/Preussen); on F. W. von Reden, see K. Wutke, *Aus der Vergangenheit des schlesischen Berg- und Hüttenlebens* (Breslau 1913) pp. 91–277. On Karl vom Stein, see *Freiherr vom Stein. Briefe und amtliche Schriften*, newly edited by Walther Hubatsch, vol. I (Stuttgart 1957). For the controversy over Prussian mercantilism, compare Gustav Croon, 'Die Wirkungen des preussischen Merkantilismus in Schlesien', *Zeitschrift des Vereins für Geschichte Schlesiens* XLII (Breslau 1908). For the rejoinder from Hermann Fechner and Gustav Croon's reply, see ibid. XLIII (1909) pp. 304–32; Hermann Fechner, 'Die Wirkungen des preussischen Merkantilismus in Schlesien', *Vierteljahrschrift für Sozial- und Wirtschaftsgeschichte* (1909) p. 315 ff.; Fechner, 'Die Fabrikengründungen in Schlesien nach dem Siebenjährigen Krieg unter Friedrich dem

Grossen', *Zeitschrift für die gesamte Staatswissenschaft* LVII (1901) p. 618ff. On Heinitz's diary, see Wutke, *Bergbau*, p. 51f. after O. Steinecke, 'Friedrich Anton von Heynitz. Ein Lebensbild', *Forschungen zur brandenburgischen und preussischen Geschichte* XV. 2 (1902) p. 106ff., here p. 128.

EAST FRIESLAND

Carl Hinrichs, 'Die ostfriesischen Landstände und der preussische Staat, 1744–1756. Ein Beitrag zur Geschichte der inneren Staatsverwaltung Friedrichs des Grossen. Teil I: 1744–1748', *Jahrbuch der Gesellschaft für bildende Kunst und vaterländische Altertümer zu Emden* XXII (1927) – based on documents in the Prussian Secret State Archive Berlin and the Emden Council Archives. The continuation of this, planned by Hinrichs, has been abandoned; Isaacsohn, III, 230–36; Tilemann Dothias Wiarda, *Ostfriesische Geschichte* vols. VI–X (Aurich and Leer 1795–1817); for Sebastian Anton Homfeld, 'Gründlicher Bericht von der Beschaffenheit des ostfriesischen Reichs-Mannlehens und der dem König-und Kurhause Brandenburg in diesem Reichsleben auf Abgang des ostfriesischen Mann-Stammes zustehenden Succession', see Reinhold Koser, *Preussische Staatsschriften* II (Berlin 1892) p. 361 ff.; Otto Schüssler, *König Friedrichs des Grossen Vertrag mit Emden*. Gymnasialprogramm (Emden 1902); Otto Hintze, 'Friedrichs des Grossen Absicht, Emden zu verkaufen', *Forschungen zur brandenburgischen und preussischen Geschichte* XIII (1900) p. 570ff.; *Acta Borussica. Behördenorganisation* VI–2, 717–24 and 717, n. 1, 923f. and n.1; ibid. VI–1, 556–614. For Homfeld's direct reports to the king, the sending of Bügel, Cocceji's negotiations and the ceremony of homage, see ibid. VI–2, 746–71. On the East Friesland revenues, see ibid. 812ff., the convention of 7 July 1744 with the East Friesland Estates, see ibid. 801–8, Cocceji's 'greatest pleasure' ibid. p. 797 – direct report of 3 July 1744; Kurt Perels, *Die allgemeinen Appellationsprivilegien für Brandenburg-Preussen* (Weimar 1908). (Quellen und Studien zur Verfassungsgeschichte des Deutschen Reichs III, 1). On the Bügel-Boden correspondence, see *Acta Borussica* VII, 30ff., 290. For the General Directory to Jhering, 7 May 1748, see Preussisches Geheimes Staatsarchiv, Generaldirektorium Ostfriesland XIX No. 2 in Hinrichs, *Landstände*, p. 246. On 18 November 1747 the Estates *Regierung* 'declared that all the complaints made by Jhering regarding the province's accounts and all his proposals for improvements had been settled once and for all' (ibid. 259). For the communication from Third Department to Department of External Affairs on 5 June 1745 on East Friesland's affairs, see *Acta Borussica. Behördenorganisation* VI–2, 900ff. On the departmental regulation (*Ressort-Reglement*) of 18 August 1746, see *Acta Borussica* VII, 114 and 120. On the rehabilitation of the former administrators of the principality of East Friesland, see Hinrichs, *Landstände*, pp. 248, 255.; *Acta Borussica* VIII, 64, 67. On Bakmeister's appointment as inspector with the administrative college at Aurich, see *Acta Borussica* VIII, ibid. For the king's instructions and direct edicts to Lentz, dating from 27 September, 26 October, 26 November, 10 December 1748, see *Acta Borussica* VIII. On Frederick the Great's visit to Emden, see H. Droysen, 'Tageskalender', in *Forschungen zur brandenburgischen und preussischen Geschichte* XXIX (1916); Wiarda, *Ostfriesische Geschichte* VIII, 362ff. On the postal service, see *Acta Borussica* VI-2, 767; H. Stephan, *Geschichte der preussische Post* (Berlin 1859) pp. 211–15; C. Esslinger, *Das Postwesen in Ostfriesland 1744–1806* (Aurich 1908). (Abhandlungen und Vorträge zur Geschichte Ostfrieslands, bk. 8/9). On East Friesland in the Seven Years War, see *Acta Borussica* XI, XII. On praise for the province, see ibid. XI, 494, 508. On the division of responsibility within the East Friesland *Regierung* in 1759: ibid. XII, 66–74. On Derschau: *Altpreussische Biographie* I (Königsberg 1941) p. 128. On Homfeld's death see *Acta Borussica* XII, 373. On Lentz: *Ostfriesisches Monatsblatt* 5 (1877); his newspaper reports: ibid. 4, pp. 131ff., 383ff. (ed. E. Friedlaender, 1876). On Lentz and Colomb, see M. Hass, 'Friedrich der Grosse und seine Kammerpräsidenten', *Festschrift zu G. Schmollers 70. Geburtstag* (Leipzig 1908) pp. 181–220. Wöllner's character sketch of Lentz is in Preussisches Geheimes Staatsarchiv, Rep. 96, 206 E.; B. Rosenmöller, *Schulenburg-Kehnert unter Friedrich dem Grossen* (Berlin 1914) p. 162ff. See ibid. 170, n. 18 for the king's cabinet order, issued in Berlin on 21 May 1785, to Schulenburg concerning land reclamation (Generaldirektorium Ostfriesland XXXVIII, 7 v. 2); Diddo Wiarda, *Die geschichtliche Entwicklung der wirtschaftlichen Verhältnisse Ostfrieslands* (Jena 1880); Fischbach, *Historische, politische, geographische, statistische und militärische Beiträge die Königlich Preussischen und benachbarte Staaten betreffend* vols. I, II (Berlin 1781–82). Here vol. I, 111–84, vol. II, 297–356. On sea-salt from East Friesland, see Frederick the Great's cabinet order of 12 October 1751 to Chamber President Lentz, also those of 16 October and 13 November 1751. See, too, *Acta Borussica. Handels-, Zoll- und Akzisepolitik* III-1, 769. For Cocceji to Podewils, 16 and 23 June 1744, see Hinrichs, *Landstände*, p. 119; *Acta Borussica* VI-2, 785. On Bügel's sea trade to France via Leer, see ibid. 203, report of 12.4.1748. On Latouche: Arnold Berney, 'Die Anfänge der friderizianischen Seehandelspolitik', *Vierteljahrschrift für Sozial- und Wirtschaftsgeschichte* XXII (1929) – also published separately. On the fitting out of merchantmen by Splitgerber and Daum, see Friedrich Lentz and Otto Unholtz, *Die Geschichte des Bankhauses Gebrüder Schickler* (Berlin 1912) p. 80ff.; Koser, *Friedrich der Grosse* II, p. 192f.; Koser, 'Der Grosse Kurfürst und Friedrich der Grosse in ihrer Stellung zu Marine und Seehandel', *Marine-Rundschau* bk. 4 (1904). Compare, in Frederick the Great's Political Testament of 1752, 'the Emden Company' with 'future phantasies'. See, too, the Political Testament of 1768 for the section on 'trade'. Viktor Ring, *Die asiatischen Handelskompanien Friedrichs des Grossen* (1890); H. Bergér, *Überseeische Handelsbestrebungen und koloniale Pläne unter Friedrich dem Grossen* (Leipzig 1899). On the refoundation of the Asiatic Company, 1769/70: Preussisches Geheimes Staatsarchiv, Rep. 95A, IV, 45; Rosenmöller, *Schulenburg-Kehnert*, pp. 173–77. On the king's deliberations, see Minüten, K. O. 26 August 1782 to Schulenburg; Rosenmöller, *Schulenburg-Kehnert*, p. 174. On shipbuilding: Frederick II to Fäsch, 1.10.1749, *Acta Borussica. Handels-, Zoll- und Akzisepolitik* III-1, 404–22. On East Friesland's sea-trade in general: ibid. 129–41. On Emden's commercial court, 1775: *Acta Borussica. Behördenorganisation* XVI-1

(1970) p. 217ff. On the herring catch: *Acta Borussica. Handels-, Zoll- und Akzise-politik* III–1, 772–79; Rosenmöller, pp. 182–216 – further reading listed there. On overseas trade: Paul Schrader, *Die Geschichte der Königlichen Seehandlung (Preussische Staatsbank) mit besonderer Berücksichtigung der neuen Zeit, auf Grund amtlicher Quellen bearbeitet*, dissertation (Münster 1911); Hermann Schleutker, *Die volkswirtschaftliche Bedeutung der Königlichen Seehandlung von 1772–1820*, dissertation (Tübingen 1920). G. Heinicke's dissertation on *Die Preussische Staatsbank (Seehandlung)* does not deal with the eighteenth century. For the Overseas Trading Company's foundation patent, see Mylius, *Novum Corpus Constitutionum* part 5, vol. I, 513ff.; Rosenmöller, pp. 268–323.

STATE SETTLEMENTS

Now that the term 'colonization' has undergone a complete change of meaning, it cannot now be used in its former sense without the danger of being grossly misunderstood. The Frederician measures for increasing the population were, in fact, based on ameliorations and settlements which were organized and financed by the state. General: Max Beheim-Schwarzbach, *Hohenzollernsche Colonisationen. Ein Beitrag zu der Geschichte des preussischen Staates und der Colonisation des östlichen Deutschlands* (Leipzig 1874); Rudolph Stadelmann, *Preussens Könige in ihrer Tätigkeit für die Landeskultur. Vol II: Friedrich der Grosse* (Leipzig 1882). (Publikationen aus den Preussischen Staatsarchiven 11); Anton Zottmann, *Die Wirtschaftspolitik Friedrichs des Grossen* (Leipzig 1937). (Gesellschaftswissenschaftliche Abhandlungen 8) p. 123ff.; Heinrich Bergér, *Friedrich der Grosse als Kolonisator* (Giessen 1896). (Giessener Studien auf dem Gebiet der Geschichte 8); Ewald Friedrich von Hertzberg, *Acht Abhandlungen, welche in der Königlichen Akademie der Wissenschaft zu Berlin an den Geburtsfesten des Königs im Jänner 1780 bis 1787 vorgelesen wurden* (Berlin and Leipzig 1789).

On the Oderbruch scheme: Frederick the Great, *Geschichte des Siebenjährigen Krieges*, German lang. ed. edited by G. B. Volz, vol. III (Berlin 1913) p. 8.; Albert Detto, 'Die Besiedlung des Oderbruchs durch Friedrich den Grossen', *Forschungen zur brandenburgischen und preussischen Geschichte* XVI (1903) pp. 163–205; P. F. Mengel, *Das Oderbruch* (2 vols., Eberswalde 1930–34).

On Pomerania: Karla König, *Friedrich der Grosse und Pommern* (Stettin 1940). (Pommern im Wandel der Zeiten 2); Beheim-Schwarzbach, *Colonisationen*, p. 367f.; Fritz Knack, *Burg Saatzig, Jacobshagen und die pommerschen Koloniegründungen Friedrichs des Grossen, Graebnitzfelde und Constantinopel* (Hildesheim 1912); P. Wehrmann, 'Friedrich der Grosse als Kolonisator in Pommern', *Jahresbericht 6 der Geographischen Gesellschaft zu Greifswald* part II (Greifswald 1898); Hans Hesse, *Die Kolonisationstätigkeit des Prinzen Moritz von Anhalt-Dessau in Pommern* (1910). (Baltische Studien, N.F. 14); E. Drumm and A. Zink, *Saarpfälzische Kolonisation in Pommern unter Friedrich dem Grossen* (Stuttgart 1938); K. Rosenow, *Der Kreis Schlawe unter Friedrich dem Grossen* (Schlawe 1927). On Brenckenhoff: A. G. Meissner, *Das Leben Franz Balthaser Schönbergks von Brenckenhoff* (Leipzig

1782); A. Berg, 'Der Brenckenhoffsche Defekt', *Forschungen zur brandenburgischen und preussischen Geschichte* XI (1898); F. Curschmann in *Festschrift Rudolf Kötzschke* (Leipzig 1927); Gustav Schmoller, 'Die preussische Einwanderung und ländliche Kolonisation des 17. und 18. Jahrhunderts', *Umrisse und Untersuchungen zur Verfassungs-, Verwaltungs- und Wirtschaftsgeschichte* (Leipzig 1898). Waldemar Kuhn, *Kleinsiedlungen aus friderizianischer Zeit* (Stuttgart 1918) – was a dissertation (Danzig 1915). Walther Kuhn, 'Die preussische Kolonisation unter Friedrich dem Grossen', *Deutsche Ostsiedlung in Mittelalter und Neuzeit* (Cologne 1971). (Studien zum Deutschtum im Osten 8), pp. 182–96; Udo Froese, *Das Kolonisationswerk Friedrichs des Grossen. Wesen und Vermächtnis* (Heidelberg 1938). (Beiträge zur Raumforschung und Raumordnung 5); Gotthardt Arndt, *Grundsätze der Siedlungspolitik und Siedlungsmethode Friedrichs des Grossen*, dissertation (Leipzig 1934).

On the Neumark: P. Schwartz, *Brenckenhoffs Berichte über seine Tätigkeit in der Neumark* (1907). (Schriften des Vereins für die Geschichte der Neumark 20); Herbert Moegelin, 'Das Retablissement des adligen Grundbesitzes in der Neumark durch Friedrich den Grossen', *Forschungen zur brandenburgischen und preussischen Geschichte* XLVI (1934) pp. 28–69, 233–74; *Acta Borussica. Behördenorganisation* XIII (1932) – edited by Ernst Posner; Erich Neuhaus, *Die friedericianische Kolonisation in Warthe- und Netzebruch, nach archivalischen Quellen dargestellt* (Landsberg am Warthe 1906). (Schriften des Vereins für die Geschichte der Neumark 18).

On the Kurmark: H. L. Schmidt, 'Friderizianische Siedlungspolitik in der Mark Brandenburg', *Jahrbuch für brandenburgischen Landesgeschichte* XII (1961); R. Jung, *Wie Friedrich der Grosse im Rhin- und Dosseluch siedelte* (1930). (Veröffentlichungen des historischen Vereins der Grafschaft Ruppin 4). Frederick the Great to Werder, 23.4.1786. Stadelmann, *Preussens Könige* vol. II. no. 619, p. 643; to the Kurmark Chamber, 12.4.1763, ibid. no. 152, p. 339. Beheim-Schwarzbach, *Colonisationen*, p. 360ff.; Helmut Kublick, *Die Siedlungspolitik Friedrichs des Grossen im Kreise Cottbus*, dissertation (Halle 1935).

On Magdeburg: Alice Reboly, 'Die friderizianische Kolonisation im Herzogtum Magdeburg', *Sachsen und Anhalt. Jahrbuch der landesgeschichtlichen Forschungsstelle für die Provinz Sachsen und Anhalt* XVI (1940) pp. 214–323 (including a map); Rosenmöller, pp. 30ff., 87ff.; Stadelmann, *Preussens Könige* vol. 2, p. 19 (for 1758).

On Silesia: Beheim-Schwarzbach, *Colonisationen*, pp. 299–358; Alfons Perlick, *Friedrich der Grosse und das Beuther Land* (Beuthen O. S. 1926); K. Räbiger, 'Koloniegründungen im Amte Herrnstedt 1776–85', *Zeitschrift des Vereins für die Geschichte Schlesiens* XXXXIV (Breslau 1910); Herbert Schlenger, *Friderizianische Siedlungen rechts der Oder bis 1800* (Breslau 1933) – supplement 1 to the historical atlas of Silesia; Johannes Ziekursch, 'Die innere Kolonisation im altpreussischen Schlesien', *Zeitschrift des Vereins für die Geschichte Schlesiens* XXXXVIII (Breslau 1914).

On East Prussia: Walter Mertineit, *Die friderizianische Verwaltung in Ostpreussen*

(Heidelberg 1958) – (Studien zur Geschichte Preussens, vol. 1); Beheim-Schwarz-bach, *Colonisationen*, p. 373ff.; E. Kobbert, *Das grosse Moosbruch, seine Urbarmach-ung und Besiedlung*, dissertation (Königsberg 1925); Frederick II's comment on fen cultivation of 1 August 1786, see A. von Taysen, *Die militärische Tätigkeit Friedrichs des Grossen während seines letzten Lebensjahres* (Berlin 1886) p. 8; August Skalweit, 'Wieviel Kolonisten hat Friedrich der Grosse angesiedelt?', *Forschungen zur brandenburgischen und preussischen Geschichte* XXIV (1911) pp. 243–48 (correction by Beheim-Schwarzbach); Stadelmann, *Preussens Könige* vol. 2, p. 37.

On West Prussia: see bibliography chapter V, 3; Walter Maas, 'Preussische Siedlungen in Westpreussen und dem Netzedistrikt 1772–1848', *Deutsche Ostsiedlung in Mittelalter und Neuzeit* (Cologne 1971). (Studien zum Deutschtum im Osten 8), pp. 197–218 (including a map); Conrad Gatz, *Sielder unter Preussens Fahnen. Zur Ansiedlung in Westpreussen und im Netzegau unter Friedrich dem Grossen* (Leipzig 1941). (Ostdeutsche Heimatbücher VI); Werner Schulz, *Die zweite deutsche Ostsiedlung im westlichen Netzegau*, dissertation (Berlin 1937) (Deutschland und der Osten, IX and X), *Darstellung und Quellenband;* Koser, *Friedrich der Grosse* vol. 3, p. 351 f.; Max Bär, *Westpreussen unter Friedrich dem Grossen* (Publikationen aus den Preussischen Staatsarchiven 83, 84).

On the Western Provinces: Minden-Ravensberg unter der Herrschaft der Hohenzollern, ed. H. Tümpel (Bielefeld 1909) p. 163; account of *Amt* Sparenberg from the documents of the War and Domains Chamber, Minden, V, 214; *Acta die geford-erten Nachrichten und Vorschläge zu reellen dem Lande unschädlichen Verbesserungen betreffend;* Rosenmöller, p. 122f.

On Cleves-Mark: Rosenmöller, p. 148f.; Walter Ring, *Kolonisationsbestrebungen Friedrichs des Grossen am Niederrhein* (Duisburg 1917) – (Schriften des Duisburger Museumsvereins VII) with 6 illustrations and 1 map.

On East Friesland: Rosenmöller, p. 171; table: A. Skalweit, 'Wieviel Kolonisten hat Friedrich der Grosse angesiedelt?', *Forschungen zur brandenburgischen und preussischen Geschichte* XXIV (1911) p. 247 f.; the quotation from Leibniz is in Dutens vol. 4, p. 502; on the Political Testament 1768: German edition Oppeln-Bronikowski, p. 135; on the *Antimachiavel*: Volz. ed., *Werke Friedrichs des Grossen* vol. 7, p. 20; *Geschichte des Siebenjährigen Krieges*, ibid. vol. 3, p. 9.

IV Safeguarding Prussia's Existence

WARTIME ADMINISTRATION

General Works: Friedrich der Grosse, *Geschichte des Siebenjährigen Krieges* in *Œuvres de Frédéric le Grand* vols. 4 and 5; German edition: *Die Werke Friedrichs des Grossen*, ed. G. B. Volz, vols. 3 and 4 (Berlin 1913). This quite extensive work confines itself to a narrative of diplomatic and military events. See also Willy Andreas *Friedrich der Grosse und der Siebenjährige Krieg* (Leipzig 1940) – reprinted from *Historische Zeitschrift* CLVIII (1938); Alfred Graf Schlieffen, *Friedrich der*

Grosse (Berlin 1912); *Die Kriege Friedrichs des Grossen*, published by the Preussichen Grossen Generalstab. Part 1: *Der I. Schlesische Krieg 1740–1742* (3 vols., Berlin 1890–3). Part 2: *Der II. Schlesische Krieg 1744–1745* (3 vols., 1895–96). Part 3: *Der Siebenjährige Krieg 1756–1763* (13 vols., Berlin 1901–14) – goes only to 1760, no more volumes published; Curt Jany 'Der Siebenjährige Krieg. Ein Schlusswort zum Generalstabswerk', *Forschungen zur brandenburgischen und preussischen Geschichte* XXXV (1923); Eberhard Kessel, *Quellen und Untersuchungen zur Geschichte der Schlacht bei Torgau* (Berlin 1937); Reinhold Koser, 'Die preussische Kriegsführung im Siebenjährigen Kriege', *Historische Zeitschrift* XCII (1903); Hans Rothfels, 'Friedrich der Grosse in den Krisen des Siebenjährigen Krieges', *Historische Zeitschrift* CXXXIV (1926), reprinted in *Bismarck, der Osten und das Reich* (Darmstadt 1960); Johann Wilhelm von Archenholtz, *Geschichte des Siebenjährigen Krieges in Deutschland* (13th ed. Leipzig 1893) – account by a serving officer; Carl Friedrich Pauli, *Leben grosser Helden des gegenwärtigen Krieges* (9 vols., Halle 1758–64) – eye-witness accounts; Winifred Baumgart, 'Der Ausbruch des Siebenjährigen Krieges. Zum gegenwärtigen Forschungsstand', *Militärgeschichtliche Mitteilungen* XI (1972).

On state administration: *Acta Borussica. Behördenorganisation* vol. VII (Berlin 1904) – 1746–48; vol. XI (Berlin 1922–25) – August 1756 to December 1758; vol. XII (Berlin 1926) – 1759 to February 1763; *Politische Correspondenz Friedrichs des Grossen*, published by the Preussischen Akademie der Wissenschaften, vols. XI–XIX (Berlin 1883–92) – 1756–60; vols. XX–XXII (Berlin 1893–95) – 1760–63; *Briefe Friedrichs des Grossen*, German edition ed. Max Hein, vol. II (Berlin 1914); *Friedrich der Grosse. Gespräche mit Heinrich Alexander de Catt*, trans. and ed. by Willy Schüssler (Leipzig 1940); Hans Droysen, 'Tageskalender Friedrichs des Grossen vom 1. Juni 1740 bis 31. März 1763', *Forschungen zur brandenburgischen und preussischen Geschichte* XXIX (1916) pp. 95–157; Georg von Frantzius, *Die Okkupation Ostpreussens durch die Russen im Siebenjährigen Kriege mit besonderer Berücksichtigung der russischen Quellen*, dissertation (Berlin 1916); Chester V. Easum, *Prince Henry of Prussia: Brother of Frederick the Great* (Wisconsin 1942); G. L. Mamlock, *Friedrichs des Grossen Beziehungen zur Medizin* (Berlin 1902); G. L. Mamlock, *Friedrichs des Grossen Korrespondenz mit Ärzten* (Stuttgart 1907); Ernst von Werlhof, 'Friedrich der Grosse und Sachsen', *Neues Archiv für Sächsische Geschichte* XXXIV (1913) p. 142ff. Up to the present no comprehensive account of Frederician state administration during the Seven Years War has been attempted, nor have the sources in the *Acta Borussica* been utilized. Within the framework of this work only a short outline was possible. Hans Portzek, *Friedrich der Grosse und Hannover in ihrem gegenseitigen Urteil* (publication of the Historische Kommission Niedersachsen XXV, 1) (Hildesheim 1958); Friedrich der Grosse, 'Betrachtungen über die militärischen Talente und den Charakter Karls XII' (1759), *Œuvres* VII (Berlin 1847) pp. 66–68, translated in *Werke*, ed. G. B. Volz, vol. VI (Berlin 1912) pp. 367–81; Richard Nürnberger 'Friedrichs des Grossen Réflexions sur Charles XII', *Spiegel der Geschichte. Festgabe für Max Braubach* (Münster 1964) pp. 590–601; indispensable for personal histories of the leading officials is C. A. L. Klaproth and C. W. Cosmar, *Der königlich preussische und kurfürstlich brandenburgische Geheime Staatsrat* (Berlin 1805).

ARMY ADMINISTRATION

Hans Helfritz, *Geschichte der preussischen Heeresverwaltung* (Berlin 1938); Eugen von Frauenholz, *Entwicklungsgeschichte des deutschen Heerwesens* vol. IV: *Das Heerwesen in der Zeit des Absolutismus* (1940) – see also S. Kaehler in *Göttingische Gelehrte Anzeigen* CCIII (1941) pp. 508–21. On the history of its formation, see Günther Gieraths, *Die Kampfhandlungen der brandenburg-preussischen Armee 1626–1807. Ein Quellenhandbuch* (Berlin 1964) – Veröffentlichungen der Historischen Kommission Berlin, 8; Curt Jany, *Geschichte der Königlich Preussischen Armee bis zum Jahre 1807* vol. II: *Die Armee Friedrichs des Grossen 1740 bis 1763* (Berlin 1928); Carl Grünhagen, 'Die Einrichtung des Militärwesens in Schlesien bei dem Beginne der preussischen Herrschaft', *Zeitschrift des Vereins für Geschichte und Altertum Schlesiens* vol. XXIII (Breslau 1889) pp. 1–28; Fred Schädrich, *Das Generalfeldkriegskommissariat in Schlesien, 1741* (Breslau 1913), (Historische Untersuchungen 2); Franz Schwartz, *Organisation und Verpflegung der Preussischen Landmilizen im Siebenjährigen Kriege. Ein Beitrag zur preussischen Militär- und Steuergeschichte* (Leipzig 1888), (Staats- und sozialwissenschaftliche Forschungen, vol. 7, bk. 4); Franz Schwartz, 'Die schlesische Gebirgs-Landmiliz 1743 bis 1745', *Zeitschrift des Vereins für Geschichte und Altertumskunde Schlesiens* vol. XXIII (Breslau 1889) pp. 145–76; Eduard Schnackenburg, *Das Invaliden- und Versorgungswesen des brandenburgisch-preussischen Heeres bis zum Jahre 1806. Mit Benutzung archivalischer Urkunden* (Berlin 1889); August Skalweit, *Die Eingliederung des Friderizianischen Heeres in den Volks- und Wirtschaftskörper* (Jena 1944) pp. 194–220 (Jahrbücher für Nationalökonomie und Statistik 108); Robert Arnold, 'Die Anfänge des preussischen Militärkabinetts', *Historische Aufsätze. Karl Zeumer zum sechzigsten Geburtstag* (Weimar 1910) pp. 169–200; A. von Taysen, *Die militärische Tätigkeit Friedrichs des Grossen während seines letzten Lebensjahres* (Berlin 1886). (Militärische Studien über die letzte Regierungs-Periode König Friedrichs II, 2f.); *Acta Borussica. Behördenverwaltung* vol. XI (Berlin 1922–25), vol. XII (Berlin 1926); 'Zwei Ranglisten des Preussischen Heeres 1713–1740', *Beiheft zum Militär-Wochenblatt* (1891) pp. 53–123 – here: the Army List of December 1740; Eduard Lange II, *Heeresschau der Soldaten Friedrichs des Grossen* (supplement to Kugler-Menzel *Geschichte Friedrichs des Grossen*) (Leipzig 1856) – new expanded edition (Krefeld 1970); Konrad Wutke 'Die Gründung des landschaftlichen Pensionsfonds für arme adlige Witwen und Waisen durch Friedrich den Grossen', *Zeitschrift des Vereins für Geschichte Schlesiens* 43 (1909) p. 183 ff.; L. von Scharfenort, *Kulturbilder aus der Vergangenheit des altpreussischen Heeres* (Berlin 1914); Friedrich Freiherr von Schroetter, 'Die Entwicklung des Begriffes "servis" im preussischen Heerwesen', *Forschungen zur brandenburgischen und preussischen Geschichte* 13 (1900) pp. 1–28; C. Kling, *Geschichte der Bekleidung, Bewaffnung und Ausrüstung des Königlich Preussischen Heeres, herausgegeben vom (Preussischen) Kriegsministerium. 3 Bände mit zahlreichen Farbtafeln, bis zum Jahre 1808 reichend*

(Weimar 1906–11); Otto Büsch, *Militärsystem und Sozialleben im Alten Preussen 1713 bis 1807* (Veröffentlichungen Berliner Historischen Kommission 7). (Berlin 1962).

FINANCES

Gustav Schmoller, 'Die Epochen der preussischen Finanzpolitik bis zur Gründung des Deutschen Reichs', *Umrisse und Untersuchungen* (1898); Adolph Friedrich Riedel, *Der brandenburg-preussische Staatshaushalt in den letzten beiden Jahrhunderten* (1866); Franz Schneider, *Geschichte der formellen Staatswirtschaft von Brandenburg-Preussen* (Berlin 1952); Manfred Wachenhausen, *Staatsausgabe und öffentliches Interesse in den Steuerrechtfertigungslehren des naturrechtlichen Rationalismus* (Berlin 1972); Reinhold Koser, 'Der preussische Staatsschatz von 1740 bis 1756', *Forschungen zur brandenburgischen und preussischen Geschichte* 4 (1891) pp. 529–51; Reinhold Koser, 'Die preussischen Finanzen im Siebenjährigen Kriege', *Forschungen zur brandenburgischen und preussischen Geschichte* 15 (1900) pp. 153–217, 329–75; Reinhold Koser, 'Die preussischen Finanzen von 1763–86', *Forschungen zur brandenburgischen und preussischen Geschichte* 16 (1903) pp. 445–76; Eduard Reimann, 'Über die Finanzpolitik Friedrichs des Grossen', *Abhandlungen zur Geschichte Friedrichs des Grossen* (Gotha 1892); Heinrich Schnee, 'Die Münzjuden in Brandenburg-Preussen, vornehmlich unter Friedrich dem Grossen', *Deutsches Archiv für Landes- und Volksforschung* 8 (1944) pp. 367–85; Th. von Dithfurth, *Zur Geschichte der Königlich preussischen Oberrechenkammer* (Berlin 1909); Walther Schultze, *Geschichte der preussischen Regieverwaltung von 1766 bis 1786. I. Die Organisation der Regie von 1766 bis 1786 und die Reform der Akzise von 1766 bis 1770* (Leipzig 1888). (*Staats- und sozialwissenschaftliche Forschungen*, vol. 7, bk. 3); Walther Schultze in *Forschungen zur brandenburgischen und preussischen Geschichte* V (1892) pp. 191–202; Gustav Schmoller, 'Die Einführung der französischen Regie durch Friedrich den Grossen 1766', *Sitzungsberichte der Akademie der Wissenschaften*, Berlin. Philosophisch-historische Klasse (1888) – in part clearly differs from Schultze; Friedrich Freiherr von Schrötter, 'Preussische Münzpolitik im 18. Jahrhundert', *Forschungen zur brandenburgischen und preussischen Geschichte* XXII (1909) pp. 134–42; Friedrich Freiherr von Schrötter, 'Die Münzverwaltung Friedrichs des Grossen', *Hohenzollern-Jahrbuch* XV (1911) pp. 91–99; Friedrich Freiherr von Schrötter, *Die Begründung des preussischen Münzsystems durch Friedrich den Grossen und Graumann 1740–1755. Das Geld des Siebenjährigen Krieges und die Münzreform nach dem Frieden 1755–65*, (*Das preussische Münzwesen im 18. Jahrhundert* vols. II–IV. *Acta Borussica. Die einzelnen Teile der Verwaltung*), (Berlin 1904–13); Konrad Wutke, 'Die Gründung des landschaftlichen Pensionsfonds für arme adlige Witwen und Waisen durch Friedrich den Grossen', *Zeitschrift des Vereins für die Geschichte Schlesiens* XLIII (1909); Friedrich Lenz and Otto Unholtz, *Die Geschichte des Bankhauses der Gebrüder Schickler* (Berlin 1912); Heinrich Schnee, *Die Hoffinanz und der moderne Staat* vol. I (Berlin 1953), vol. V (Berlin 1965); Otto Hintze, 'Friedrich der Grosse nach dem Siebenjährigen Krieg und das Politische Testament von 1768', *Geist und Epochen der preussischen Geschichte*, ed. Fritz Hartung (Leipzig 1943), see pp. 514–36; Marcus C. von Niebuhr, *Geschichte der Königlichen Bank in Berlin 1765–1845* (Berlin 1854); Heinrich Poschinger, *Bankwesen und Bankpolitik in Preussen* vol. I (Berlin 1878); Melle Klinkenborg, 'Über den Anteil Friedrichs des Grossen an der Begründung der preussischen Bank (Reichsbank)', *Forschungen zur brandenburgischen und preussischen Geschichte* XXIX (1916) pp. 474–80; Bernhard Rosenmöller, *Schulenburg-Kehnert unter Friedrich dem Grossen* (Berlin 1914) – § 17: 'Die Bank'; C[hristian] A[ugust] Zakrzewski, *Die wichtigeren preussischen Reformen der direkten ländlichen Steuern im 18. Jahrhundert* (Leipzig 1887), (*Staats- und sozialwissenschaftliche Forschungen* vol. 7, bk. 2); Heinrich von Beguelin, *Historisch-kritische Darstellung der Accise- und Zollverfassung in den preussischen Staaten* (Berlin 1797); Arnold Borel, *Le Conflit entre les Neuchâtelois et Frédéric le Grand sur la question de la ferme des impôts du pays de Neuchâtel* (1766–1768), dissertation (Berne 1889); R. Witschi, *Friedrich der Grosse und Bern* (Berne 1926); Oliver Eisenmann, *Friedrich der Grosse im Urteil seiner schweizerischen Mitwelt*, dissertation (Zurich 1972); Erich Paul Reimann, *Das Tabaksmonopol Friedrichs des Grossen*, dissertation (Berlin 1912); Ludwig Beutin, 'Die Wirkungen des Siebenjährigen Krieges auf die Volkswirtschaft in Preussen', *Vierteljahresschrift für Sozial- und Wirtschaftsgeschichte* vol. XXVI (1933) pp. 209–43; Leopold Krug, *Geschichte der preussischen Staatsschulden*, ed. C. G. Bergius (Breslau 1861); Friedrich der Grosse, 'Denkwürdigkeiten vom Hubertusburger Frieden bis zum Ende der Polnischen Teilung', ch. 2: 'Finanzwesen', *Œuvres* vol. VI, pp. 73–90 (Berlin 1847). Trans. in G. B. Volz (ed.), *Die Werke Friedrichs des Grossen* vol. V (Berlin 1913) pp. 56–68; G. B. Volz on finances in the Political Testaments of 1752 and 1768; edicts, *Novum Corpus Constitutionum Prussico-Brandenburgensium praecipue Marchicarum 1751–1810* (14 vols., Berlin 1753–1822).

V The Second *Rétablissement*

ADMINISTRATIVE REFORM

Reinhold Koser, 'Zur Bevölkerungsstatistik des preussischen Staates von 1756–1786', *Forschungen zur brandenburgischen und preussischen Geschichte* XVI (1903) pp. 583–89; Reinhold Koser, ibid VII (1894) pp. 540–48; Martin Hass, 'Die preussischen Adresskalender und Staatshandbücher als historisch-statistische Quelle', *Forschungen zur brandenburgischen und preussischen Geschichte* XX (1907) p. 170ff.; Otto Behre, *Geschichte der Statistik in Brandenburg-Preussen bis zur Gründung des Königlich Statistischen Büros* (Berlin 1905); Max Hanke, *Geschichte der amtlichen Kartographie Brandenburg-Preussens bis zum Ausgang der friderizianischen Zeit*, ed. Hermann Degner (Stuttgart 1935) (*Geographische Abhandlungen* series 3, bk. 7); Adolf Poschmann, 'Die Landesaufnahme des Ermlandes im Jahre 1772', *Zeitschrift für Geschichte des Ermlandes* XXIII (1928) pp. 382–445; *Acta Borussica. Behördenorganisation* vols. 7–10, 13–16, 1 (Berlin 1904–70); Boden's answer to Frederick II, ibid. vol. 12 (1926) pp. 63–65; Instruction of 20 May 1748 in vol. 7 (1904) pp. 552–839; lists of officials in vol. 8 (1906) pp. 190–223; see also

Martin Hass 'Zur Aufnahme des Personalbestandes der preussischen Provinzial- und Lokalbehörden im Jahre 1748', *Forschungen zur brandenburgischen und preussischen Geschichte* XXI (1908) pp. 549–58. Collection of edicts: Christian Otto Mylius, *Corpus Constitutionum Marchicarum*, 6 parts (1298–1736). Part 1–3 in one volume. Important for this chapter are: *4 Continuationes* (*1737–1750*) and *Supplement zu Continuationes 1–3* (*1737–1747*) with registers (Berlin and Halle 1737–55); *Novum Corpus Constitutionum Prussico-Brandenburgensium praecipue Marchicarum* [*for the years 1751–1810*], ed. by the Königlich Preussische Akademie der Wissenschaften, 12 vols., additionally 1 vol. of registers each for 1751–75 and 1775–1800 (Berlin 1753–1822); George Grube, *Corpus Constitutionum Pruthenicarum* (Königsberg 1721) – important because of the record of the continuing valid rights of the Estates and Church. For the appropriate collections of edicts for Pomerania see: David Friedrich Quickmann, *Ordnung oder Sammlung derer in dem königlich preussischen Herzogtum Pommern und Fürstentum Cammin bis Ende des Jahres 1747 publicirten Edikten, Mandaten und Rescripten* . . . (Frankfurt 1750); for Cleves-Mark: Johann Joseph Scotti, *Sammlung der Gesetze und Verordnungen, welche in den ehemaligen Herzogthümern Jülich, Cleve und Berg* . . . *ergangen sind,* 4 parts [1418–1816] (Düsseldorf 1821–22); Ed. Cauer, 'Ein Regierungsprogramm Friedrichs des Grossen [*Instruktion* of 1748], *Preussische Jahrbücher* X (1862) pp. 335–62; August Skalweit, 'Die Entlassung des Plusmachers Eckart', *Forschungen zur brandenburgischen und preussischen Geschichte* XX (1909) pp. 594–602; Heinrich von Friedberg, 'Friedrich der Grosse und der Prozess Goerne', *Historische Zeitschrift* LXV (1890) pp. 1–43; on Knyphausen: H. Hoffmann, *Die gewerbliche Produktion Preussens* (1956); on A. H. von Borcke: Stephan Skalweit, 'Edmund Burke und sein "Prussian gentleman"', *Festgabe für Max Braubach* (Münster 1964) pp. 613–26; Walther Schultze, 'Ein Angriff des Ministers von Heinitz gegen die französische Regie in Preussen', *Forschungen zur brandenburgischen und preussischen Geschichte* V (1892) pp. 191–202; Otto Steinecke, 'Friedrich Anton von Heinitz. Ein Lebensbild', *Forschungen zur brandenburgischen und preussischen Geschichte* XV (1902) pp. 421–70; Otto Steinecke, 'Des Ministers von Heynitz Mémoire sur ma gestion du 4e et 5e département', ibid. XXII (1909) pp. 183–91; F. J. Kühns, 'Die Ressortverhältnisse des Preussischen Geheimen Staatsrats bis in das 18. Jahrhundert', *Zeitschrift für preussische Geschichte und Landeskunde* VIII (1871) pp. 141–70; Edgar Loening, *Gerichte und Verwaltungsbehörden in Brandenburg-Preussen* (Halle 1913). (*Abhandlungen und Aufsätze* 1); Richard Ecker, *Die Entwicklung der Königlich Preussischen Regierung von 1701–1758,* dissertation (Königsberg 1908); Ed. Rudolf Uderstädt, 'Die ostpreussische Kammerverwaltung 1713–1756', *Altpreussische Monatsschrift* IL–LI (1912–14); August Skalweit, 'König Friedrich der Grosse und die Verwaltung Masurens', *Forschungen zur brandenburgischen und preussischen Geschichte* XXI (1908) pp. 139–73; Walter Mertineit, *Die friderizianische Verwaltung in Ostpreussen* (Heidelberg 1958). (*Studien zur Geschichte Preussens* 1); renewed Instruction of 30.7.1774 for the East Prussian *Regierung* in the former Stadt-Archiv Königsberg, Et. Min. 121; Georg Rohde, *Die Reformen Friedrichs des Grossen in der Verfassung und Verwaltung des Herzogtums Geldern 1763–1770,* dissertation (Göttingen 1913); P. Steffens, *Die*

Entwicklung des Landratsamtes in den preussischen Staaten bis zum Ausgang des 18. Jahrhunderts, dissertation (Berlin 1914); O. Kutzner, *Das Landratsamt in Schlesien 1740–1806,* dissertation (Breslau 1911); Ludwig Wilhelm Brüggemann, *Ausführliche Beschreibung des gegenwärtigen Zustands des Königlich-Preussischen Herzogtums Vor- und Hinter-Pommern* I. II. 1.2. (Stettin 1779 and 1784); Adolf Schill, 'Die Einführung des Landratsamtes in Cleve-Mark', *Forschungen zur brandenburgischen und preussischen Geschichte* XXII (1909) pp. 321–74; Otto Hintze, 'Die ständischen Elemente in dem Regierungssystem Friedrichs des Grossen', (Vortragsbericht), *Forschungen zur brandenburgischen und preussischen Geschichte* IX (1897) p. 595f.; Leo Wollenhaupt, *Die Clevisch-Märkischen Landstände im 18. Jahrhundert (Historische Studien* 159). (Berlin 1925); Martin Hass, 'Friedrich der Grosse und seine Kammerpräsidenten', *Beiträge zur brandenburgischen und preussischen Geschichte, Festschrift zu Gustav Schmollers 70. Geburtstag* (Leipzig 1908) pp. 191–220; R. von Flanss, 'Quos ego! Bescheide König Friedrichs II an die Westpreussische Kriegs- und Domänenkammer 1779ff.', *Zeitschrift des Historischen Vereins für den Regierungsbezirk Marienwerder* V (1881) pp. 243–50; Johannes Ziekursch, *Beiträge zur Charakteristik der preussischen Verwaltungsbeamten in Schlesien bis zum Untergang des friderizianischen Staates* (Breslau 1907). (*Darstellungen und Quellen zur schlesischen Geschichte* 4); see also: Martin Hass in *Forschungen zur brandenburgischen und preussischen Geschichte* XX (1907) p. 568ff., and XXI (1908) p. 331ff.; W. Naudé, 'Zur Geschichte des preussischen Subalternbeamtentums', *Forschungen zur brandenburgischen und preussischen Geschichte* XIIX (1905); H. A. Mascher, *Das Institut der Landräte in Preussen* (Berlin 1868); Franz Gelpke, *Die geschichtliche Entwicklung des Landratsamtes der preussischen Monarchie unter besonderer Berücksichtigung der Provinzen Brandenburg, Pommern und Sachsen* (Berlin 1902). (*Verwaltungsarchiv* 10); G. A. H. von Lamotte, *Von den Landräten in der Churmark u.a.m.* (Berlin 1783); Hans Delbrück, 'Landrath und "Regierung" in Preussen', *Preussische Jahrbücher* LIV (1884) pp. 518–32; S. Isaacsohn, *Geschichte des preussischen Beamtentums* vol. III (Berlin 1884) – new impression 1962; Martin Hass, 'Über das Aktenwesen und den Kanzleistil im alten Preussen', *Forschungen zur brandenburgischen und preussischen Geschichte* XXII (1909) pp. 521–75; Hans Haussherr, 'Die Auflösung der Einheitsverwaltung in Preussen', *Verwaltungseinheit und Ressorttrennung vom Ende des 17. bis zum Beginn des 19. Jahrhunderts* (Berlin 1953). On the office of *Landrat* in East Prussia: *Acta Borussica* vol. IX (1907), no. 247; in Cleves-Mark: ibid. nos. 320 and 333.

On the dismissal of leading officials: among others Chamber Director Kellner in Königsberg 1746 (*Acta Borussica* vol. VII); Chamber Director Ernst Gottlieb Cautius in Magdeburg 1769 (ibid. vol. XV); Minister of State Fabian Abraham von Braxein in Königsberg 1768 (ibid. vol. XIV); see also in various volumes of *Acta Borussica* the index entries for the following words: 'Entlassungen', 'Cassation', 'Strafen'. On remunerations and salaries: ibid. under the appropriate index entries. [Hengst], *Die Ritter des Königlich Preussischen Hohen Ordens vom Schwarzen Adler und ihre Wappen* (2nd ed. 1901); Colmar Grünhagen, *Die Entstehung eines schlesischen Sonderministeriums*; Colmar Grünhagen, 'Die beiden ersten schlesischen

Sonderminister'. *Forschungen zur brandenburgischen und pressischen Geschichte* XX (1907) pp. 105ff., 429; G. W. von Raumer, 'Landräte und Kreisstände der preussischen Monarchie', *Berliner Politisches Wochenblatt* (1832–33); Otto Hintze, 'Die Wurzeln der Kreisverfassung in den Ländern des nordöstlichen Deutschland', *Gesammelte Abhandlungen*, ed. Fritz Hartung. I: *Staat und Verfassung* (Leipzig 1941) pp. 176–205.

On the collection of edicts: Sammlung aller in dem souveränen Herzogtum Schlesien und dessen incorporierten Grafschaft Glatz in Finanz-, Justiz-, Criminal- usw. Sachen publicierten und ergangenen Ordnungen, Edicten, Mandata (Breslau n.d.) bei Joh. Jacob Korn; H. F. Diez, *Archiv Magdeburgischer Rechte* T.I. (Magdeburg 1781); *Sammlung gemeiner und besonderer Pommerscher und Rügischer Landes-Urkunden, Gesetze, Privilegien, Verträge, Constitutionen und Ordnungen* vols. I–III, ed. Johann Carl Dähnert (Stralsund 1765–69) – *Supplement und Fortsetzungen*, 4 vols., ed. G. von Klinckowström (Stralsund 1782–1802).

On the history of the General Directory: Privy Finance Councillor Franz Rembert Roden, who in 1768 was appointed First President of the *Oberrechenkammer*, drew up, in March 1781, a 'Historisch-chronologische Beschreibung von der Stiftung des General-Directorii usw.', (Preuss. Geh. Staatsarchiv R. 94 II C 4); on 16 April 1767 he sent notes on this work to minister von Hagen (*Acta Borussica. Behördenorganisation* vol. XIV, no. 119, p. 290); see J. D. E. Preuss, *Friedrich der Grosse. Eine Lebensgeschichte* (1832) vol. III, p. 444ff. For the personal histories of the leading officials: indispensable, Ch. A. L. Klaproth and C. W. Cosmar, *Der königlich preussische und kurfürstlich brandenburgische Geheime Staatsrat* (Berlin 1805).

REFORM OF THE DOMAINS AND OF AGRICULTURE

Otto Behre, *Geschichte der Statistik in Brandenburg-Preussen bis zur Gründung des Königlich Statistischen Bureaus* (Berlin 1905); W. Naudé and A. Skalweit, *Die Getreidehandelspolitik und Kriegsmagazinverwaltung Preussens 1740–1756*, (*Acta Borussica. Getreidehandelspolitik* vols. III and IV). (Berlin 1910–31); Rudolph Stadelmann, *Preussens Könige in ihrer Tätigkeit für die Landeskultur* vol. II (Leipzig 1882). (Publikationen aus den Preussischen Staatsarchiven 11); Hans Plehn, 'Zur Geschichte der Agrarverfassung von Ost- und Westpreussen', *Forschungen zur brandenburgischen und preussischen Geschichte* XVII (1904) pp. 383–466; vol. XVIII (1905) pp. 61–122; Gustav Aubin, *Zur Geschichte des gutsherrlich-bäuerlichen Verhältnisses in Ostpreussen vor der Gründung des Ordensstaates bis zur Steinschen Reform* (Leipzig 1902); Wilhelm von Brünneck, 'Die Aufhebung der Leibeigenschaft durch die Gesetzgebung Friedrichs des Grossen und das Allgemeine Preussische Landrecht', *Zeitschrift der Savigny-Stiftung für Rechtsgeschichte. Germanische Abteilung* vol. X (1889) pp. 24–69, vol. XI (1890) pp. 101–50; Peter Schutiakoff, *Die Bauerngesetzgebung unter Friedrich dem Grossen*, dissertation (Strasbourg 1893; Darmstadt 1895); Johannes Ziekursch, *Hundert Jahre schlesi-*

scher Agrargeschichte. Vom Hubertusburger Frieden bis zum Abschluss der Bauernbefreiung (Breslau 1915). (Darstellungen und Quellen zur Schlesischen Geschichte 20); Otto Hintze, 'Zur Agrarpolitik Friedrichs des Grossen', *Forschungen zur brandenburgischen und preussischen Geschichte* X (1898) pp. 275–309. This eminent expert on the documents of the Mehring Legend (Franz Mehring, *Die Lessinglegende* [1893]) has rightly and authoritatively countered Mehring's 'tendentiously sharp exposition' of the Instruction of 22 May 1763 (*Acta Borussica* XIII, p. 113ff.) and its misinterpretation. *Acta Borussica. Behördenorganisation* vol. VII (1904) to vol. XVI (1970); Walter Mertineit, *Die friderizianische Verwaltung in Ostpreussen* (Heidelberg 1958). (Studien zur Geschichte Preussens, vol. 1); Friedrich Wilhelm Henning, *Herrschaft und Bauernuntertänigkeit ... vor 1800* (Würzburg 1964); Friedrich Wilhelm Henning, *Bauernwirtschaft und Bauerneinkommen in Ostpreussen im 18. Jahrhundert* (Würzburg 1969); E. Schwenke, *Friedrich der Grosse und der Adel*, dissertation (Berlin 1911); Otto Meinardus, 'Das Gnadengeschenk Friedrichs des Grossen für den schlesischen Landadel', *Zeitschrift des Vereins für Geschichte Schlesiens* XXXXIV (1910); Konrad Wutke, 'Über die Einladung schlesischer Vasallen zur Hochzeit des Prinzen von Preussen im Jahre 1765', *Zeitschrift des Vereins für Geschichte Schlesiens* XXXXII (1908); H. Mauer, *Das landschaftliche Kreditwesen Preussens* (Strasbourg 1907); Theodor von der Goltz, *Geschichte der deutschen Landwirtschaft* (2 vols., Stuttgart 1902–3); P. Habernoll, 'Die Versuche Friedrichs des Grossen, das englische System der Fruchtwechselwirtschaft in Preussen einzuführen', *Landwirtschaftliche Jahrbücher* (1900) p. 89f.; Schlabrendorff: 'to govern reasonably': see: *Acta Borussica. Behördenorganisation* vol. XII, p. 388; Friedrich Lütge, *Geschichte der deutschen Agrarverfassung vom frühen Mittelalter bis zum 19. Jahrhundert* (2nd ed. 1967). (This supersedes the long outdated but still frequently quoted work by Georg Friedrich Knapp, *Die Bauernbefreiung und der Ursprung der Landarbeiter in den älteren Teilen Preussens* (2 vols., Leipzig 1887).

WEST PRUSSIA

G. F. von Martens, *Recueil des principaux traités*, vol. VI p. 89 and 93 (Göttingen 1801); A. Beer, *Die erste Teilung Polens* (2 vols. and a volume of documents, Vienna 1873); H. H. Kaplan, *The First Partition of Poland* (New York 1962); W. Hubatsch and H. Jablonowski, *Epochen politischer Gestaltung im nordostdeutschen Raum* (Wiss. Buchgesellschaft, Reihe Libelli vol. CCLXIV). (Darmstadt 1968), p. 40ff. – contains a fuller bibliography of the whole problem; M. Bär, *Westpreussen unter Friedrich dem Grossen* vol. I, II (Publikationen aus den Preussischen Staatsarchiven 83, 84). (Leipzig 1909), p. 38ff.; Th. von Moerner, *Kurbrandenburgs Staatsverträge 1601–1700* (Berlin 1867) p. 809f.; H. Jablonowski, *Die erste Teilung Polens* (Beiträge zur Geschichte Westpreussens 2, 1969) p. 47ff. – footnote 14 proposes that it was preferable to speak of the 'dismemberment of Poland Lithuania in 1772' rather than of the 1st Partition of Poland; Th. Schieder, *Deutscher Geist und ständische Freiheit im Weichsellande* (Königsberg 1940); E. Bahrfeldt, *Die Münzen und Medaillensammlung in der Marienburg* vol. II (Danzig

1904) p. 102; E. Joachim, *J. F. von Domhardt* (Berlin 1899); A. G. Meissner, *Das Leben F. B. Schönbergks von Brenckenhoff* (Leipzig 1782); M. Miller, *Die Auswanderungen der Württemberger nach Westpreussen und dem Netzegau 1776–1786* (Stuttgart 1935). (Veröffentlichung der Württembergischen Archiv-Verwaltung 1); reprint 1972 (Sonderschriften des Vereins für Familienforschung in Ost- und Westpreussen e. V. no. 22). Elbing: the mortgaging of the town and territory to the electorate of Brandenburg through a secret treaty concluded in Johannisburg on 28 May/7 June 1698 between Elector Frederick III of Brandenburg and King Augustus II of Saxony-Poland; the Brandenburg-Elbing Treaty, concluded in Elbing on 11 November 1698, in which reference was made to Brandenburg's right of occupation through the Wehlau and Bromberg Treaties of 1657. The town was finally taken over in 1703. Theodor von Moerner, *Kurbrandenburgs Staatsverträge von 1601 bis 1700* (Berlin 1867) 121c, 418, 423, 432, Appendix XXV; Walther Maas, *Preussische Siedlungen in Westpreussen und Netzedistrikt 1772–1848* (Studien zum Deutschtum im Ausland 8). (Cologne 1971) pp. 197–218; Emilian von Zernicki, 'Vasallen-Liste des im Jahre 1772 Preussen huldigenden polnischen Adels in Westpreussen. Den im König Geheimen Staats-Archiv zu Berlin befindlichen Huldigungsakten entnommen', *Vierteljahresschrift für Wappenkunde* 20 (1892) pp. 1–72; Max Beheim-Schwarzbach [a professor in the Gymnasium at Ostrau bei Filehne], 'Der Netzedistrikt in seinem Bestande zur Zeit der ersten Teilung Polens', *Zeitschrift der Historischen Gesellschaft für die Provinz Posen* 7 (1892) pp. 188–262, 381–426; 8 (1893) pp. 47–70, 121–210; J. Meisner [chief provincial judicial councillor in Posen], 'Gerichtsverfassung und Rechtspflege im Netze-Distrikt unter Friedrich dem Grossen', *Zeitschrift der Historischen Gesellschaft für die Provinz Posen* 7 (1892) pp. 263–336 (from: *Acten der Besitznahme-Kommissarien Rep. II B 1* in the Staatsarchiv Posen); Martin Meyer [a government councillor], 'Mitteilungen aus der Geschichte der preussischen Domänenverwaltung im Netzedistrikt zur Zeit Friedrichs des Grossen', *Jahrbuch der Historischen Gesellschaft für den Netzedistrikt zu Bromberg* (Bromberg 1895) pp. 27–68; Acta Camerae concerning the surveying, establishment and leasing of Starosti estates in the province of Klein-Preussen and other papers. Probably in Bromberg, origin not given. Hans Kiewning [assistant archivist in Posen], 'Seidenbau und Seidenindustrie im Netzedistrikt von 1773–1805' – the equivalent, for provincial history, of the *Acta Borussica* – *Zeitschrift der Historischen Gesellschaft für die Provinz Posen* 10 (1895) pp. 1–116, 169–238; 11 (1896) pp. 53–121, 257. From the documents of the Staatsarchiv Posen, Kriegsarchiv Bromberg III. 17.2. vols. I–XII. Vols. III–XI are missing for 1781–97. Supplement: private enterprises. Christian Meyer [state archivist in Posen. ret.] ed., *Friedrich der Grosse und der Netzedistrikt* (2nd ed. Bromberg and Leipzig 1908); Rodgero Prümers, *Der Netzedistrikt unter Friedrich dem Grossen* (Historische Monatsblätter für die Provinz Posen XIII no. 2). (1912); Ludwig Boas, 'Friedrichs des Grossen Massnahmen zur Hebung der wirtschaftlichen Lage Westpreussens', *Jahrbuch der Historischen Gesellschaft für den Netzedistrikt* (1891) pp. 33–65 and (1892) pp. 5–26; part I, also, Dissertation (Berlin 1890); Johann Friedrich Goldbeck, *Vollständige Topographie des Königreich Preussen*, part II: *Westpreussen* (Marienwerder 1789; reprinted Hamburg 1969).

(Sonderschriften des Vereins für Familienforschung in Ost- und Westpreussen e. V. no. 7); Max Toeppen, *Historisch-comparative Geographie von Preussen* (Gotha 1858); Erich Keyser, *Das Preussenland (Staats- und Verwaltungsgrenzen in Ostmitteleuropa, Historisches Kartenwerk II)*. (Munich 1954); H. and G. Mortensen, R. Wenskus, *Historisch-geographischer Atlas des Preussenlandes* part II (Wiesbaden 1970) – administrative chart of East and West Prussia at the end of the 18th century. The protocols of occupation: 1772: *Zeitschrift des Historischen Vereins für den Regierungsbezirk Marienwerder* bk. 7 (Marienwerder 1883) pp. 87–106; Otto Hintze, *Die Industrialisierungspolitik Friedrichs des Grossen in Westpreussen* (Danzig 1903), reprinted in *Historische und politische Aufsätze* (1927) vol. II, pp. 107–30; Margot Herzfeld, 'Der polnische Handelsvertrag von 1755', *Forschungen zur brandenburgischen und preussischen Geschichte* XXXII (1920), XXXV (1923), XXXVI (1924); see also Adalbert Hahn, ibid. LI (1939); Hans Haussherr 'Provinz und Staat in der altpreussischen Finanzwirtschaft (Westpreussen unter Friedrich dem Grossen)', *Forschungen zu Staat und Verfassung. Festgabe für Fritz Hartung* (Berlin 1958) pp. 269–88; Ilse Rhode, 'Das Nationalitätenverhältnis in Westpreussen und Posen zur Zeit der polnischen Teilungen', *Deutsche wissenschaftliche Zeitschrift für Polen* 7 (1926) pp. 3–79; Walther Recke, 'Friedrich der Grosse und Westpreussen', *Westpreussen-Jahrbuch* (1951/52) pp. 80–86; Robert Schück, 'Die Organisation der Posten in Westpreussen (1772/73)', *Altpreussische Monatsschrift* 10 (1873) pp. 52–60; J. Borngräber, 'Die Einrichtung der Preussischen Post in Westpreussen 1772', *Deutsche Postgeschichte* 2 (1941) pp. 59–74; Ruth Bliss, 'Zur Überlieferung der Friderizianischen Landes-Aufnahme für Westpreussen und den Netzedistrikt in den Jahren 1772/73', *Preussenland* 6 (1968) pp. 49–56; Ad. Poschmann, 'Die Landesaufnahme des Ermlandes im Jahre 1772', *Zeitschrift für Geschichte des Ermlandes* 23 (1928); Max Aschkewitz, 'Die Bevölkerung im südlichen Pommerellen vom 13. – 18. Jahrhundert', *Altpreussische Forschungen* (1942) pp. 155–84.

VI The Old King

CHURCH AND SCHOOL ADMINISTRATION

On church affairs: Carl Hinrichs, *Preussentum und Pietismus* (Göttingen 1971); Behre, *Statistik; Acta Borussica. Behördenorganisation (passim,* among others: vol. VII: Königliches Patronat; vol. VIII: Ober-Konsistorium; vol. IX: General-Visitationen, Pomeranisches Konsistorium, Provinzial-Synode Cleve; vol. XIII: Geistliches Departement; vol. XIV: Bekanntmachung amtlicher Edikte in den Kirchen; Revision der Kirchenrechnungen in den Ämtern; vol. XVI: Ablösung der Naturalbezüge der Pfarrer). Johann Heinrich Friedrich Ulrich, *Über den Religionszustand in den preussischen Staaten seit der Regierung Friedrichs des Grossen* (2 vols., Leipzig 1778–80); Friedrich Brandes, *Geschichte der kirchlichen Politik des Hauses Brandenburg. I: Geschichte der Evangelischen Union in Preussen* part II (Gotha 1873) – see chs. 20 and 21: 'Die Stellung Friedrichs des Grossen zu den kirchlichen Fragen'; Heinrich Pigge, *Die religiöse Toleranz Friedrich des Grossen nach ihrer theoretischen und praktischen Seite* (Mainz 1899); Max Lehmann, *Preussen und die katholische Kirche seit 1640* parts 2–5 (1740–1786). (Leipzig 1881ff.) – Publikationen aus den Preussischen Staatsarchiven, vols. X, XIII, XVIII, XXIV, LIII; O. Hegemann, *Friedrich der Grosse und die katholische Kirche in den reichs-rechtlichen Territorien Preussens,* dissertation (Heidelberg 1904); L. Witte, *Friedrich der Grosse und die Jesuiten* (2nd ed. Halle 1901); Th. Mommsen, 'Friedrich der Grosse und das katholische Vicariat in Berlin', *Preussische Jahrbücher* XXXIX; W. Schneider, 'Die Kirchenpolitik Friedrichs des Grossen', *Historische Viertel-jahresschrift* XXXI (1937) pp. 275–92; Ed. Cauer 'Die Umgestaltung der kirch-lichen Verhältnisse Schlesiens unter Friedrich dem Grossen', *Schlesische Provinzial-blätter* (1862), see also: Ed. Cauer, *Zur Geschichte und Charakteristik Friedrichs des Grossen* (Breslau 1883); C. Weigelt, 'Die evangelische Kirche in Schlesien zur Zeit der preussischen Besitzergreifung und ihre Entwicklung von 1740 bis 1756', *Zeitschrift des Vereins für Geschichte Schlesiens* XXIII (1889); Augustin Theiner, *Zustände der katholischen Kirche in Schlesien 1740 bis 1758* (2 vols., Regensburg 1852); Ludwig Petry, 'Die Errichtung schlesischer Ordensprovinzen unter Friedrich dem Grossen', *Der Oberschlesier,* June/July 1936, pp. 1–8; Hartwig Notbohm, *Das evangelische Kirchen- und Schulwesen in Ostpreussen während der Regierung Friedrichs des Grossen* (Heidelberg 1959). (Studien zur Geschichte Preussen V); Walther Hubatsch, *Geschichte der evangelischen Kirche Ostpreussens* (3 vols., Göttingen 1968); Heinz Neumeyer, *Kirchengeschichte von Danzig und Westpreussen aus evangelischer Sicht* vol. 1 (Leer 1971); Hellmuth Heyden, *Kirchen-geschichte Pommerns* vol. 2 (Cologne 1957); Hellmuth Eberlein, *Schlesische Kirchen-geschichte* (4th ed. Ulm 1962); Heinrich Friedrich Jacobson, *Geschichte der Quellen des Kirchenrechts der Provinzen Preussen, Posen, Rheinland und Westfalen* (3 vols., Königsberg 1837–44) – with documents and registers; D. H. Hering, *Beiträge zur Geschichte der reformierten Kirche in den preussisch-brandenburgischen Ländern* (2 parts, Breslau 1784–85) – *Neue Beiträge,* 2 parts (1786–87); Rudolf von Thadden, *Die brandenburgisch-preussischen Hofprediger im 17. und 18. Jahrhundert* (Arbeiten zur Kirchengemeinde 32). (Berlin 1959); Julius Langhäuser, *Das Militär-Kirchen-wesen im kurbrandenburgischen und königlich preussischen Heer. Seine Entwicklung und derzeitige Gestalt,* dissertation (Strasbourg/Metz 1912); Alexander Lyncker, *Die Altpreussische Armee 1714–1806 und ihre Militärkirchenbücher* (Berlin 1937) (Schriftenreihe der Reichsstelle für Sippenforschung 1); E. Schild, *Die preussischen Feldprediger* (2 vols., Eisleben and Halle 1889–90); Richard Graewe, 'Die Feld-prediger der Armee im 17., 18. und 19. Jahrhundert', *Zeitschrift für Heereskunde* Jg. 29 (1965), 33 (1969), 34 (1970). On chorale singing on campaign: C. Jany, *Geschichte der preussischen Armee* vol. 2 (1928); Selma Stern, *Der preussische Staat und die Juden* vol. III, 1–2, 1, 2. *Die Zeit Friedrichs des Grossen. Darstellung und Akten* (3 vols., Tübingen 1971) – with full bibliography.

On school affairs: Acta Borussica. Behördenorganisation (passim, among others: vol. VIII: Verbot des Besuchs auswärtiger Schulen; vol. X: Clevesche Stadtschulen; vol. XIII: Landschulwesen, Besoldung, Schulbücher; vol. XIV: Überprüfung des General-Schul-Reglements durch die Landräte); Eduard Cauer, *Friedrichs des*

Grossen Grundsätze über Erziehung und Unterricht. Programm Gymnasium (Danzig
1873): Alfred Heubaum, *Das Zeitalter der Staats- und Berufserziehung. 1: Bis zum
Beginn der allgemeinen Unterrichtsreform unter Friedrich dem Grossen 1763 ff.* (Berlin
1905) – (Geschichte des Deutschen Bildungswesens seit der Mitte des 17. Jahrhunderts); Justus Bona-Meyer, *Friedrichs des Grossen pädagogische Schriften und
Äusserungen. Mit einer Abhandlung über Friedrichs des Grossen Schulregiment nebst
einer Sammlung der hauptsächlichsten Schul-Reglements, Rescripte und Erlasse*
(Langensalza 1885); Robert Stein, *Die Schule als Staatsanstalt in Schulgeschichte
und Staatslehre bis 1794,* dissertation (Leipzig 1906); Conrad Rethwisch, *Der
Staatsminister Freiherr von Zedlitz und Preussens höheres Schulwesen im Zeitalter
Friedrichs des Grossen* (2nd ed. Strasbourg 1886); Ferdinand Vollmer, *Die Preus-
sische Volksschulpolitik unter Friedrich dem Grossen* (Berlin 1918) – (Monumenta
Germaniae Paedagogica LVI); Kurt Wöhe, *Die Geschichte der Leitung der preus-
sischen Volksschule von ihren Anfängen bis zur Gegenwart,* dissertation (Halle
1933); A. M. Kosler, *Die preussische Volkschulpolitik in Oberschlesien 1742–1848*
(Breslau 1929); Georg Froelich, 'Ein Landschulkatalog des Kirchspiels Georgen-
burg vom Jahre 1766', *Altpreussische Monatsschrift* XXXI (1894) pp. 470–90; B.
Poten (ed.), *Geschichte des Militär-, Erziehungs- und Bildungswesens in den Landen
deutscher Zunge* (Berlin 1896) – (Monumenta Germaniae Paedagogica XVII);
F. Wienecke, 'Das preussische Garnisonschulwesen', *Mitteilungen der Gesellschaft
für deutsche Erziehungs- und Schulgeschichte,* supplement 14 (1907); J. Grüner, *Das
Schulwesen des Netzedistrikts zur Zeit Friedrichs des Grossen (1772–1786)* (Breslau
1904); E. Clausnitzer, *Die Volksschulpädagogik Friedrichs des Grossen und der
Preussischen Unterrichtsverwaltung seiner Zeit* (Die pädagogischen Klassiker 7).
(Halle 1902); E. Reimann, 'Über die Verbesserung des niederen Schulwesens in
Schlesien in den Jahren 1763–1769', *Zeitschrift des Vereins für die Geschichte
Schlesiens* XVII (1883) pp. 317–51; Emil Waschinski, 'Das Schulwesen der Lande
Lauenburg und Bütow bis 1773', *Zeitschrift für Geschichte der Erziehung und des
Unterrichts* IV (1914) pp. 84–115.

On academic affairs: Adolf Harnack, *Geschichte der Königlich Preussischen Akademie
zu Berlin* (Berlin 1900); Reinhold Koser, 'Friedrich der Grosse und die preussischen Universitäten', *Forschungen zur brandenburgischen und preussischen Geschichte*
XVII (1904); Walther Hubatsch, 'Die Königsberger Universität und der preussische Staat', *Jahrbuch der Albertus-Universität zu Königsberg/Pr.* vol. 17 (1967) pp.
63–79; Wilhelm Dilthey, *Friedrich der Grosse und die deutsche Aufklärung* (Gesammelte Schriften 3). (2nd ed. Leipzig 1942); Walther Ring, *Geschichte der Universität Duisburg* (1920); *Dem Andenken der Universität Frankfurt [Oder], 26. April
1506 bis 10. August 1811. Festschrift zur 400. Wiederkehr ihres Gründungstages*
(1907); Götz von Selle, *Geschichte der Albertus-Universität zu Königsberg in
Preussen* (2nd ed. Würzburg 1956); *450 Jahre Martin-Luther Universität Halle-
Wittenberg* vol. 2: *Halle 1694–1817* (Halle [1952]); W. Schrader, *Geschichte der
Friedrichs-Universität zu Halle* vol. 1 (Berlin 1894); Friedrich Andreae, 'Geschichte
der Jesuitenuniversität', *Die Universität Breslau,* eds. Friedrich Andreae and A.
Griesebach (Breslau 1928); Ludwig Petry, 'Geistesleben des Ostens im Spiegel

der Breslauer Universitätsgeschichte', *Deutsche Universitäten und Hochschulen im Osten* (Cologne 1964) – (Wissenschaftliche Abhandlungen der Arbeitsgemeinschaft für Forschung des Landes Nordrhein-Westfalen XXX); Helmuth Fechner, *Friedrich der Grosse und die deutsche Literatur* (Braunschweig 1968); Ludwig Geiger, *De la littérature allemande (1780) von Friedrich dem Grossen* (2nd ed. Berlin 1902; reprinted Darmstadt 1969).

LEGAL REFORM

F. J. Kühns, 'Die Ressortverhältnisse des Preussischen Geheimen Staatsrats bis in das 18. Jahrhundert', *Zeitschrift für Preussische Geschichte und Landeskunde* VIII (1871) pp. 141–70; Conrad Bornhak, *Preussische Staats- und Rechtsgeschichte* (Berlin 1903); Hermann Conrad, *Deutsche Rechtsgeschichte* vol. 2: *Neuzeit bis 1806* (Karlsruhe 1966); Albert Lotz, *Geschichte des deutschen Beamtentums* (1909; 2nd ed. 1914); Edgar Loening, *Gerichte und Verwaltungsbehörden in Brandenburg-Preussen* (Halle 1914); Otto Hintze, 'Preussens Entwicklung zum Rechtsstaat (Auseinandersetzung mit Edgar Loening)', *Forschungen zur brandenburgischen und preussischen Geschichte* XXXII (1920) pp. 385–451; Adolf Stölzel, *Brandenburg-Preussens Rechtsverwaltung und Rechtsverfassung* vol. 2 (Berlin 1888); Siegfried Isaacsohn, *Geschichte des preussischen Beamtentums* III, pp. 289–343; Friedrich Holtze, *Geschichte des Kammergerichts in Brandenburg-Preussen (Beiträge zur brandenburg-preussischen Rechtsgeschichte* part 3: *Das Kammergericht im 18. Jahrhundert* (Berlin 1901); Erik Amburger, *Das Kammergericht und seine Präsidenten* (Berlin 1955); Eberhard Schmidt, *Kammergericht und Rechtsstaat* (Schriftenreihe der Juristischen Gesellschaft Berlin XXXI). (Berlin 1968); Otto Behre, *Geschichte der Statistik in Brandenburg-Preussen* (Berlin 1905) p. 295f.; Hans Neufeld, *Die Friderizianische Justizreform bis zum Jahre 1780*, dissertation (Göttingen 1910); Otto Hintze, 'Friedrich der Grosse und die preussische Justizreform des 18. Jahrhunderts', *Recht und Wirtschaft*, Jahrgang 1, bk. 5 (1912) pp. 129–35; Max Springer, *Die Coccejische Justizreform* (1914); E. Döhring, 'Samuel von Cocceji', *Neue deutsche Biographie* vol. 3 (1957); Wolfgang Rüfner, *Verwaltungsrechtsschutz in Preussen von 1749 bis 1842* (Bonner rechtswissenschaftliche Abhandlungen LIII). (Bonn 1962); Karl Dickel, *Friedrich der Grosse und die Prozesse des Müllers Arnold* (1891); see also: F. Graner, *Forschungen zur brandenburgischen und preussischen Geschichte* XXXVIII (1962) p. 77ff.; H. von Friedberg, 'Friedrich der Grosse und der Prozess Goerne', *Historische Zeitschrift* LXV (1890) pp. 1–43; W. Hülle, 'Friedrich und Trenck,' *Zeitschrift für die gesamte Strafrechtswissenschaft* LXXXI (1969) p. 834f.; Eberhard Schmidt, *Rechtssprüche und Machtsprüche der preussischen Könige* (Leipzig 1943); Gustav Berthold Volz, *Friedrich der Grosse und Trenck. Urkundliche Beiträge zu Trencks merkwürdiger Lebensgeschichte* (Berlin 1926); Werner Hülle, *Das Auditoriat in Brandenburg-Preussen. Ein rechtshistorischer Beitrag zur Geschichte seines Heerwesens mit einem Exkurs über Österreich* (Göttinger rechtswissenschaftliche Studien LXXXIII). (Göttingen 1971); Johann von Hymmen, *Beiträge zur juristischen Literatur in den preussischen Staaten* (8 vols. and commentary, Berlin 1775–90); Hans Hattenhauer (ed.), *Allgemeines Landrecht für die Preussischen*

Staaten von 1794, text (reprinted Frankfurt on Main 1970); Wilhelm Dilthey, *Das Allgemeine Landrecht (Gesammelte Schriften* vol. XII). (Leipzig 1936); Hermann Conrad, *Die geistigen Grundlagen des Allgemeinen Landrechts für die preussischen Staaten von 1794* (Arbeitsgemeinschaft für Forschung des Landes Nordrhein-Westfalen, Geisteswissenschaften LXXVII). (Cologne 1958); Hermann Conrad, *Das Allgemeine Landrecht von 1794 als Grundgesetz des friderizianischen Staates* (Schriftenreihe der Juristischen Gesellschaft Berlin XXII). (Berlin 1965); Erik Wolf, 'Carl Gottlieb Svarez', *Grosse Rechtsdenker der deutschen Geistesgeschichte* (4th ed. Tübingen 1963); Hermann Conrad and Gerd Kleinheyer (ed.), *Vorträge über Recht und Staat von Carl Gottlieb Svarez (1746–1798)* Wissenschaftliche Abhandlungen der Arbeitsgemeinschaft für Forschung des Landes Nordrhein-Westfalen X (Cologne 1960); Eberhard Schmidt, *Johann Heinrich von Carmer* (Schlesische Lebensbilder, vol. 2, 1926); *Acta Borussica. Behördenorganisation,* see vol. VII: Cocceji's reform of justice; vol. VIII: as before and Codex Fridericianus; vols. IX and X: as before and the administration of justice in the provinces (u.a. Justiz-Visitations-Ordnung, vol. 10, p. 6of.); vol. XIII: the Department of Justice and visits of inspection; vol. XIV and XV as before: vol. XVI/I: fragments only; Ludwig Tümpel, *Die Entstehung des brandenburg-preussischen Einheitsstaates im Zeitalter des Absolutismus 1609–1806* (Breslau 1915; reprint 1965); Hermann Conrad, *Rechtsstaatliche Bestrebungen im Absolutismus Preussens und Österreichs am Ende des 18. Jahrhunderts* (Arbeitsgemeinschaft für Forschung des Landes Nordrhein-Westfalen XCV). (Cologne 1961); Hermann Conrad, *Staatsgedanke und Staatspraxis des aufgeklärten Absolutismus* (Vorträge G 137 der Rheinisch-Westfalischen Akademie der Wissenschaften). (Opladen 1971); G. von Ising, 'Aus dem Leben des Grosskanzlers von Jariges', *Mitteilungen des Vereins für die Geschichte Berlins* XLIV (1927) p. 59ff.; Hermann Weil, *Frederick the Great and Samuel von Cocceji: A Study in the Reform of the Prussian Judicial Administration, 1740–1755* (Madison, Wisconsin 1961).

CABINET GOVERNMENT

Heinrich Otto Meisner, *Urkunden- und Aktenlehre der Neuzeit* (2nd ed. Leipzig 1952); expanded edition under the title: *Archivalienkunde vom 16. Jahrhundert bis 1918* (Leipzig 1969); Melle Klinkenborg, 'Die Stellung des Königlichen Kabinetts in der preussischen Behördenorganisation', *Hohenzollern-Jahrbuch* XIX (1915) pp. 47–51; on the secrecy of cabinet orders 1768 see: *Acta Borussica, Behördenorganisation* vol. XIV, p. 483 (von Massow's order of 17 May 1768); Martin Hass, 'Über das Aktenwesen und den Kanzleistil im alten Preussen', *Forschungen zur brandenburgischen und preussischen Geschichte* XXII (1909) pp. 521–75; Hermann Hüffer, *Die Kabinettsregierung in Preussen und Johann Wilhelm Lombard* (Leipzig 1891) – on the cabinet government under Frederick the Great see pp. 48–57; Hermann Hüffer, 'Die Beamten des älteren preussischen Kabinetts von 1713–1808', *Forschungen zur brandenburgischen und preussischen Geschichte* V (1892) pp. 167–90; Carl Hinrichs, *Der allgegenwärtige König. Friedrich der Grosse im Kabinett und auf Inspektionsreisen* (2nd ed. Berlin 1942) p. 33; *Das Tagebuch des Marchese*

Lucchesini (1780–1782). *Gespräche mit Friedrich dem Grossen*, ed. Friedrich von Oppeln-Bronikowski and Gustav Berthold Volz (Romanische Bücherei no. 5) (Munich 1926); Franzisco Agramonte y Cortijo, *Friedrich der Grosse. Die Letzten Lebensjahre* (Berlin 1928) p. 327f. Fuller bibliography under chapters II–1, V–1 and VI–2. Hans Friedrich von Diebitsch, *Specielle Zeit- und Geschäftseinteilung König Friedrichs II* (St Petersburg 1802); Friedrich August Ludwig von der Marwitz, *Ein märkischer Edelmann im Zeitalter der Befreiungskriege*, ed. F. Meusel – see here: vol. I (1908); Willy Andreas, 'Marwitz und der Staat Friedrichs des Grossen', *Historische Zeitschrift* CXXII (1920); for Mencken's memoir of October 1797 see excerpt in: C. Hinrichs, *Der allgegenwärtige König* (2nd ed. Berlin 1942) p. 96; Elliot, 1777: cited in Koser, III, p. 522.

Epilogue

Compare the Political Testaments of Frederick the Great from 1752 and 1768 as well as the personal testament of 1769. See in addition: 'Abriss der preussischen Regierung und der Grundsätze, auf denen sie beruht, nebst einigen politischen Betrachtungen' (1776). Volz, VII, pp. 210–16; Goethe, *Dichtung und Wahrheit* part 3; on Stein see: W. Hubatsch (ed.), *Briefe und amtliche Schriften* vol. IX, pp. 711f., 735f., 866; Gustav Berthold Volz, *Friedrich der Grosse im Spiegel seiner Zeit* (3 vols., 1926–27); H. G. de Mirabeau, *De la monarchie Prussienne sous Frédéric le Grand* (4 vols., London 1788) – in German in 2 parts (1790–91). It should be noted that Mirabeau, despite his personal respect for the king, was an enemy of the Prussian state and was in Berlin in the capacity of a spy, where much loose opinion was passed on to him by numerous informers. Denied an understanding of Prussia's administrative achievements he was hardly in a position to offer factual opinions on this subject. Serious preoccupation with Frederick the Great first began with the publication of the Frederician legacy by J. D. E. Preuss in the years between 1832 and 1856. Franz Kugler's popular biography of Frederick (1839–42), based on Preuss, was illustrated by the drawings of Adolph Menzel. These, with their blend of realism and refined emotionalism, brought about something of a Frederician renaissance among broad sections of the population which lasted for almost a century. Menzel's 'Tafelrunde' and 'Flötenkonzert', together with hundreds of little works, among them those on the history of the uniform, form an integral part of the historiographical awakening and the consolidation of Frederick's image. Thomas Babington Macaulay, *Frederick the Great* (1842) – many times reprinted, new German edition with commentary by Alexander von Hase (Berlin 1971); Thomas Carlyle, *History of Frederick the Great* (6 vols., 1857–65); Gustav Schmoller, Academy Address of 21 April 1892, printed in *Umrisse und Untersuchungen* (Leipzig 1898) p. 560. Following the personal legacy Frederick William I's and Frederick II's accomplishments in the field of administration were rediscovered from 1892 onwards with the publication of the *Acta Borussica* (still in progress). Only with the activity of the eighteenth-century administrative authorities can the industrious and unselfish labour of the scholars who worked on this publication be compared. The names of Gustav

Schmoller, Otto Hintze, Martin Hass, Ernst Posner and numerous others can, therefore, only be recalled with awe and gratitude, as well as those of Gustav Berthold Volz and Reinhold Koser. Few modern historians trouble themselves to work so directly from the sources as did all of these men. Therefore to disparage them today as conservatives denotes nothing more than simplistic snobbery. Parallel to Koser and Ritter were broadly based solid works such as those of Ernest Lavisse and later Gaxotte and finally of George Peabody Gooch. Work on Frederick since the Second World War indicates a more general international interest in the person and effectiveness of the king, mirrored in research reports and publications. In conclusion some of these are here mentioned: Walther Hubatsch, 'Preussen als internationales Forschungsproblem', *Geschichte in Wissenschaft und Unterricht* (1962) pp. 71–86; Thomas Ellwein and Waldemar Brückmann, 'Friedrich der Grosse im Spiegel der Nachwelt', *Zeitschrift für Religions- und Geistesgeschichte* (1948) pp. 2–24; Walter Bussmann, 'Friedrich der Grosse im Wandel des europäischen Urteils in Deutschland und Europa', *Festschrift für Hans Rothfels*, ed. Werner Conze (Düsseldorf 1951) pp. 375–408; Stephan Skalweit, 'Das Problem von Recht und Macht und das historiographische Bild Friedrichs des Grossen', *Geschichte in Wissenschaft und Unterricht* (1951); Karl Erich Born, 'Friedrich der Grosse im Urteil der preussischen Konservativen', *Geschichte in Wissenschaft und Unterricht* (1955); Walther Hubatsch, *Das Problem der Staatsräson bei Friedrich dem Grossen* (Göttingen 1956); Stephan Skalweit, *Frankreich und Friedrich der Grosse. Der Aufstieg Preussens in der öffentlichen Meinung des 'ancien régime'*, Bonner Historische Forschungen 1 (Bonn 1952); Manfred Schlenke, *England und das friderizianische Preussen 1740–1763* (Munich 1963); Henry M. Adams, *Die Beziehungen zwischen Preussen und den Vereinigten Staaten 1775–1870* (Würzburg 1960); Thomas M. Barker (ed.), *Frederick the Great and the making of Prussia* (New York 1972); on F. A. von Heinitz (Heynitz): W. Schellhas, in *Neue Deutsche Biographie* 9 (1972) p. 96 ff.

List of Illustrations

24 Johann Friedrich von Domhardt (1712–81); engraving by J. F. Bause.

25 F. B. Schönberg von Brenckenhoff (1723–80); portrait by C. F. R. Lisiewski, c. 1775. Schloss Grunewald, Berlin.

26 Freiherr H. F. K. vom und zum Stein (1757–1831); engraving after P. J. Lützenkirchen. Photo Bildarchiv Preussischer Kulturbesitz, Berlin.

27 F.A. von Heinitz (1725–1802); contemporary version of portrait by A. von Graff (1736–1813).

28 Count Heinrich von Podewils (1695–1760); contemporary engraving.

29 Frederick II visiting colonies in the Havelland; painting by J. C. Frisch (1730–1815). Schloss Charlottenburg. Photo Staatsbibliothek, Berlin.

30 Head of Frederick II and Frederick II receiving the homage of the West Prussian Estates, 1772; contemporary silver medal. Staatliche Museen, Berlin.

31 Samuel von Cocceji (1679–1755); bust by Adam and Michel.
Formerly Lawcourts, Berlin.

32 K. G. Svarez (1746–98); bust by Melchior zur Strassen. Photo Staatsbibliothek, Berlin.

33 Title page of royal decree, 1783. Photo Geh. Staatsarchiv, Berlin-Dahlem.

34 Frederick II discussing building plans; etching by P. Haas c. 1788.

35 Frederick being received by a local mayor; engraving by W. Jury (1763–1829). Geh. Staatsarchiv, Berlin-Dahlem.

36 Frederick II taking leave of a rural commissioner; illustration from D. Chodowiecki's *Anekdoten und Charakterzüge Friedrichs des Zweyten König von Preussen*, 1788.

37 Frederick II, his queen Elisabeth Christina of Brunswick-Wolfenbüttel and a view of Breslau, 1768; woodcut by Strachowsky. Geh. Staatsarchiv, Berlin-Dahlem.

38 Concluding sentence and signature of Frederick II's last will, 1769.

39 Frederick II visiting a weaving-mill; drawing by A. von Menzel (1815–1905). Staatsbibliothek, Berlin.

40 Frederick II; Wedgwood cameo by Tassie, 1780–1800. Victoria and Albert Museum.

Index